D1161121

SAN MARTÍN

SAN MARTÍN

ARGENTINE SOLDIER
AMERICAN HERO

JOHN LYNCH

YALE UNIVERSITY PRESS
NEW HAVEN AND LONDON

For information about this and other Yale University Press publications, please contact:
U.S. Office: sales.press@yale.edu   www.yalebooks.com
Europe Office: sales@yaleup.co.uk   www.yaleup.co.uk

Set in Minion by IDSUK (DataConnection) Ltd.
Printed in Great Britain by TJ International, Padstow, Cornwall

Library of Congress Cataloging-in-Publication Data

Lynch, John, 1927-
   San Martín : Argentine soldier, American hero / John Lynch.
      p. cm.
Includes bibliographical references and index.
ISBN 978-0-300-12643-3 (ci : alk. paper)
1. San Martín, José de, 1778-1850. 2. South America—History—Wars of
Independence, 1806-1830. I. Title.
   F2235.4.L95 2009
   980'.02092—dc22

A catalogue record for this book is available from the British Library.
10 9 8 7 6 5 4 3 2 1

For

George, Olivia, Edward,
Kento and Rui

Contents

Illustrations

Maps

Preface

In the age of revolution and the time of liberation José de San Martín excelled by the brilliance of his strategy and the strength of his leadership. He is known to history as the *hombre necesario*, the indispensable one, of the South American revolution. Yet he spent more than two-thirds of his life in Europe. His career as a liberator was marked by a curious chronology: thirty-four years of preparation, ten years in action, twenty-eight years in exile. His American career was concentrated in one brief decade, from the time he arrived in Buenos Aires on 9 March 1812 to his retirement from Peru on 20 September 1822. The apprenticeship was important. During his twenty-two years service in the Spanish army, in the course of which he was promoted from infantry lieutenant to lieutenant-colonel of cavalry, he served on numerous fronts in North Africa and Spain, and for the last three years against the French invaders of the peninsula. He acquired a combination of talents unique among all the liberators: military skill as a strategist and tactician, a knowledge of enlightened ideas, and above all perhaps an authority born of participation in some of the crucial events of modern history.

San Martín's greatness consisted in his ability to inspire the peoples of South America to follow his armies and accept his strategies, taking independence outside national frontiers and beyond national interests and giving it an American identity. As far as we can judge, he did not respond to any particular interest, social or economic, or care for power and glory. War and peace were his priorities. The military objectives were more easily resolved than the political. San Martín always said that America's great trial would arrive not in winning independence but in the subsequent protection of freedom in societies unprepared for the task. The historian has to decide whether San Martín's own qualities of leadership—professional experience, strategic judgement, clarity of purpose and force of willpower—were better displayed making revolution than making peace.

We should judge him on his own merits, not by constant comparison with the other great leader of South American independence, Simón Bolívar. Comparisons are invidious but inevitable. It is not difficult to write a life of Bolívar. Given half a chance he will write it for you himself. The historian has to defend himself against Bolívar and to preserve his own version of independence against the torrent of words with which Bolívar seeks to explain and persuade. San Martín is different. He lacks the style and panache of Bolívar, preserves a decent reticence about his private life and maintains a natural reserve about his role in the revolutions for independence. So it is a challenge for the historian, to bring him out and discover the man behind the silence. Of the two liberators, San Martín was in many ways the pioneer whose strategy and methods were a necessary preliminary to the Bolivarian conclusion. He has not suffered the fate of Bolívar or been appropriated by particular regimes, but he has not entirely escaped the polemicists. In Argentina historians, writers and politicians still fight the wars of independence and keep alive the controversies of San Martín's career, especially the three turning points in his life: his decision to abandon Spain for Argentina in 1812, his adoption of the trans-Andean strategy in 1816 and his abandonment of leadership in 1822. And while one Argentine historian discovers a British author for the grand strategy, another denounces San Martín as a British spy, herald of a third British invasion.

San Martín was a professional soldier, taciturn in public but articulate in the cause of liberation, convinced of his mission to change the Hispanic world. He was an enigmatic character, austere, stoic and deeply committed to American independence. He kept his emotions to himself, aloof from the extravagant gesture. Discipline was the guide to his conduct, on and off the battlefield. He drove his armies hard, though concern for his troops earned him their respect. As a soldier San Martín had two sublime talents, the ability to think big and a genius for organization. His strategy was based on the concept that the South American revolution could not be complete until the base of Spanish power in Peru had been destroyed; that the route north from Argentina to Peru was closed by the hostility of men and nature; and that the only way ahead was by a vast flanking movement, across the Andes to Chile, then up the Pacific in a seaborne invasion of Peru. He had to sell this extraordinary idea to allies and critics alike, and, as if this were not enough, to crown it with his concept of revolution without war, a position that proved to be his sternest test and led to his deepest disillusion.

Studies of San Martín are rare in English. The few that exist are old and at the moment there is no modern biography of him. He has been studied almost exclusively by Argentine scholars, preeminently by Ricardo Piccirilli

(1957), A.J. Pérez Amuchástegui (1966 and 1976), and more recently by Patricia Pasquali (1999), whose distinguished biography is a worthy successor to the classic work of Bartolomé Mitre (1887). For over a century Argentine historians have also been publishing the manuscript sources of San Martín's life and work, and have placed him securely in the documentation of independence. These primary sources, together with modern research, are the basis of the present book.

The revolutionary career of San Martín is significant at various levels: first as a display of a masterly war strategy and a great feat of arms in the Andes and the Pacific comparable to anything achieved in the Napoleonic age in Europe; then as a series of dramatic set pieces, the confrontation with Lord Cochrane in Peru and the standoff with Bolívar in Guayaquil, an encounter that darkened San Martín's last days in South America; and finally as a study in the making and undoing of a leader. These and other events in the southern war of independence have involved endless controversy, and invite restatement and revision. As for method, this has to vary, following a central narrative course in which San Martín develops his policies and leads his armies in pursuit of liberation. Meanwhile the historian has to alternate movement with standing still in order to survey the conditions in which the liberator operated; thus analysis accompanies narrative and perhaps enables the reader to escape from the labyrinth of simultaneous events.

San Martín's career is a commentary on the Spanish American revolutions, no longer seen as purely political and military events. Historians have been exploring the economic and social dimensions of independence; they seek its ideological origins, examine its influence on the formation of national identities and consider its meaning for race relations. As a soldier and a statesman leading from the front, San Martín had to concentrate on winning the war; but he had to find the resources of war and to guarantee military and naval supplies from three different countries and from abroad. He had to know and organize his economic bases from Mendoza, Santiago and Lima, and exert pressure on different sectors of Spanish American society. This provoked further tests of his leadership. The ruling classes were not natural allies of San Martín and people did not automatically accept the cost of revolution. Argentines came to suspect the general who moved away from Argentina; Chileans became irritated by the burden of a foreign war; and the Peruvian elites were distinctly cool. His liberal instincts about slavery and his sympathy towards Indians provoked the hostility of landed interests, and brought his social policies into conflict with property owners. His political ideas, too, alerted his contemporaries and produced a number of contradictions. His repudiation of Spain and decision to abandon Europe in favour of South America revealed his feeling for Argentine identity, yet he did not share the exclusive nationalism of his countrymen or receive their unqualified support. While his war on Spain marked him as a revolutionary, he was no republican; his constitutional ideas were traditional and he regarded strong monarchy as the best form of government for South America, a view out of harmony with the spirit of the age.

I am grateful to Yale University Press and particularly to Robert Baldock for suggesting this book, and to the Yale editorial team for helping to produce it. I am grateful too to Peter Blanchard for his guidance on the subject of slaves and slavery during the wars of independence, and for showing me the manuscript of his book in advance of publication. Margarita Suárez kindly provided bibliographical advice on Peruvian independence. I warmly thank Samuel Amaral for his great help in obtaining illustrations from the Museo Histórico Nacional in Buenos Aires, and the Director of that institution for kindly giving me permission to reproduce the images. I thank my grandson George Archer for supplying computer skills when they were needed. In London the National Archives (Public Record Office), the British Library, the Institute of Historical Research and the Library of University College London have been indispensable in the search for material.

Last and most of all I wish to thank my wife Wendy, who has invariably been able to supply an appropriate word or idiom, and whose support and encouragement over many years have been my constant mainstay.

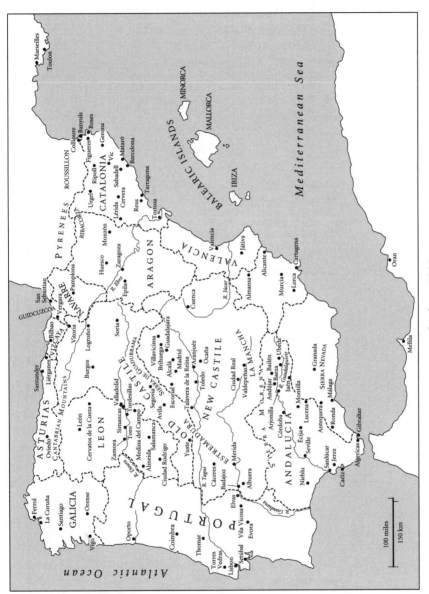

Spain *c.* 1800

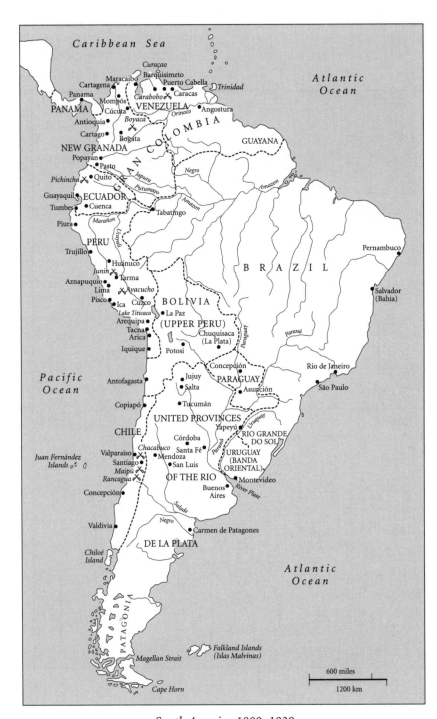

Caribbean Sea

Curaçao

Maracaibo • Barquisimeto
Cartagena • • • Puerto Cabella ⌒ Trinidad
Panama • Mompós • Carabobo • Caracas
PANAMA • Cúcuta VENEZUELA
Antioquia • Boyacá Orinoco • Angostura
Cartago • Bogotá
NEW GRANADA GUAYANA
Popayán • Pasto
Pichincha ✕ Quito Japura Negro
Guayaquil • ECUADOR Putumayo Amazon
Tumbes • • Cuenca Tabatingo
Piura • Marañon Amazon

PERU
Trujillo •
Huánuco •
Junín ✕ Tarma B R A Z I L Pernambuco •
Aznapuquio • Ayacucho
Lima ✕ Cuzco Salvador
Pisco • Ica BOLIVIA (Bahia) •
Lake Titicaca • La Paz
Arequipa (UPPER PERU)
Tacna Chuquisaca
Arica (La Plata)
Iquique • Potosí Paraná Rio de Janeiro •

Pacific Concepción São Paulo •
Ocean Antofagasta • Jujuy PARAGUAY
• Salta • Asunción
Copiapó • Tucumán
UNITED PROVINCES Uruguay
CHILE Yapeyú
Córdoba • RIO GRANDE
Valparaíso • Chacabuco Santa Fé DO SOL
Santiago ✕ • Mendoza URUGUAY
Maipú ✕ • San Luis (BANDA
Rancagua OF THE RIO ORIENTAL)
Concepción • • Montevideo
Buenos River Plate
Aires
Valdivia • Negro
• Carmen de Patagones
Chiloé DE LA PLATA
Island

Juan Fernández
Islands

Atlantic
Ocean

Atlantic
Ocean

PATAGONIA

Magellan Strait Falkland Islands
(Islas Malvinas)

Cape Horn

600 miles
────────
1200 km

South America 1800–1830

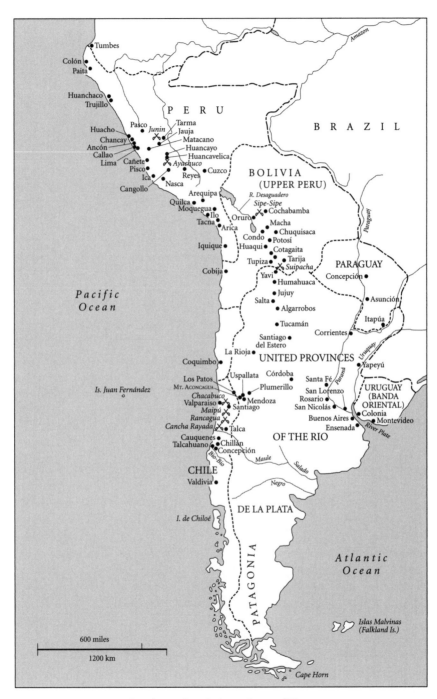

Southern South America and Peru

CHAPTER 1

Soldier of Spain

The Road from Yapeyú

Yapeyú—an obscure village on the west bank of the River Uruguay, once a thriving community in the heart of a stable society, now in 1778 a melancholy outpost on the fringe of the Hispanic world, struggling to survive. Yapeyú was the victim of two recent disasters. A violent smallpox epidemic in 1770 had reduced its population from eight thousand to three thousand in the space of two years and returned its economy to little more than subsistence. Its prosperity had already been wrecked by another event, a decision taken at the royal palace in Madrid and applied on this distant frontier in a single dramatic action. This was Jesuit territory, within living memory part of the extensive Guaraní missions, whose protected Indians were the targets alike of Portuguese slave hunters and Spanish settlers. The frontiers were vulnerable and Spain still needed to defend them after their traditional defenders, the Jesuit fathers, were expelled from Spain and its empire in 1767. It was a ruthless operation, characteristic of the Bourbon state, and one with few parallels in imperial history. Casualties of a despotic act, the Jesuits were replaced by colonial officials, and the once benevolent management of people and resources became a nightmare of neglect and incompetence. In 1778 the Bourbon state in Yapeyú was represented by Juan de San Martín, a military officer, whose modest career in the Spanish army reached its American peak in this distant province. There his youngest son was born on 25 February 1778 and was baptized José Francisco de San Martín on the following day.[1] A curious irony. In a remote corner of the Hispanic world a loyal defender of empire had produced its nemesis.

Colonial society was sensitive about race and anyone born in Indian country could expect to have his origins queried. Juan Bautista Alberdi,

Argentina's leading political theorist of the time, interviewed San Martín in France in 1843: 'I believed him to be Indian, as he had so often been described to me; yet he is simply a man with a dark complexion'.[2] He himself, in a parley with Indian chiefs in 1816, mocked the Spaniards who would cross the Andes to kill them and rob their women and children, and declared, 'I too am an Indian', a rhetorical flourish not to be taken literally.[3] In his classic history of San Martín, Bartolomé Mitre gave what became the authorized version of his birth: José Francisco de San Martín was born in Yapeyú on 25 February 1778, the fifth child of Captain Juan de San Martín. He referred to San Martín's dark skin and told the anecdote of his meeting with the defeated Spanish general, Marcó del Pont, who had referred disdainfully to his enemy's 'black' hand of disloyalty and was now invited ironically to 'give me your white hand!'[4] There is no baptismal record, an absence possibly explained by the destruction of Yapeyú by Portuguese troops in 1817. But there is other evidence, particularly the death certificate for San Martín issued on 18 August 1850 by the mayor's office in Boulogne, where San Martín died, which states, 'born in Yapeyú, province of Misiones (Argentine Confederation), of 72 years, 5 months and 23 days', and the burial certificate issued by the parish priest of the church of Our Lady in Boulogne, which specifies the date of birth 25 February 1778 and the parents as Juan de San Martín and Gregoria de Matorras.

Most observers refer to San Martín's dark skin. His English naval friend, Commodore William Bowles, described him as he approached his fortieth year as 'tall, strongly-formed, with a dark complexion and marked countenance'.[5] Argentine revisionists, however, go further. They claim that the true mother of San Martín was a Guaraní woman and they see him as a man of two worlds, a mestizo son of a Spanish officer and an Indian woman, who was to return to South America in search of his roots and to fight Spanish domination. It is true that Spaniards isolated on this remote frontier often found solace with Guaraní girls, and their offspring joined the ranks of mestizos who populated the northern reaches of the Río de la Plata. There is no evidence that Juan de San Martín ever took an Indian lover, but this has not prevented Argentine historians speculating on the race of his youngest son.[6]

The San Martíns came from the Spanish province of Toro in Old Castile. Juan de San Martín, José's father, was born on 3 February 1728 in the village of Cervatos de la Cueza, son of Andrés de San Martín and Isidora Gómez.[7] Not far away, in Paredes de Navas, Gregoria Matorras was born to Domingo Matorras and María Del Ser on 12 March 1738. Juan and Gregoria met, not in Spain but in America, where they were seeking something more than the routine life of the Castilian *llanos*, a land of blue summer skies and grey winters, hot and dusty for half the year, cold and wet for the rest. These were small villages typical of rural Castile, where primitive agriculture produced a limited range of products for local trade, prime territory for emigration. Cervatos de la Cueza, close to the Camino de Santiago, was the home of peasant farmers, day labourers and shepherds, and perhaps a few tradesmen.[8] The San Martíns were village people of modest resources, smallholders with house and land, commoners in a society dominated by nobles. Juan de San Martín, who seems to have been orphaned while young, left the village to strike out for a military career, though not one favoured by the elite; at the age of eighteen he enlisted in the ranks of the Lisbon Regiment on 18 December 1746 and was promoted to sergeant in 1753. He was posted first to Melilla in Morocco and Oran in Algeria, where there were few opportunities for accelerated promotion, then at last to America in 1764, not to a great viceroyalty such as Mexico or Peru but to the fringe of empire, the Río de la Plata.

In the southern hemisphere, however, Spain was reordering its imperial priorities. Soon the Río de la Plata became a major focus of interest and resources, and Buenos Aires became a viceregal capital at the leading edge of empire. Spain was alerted by the growing power of Britain in the Americas, its encroachment on Spanish territorial and trading positions, and its new interest in the southern seas. A Spanish expedition to the Río de la Plata in 1776 not only captured Colonia from Portugal and gave Spain undisputed dominion over the region, it also led directly to the creation of the viceroyalty of the Río de la Plata in 1778 and the reorientation of Spanish imperial strategy in South America. Pedro de Cevallos, the first viceroy, insisted that the Río de la Plata 'is the true and only defensive wall in this part of America, and its development must be vigorously promoted . . . for it is the one point where South America will be retained or lost.'[9] The geopolitical change involved action on the east bank of the River Plate where Spain took measures to strengthen its presence in the Banda Oriental and to establish peace with the Portuguese. This gave Juan de San Martín his first opportunity for career advancement, when he was promoted to lieutenant in the Battalion of Spanish Volunteers of Buenos Aires. The second opportunity came in the aftermath of the expulsion of the Jesuits in 1767, and he was appointed to administer their large estancia Las Caleras de las Vacas. Meanwhile, Gregoria Matorras, still unmarried at twenty-nine, arrived in Buenos Aires in the company of a cousin. Spanish girls were few and much valued in the colony and, once she had met her compatriot Juan de San Martín, both far from their native land, his marriage proposal quickly followed. Juan, now adjutant of the Battalion of Spanish Volunteers, was stationed on the other side of the River Plate, and he married Gregoria by proxy on 1 October 1770.

The couple soon moved temporarily to the ex-Jesuit estancia, of which Juan was still administrator. There, in the years 1771–4 they had a daughter, María Helena, and two sons, Manuel Tadeo and Juan Fermín Rafael; a third son, Justo

Rufino, arrived in 1776. Meanwhile the father pressed hard for a posting to military duties and promotion in the army, but this was a case of good conduct turning against him: reports of his excellent administration of estates and maintenance of law and order condemned him to civilian duties, while his military career stagnated. Eventually, in 1775, he took up a new posting as lieutenant-governor of Yapeyú with jurisdiction over the extensive former Jesuit territory, recently abandoned to inferior secular officials and threatened once more by the incursion of the feared Paulistas, bandits and slave hunters from São Paulo in Portuguese Brazil. In spite of their potential for growing crops and raising cattle, and their trade downriver in hides and meat, the former missions languished in the beauty of their tropical setting and continued to decline from previous splendours, their population and production down from Jesuit levels. But the Jesuit buildings were still there, real houses for the Indians and not mere adobe huts, and Juan de San Martín took up residence with his family in the former College, a well-appointed structure with an extensive library situated in the main square of Yapeyú next to the church. He was soon in action raising troops, resisting Portuguese incursions, repelling raids on estancias and on Indians, and then beginning the work of reconstruction.

San Martín's confrontational policy towards the Minuan Indians, allies of the Portuguese, led to his investigation for exceeding his brief. He was cleared and promoted captain in 1779. Meanwhile, during his father's tour of duty in Yapeyú, José Francisco de San Martín was born on 25 February 1778, the fifth and last child of Juan and Gregoria. His baptism, by a Dominican friar, Francisco de la Pera, parish priest of Yapeyú, was a happy event for the tiny Spanish community in this distant land amidst a mass of Guaraní Indians, a strange location that would come to have extraordinary meaning for Argentina, for the life of José Francisco and for the labours of future historians. Juan de San Martín's appointment in Yapeyú terminated in 1781 when he left with his family for Buenos Aires; two years later his service in America was also brought to a close and he was posted along with other military units back to Spain. The San Martíns sailed from Buenos Aires at the end of 1783 in the frigate *Santa Balbina* and arrived at Cádiz on 23 March 1784, leaving the summer heat of Buenos Aires for the early spring of Andalucía, and exchanging a developing colony for a declining metropolis. The five-year-old José thus abandoned his native land for a new homeland, and Spain became his prime allegiance for the next thirty years.

The Making of a Spaniard

The Spain to which Juan de San Martín took his family was a country enacting its own version of the *ancien régime*. Spanish imperial power, it seemed, had never been greater. American trade was free and protected, revenues were high, defences secure. In the Iberian Peninsula agricultural exports from Andalucía, Catalonia, and even Castile were earning profits for producers and income for Spain. Public works, the construction industry, textile factories, these and other enterprises were visible signs of material progress and prosperity. While ministers, architects and planners worked to improve the face of Bourbon Spain, bureaucrats in Madrid, shippers in Cádiz, merchants in Barcelona, all could face the future with confidence in their country and reliance on its resources. Life in Madrid and provincial capitals was superior to anything the San Martín family had known in the Río de la Plata, and a soldier from the lower ranks of the officer corps could only wonder at the ostentation of the rich and the gulf between these and the mass of the population. And in spite of appearances he could hardly be blind to the underlying recession that Spain endured in the last decade of the eighteenth century.

The reign of Charles III ended in 1788 with its two policy objectives—the modernization and aggrandizement of Spain—still unfulfilled. In the following years both were further undermined, the first by the advance of French revolutionary ideas, the second by the invasion of French armies in 1793–5. These extraordinary shocks had to be met in worsening economic conditions and by a Spanish government unequal to the task. The moderate prosperity experienced in the middle decades of the century was drawing to a close, as population growth, agrarian expansion and industrial output reached a plateau and began to recede. The country lurched into a series of subsistence crises worse than any before and beyond the control of a regime encumbered by the most discredited institutions of Bourbon Spain—the Inquisition, oligarchic town councils, seigneurial jurisdiction, entails, corporate *fueros*, the whole panoply of privilege. Spain's problems would have tested any regime, but this was a special regime. Within a few years Charles III, who had provided stability and some economic growth, gave way to Charles IV, whose empty benevolence, famously depicted by Francisco de Goya, was also characteristic of his political attitudes, and First Minister Manuel Godoy recalled how each night the king would ask him, 'What have my subjects being doing today?'[10] Queen María Luisa of Parma, whose royal role was to produce an heir to the throne and a host of reserves, was a woman of character, but it was not a character liked by Spaniards who believed that she took lovers before and after she met Godoy, then a young officer in the household guards, and launched him on his astonishing career. Whatever the truth, she knew what she was doing in selecting Godoy and grooming him to be first minister, creature of the monarchs, their aide and counsellor in an uncertain world, whose anteroom was invariably full of young women sent by their families to seek favours.

Godoy was expected to stand up to France, but he responded to the French invasion by taking Spain into a ruinous war with its neighbour and then into an expensive peace, when he signed the treaty of San Ildefonso (18 August 1796) and delivered Spain to France as an ally against Britain. The Spain in which San Martín spent his formative years, therefore, was a satellite of France and an enemy of Britain, a fatal dilemma from which Spain would only escape after a decade of destruction.

The San Martín family had returned to Spain in 1784 in relative poverty and had to exist on an officer's half-pay, often in arrears, and without possibility of any increase through promotion, firmly denied to Juan after thirty-eight years' service. In 1785 he was posted as a retired infantry captain to a staff appointment in Málaga with a lieutenant's pay of 300 reales a month.[11] So family circumstances were poor and hardly alleviated by their meagre savings from America; the parents were left struggling to educate and provide for their children, though this was not something that embittered San Martín in later life or that he allowed to retard his career.

Málaga was not the leading edge of Bourbon ambitions but it was a port of moderate prosperity, cradled between the Mediterranean and inland hills, and celebrated for its subtropical climate and fine muscatel wines. The English traveller Joseph Townsend was appalled by the 'multitude of beggars' infesting the streets, and recorded that mugging was common, industry rare and hygiene non-existent. People stayed indoors during the day to avoid the over-whelming heat; in the cool of the evening young people came out to swim in the sea for hours, though there was strict segregation of the sexes and 'the spot where the ladies are is guarded by sentinels with loaded muskets.'[12] In Málaga, José received a primary education in a free school in the public sector, an ex-Jesuit college, until he was thirteen years old. Jesuit schools had been forcibly converted into state institutions after the expulsion of 1767 and standards were no longer of the highest. So José's education was fairly basic. He learnt Latin grammar, mathematics, drawing, and he had some talent with the guitar, later improved by lessons from the distinguished composer Fernando Sor. Given the circumstances of the family—a military background, poor prospects and a modest education—virtually the only respectable career open to San Martín and his brothers was to follow their father into the army, and this was the decision their father took for them. In the army José would enjoy no privilege of birth but would have to make his way through merit and character. What kind of army was he joining?

Charles III and his ministers, obsessed by foreign and imperial policy, were determined to give Spain the armed forces of a world power. Defeat in the Seven Years War (1756–63) called for a radical reappraisal. Rearmament was therefore accompanied by military reform, for which the preferred model was

Prussia. Impressed by the victories of Frederick the Great, Charles III sent teams of officers to study the Prussian military system and return to teach Prussian tactics to the Spanish army; and though Spain did not have a central military academy for training officers, it developed a military academy at Avila for infantry, cavalry and engineers, and an artillery academy at Segovia. With these precedents the Spanish army adopted a three-deep line of infantry tactics, which gave a high rate of firepower and depended on strict discipline instilled by ruthless officers. The cavalry also followed Prussian methods of using masses of heavy cavalry to deliver death-or-glory charges, though the dragoons retained the original role of mounted infantry. A permanent problem was recruitment of troops. Military service was unpopular and the government was sensitive to resistance from conscripts, preferring instead to recruit volunteers and foreigners, supplemented by the *leva*, the levy, a device by which magistrates were empowered to impress into the army convicted criminals, beggars and vagrants. So the army, or at least the infantry, was composed not of the dregs of society, as is sometimes said, but of *campesinos* without the means of escape.

Deficient in recruitment, the Spanish army was also badly led. The officer corps, to which San Martín aspired, was not a cohesive body but divided by social origins and career prospects.[13] The Spanish nobility enjoyed privileged access to the officer corps, especially to its senior ranks, and were regarded by the Crown as its natural leaders. Only nobles could become officer cadets, though nobility was a broad concept in the country of *hidalgos*. In the infantry and cavalry, while two-thirds of the officers came from the nobility, the rest could be promoted from the ranks; this concession later included *hidalgos*, sons of officers and qualified sergeants. San Martín's father, who had entered as a soldier in the ranks, never received promotion beyond captain, and although San Martín joined as a cadet he too would suffer in promotion prospects from the existing system. *Hidalgos* and commoners tended to stay at the bottom, while the upper ranks were dominated by the higher nobility who often moved straight to the top through wealth and influence at court. In 1788 his two elder brothers, Manuel Tadeo and Juan Fermín Rafael entered the Infantry Regiment of Soria as cadets. And on 21 July 1789 at the age of eleven José was accepted as a cadet in the Infantry Regiment of Murcia, whose barracks were in Málaga, where his father had to contribute towards his subsistence. The bias against less privileged officers was exacerbated by the lag of military salaries behind inflation, especially in the period 1780–98; officers' salaries remained fixed at the 1768 level until 1791, when they were raised by an average of 16.5 per cent; five years later the severe financial difficulties of Charles IV's government forced it to reduce officers' salaries by some 21 per cent. On the other hand officers benefited from possession of the *fuero militar*, which gave them fiscal and legal privileges not enjoyed by the rest of the population. The officer corps remained divided between a privileged minority drawn from the upper nobility with influence at court and good promotion prospects, and a mass of lower officers living a life of boredom and poverty with little prospect of promotion. The secretary of the French embassy in Madrid was not far wide of the mark:

> Let us add, as an apology for the Spanish officers, that the life they lead is such as to benumb all their faculties. Most of their garrison towns are lonely places without resources either in respect of instruction or genteel amusements. Deprived entirely of furloughs, they seldom obtain leave to attend to their affairs . . . the obscure and monotonous life they lead, without any manoeuvres on a great scale, and without any reviews, at length deadens all activity.[14]

Yet the Spanish army could fight impressively when it was well led and equipped. The expedition to Algiers in 1775 was a model of military incompetence but within six years a Spanish army from Cuba, its main component European, crowned a successful campaign against the British with the capture of Pensacola, Florida, overcoming far greater planning, logistic and military difficulties than had ever presented themselves in the Mediterranean.

San Martín received his military training in his own regiment in Málaga. It was a practical training, with little theoretical content, though there were certain texts, particularly the *Ordenanzas militares* of 1768, the basic regulations for the Spanish army which officer recruits were expected to learn, and a short text *Instrucción militar cristiana para el Ejército y Armada de su Majestad*, a military catechism which had long been obligatory for cadets and offered a model for 'the Christian soldier', including Catholic prayers and encouragement for moral behaviour as well as military advice. Arithmetic and geometry, tactics and troop manoeuvres completed the training, and alongside these the young San Martín learnt the basics of soldiering, and acquired practical experience of discipline and leadership.

While still in his teens San Martín gained his first military experience in North Africa, where Spain had a number of fortified enclaves—Ceuta and Melilla (Morocco), and Oran (Algeria)—regarded as essential for security against Islam and to exert a Spanish presence in the western Mediterranean. Morocco was a target of diplomacy rather than force, being of some economic interest to Spain and a useful source of grain for Andalucía in times of dearth. The Algerians were more recalcitrant and recent Spanish expeditions against them had been abject failures. Oran, a fortified Spanish outpost consisting of the citadal, palaces, a market and a church, was struck by a severe earthquake in 1790 which killed the Spanish governor and thousands of inhabitants, and shattered many buildings; the crisis invited hostile pressure from Algiers and the Barbary pirates, and was exploited as usual by Spain's maritime enemies. It was decided to take action, if that is the right word for a stuttering perform-ance by the military planners. After a brief stay in Melilla, northern Morocco, San Martín's company was posted to Oran in April 1791, but a decision not to provoke a Muslim attack caused its withdrawal to Málaga. A further change of tactics took the Murcia Regiment back to relieve Oran from a Muslim siege, and San Martín spent seventeen days there before negotiations again halted operations; the pause was only temporary, for his unit was sent back to resist the siege in June 1791. San Martín's battalion was in action from 28 June in a series of bloody encounters in which the thirteen-year-old cadet received his baptism of fire; the campaign was hard—thirty-three days of close fighting, in which he found inspiring leadership from his company officer and true comradeship from his fellows. The Spanish government was less impressive. Having previously boasted that Spain would teach Europe how to treat these barbarians, it now decided that Oran was a source of friction rather than profit; on 12 September 1791 by the Convention of Algiers Spain relinquished Oran and began the evacuation of the once famous conquest of Cardinal Jiménez. San Martín was in the rearguard, among the last to leave in February 1792, and as he watched the military embarking with their flags unfurled but less than victorious, he could only conclude there was not much to show for his first experience of active service.[15]

On leaving Oran San Martín was stationed with his regiment in Cartagena where he had time to reflect on his North African experience. On the personal side, to have served there as a cadet and therefore presumably as a volunteer could not have harmed his prospects, and his brave conduct was the first mark of distinction in his military record. While his qualifications were improving, his progress was checked just when a looming war with France created vacan-cies in the officer corps. His promotion was halted by a malicious report from his colonel, who favoured another candidate. But the Inspector of Infantry overturned the decision, having found that San Martín's conduct in Oran was exemplary: he had done his duty calmly and bravely against the Moors, and his application, ability and conduct in 1791 were all described as good. So he received accelerated promotion to second lieutenant (19 July 1793), exchanging the bayonet for the officer's sword. On the other hand, in terms of Spain's credibility his first combat experience was disillusioning, an early cloud over his Spanish career. The long series of orders and counter-orders, the useless journeys in the western Mediterranean, the doubts hanging over the purpose of these isolated fortresses, and the final surrender with no mili-tary defeat to justify it, produced a sense of futility in the ranks of the regiment and challenged the morale of the young soldier.

Baptism of Fire

San Martín soon experienced a more serious challenge and a military response he could share with government and people alike. France's revolutionary expansionism and imperial ambition were making it a difficult neighbour, and the new National Convention (September 1792) declared war on Spain on 7 March 1793, a war to remove another Bourbon from his throne and to carry the French Revolution to the Spanish people. The Spanish people, however, did not want the Revolution, and French aggression provoked one of the most spontaneous war efforts in Spanish history. Priests preached it from their pulpits. Gifts of money poured into the government. The rush of volunteers came faster than the government could arm them. The Spanish people's traditional passion for their religion and their monarchy reasserted itself, and they rejected the Revolution with a fervour which was soon reflected in the advance of the armed forces. To the surprise of the Revolutionaries a Spanish army under General Antonio Ricardos invaded Roussillon in southeastern France in April, a premature success to be sure, but during the rest of 1793 the French army of the Eastern Pyrenees was occupied in repulsing the Spanish invasion. San Martín was among the invaders. He reached the front with the Murcia Regiment, sailing to the port of Los Alfaques, and marching from there to Zaragoza and finally to the mountain valleys of Arán and Tena, an abrupt introduction to long route marches and mountain terrain.

This was a war for God, king and country, but the Church was helpless, the king uninspiring and the country vulnerable. The truth was that the army was not fit for fighting. The Spanish forces were always inferior to the enemy in effective numbers. When the French struck back in Roussillon in April–May 1794 they had forty thousand men against twelve thousand on the Catalan front; in October 1794 the French had fifty thousand men in Navarre and Guipúzcoa, the Spaniards only twenty-three thousand to defend Pamplona. Poor generalship helped to lose the war for Spain. The military talents of the higher command fell far short of what was needed and reflected badly on the Spanish aristocracy; on the Roussillon front the generals were unbelievably inert. Godoy himself was found wanting, a decorative soldier masquerading as a war minister. The campaign itself was fought with staggering ineptitude and the leaders failed to match the prodigious war effort of the Spanish people.

The campaign began in April 1793 with Spanish forces dispersed along the frontier in a thin line. The offensive in Roussillon under the impetuous General Ricardos, who had his forces spread out between Boulou at the foot of the Pyrenees and Banyuls on the coast, was not strong enough in depth and, after a few offensive operations such as the attacks on Mont-Boulou, Tour de Batére and Banyuls, in all of which San Martín fought with his regiment, the offensive came to a halt in a fruitless blockade operation. This allowed the French to recover and hit back from April 1794. The Spaniards were repulsed across the Pyrenees and soon a large part of northern Catalonia was lost to the French. A similar course of events followed in the Basque provinces, and by April 1795 the Spanish war effort appeared to have broken and the will to win to have vanished as the French army pressed forward. At this point Godoy and his colleagues lost their nerve and decided to cut their losses. The Peace of Basle brought the war to a conclusion on 22 July 1795, when Spain was fortunate to recover all the territory lost in the pensinsula but, in the subsequent alliance, was forced to place troops, ships and money at France's disposal, becoming in effect a satellite of France for the rest of the century and beyond.

The events of 1793–95 revealed that Spain was utterly unprepared for total war and they left a lasting impression on San Martín. The army was ill-equipped to face a conflict and an enemy of this kind, an eighteenth-century army against a nation in arms, a dynastic cause against a revolutionary struggle. In March 1794 some of these points had been made by the count of Aranda, one of the few dissidents in the Spanish ruling class, in a confrontation with Godoy in the council of state. Aranda argued that the war with France was unjust, impolitic, beyond Spain's resources and risky to the monarchy. The French were fighting for liberty and independence, unlike the Spanish army; their cause was superior to that of Spain.[16] Thoughts of this kind—the power of a national cause and the irresistibility of an army representing the people in arms—foreshadowed the future thinking of San Martín when, in the years after 1810, he surveyed the prospects of Spanish America.

Meanwhile as the Spanish offensive in Roussillon came to a halt, the capitulation of the besieged Spanish troops in the nearby coastal town of Collioure (27 May 1794), for whom no fleet came to the rescue, converted San Martín and his comrades into prisoners-of-war; they were exchanged and repatriated to Barcelona on condition that they took no further action against France, a common practice at the time. There, in July 1794, San Martín was promoted to first lieutenant. The campaign in Roussillon was not entirely wasted on him. He had gained further experience in manoeuvres and combat, specifically in the tactics of light infantry, a more mobile and less routine arm than the regular infantry, and he had fought in the highlands as well as the plains, combat terrain which rehearsed the conditions that awaited him in South America.

The Spanish alliance with France, sealed in the Treaty of San Ildefonso on 18 August 1796, was a prelude to French ideological influence in books and revolutionary literature, not least in Cartagena, southeastern Spain, where San Martín was now stationed and where he had contact with French culture, acquired numerous French books and some knowledge of the language. The alliance was also followed by war with Great Britain and exposure to British sea power, dominant after the battle of Cape St Vincent in 1797. To improve security against Britain, resist enemy corsairs and keep the maritime routes open, Spain launched a fleet of rapid frigates in the western Mediterranean. San Martín volunteered to serve as an infantry marine and was posted to the *Santa Dorotea*, a forty-gun frigate operating out of Cartagena from mid-1797. He remained on board for over a year as it escorted merchant vessels, carried arms and supplies, pursued corsairs and saw action against the enemy. He was in Toulon in May 1798 as a French expedition led by Napoleon was preparing to sail to Egypt. According to tradition, Napoleon stopped in front of San Martín during an inspection of a naval parade and, attracted by his different uniform, read out the name of the Murcia Regiment from a jacket button. In July 1798 the *Santa Dorotea* sailed on what was to be its last mission, from Cartagena to Algiers, and on returning to base was damaged in a sudden storm, losing its topmast and mizzen sail. On 15 July it encountered a British ship of seventy-four guns, the *Lion*, which attacked the crippled vessel and launched a boarding operation that lasted two hours.[17] The Spanish ship lost thirty of its crew killed in action and thirty-two gravely wounded, and after a spirited resistance was obliged to surrender, the survivors being transferred to a neutral vessel and shipped first to Mahon, then on 9 August to Cartagena, on an undertaking not to fight against the British until there was an exchange of prisoners. San Martín remained under this honorary imprisonment until 1801. Again, the experience was not lost on him; naval service was uncommon among infantry officers and ensured that he was not a complete novice when the time came to launch the invasion of Peru from the Pacific.

Spain had to deliver on its alliance with France, partly in subsidies and partly in military collaboration. In 1801 it was required to move against Portugal to force it to abandon its alliance with Britain and close its ports to British trade and influence. Godoy saw Napoleon as a man 'whose loyalty and good faith were not things obvious from his previous record', and he sought to anticipate the projected French invasion by making a preemptive strike, which would overcome Portugal without the intrusion of France. So he acted rapidly. Spanish generals were not known to be willing volunteers and several excused themselves or refused outright to command this operation; so Charles IV appointed Godoy himself as supreme commander of the invading army. The divisions led by the marquis of Castelar took the initiative in the first assault on the fortresses of Olivenza and Jurumeña, and San Martín fought in these actions. Portugal sued for peace, signed at Badajoz on 6 July 1801, agreeing to close its ports to British shipping. Thus ended the 'war of the oranges', referring to the trophies taken from the orange trees at the fortress of Elvas, which Godoy presented to Queen María Luisa. San Martín was unscathed in this inglorious war but not in its aftermath. Late in 1801 one of his duties was to take reinforcements to his Murcia Regiment from volunteers he had recruited in Old Castile. Lack of horses in one of the villages he passed through separated him from the rest of his unit. Once mounted he hastened to catch up with his men. On the road from Valladolid to Salamanca four bandits attacked him; he drew his sword and resisted, receiving two wounds, one in the chest and quite serious, the other in his right hand, and he was robbed of his baggage, including the money left over from his mission. Wounded and bleeding, he was picked up by passing travellers who took him to the village of Cubo de la Tierra del Vino. His military superiors approved his conduct and he was exonerated for the loss of 3,350 reales. So far so little. After a false start in the Pyrenees and a brief campaign in Portugal his military career stagnated in the years after 1800; he continued as second lieutenant, without promotion, surveying an international situation that held no better prospects for Spain.

In 1802, taking advantage of the respite offered by the Peace of Amiens, Godoy turned his attention to Spain's failing army; his reforms involved adjustments to existing regiments and the creation of new units. A battalion of light infantry, the Voluntarios de Campo Mayor, was formed in Seville in March 1803, and San Martín was appointed second adjutant; while not an advancement in rank it was a new experience, one in which he could learn to organize, equip and train a new unit. At the end of 1803 the Voluntarios de Campo Mayor were transferred to Cádiz, a place that would always carry a special meaning for San Martín. Cádiz was Spain's leading port, a promontory at the end of a peninsula, joined to the Isla de León by a causeway. Defended by sea walls, enriched by trade with America, its harbour was a focus for merchant and naval vessels, many of them built in its own shipyards. The population was divided between those enriched by trade and others marginalized by poverty, though relief was provided in the *hospicio*, a large workhouse for the poor, destitute and orphans.[18] Cádiz was soon to be famous for its defence of Spanish independence and its debates on a liberal constitution. For Americans the imperial role of Cádiz made it a vital link to their homelands but also an obstacle to their liberation. Cádiz became a beacon in the life of San Martín, at once a welcome and a warning on the road to America.

In Cádiz San Martín became close to a new senior colleague, whose friendship left a permanent impression on him. Lieutenant General Francisco María Solano, marquis of Socorro, native of Caracas, captain general of Andalucía, and civil and military governor of Cádiz, was a rare talent in the military hierarchy of Bourbon Spain. He had served in the major campaigns of the time, including a period in the French Army of the Rhine. He was active in introducing French tactics into the Spanish army, not least in the Voluntarios de Campo Mayor, which became a model for purposes of instruction. San Martín now acquired a special expertise in the methods of training troops, under the influence of an expert whom he respected. In Cádiz he also endured the ordeal of a yellow fever epidemic that decimated the ranks of the Voluntarios; his exemplary conduct was treated as war service and earned him promotion in November 1804 to second captain in the second company, a position that would place him in the front line of any action. For the moment active service meant garrison duty and patrols against the contrabandists and criminals swarming in Andalucía, but he earned further distinction as an aide to lieutenant General Solano.

The predictable renewal of war with Britain was to draw attention to the flaws in Spanish policy and military planning which fitful modernization did little to overcome. Conservative opposition prevented Godoy from introducing new French tactics, and the army's supply system continued to be neglected. Godoy, a favourite who bred favourites, created too many generals, a corrupt form of patronage and recruited too few troops. Once Britain renewed the war with France, in May 1803, treasure shipments were at risk, yet Godoy never wavered in his choice, or fear, of the French ally. The Spanish government had manoeuvred itself into the weakest of positions. Peninsular defences had not improved since 1783; colonial trade was threatened by Britain; and treasure receipts were drained by France to the tune of a monthly subsidy of six million livres.

Spain now lost the last shreds of its sea power. In October 1804, anticipating formal war, a British squadron intercepted a large treasure shipment from Callao and Buenos Aires, sank one Spanish vessel and captured three others carrying 4.7 million pesos, of which 1.3 million were for the Crown.[19] Among the survivors was Captain Diego de Alvear and his fifteen-year-old son Carlos, future friend and eventual nemesis of San Martín, while the rest of the Alvear family perished. On 12 December Spain declared war on Britain, entered a maritime alliance with France on 4 January 1805, and ten months later suffered disaster at Trafalgar, the preparations and aftermath of which San Martín observed from the home port of Cádiz. Spain now entered unknown territory, an imperial power without a fleet, colonies without a metropolis.

Soon San Martín received news of another blow to the Spanish empire. In 1806 a British expeditionary force from the Cape of Good Hope crossed the south Atlantic, entered the Río de la Plata and occupied Buenos Aires. The invaders were experts in combined operations but they underestimated the will and the ability of the people of Buenos Aires to defend themselves. While the Spanish viceroy, the marquis of Sobremonte, fled into the interior and the wealthy citizens of Buenos Aires sought the shelter of their country houses, the lower classes and many of the younger generation took to the streets to hurl defiance and confront the British. Creoles rather than Spaniards formed a volunteer army which defeated the British force and took its commander and twelve hundred troops captive. Creole initiative was also evident in the following year, 1807, when the viceroy was deposed and reinforcements from Britain were overcome and forced to capitulate.

To the American San Martín the British invasions of the Río de la Plata taught a number of lessons. They showed that his countrymen were unwilling to exchange one imperial master for another. They also exposed gaping holes in Spain's southern empire, its fragile administration, its feeble defences. It was the local inhabitants, not Spain, who had defended the colony; the creoles had discovered their strength and acquired a sense of identity. Cornelio de Saavedra, the creole militia leader, spoke of 'the merit of those born in the Indies . . . not inferior to European Spaniards', and pointed out that 'Buenos Aires accomplished this memorable and glorious defence with its own sons and its own people alone'.[20] San Martín, born in the Indies and surrounded by European Spaniards, had much to think about.

The Peninsular War

Napoleon was determined to reduce the Iberian Peninsula to French control, close the ports to British trade and impose his own rulers. But the French invasions of Portugal and Spain in 1807–8 had mixed results. The Portuguese royal family together with a crowd of courtiers, the bureaucracy and many of the ruling elite embarked in the Tagus to seek refuge in Brazil, taking with them a great quantity of treasure and most of the British merchant community. Out of Lisbon they were met by British warships, which convoyed them to the safety of Brazil. So this was a prize that eluded Napoleon. The Spanish response was not so adroit. While French armies crossed Spain to get to grips with Portugal, Spain was also required to invade its neighbour. But the Spanish army was not ready for war. Its shortcomings were predictable: there was no advance planning, no liaison with its ally and no ready reserves of men or resources. Full of misgivings, General Solano was charged in 1807 with leading the invasion of the southern frontier by a Spanish division of six thousand men, and he was fortunate to meet little opposition. San Martín participated in this ramshackle expedition as 'capitán de guías', personally appointed by Solano. Alentejo and Extremadura were occupied without fighting in December 1807 and Solano's forces encamped at Setúbal, while the army of the French General Jean-Andoche Junot occupied Lisbon on 30 November. It was a brief campaign, a mere pretext for a large army of French troops to occupy Spain. Reacting to French duplicity, Godoy ordered the Spanish troops in Portugal to return to Spain. His government, however, was running out of time.

On the night of 17 March, 1808, there was a riot at Aranjuez by a mob of soldiers, peasants and palace workers. Godoy, whose home had been heavily guarded for years, was suddenly left unprotected; he went into hiding inside a rolled-up carpet in an attic of his house, to emerge hungry and thirsty to face a bleak future, first arrest, then pardon and finally exile, while his royal patron Charles IV was forced to abdicate in favour of his son and heir Ferdinand VII. This was not a 'popular' rebellion. It was headed by Ferdinand and his partisans, organized by the grandees and titled nobility, implemented by the army and the mob, in the cause of an aristocratic government as against one of favourites and bureaucrats. Miserable the country with choices like these! Charles IV and María Luisa were sent to France, but the *fernandistas* found that they had miscalculated. Napoleon had sent his troops not to rid them of Godoy but to rob them of Ferdinand. He too was sent to France and at Bayonne on 10 May, in a grotesque parody of kingship, the Spanish Bourbons were forced to abdicate in favour of the emperor's candidate, his brother Joseph Bonaparte. But Napoleon did not win either.

At first the Spanish people blamed Godoy for everything. They soon discovered that things were not so simple and that Spain had many problems, some of its own making, some from across the Pyrenees. They rose against the French. The rising in Madrid on 2 May 1808, wild, unplanned and poorly armed, was easily crushed by the Imperial Guard, which moved through the streets shooting and killing and dispensing summary justice. One scene on the night of 2 May was captured by Goya, a group of men kneeling, one at the front with his arms flung wide and his mouth open, and the firing squad aiming their muskets. Gradually rebellion became more organized, as the Spanish army opened its ranks to volunteers; guerrillas were recruited, provincial juntas organized resistance, and a Junta Central sought the role of a central government. Drawn from the regular army and new recruits, Spanish resistance acquired a rudimentary military structure in the form of field armies based on Asturias, Galicia, Old Castile, Extremadura, Andalucía, the Levant and Catalonia. Two of the regional juntas, first Asturias then La Coruña, made contact with London. Alliances were reversed: Spain joined the British, and re-enacted with greater confidence, stronger interests, and eventually more success, the alliance of 1793. The scene was set for the Peninsular War, known to Spaniards as their War of Independence.

San Martín was not a passive spectator of these events. His critical observation of Spain's decline now became a deep disillusion, and the English alliance was soon to affect him personally. Solano returned from Portugal, and at Badajoz attempted to rally the Spanish army against the French invaders, a futile exercise. The Spanish army was in no condition to resist. Solano decided that discretion was the better part of valour, but he was now a marked man by those who wanted to resist, namely the Junta of Seville, which at the beginning of the uprising had given itself the title of 'Supreme Junta of Spain and the Indies' and disputed the role of central government with the Junta Central, now also located in Seville. The Junta of Seville sent emissaries to provoke insurrection in Cádiz, where the mob was stirring. Solano faced a painful dilemma. Should he join the anti-French movement, now being 'organized' by the Junta of Seville? Or should he wait and see? He and other generals sought to contain Spaniards within existing military institutions, encouraging them either to join the army or stay at home. But this did not satisfy the insurgents in Cádiz, pushed by the Junta of Seville, and they made to storm the governor's house, seeking the general whom they identified as a supporter of the French. Now Solano's dilemma was also the dilemma of San Martín.

The officer in charge of the guard drew up defensive positions to block the way and ordered two bursts of fire in the air. Was this San Martín? Possibly. He despised the *populacho* (mob). It would not have been surprising had he stood by Solano, and fearing for his friend's life, confronted the insurgents using his authority over the Voluntarios de Campo Mayor, giving Solano a chance to escape. The insurgents turned canon on the entrance to the governor's house and stormed in. Solano escaped over the roof to the house next door belonging to an Irish lady, but he came out of hiding to spare the neighbours and face the mob; he managed to stagger wounded as far as the plaza of San Juan de Dios, where he was killed by a sword thrust. San Martín, frustrated in his efforts to save Solano, sought refuge in the house of a friend until he could escape to Seville.[21]

Other sources tell another story: San Martín arrived from duty in the Isla de León to find that the mob had just killed Solano. He fought his way through the crowd to his friend's body but he was surrounded and pushed away amidst shouts of 'Kill him!' from some who mistook him for Solano. His sword was broken in the struggle but he resisted his attackers and ran in the direction of the port. He took refuge in the church of the Capuchinos, where a friar raised a crucifix and stood between him and the mob, affirming that this was not Solano but San Martín and he wanted him saved. So San Martín was able to escape; he took the friar's hand and said 'I'll not forget this', and ran off.[22] It was a day of grief he never forgot.

As associates of San Martín were persecuted in the following days, Lieutenant Colonel Juan de la Cruz Murgeón hid him in his house until he was able to leave for Seville; from there he managed to rejoin his unit, the Voluntarios de Campo Mayor, then stationed in Ronda. He now abandoned his policy of 'wait and see' and decided to join the Spanish rising against the French. It was not an uncomplicated decision. The memory of the *populacho* never left him, and he retained a permanent hatred of political extremism and popular power.

At the beginning of June 1808 the Junta of Seville had appointed San Martín major-general in the forces commanded by Colonel Francisco Torres in Jaén. But before he could take up the appointment he was posted with his regiment, the Voluntarios de Campo Mayor, to the Army of Andalucía led by General Francisco Javier Castaños, who was recruiting, organizing and training Spanish troops in Utrera. A shock force, the Agrupación de Montaña volante was led by Murgeón, whose vanguard was commanded by San Martín. On 23 June in the vicinity of Arjonilla, San Martín was leading a small joint force of cavalry and infantry as an advance party when he came up against an enemy reconnaissance force. Murgeón ordered an attack but the French withdrew. San Martín marched by a short cut to intercept them, and although apparently outnumbered ordered an attack which was vigorously conducted and killed twenty French dragoons. He put the rest to flight and would have continued the pursuit had not the retreat sounded, as Murgeón was aware that the French were bringing up 100 cavalry reinforcements. San Martín was disappointed that the remainder of the enemy detachment and its commanding officer were allowed to escape, but, as the official report made clear, he preferred obedience to 'his ambition for glory' and held back.[23] It was only a skirmish but he displayed two marks of a professional soldier, bravery and discipline; and up to then it was one of the few victories to Spain's account. He was promoted on 27 June to first adjutant of his regiment, then advanced to aide-de-camp of the Spanish commander, the marquis of Coupigny; and he acquired further status (6 July) as acting captain of Bourbon cavalry.[24]

The French commander, Pierre Dupont, vainly striving to subjugate Andalucía, held back from Córdoba and unaccountably stationed his forces at Andújar, where he had seventeen thousand troops against a much larger army of Spaniards.[25] At the end of June 1808 the army of Francisco Castaños left Utrera, and moved towards Córdoba following the River Guadalquivir. To this was joined the forces proceeding from Granada commanded by Teodoro Reding, a Swiss officer in the service of Spain. The reorganized force consisted of at least thirty-three thousand, plus numerous volunteers recruited by the various juntas. General Castaños divided his force into four divisions. The first, under his command, was deployed to threaten the main force of Dupont and pin it down in Andújar; another group, made up of the divisions of Reding and the marquis of Coupigny, was manoeuvred to make a detour across the Guadalquivir and join up in Bailén; after routing the French there, they would return towards Andújar, remaining in position to attack the enemy from behind and then surround him. A fourth division would attack Dupont from the north. To divide the attack in this way was not best strategy and ran the risk of exposing each Spanish component to piecemeal destruction by a united French force. In the event the Spaniards were lucky. By chance or good judgement, in a series of confused operations beginning on 14 July, they left Dupont and his commanders to make a succession of mistakes, moving the French forces to counter non-existent threats and to leave their own strategic position divided. It was becoming clear that the Spanish artillery was superior to that of the French and consistently outgunned the enemy. Both forces suffered from the climate, the heat oppressive in a brown landscape, relieved only by occasional olive groves and the ruins of Moorish sites.

Coupigny's force, in which San Martín was serving as his aide, defeated the French battalions in the battle of Villanueva de la Reina. After crossing the Guadalquivir and joining up with Reding's division, they marched towards Bailén and from there west to Andújar to attack the headquarters of Dupont, forcing him to evacuate his centre and finally fall back on Bailén. At daybreak on 19 July the French vanguard encountered the forward troops of Reding and Coupigny, and for nine hours there followed a hard battle under a burning sun among the olive groves and ilex trees; Coupigny and his forces took the major part, as Reding acknowledged, and forced the capitulation of almost eighteen thousand French troops. 'Thus ended a day of confusion and slaughter.' Handing his sword to Castaños, Dupont remarked, 'You may well, General, be proud of this day; it is remarkable because I have never lost a pitched battle until now—I who have been in more than twenty'. The reply of Castaños was ironic: 'It is the more remarkable because I was never in one before in my life'.[26] Spain rejoiced. Napoleon was furious: 'In all the history of the world there has never been anything so stupid, so inept or so cowardly'. For his active combat role in the battle San Martín was promoted to lieutenant colonel of cavalry and decorated with the Bailén medal by the Junta of Seville. Coupigny congratulated him and commiserated too for the ill health he was then suffering.[27] His problem was a chest complaint that took him out of action to Seville to seek a cure, and Castaños gave him a job in the military inspectorate.

Bailén dented the myth of the invincibility of French armies. It was also a propaganda coup for the Spaniards, who made more of it than it deserved. Sir Arthur Wellesley, the future Duke of Wellington, believed that 'no-one was more surprised at the result of Bailén than Castaños himself'.[28] But Joseph Bonaparte, foolish victim of his brother's favour and Spanish ridicule, promptly backed out of Madrid, seeking a safer base first in Burgos then Vitoria, and the French abandoned the siege of Zaragoza. While Joseph was mocked for his loss of nerve—and his alleged drinking—Castaños entered Madrid in triumph on 23 August. With Wellington and Sir John Moore in Portugal, England was entering the fight. And three Spanish armies—Galicia, Andalucía and Aragon—brought in more Spanish volunteers. But France soon fought back and the Junta Central beat a hasty retreat to Seville before the end of the year. Napoleon took over, and with his best marshals and an army of two hundred thousand he personally, if briefly, commanded his forces in Spain. The Spanish armies were defeated on numerous fronts, and on 3 December Napoleon entered Madrid in victory. When he left a month later, French power was firmly consolidated.

San Martín was still recuperating from his chest condition when Coupigny asked him to accompany him in his new command to the Army of Catalonia, where 'being immediately under me could advance you in your career'.[29] In May 1809 San Martín was sufficiently recovered to accept and to ask the Junta Central for leave to go. This was granted, and he remained in his new appointment for six months, during which he worked on supply and training of cavalry troops, and organizing the operations of the *somaténes*, the region's guerrillas, in so far as anyone could organize these unruly hordes.

But the crisis of Spanish arms worsened. The fall of Madrid to the French in late 1808 prefaced the collapse of the Spanish position in central Spain. Joaquín Blake, the grandson of a Scottish Jacobite, suffered sucessive defeats. The retreat of Sir John Moore's army westwards to La Coruña, where Moore himself was fatally wounded, was a crushing disaster, a blow to British prestige as well as to Spanish morale, though raised to glory in the ode by Charles Wolfe.

> *Not a drum was heard, not a funeral note,*
> *As his corse to the rampart we hurried.*
> *Not a soldier discharged his farewell shot*
> *O'er the grave where our hero we buried.*

Buried too were the hopes of an early end to the war. The French occupied Zaragoza, and Marshal Soult's victory at Ocaña in November 1809 left Andalucía open to the invaders. Patriot Spain was in full retreat. The Junta Central was driven into a corner; having already retreated to Seville, it then moved to Cádiz, and finally to the Isla de León; in January 1810 it dissolved itself, leaving in its place a Council of Regency, a highly conservative body, spiritual heir of the old regime, but responsible for convoking a cortes, on which liberals pinned their hopes. In Extremadura the marquis of La Romana led the Army of the Left on the frontier with Portugal, and Coupigny followed by his aide, San Martín, joined this in January 1810. But he could only observe further defeats, as Ciudad Rodrigo and Almeida were besieged and capitulated in August 1810. In October San Martín joined the Lines of Torres Vedras set by Wellington to block the French advance on Lisbon; there he was able to observe English strategy in operation, and the use of fortifications and trenches in combination with guerrilla attacks to create an impregnable system of defence.

From February 1811 San Martín was in Cádiz with Coupigny. Cádiz, besieged by Marshal Victor, duke of Belluno was the ultimate bastion of Spanish independence and government, from which San Martín was at last able to claim and receive his arrears of pay, and to receive instructions to accompany Coupigny, now general in chief of the second army in Valencia. But these orders were changed and after the battle of Chiclana on 5 March Coupigny was placed in command of the fourth army defending Cádiz. Disputes between General Sir Thomas Graham commanding the Anglo-Portuguese division and the incompetent Spanish general Manuel la Peña (known even to Spaniards as Doña Manolita), who took the feeble decision to fall back upon the Isla de León, allowed the French besieging forces a victory they did not merit, and La Peña was justifiably replaced.[30] San Martín remained with Coupigny, even after his own appointment (26 July 1811) as commander of the regiment of Dragoons of Sagunto. He had already made up his mind on his future.

His true identity, long dormant, now revived at a time of weakness of Spain and opportunity for America. A failing state in the Old World and the prospect of emerging states in the New, these two factors stirred the embers of his American conscience. It was an opportunity for San Martín, conscious as he was that Americans could not normally satisfy their highest ambitions in the mother country. When, in 1808, the metropolis was severed from its colonies by the French invaders, a crisis of authority arose. Who ruled in America? Who should be obeyed? As legitimacy and loyalty were disputed San Martín had every reason to question his own position. Spanish liberals were no less imperialist than Spanish conservatives. The cortes of Cádiz was working on a new constitution, which would declare Spain and America a single nation. But while Americans were granted representation they were denied equal representation, and while they were promised reform they were refused freedom of trade.

Time of Decision

These years brought San Martín into touch with a number of Spanish Americans who were in the peninsula for a variety of reasons, messengers or perhaps exponents of new political ideas, more or less influenced by current liberalism and opposition to absolutism, and focusing more pointedly on freedom for their own countries. Groups of American dissidents, some of them in contact with the Venezuelan precursor of independence, Francisco de Miranda, held meetings in Madrid, Seville and Cádiz in the years 1807–11, and with the Napoleonic invasion many returned to America, believing that the time had come for action. During his time in Cádiz from February 1811,

San Martín was known to participate in meetings of the American group, reassembled after its dispersion from Seville, sometimes called the *Sociedad de Caballeros Racionales* and regarded by later historians as a secret society indirectly linked to masonry, professing liberal and enlightened principles, and using rites, codes and entry rituals. The evidence for masonic identity is meagre and in view of the secrecy impossible to obtain, though some members probably belonged to masonic lodges outside their American activities; their function was essentially political, to recruit the future leaders of independence and keep the cause alive. One of San Martín's former Cádiz associates, General José Rivadeneira, met him again in Huaura in 1821: 'He embraced me and recalled our old friendship, our endeavours in the society in Cádiz, where we worked to make America independent.'[31] San Martín at least knew of the existence of a lodge in Cádiz, of which Carlos de Alvear was a member, even if there is no proof that he actually swore into it.[32]

San Martín was on active service in Portugal when news first arrived of the events of 1810 in Spanish America, rebellion against colonial authorities and rejection of Spanish officials. On his return to Cádiz in February 1811 he could learn more of events in Buenos Aires and perhaps have contact with those disposed to rebellion, and enrol in the Sociedad de Caballeros Racionales. Looking beyond Cádiz he could not ignore the irresistible waves of French advance across the peninsula and the impotence of the Spanish authorities. His dilemma seemed hopeless. On the one hand his personal prospects were getting worse and difficult to foresee, and Spain was not generous towards Americans of humble birth. What hope could he have in a failed Spain? On the other hand he saw a modern France with some liberal appeal but basically an enemy invader intent on conquest and dominion. He was on the side of resistance to the invaders but he had little faith in the disorderly and incompetent juntas, much less in the five-person Regency, of doubtful legitimacy and tied to the interests of the Cádiz merchants who looked upon America as a captive market. As for the cortes, it was debating a constitution for a non-existent state and for a society in which privilege and hierarchy were deeply embedded. As the Spanish monarchy had vanished, where did that leave allegiance to the king? San Martín's own convictions were liberal, though he had a horror of populism and demagoguery, as well as an aversion to absolutism.

After twenty-two years in the service of Spain he could not identify with any point of allegiance. Juntas, absolutists, the French, all were repugnant, while the Spanish army was no longer a profession for a man of ambition. He could not deny that Spain's war of independence was a noble cause. But it was not at first brilliantly fought. The years 1810–11 were desperate years for the Spanish army. The war in the peninsula seemed to be slipping away from patriot control. The fall of Ciudad Rodrigo on 9 July 1810 after relentless bombardment and the surrender of Badajoz in March 1811 in needless haste cancelled out Wellington's triumph in Portugal, and left the Spaniards blaming the British and the British furious with the Spaniards.[33] The Spanish army redeemed itself in the bloody battle of Albuera (16 May 1811), Byron's 'glorious field of grief' in the arid plains of Extremadura, which showed that Anglo-Spanish cooperation could at least contain the French. The way was now open for greater victories in 1812. The recovery of Ciudad Rodrigo (January 1812), where Wellington threw his army into the breaches and the guerrillas of Julián Sánchez harried the French everywhere, was followed by the violent pounding of Badajoz which fell in March. Wellington was now free to march on Salamanca. There, watching the French through his telescope, he pounced on the tactical mistake of his opponents marching across his front in an overstretched line, threw his half-finished chicken leg over his shoulder, and shouting 'By God, that will do!' leaped on his horse, and rode off to inspire a legendary victory on 22 July 1812, 'Wellington's masterpiece.'[34] Now the controversial—to Spaniards—appointment of Wellington as commander-in-chief of the Spanish army was no more than realistic and Spaniards could believe at last that their war of independence was winnable.

Did San Martín share these beliefs? He did not say. The Peninsular War was a paradox. A war of liberation for Spain, it was an imperial war in the eyes of San Martín, fought to restore Spain's power in America as well as its independence in Europe. The experience caused him to re-examine his Spanish allegiance. America was showing another way. In Buenos Aires Americans had resisted and rejected British invaders, then shown indifference to Napoleon's emissaries, and finally rose in rebellion against the colonial authorities. Yet San Martín's case was not the same as that of other Americans in Spain and Europe, different too from that of the revolutionaries in Buenos Aires. He was an officer of Spain with twenty-two years service, a record not easily disavowed. So his next decision was difficult. He needed an even stronger cause to convince him and give him an alternative loyalty—a national cause of his own. Towards mid-1811 the American group in Cádiz, knowing of events in Buenos Aires since 1808 and the hostile reaction of Spain, and aware of the interest of Napoleon, secretly prepared to get patriot members back to the Río de la Plata. San Martín had to plan his own route.

He later gave three versions of his decision to change allegiance.[35] The first was in 1819 when he sent his resignation from command of the Army of the Andes to the Supreme Director in Buenos Aires. 'In 1811, when I was in the service of Spain as Squadron Commander in the Cavalry Regiment of Bourbon, I heard the first news of the movements in the Americas on behalf of emancipation from the tyrannical government of Spain. From this moment I decided to employ my modest services to wherever insurrections were occurring: I preferred to come to my country of birth, and here I have done whatever has been within my powers: my country has repaid my modest services, loading me with honours I scarcely deserve'[36] The second occasion was in April–May 1827; he was replying, in the third person, to General William Miller on various questions of detail when the latter was preparing his memoirs. 'General San Martín had no other object in going to America than to offer his services to the Government of Buenos Aires. A prominent English resident in Cádiz at that time, a friend of the General, to whom he confided his decision to go to America, obtained passage for him on an English warship as far as Lisbon, offering him with the greatest generosity his monetary assistance, which while not accepted has always been much appreciated'. The third is a much-quoted explanation written in 1848 towards the end of his life to the Peruvian statesman, General Ramón Castilla, in a letter that was the nearest San Martín ever came to an *apologia pro vita sua*: 'Like you, I served in the Spanish army, in my case in the Peninsula, from the age of thirteen to twenty-four, reaching the rank of lieutenant colonel of cavalry. In a meeting of Americans in Cádiz, knowing of the first movements which had occurred in Caracas, Buenos Aires and elsewhere, we resolved to return each to our country of birth, in order to offer our services in the struggle which we considered was bound to grow'.[37] For San Martín this meant a return to Argentina, and his explanations were simple and consistent.

San Martín's life so far had been an exemplary if conventional career as a Spanish officer, who had never stepped out of line, criticized policy, queried an order or departed from the austerity that seemed to be the hallmark of his character. Behind the veil of correctness, however, there lay a mind and a will capable of rising beyond present discontents. There was already a sense of destiny in San Martín. His preference for his native land was a calculated decision, based on an inner compulsion which almost precluded choice. Some years later he confessed that he had to accept 'the misfortune of being a man in public life; yes, my friend, the misfortune, because I am convinced that you are what you have to be, otherwise you are nothing'.[38] He seemed to be saying that you have to take decisions without fear of the personal consequences, driven by stern necessity; more than this, you have to accept and preserve your own identity. In 1811 he saw what he had to do: if he remained in Spain he would be nothing. If he returned to Argentina he could achieve great things in a greater cause.

He appears to have been motivated, therefore, not by private ambition or search for power, but by liberal political ideas, disillusion with Spain, and a sense of personal and national identity. Place of birth was decisive for identity in the Hispanic world. Theoretically Spaniards born in the New World were no less Spaniards than those born in the peninsula. But they were known as *criollos* as distinct from *peninsulares* and in practice they suffered discrimination in social perception and in appointments to higher office in Church and state, in Spain and in America. San Martín admitted that his status of *indiano* (in the sense of *americano*) had not prejudiced his military career in Spain: 'twenty years of honourable service had brought me some consideration, in spite of being American; I knew of the revolution in my country, and in abandoning my hopes and sacrificing my career I only wanted to contribute to the freedom of my native land.'[39] But the creole awareness of *patria* was so strong that it overcame his long association with the Spanish cause and the Bourbon regime. Yet San Martín wanted a firmer launching pad than a decrepit metropolis, which although it was fighting for its own liberation from France was still opposed to Spanish America's liberation from Spain. He wanted the experience, the contacts and the prestige that he could only gain from a visit to England.

He decided to resign from the Spanish army, setting the authorities a false trail and inviting a favourable reply. In his request to the Regency (26 August 1811) he stated that he had to go to Lima to regulate his financial interests, lately abandoned for lack of attention; the visit would improve his income and, as a taxpayer, that of the treasury too. He calculated well in specifying Lima, which was a bulwark of the royalist cause in America and would thus reassure the authorities in Cádiz; he also mentioned the interests of two of his brothers serving in the Spanish army in the peninsula, invoking family loyalty. He did not request a pension, only the use of his uniform and the protection of the *fuero militar*. To use such an argument in time of war, that they would save an officer's salary, showed a certain contempt for the Regency government.[40] The authorities accepted that after twenty-two years' service his war record merited consideration; they accepted too his motives for retiring, to look after his neglected affairs in Lima. His request was granted and he was given permission to resign. So the Regency saved an officer's salary, and South America gained a liberator.

He left Cádiz towards the end of September, his destination not Lima but London. In Cádiz the members and motives of the American group were already known to British agents. The two sides were far apart in political ideas. The Americans wanted liberation for their countries and some looked to Britain for support. The British government had already in 1808 made it clear that its priority was not the independence of Spanish America from Spain but the independence of Spain from France, and the expeditionary force assembled at Cork under Sir Arthur Wellesley had sailed not for America but for the Spanish peninsula.

San Martín was not disturbed by these differences. In Cádiz he had a valued British friend in James Duff, an army officer in the Spanish service, an Oxford graduate, whose wife had died young of rabies in Edinburgh. To assuage his loss he had volunteered to join the Spanish in their war against Napoleon; he became a staff officer, and fought at the battle of Talavera and the siege of Cádiz, where he was severely wounded. In 1811 he became fourth Earl of Fife and returned to England.[41] Duff became a bridge for San Martín between Spain and England. He had good memories of San Martín and years later wrote from Edinburgh, 'I have always held a great friendship with you and since my return from Spain I have always been saying to my friends, Patience, there is a man over there who will surprise you all. I have always been convinced that a great blow would be delivered by your strong arm. For the moment I won't enter into the political history of your affairs, nor the motives, I only want to say that you can count on me as a good friend, highly interested in what is best for San Martín'. San Martín's reply, referring to his Chilean campaign, included a typical disclaimer: 'My warmest thanks for your congratulations upon the successful expedition to Chili, which though it ought alone to be attributed to the bravery of the troops and not to any moderate skill I may possess, is yet by Your Lordship ascribed to the latter, owing to the sentiments of friendship which you have ever entertained for me, and of which you have given me so many proofs'.[42]

It is easy to conjecture that Duff suggested the tactics and wording of his resignation, if not the basic idea. Through the good offices of Sir Charles Stuart, British minister at Lisbon and member of the Portuguese regency council, Duff obtained a passage for San Martín on 14 September 1811 on a British warship to Lisbon and thence to London. He abandoned Spain during a pause in its war of independence, when Wellington was still contained on the Portuguese frontier and the French were still in successful occupation of western Spain. He suffered no crisis of conscience. A soldier of his rank and seniority could not expect to make a difference in the strategy of the war; that would depend on the major ally, Britain, and not on Spain. The Spanish army as a career could guarantee him nothing; a victory for reaction would bring no satisfaction, while the liberal opposition was known to be anti-military.[43] In any case, his allegiance now lay elsewhere, and his new friends respected that allegiance. San Martín was well regarded among British army and naval officers. Commodore William Bowles subsequently gave him an excellent reference: 'I understand he was considered to possess considerable military talents, and was employed on the staff under General Castaños at the surrender of Dussault [Dupont], and subsequently with the Marquis Romana and General Peña, in which situation he must be known to many British officers. He is extremely friendly to the English, and I have every reason to believe entertains a sincere dislike to the French, whose cruelties and enormities in Spain I have heard him frequently relate and enlarge upon in public'.[44] San Martín not only left Spain, the Spanish army and his comrades in arms, but also his family. With the exception of his father, who had died in Málaga on 4 December 1796, he still had those with whom he had arrived in Spain. Two brothers Manuel Tadeo and Justo Rufino continued to fight in the Spanish service while Juan Fermín was stationed in Manila. His mother, Doña Gregoria, now seventy-three and living in Orense, Galicia, was cared for by her daughter, María Helena, who remained at her side until 28 March 1813, the day of her death.

San Martín stayed in London for four months, from September 1811 to 19 January 1812, too late to meet the Venezuelans Simón Bolívar and Francisco de Miranda but long enough to converse with their colleagues Andrés Bello and Luis López Méndez, with the Mexican Fray Servando Teresa de Mier, and the Argentines Carlos de Alvear and José Matías Zapiola, all of whom he met at Miranda's house of hope in Grafton Street, still haunted by the presence of the Precursor. Miranda was a man of the Enlightenment and a freemason from his time in France in the 1790s; he subscribed to the movement's ideals of fraternity, justice, toleration, liberty, and was seduced by its organization and secretiveness, which made it ideal for planning and dissidence. In London he had founded a Spanish American lodge, variously known as the *Gran Reunión Americana* or the *Sociedad de los Caballeros Racionales*, one of a network of pseudo-masonic lodges which Spanish Americans formed in Europe and America to plot independence and which were secret political societies, covers for revolutionary planning, rather than affiliates of pure freemasonry. Miranda's Spanish American lodge in exile, whose members swore to promote the independence of America and republican government, attracted many future liberators, who subsequently became leaders of affiliated societies in Spanish America.[45]

In London San Martín did not reproduce the role or the resonance of Miranda. That was not his style and it was not in his character to anticipate his prospects, which at the time he knew were modest and unpredictable. As he waited for a passage to Buenos Aires, he could ponder his assets. He still had to make his way in Argentina. Now aged thirty-four, he was a Spanish officer returning to the port he had left when he was barely six. It was not so much a return voyage as a journey to a new world. But he calculated that his presence in Britain, the greatest naval power in the world, the defender of freedom against despots and the home of liberal ideas, followed by his return to Buenos Aires with important, if informal, British contacts, gave him qualifications and legitimacy as a revolutionary leader that enabled him to overcome his Spanish past and to occupy immediately a position of authority in the revolution against Spain.

CHAPTER 2

The Revolution Calls

Decline and Fall of an Empire

The life of San Martín unfolded amidst turmoil in the Hispanic world. Spain ruled in America by virtue of conquest. But conquest was not the same as control: from the beginning of empire the claims of conquest had outstripped the capacity to enforce them and Spain always felt the danger of overstretch. For three centuries Spain had compensated for its military weakness in America by coopting Americans in the task of government and defence. Now, having lost power in the Atlantic to Britain and with it the route to its own possessions, Spain was unable to secure the trade and loyalty of its colonial subjects. San Martín could see that the fall of the Bourbons left government in terminal disarray. Once the metropolis lost its authority, he and others asked, who was their sovereign in America? And whom should they obey? As legitimacy and loyalty were disputed, argument gave way to violence, and resistance escalated into revolution. But if the war of independence was sudden and apparently unplanned, it had a long prehistory, during which colonial societies acquired identity, economies developed and ideas advanced to new positions. Demands were now made for autonomous institutions and a free economy, at the same time as the metropolis was threatened nearer home by France.

Most of the independence movements began as the revolt of one minority against a smaller minority, of creoles (Spaniards born in America) against *peninsulares* (Spaniards born in Spain); some creoles were royalists and the conflict often assumed the appearance of a civil war; and many simply stayed at home and waited for results. Around 1800, in a total population of 16.9 million, there were 3.2 million whites, of whom only some 30,000 were *peninsulares*. In demographic terms political change was overdue, not an accident of 1808. The aim of the revolutionaries was self-government for creoles, not necessarily for Indians, blacks or mixed races, who together comprised over 80 per cent of the population of Spanish America. The imbalance reflected the existing distribution of wealth and power. The newly aware creole groups of the late colonial period were indispensable for independence, to administer its institutions, defend its gains and conduct its trade.

The Spanish empire was not an evil empire. It had much to its credit in the development of institutions, the organization of the economy, the incorporation of social groups, the evangelization and education of peoples, and the exploration of the environment. Creole discontent was not the result of three centuries of oppression but a reaction to recent Spanish policy. Creoles in the late eighteenth century were heirs of a distinct tradition, and recalled a time, roughly 1650–1750, when their families had broken through imperial barriers, gained access to the bureaucracy, bargained over taxes and bypassed the Spanish trade monopoly. Political devolution was accompanied by economic autonomy: America had developed a strong internal market, producing agricultural products and manufactured goods, and selling them from region to region in a vital demonstration of self-sufficiency. In this way imperial government and commercial relations proceeded by compromise, and Americans reached a kind of colonial consensus with their metropolis. As they advanced into the regional oligarchy to become senior partners in the colonial compact, the creoles were living proof of the Baron de Montesquieu's dictum that while the Indies and Spain were two powers under the same master, 'the Indies are the principal one, and Spain is only secondary'.[1] This was the first Spanish empire, an empire of consensus, soon to be overtaken by a second empire, one of coercion.

Bourbon planners led by José de Gálvez, minister of the Indies, decided to bring the creole age to an end and to turn the clock back to more primitive political times. The object of the misnamed 'Bourbon reforms' from 1765 was to restore Spain to imperial greatness and to recover the colonies for the metropolis. But the policy backfired and helped to alienate the colonies beyond recall. Manuel Godoy, whose mind was usually on other things than America, taunted the policy of Gálvez, who had thought of little else. You should not deprive Americans of gains already made, he argued: 'It was not feasible to turn back, even though it might have been profitable to do so. People endure with patience the lack of benefits they have not yet enjoyed; but granted that they have acquired them as of right and enjoyed the taste, they are not going to agree to have them taken away.'[2] Hard imperial policy and resolute colonial responses were nowhere more evident than in the Río de la Plata, birthplace of San Martín.

The Río de la Plata underwent its first economic development in the eighteenth century, when an incipient cattle interest emerged, responding to *comercio libre* (free trade) and ready to expand the export of hides to Europe, and salted meat to Brazil and Cuba. From 1778 the Cádiz merchant houses with capital and contacts secured firm control of the Buenos Aires trade, and interposed themselves between the Río de la Plata and Europe. But in the 1790s these were challenged by independent *porteño* merchants, who procured slave concessions and with them permission to export hides. They employed their own capital and shipping, and offered better prices for hides than did the Cádiz merchants, freeing the *estancieros* from the grip of monopoly.[3] The normal *estancia* was small or medium size, capital investment was low and the lifestyle of its owner was austere.[4] The *estancieros* were not yet a political elite, but they formed a third pressure group, allies of the creole merchants against Spanish monopolists. These *porteño* interests had a spokesman in Manuel Belgrano, close collaborator of San Martín in the Andes campaign, and secretary of the *consulado*, or merchant guild, which he made a focus of liberal economic thinking.

Independence was more than a simple movement for free trade. Many freedoms had already been won: concessions such as trade with foreign colonies from 1795, and in neutral vessels from 1797, made the economic argument appear less urgent. But not less relevant. Americans had experienced the possibilities of economic growth within an imperial framework during the years of trade-induced prosperity, from 1776 to 1796. Now Spain's imperial world was collapsing, as the trade routes were cut by the British navy and interlopers came and went at will. In the course of 1797 American ports, including Buenos Aires, with the connivance of local officials traded directly with foreign ports. Spain was forced to allow a legal trade with Spanish America in neutral vessels, and was finally reduced to selling licences to various European and North American companies to trade with colonial ports, and the cargoes were often British manufactures. 'During a dozen years of warfare', a recent study has concluded, 'the commercial barriers surrounding the Spanish colonies collapsed, until by 1807 the British alone did business there to the extent of at least 13,000,000 pesos. This represented a first moment of something approaching free trade with foreign nations, managed and promoted moreover in no small part by Spanish Americans themselves'.[5] It seemed that Spanish Americans at last had an outlet to the world market, bypassing their own metropolis. In 1807 Spain received not one shipment of colonial treasure and to all appearances was no longer an Atlantic power.[6] Yet Spain did not abandon her claims, and Americans knew, and had it confirmed by experience in 1810, that no matter how unrealistic these claims were, the monopolists of Cádiz would never admit a full free trade and the Crown would never grant one. Only independence could destroy monopoly.

Conflict of economic interests did not exactly follow social divisions. Some creoles were associates of the monopolists, others sought alliance with royal officials. But there was a rough alignment of society according to interests. In Buenos Aires the merchant community itself split along Spanish–creole lines, the latter offering better prices to local ranchers, demanding freedom to trade with all countries and in 1809 urging that Buenos Aires be opened to British trade. The loathing of the *porteños* towards *peninsulares* can be read in the words of Mariano Moreno, radical lawyer and political activist, once the May Revolution had stripped away pretence:

The European Spaniard who set foot in these lands became noble as soon as he arrived, and was rich within a few years, master of all employment and thereby all powerful over subordinates, with the arrogance typical of those who are in command far from home. . . . And although they were well aware that, lacking the immediate presence of their country, supporters, and family, they were entirely dependent on the good will of their so-called brothers, they still bawled at them with contempt: 'Americans, keep your distance, you are not our equals, spare us that degradation, for nature has created you to vegetate in obscurity and dejection.'[7]

The new wave of *peninsulares* after 1760 encroached on the political space of the creoles as well as on their economic position. The policy of the later Bourbons was to increase the power of the state and apply to America closer imperial control. The clergy were pressured, their privileges curtailed, the Jesuits expelled, taxes extended and raised, and creoles demoted. This was a reversal of previous trends and took from Americans gains they had already made. Thus the great age of creole America, when the local elites bought their way into treasury, *audiencia* and other offices, and secured an apparently permanent role in administration, was followed from 1760 by a new order, when the government of Charles III began to reduce creole participation and to restore Spanish supremacy. Higher office in the *audiencias*, the army, the treasury and the Church was now reserved almost exclusively for *peninsulares*, at the same time as new opportunities in the transatlantic trade were made their special preserve. There was indeed a Spanish 'reaction' against creole influence in government, and this was experienced in most parts of America.

The experience was nowhere more striking than in the Río de la Plata. A new viceroyalty, it soon became a model of the new empire, a test for Spanish leadership in the South Atlantic. The arrival of more bureaucrats, military officers and churchmen increased the Spanish presence in Buenos Aires, and sharpened the division between *peninsulares* and creoles. Previously the minor strategic role of the port had created less need for imperial controls; creoles in the *cabildo* handled many matters of routine administration, while Spanish governors and officials were agents of inertia not of change. But the establishment of the viceroyalty and the appointment of intendants ended the creole age. While Spanish judges, intendants, commanders and clerks usurped the best offices, creoles were confined to minor positions. The effect of Bourbon innovation in Buenos Aires was to increase the power of the colonial state—now unmistakably a Spanish state—reminding creoles of their colonial status and making them more conscious that they were different from *peninsulares*. Of the eleven viceroys between 1776 and 1810 only one, Juan José de Vértiz, was an American, though not from the Río de la Plata. Of the thirty-five ministers of the *audiencia* of Buenos Aires in 1783–1810, twenty-six were born in Spain, six were creoles from other parts of America and only three were creoles of Buenos Aires.[8] No native of the Río de la Plata managed to obtain a confirmed royal appointment as an intendant in the viceroyalty. The bureaucracy of Buenos Aires was dominated by *peninsulares*; in the period 1776–1810 they held 64 per cent of appointments, natives of Buenos Aires 29 per cent and other Americans 7 per cent.[9]

By 1810 Buenos Aires was home to a Spanish party and a revolutionary party. The Spanish party consisted of peninsular officials and monopoly merchants, but also included some creole merchants who profited from trading links with Spain. The revolutionary party comprised creole bureaucrats and military who were critical of Spanish rule, creole merchants who specialized in neutral and other non-monopoly trade, smaller retail merchants and a few Spanish merchants of similar exporting interests. In other words, division between privileged and marginal merchants, between higher and lower bureaucracy, was also, though not absolutely, a division between Spaniards and creoles. The roots of independence, it is sometimes argued, are to be found in economic interests and social perceptions, or in an ideological division between conformists and dissidents, rather than in a simple Spanish-creole dichotomy. Neverthless, Americans were becoming conscious of their identity and interests, and aware that these were different from those of Spaniards. The viceroyalty brought the age of absolutism to Buenos Aires; it provided a new bureaucracy, more trade and an improved infrastructure. But it also brought a heavier burden of government, greater exploitation, a more peremptory policy.

The de-Americanization of the colonial state did not apply completely to its military arm. To recruit and pay a large standing army from the peninsula itself was not feasible, and for imperial defence Spain relied on colonial militias backed by a small regular army. By 1800–10 regular officers were predominantly creole and over 90 per cent of the militia officers were American-born; virtually all the soldiers were Americans.[10] In the Río de la Plata strategic reorientation and the establishment of the viceroyalty were supported by military reinforcements from Spain, among them San Martín's father. But in a shortsighted economy these were withdrawn in the 1790s and Buenos Aires was left exposed in a dangerous world. In 1806 the British invaders met with little opposition until local militias dominated by lower-class creoles were organized, to the surprise of the British and in due course the subversion of Spain. The creoles of the militias now elected their officers, which gave opportunity to men without fortune or training but with some prestige among the troops. There were also financial implications: the local administration had to pay for the new military, at the expense of remittances to Spain, and there was thus a transfer of resources to the urban creole sector which saw in the expanding military a means of profitable employment. This changed the balance of power in Buenos Aires towards the creoles and simultaneously raised the prestige of the military.[11] These developments had a double significance for San Martín: they meant that he would join a military establishment that had a higher social status than it had enjoyed before the British invasions, and one that carried sufficient political weight to launch him on a new career.

The Spanish American revolutions responded first to interests, and interests invoked ideas. The outbreak of the French Revolution in 1789 raised expectations, and many young creoles were fascinated by the ideas of liberty and equality, and by the war against tyrants. 'Since I was in Spain in 1789,' wrote Manuel Belgrano, 'at a time when the French Revolution was causing a change in ideas, particularly among the men of letters with whom I associated, the ideas of liberty, equality, security, and property, took a firm hold on me, and I saw only tyrants in those who would prevent a man, whatever his origins, from enjoying the rights with which God and Nature had endowed him, and which even human societies had agreed, directly or indirectly, to establish.'[12] The career of Belgrano exemplifies many of the stages of disillusionment experienced by educated creoles. Belgrano was born in Buenos Aires, educated at the Universities of Salamanca and Valladolid in Spain, and made a name for himself in the last years of colonial rule as an economist and secretary of the merchant guild in Buenos Aires. He played a prominent part in the revolution of May 1810, was a member of the governing junta which was then established in Buenos Aires, and finally became a general leading the armies of the revolution to distant provinces. There he became a close collaborator and admirer of San Martín, and he was the intellectual model who most inspired the soldier-liberator.

Before 1810 liberty was a dangerous call in Spanish America, a project without power. The French Revolution drew from the colonial authorities a fierce reaction that caused creole radicals to run for cover and enlightened ideas to go into hiding. Equality too was an illusion. The more radical the

French Revolution became the less it appealed to the creole elite. They saw it as a monster of extreme democracy, which, if admitted into America, would destroy the social order they knew, as it had destroyed the French slave colony of Saint-Domingue. During the course of the May Revolution in Buenos Aires, Mariano Moreno was regarded by the moderates led by Cornelio de Saavedra as an extremist, a '*malvado de Robespierre*' who would reproduce all that was worst in the French Revolution; they therefore moved quickly to marginalize him and protect the revolution from his influence. This was a characteristic response. Nevertheless the French Revolution in its imperial phase continued to cast its spell. Indirectly, in terms of military and strategic consequences, events in France had a resounding impact on Latin America. First, from 1796, the French connection drew the hostility of Britain on France's ally, Spain, and British sea power was instrumental in isolating the metropolis from its colonies; then in 1808 when France invaded the Iberian Peninsula and deposed the Bourbons, the collapse of the Spanish state precipitated in America a crisis of legitimacy and a struggle for power.

The influence of Britain was forceful but finite. From 1780 to 1800 the industrial revolution began to bear fruit and was powerfully attracted to the Spanish American market, a captive market without a rival industry and one that had a vital medium of trade, silver. Britain, therefore, valued its trade with Spanish America and sought to expand it, either via Spain and the Caribbean or by more direct routes. During times of war with Spain, while the British navy blockaded Cádiz, British exports supplied the consequent shortages in the Spanish colonies—a new economic metropolis was displacing Spain in America. It would be an exaggeration to say that British trade undermined the Spanish empire or made revolutionaries out of opponents of monopoly, but the stark contrast between Britain and Spain, between growth and depression, left a powerful impression in Spanish America. And there was a further sting in the argument that would not escape the Anglophile San Martín. If a power like Britain could lose an empire in America, why should the Spanish empire survive?

Spanish Americans were familiar with theories of natural rights and social contract. From these they could follow the arguments in favour of liberty and equality, and accept the assumption that these rights could be discerned by reason. The object of government, they would agree, was the greatest happiness of the greatest number, and many of them would define happiness in terms of material progress. So much they could learn from Thomas Hobbes and John Locke, Montesquieu and Jean-Jacques Rousseau, Thomas Paine, Abbé Raynal and Jeremy Bentham. The texts of liberty were read by San Martín, whose library contained works by Paine, Rousseau, Montesquieu, Denis Diderot and Voltaire.[13] Rousseau had numerous followers in America, and in Buenos Aires Mariano Moreno found in his political thought an instrument of revolution and justification for a contractual solution to the political situation in 1810.

But liberty was not enough. Liberty could be an end in itself and stop short of liberation. This was the belief of the Spanish liberals in the cortes of Cádiz, who subscribed to the freedoms of the Enlightenment and offered them to Spanish Americans, but with equal determination refused them independence. The Enlightenment, in other words, could be invoked to grant greater freedom within a Hispanic framework, to justify reformed imperialism. In Cádiz in 1810–11 San Martín saw imperial Spain in its heartland, its government, its navy and its commerce. He also saw its critics and dissenters and became one himself. San Martín walked away from Cádiz, unconvinced by the ideas of Spanish reformers. The leading thinkers of the European Enlightenment seem to have been totally unaware of the possibility of new and embryonic nation-alities, of the need to apply ideas of freedom and equality to relations between peoples, or of any right of colonial independence. The leading exceptions were Paine and Raynal, who provided outright justifications for colonial rebellion. These apart, Spanish Americans had to develop their own concept of colonial liberation, as did Juan Pablo Viscardo, Francisco de Miranda and Simón Bolívar. For liberators these were the principal teachers. As for San Martín, he taught by his example.

If it was not a 'cause' of independence, the Enlightenment was an indispen-sable source from which leaders drew to justify, defend and legitimize their actions, before, during and after the May Revolution. In the interests of their own safety creoles were more likely to invoke its ideas after than before 1810. In the course of this year Mariano Moreno turned from moderate to radical policies, and was soon described by his enemies as a Jacobin because of his political aggression, egalitarianism, pretensions to absolutism, and terrorism against the revolution's enemies. It is true that the essential idiom of the May Revolution was that of 1789: liberty, equality, fraternity, popular sovereignty and natural rights. But influence is not to be judged by language alone.[14] In practice the terms of revolution did not have the same meaning in Buenos Aires as they did in France. The two revolutions were twenty years apart, and while in Buenos Aires demo-cratic principles were debated and proclaimed, political procedure was more cautious and less 'popular' than the discourse of the time. The *morenistas* were ready to propagate revolutionary ideas among the popular sectors, but they saw the revolution as a controlled and guided force, not a spontaneous movement.[15] The balance between tradition and innovation is seen in the decision of Moreno to suppress from his translation of Rousseau's *Social Contract* the chapter on reli-gion, while at the same time he ordered two hundred copies to be printed for use as a textbook to teach students 'the inalienable rights of man.'

Colonial societies do not stand still; they have within them the seeds of their own progress and, ultimately, of independence. This was the silent factor, the metamorphosis overlooked by Spain: the maturing of colonial societies, the development of distinct identity, the new age of America. The signs were there; the demands for equality, for office and for opportunities expressed a deeper awareness, an increasing sense of nationality, a conviction that Americans were not Spaniards. Recent experience sharpened these perceptions. Since 1750 creoles had observed a growing Hispanization of American government; by 1780 they were aware that their political space was shrinking and they had no redress. If Americans had once gained access to office, bargained over taxation, and traded with other nations, if they had already experienced intimations of independence and tasted its benefits, would not this in itself increase their awareness of *patria*, consciousness of identity and desire for further freedoms? And would not a reversion to dependency be regarded with a sense of loss and as a betrayal, not only of their material interests, but of their pride as Americans?

Incipient nationalism was a predominantly creole nationalism, not shared by the Indians, the blacks and the slaves, who had a lesser stake in colonial society and only an obscure sense of the nation. It was the nationalism expressed by Juan Pablo Viscardo, the Peruvian Jesuit writing from exile, who used the language of the eighteenth century, that of 'inalienable rights', 'liberty' and 'natural rights', and invoked Montesquieu to deny the right of the lesser power (Spain) to rule the greater (America). Viscardo presented access to office and political control as matters of national interest: 'The interests of our country are precisely our interests . . . and we alone have the right to exercise the functions of government, to the benefit of the *patria* and of ourselves.' This was the argument of his *Lettre aux Espagnols-Américains*, published in 1799 and quickly recognized as a classic statement of colonial grievance and national independence. 'The New World is our homeland, and its history is ours, and it is in this history that duty and interest alike oblige us to seek the causes of our present situation, to make us determined thereby to take the necessary action to save our proper rights and those of our successors.'[16]

The May Revolution

By 1810, when the armies of Napoleon engulfed the Iberian Peninsula, the balance of social forces in Buenos Aires had changed. The administration had lost ground during the British invasions and the ambiguous rule of the pro-creole viceroy Santiago de Liniers. The Church had been reduced by Bourbon regalism and stripped of any independence it had once had. The wealthy Spanish class had staged a reactionary coup in January 1809 but been defeated by creole troops led by Cornelio Saavedra. This left the way open to two creole groups, the military and the intellectuals, who possessed the arms and ideas to take the initiative. On 13 May 1810 a British vessel brought to Montevideo news that French armies had occupied Andalucía and entered Seville. The Junta Central had fled to Cádiz and dispersed, providing for a council of regency to be established in its place. This was the opportunity for which the revolutionaries had been waiting.[17]

A creole underground movement was already in being, reinforced by Saavedra and senior officers of the militia, hitherto thwarted by Spanish prejudice and now lured by prospects of promotion. The viceroy was pushed aside and the *cabildo* forced to take account of an armed band of about six hundred young activists mobilized under the leadership of two radical creoles, Domingo French and Antonio Beruti. These were the spearhead of the revolution, the nearest approach to popular forces; they controlled the streets, and they constituted in effect the 'people' who congregated in the main square. On 22 May an open *cabildo* met, its intention to depose the viceroy and create a new government. It was a representative assembly only in a limited sense. The population of Buenos Aires was over fifty thousand, the revolutionaries perhaps were three thousand, and the hardcore militants in the main square no more than six hundred. To the *cabildo* only 450 people were invited; of these 251 accepted and actually attended, all of them people of substance, officials, clerics, lawyers and professional men, merchants, military, and ordinary citizens.

Masters of the streets, the revolutionaries quickly dominated the assembly and soon their leaders were claiming that in the absence of legitimate government, power reverted to the people of Buenos Aires. The voting yielded a decisive majority in favour of change; this majority was predominantly creole and it had a decisive military advantage. A British naval observer was impressed by 'the great power, which is the troops, being in the possession of one party', and it was this balance of power that forced the *cabildo* to form a patriotic junta cleared of Spanish conservatives.[18] 'Where are the people?', asked a *cabildo* official on 25 May from the balcony overlooking the main plaza. Only a few had assembled, those allowed into the square by the military. The May Revolution, like most revolutions, was initiated by a minority who sought to mobilize—and manipulate—a majority. The leadership set the doctrine: as secretary of the junta Moreno's declared aim was 'to destroy the oppressive administration, to promote a new and unprecedented government activity.'[19]

The revolution was directed precisely against the administration then holding power. Spanish officials were removed, and the viceroy and judges of the *audiencia* shipped off to the Canary Islands. This policy was soon extended to all Spaniards known or suspected to be hostile to the junta; they were subject to 'violence and unprecedented oppression', and where there was resistance, as in Córdoba, they were executed.[20] In January 1811 the junta created a Committee of Public Safety, to search out opposition and to receive denunciations against counter-revolutionaries.[21] The strategy of terror to save the revolution strongly suggests that the junta considered itself permanently independent of Spain, and of the Spanish Crown, for the changes wrought were so substantial and the link with the Crown so tenuous that a restoration of royal sovereignty was hardly conceivable. The May Revolution was thus more than an extension of the resistance and junta movement in Spain, more than a bid for self-government under the Crown. It was the revolt of a colony, led by radical and violent revolutionaries, whose loyalty to a captive king cannot be taken seriously. If some wore a mask of monarchy it was soon torn aside.

In the following years the executive changed form—and changed hands—many times, but it did not lose its revolutionary credentials or abandon its twin objectives, a liberal system in a unitary state.[22] The new leaders were professional revolutionaries, men who saw independence as a career as well as a policy and who promoted individual as well as collective interests. They needed allies, in particular a militia to protect the revolution at home and an army to carry it abroad. In creating these things they further enhanced the importance of the armed forces and increased the prestige, and the budget, of the military; for these too the revolution became a business.[23]

It soon became obvious, however, that the May Revolution was not immediately popular among regional elites, whose political, social and economic interests were often different from those of the capital, and whose reactions in due course would be studied more closely by San Martín. The claims of the junta were not acceptable to the Banda Oriental, to Paraguay or to Upper Peru, and these regions opposed the expeditionary forces sent by the capital. It soon became clear that the *porteño* army aimed not only to liberate Upper Peru but also to attach it in a subordinate position to Buenos Aires. Up to the May Revolution this mining province in the distant Andes had been part of the viceroyalty of the Río de la Plata and when Buenos Aires revolted, Lima moved quickly to claim its ancient patrimony and reintegrate it into the royalist stronghold of Peru. Buenos Aires refused to accept this secession and made the liberation of Upper Peru one of the essential objects of the revolution. Politically Upper Peru, a land of graduates, caudillos, guerrillas and Indians was a challenge to the ideals of 1810 and to any outsider who intervened; prime loyalties were centred on the regional interests of Upper Peru and minds were not easily captured either by the liberals of Buenos Aires or the royalists of Lima, though each gained temporary advantages in the years after 1810.[24] Economically its silver production had become an important item in the overseas trade of Buenos Aires. And strategically it was an obvious springboard for Spanish counter-insurgency operations. But there was no easy passage to victory. The reluctance of the creole aristocracy to subvert the social order in a population where they were vastly outnumbered by Indians and mestizos, and the military resourcefulness of the viceroy in Lima, all made it difficult for the forces of liberation, or the 'Argentine auxiliary armies' as they were called, to secure Upper Peru. After an orgy of terror and plunder, the first of the liberating armies was defeated by the royalists at Huaqui on 20 June 1811 and retreated in disorder to Salta. Military weakness alone was not the cause of its defeat. The position of the *porteños* in Upper Peru was already undermined by their own reputation. They bore the unfortunate stigma not only of plunderers but also of social reformers. They promised to free the Indians from charges and tributes, to suppress abuses, to distribute land and to grant equality. Without gaining the confidence of the Indians, the liberal demagogy emanating from Buenos Aires did enough to alienate the Upper Peruvian aristocracy of mines and land, and drive them into the royalist camp. Upper Peru was an object lesson in the pitfalls of revolution, a case study awaiting the attention of San Martín, and a problem that would retard his own strategy of independence.

Closer to home even the interior provinces had little sense of national unity, and the term 'Argentina', though convenient in a general and geographical sense, did not yet signify a unitary state. To its provinces, Buenos Aires sent emissaries not armies. In the north and west, in Tucumán and Cuyo, its political agents were forced to delegate power to local oligarchies, and to leave the revolution in the hands of conservative interests and their dependent militias. To some degree these reservations reflected differences of political opinion as to the future organization of the area. Some saw the Río de la Plata as a single entity with Buenos Aires its capital. Others argued that separation from Spain left each province master of its own destiny, a destiny that might include association with Buenos Aires but in freedom not subservience. These were not simply differences of political theory. They reflected also deep economic divisions accompanied by social differences. The interior was the home of conservatism. The large hacienda, with its Indian and mestizo labour force and its seigneurial values, was more firmly planted in the northwest and far west than in the littoral, where to a large extent the gaucho was still untamed and the land unclaimed. Provincial conservatism sought to preserve an economic structure which gave local products protection against the open trade policy of Buenos Aires. And socially it stood for hierarchy, for a *patrón–péon* relationship, as against the more mobile society of Buenos Aires and the relative freedom of the pampas.

The revolution was also under pressure from within, as liberal and conservative factions struggled for control. The military disaster of Huaqui in June

1811 ruined the reputation of Saavedra and the conservative junta, and by September the young *morenistas,* heirs of the late Mariano Moreno (who died 4 March), were making a comeback. Grouped in the Sociedad Patriótica and meeting in the Café Marco, they continued to work for an uncompromisingly liberal revolution. They sought to renew the revolutionary spirit of May, declare independence and produce a constitution. They did not seek democracy. Membership of the Society was restricted to people of education and did not automatically confer a right to participate in discussions.[25] Under popular pressure the junta was forced to establish a new executive, a triumvirate consisting of Manuel Sarratea, Juan José Paso and Martín Pueyrredón, while the junta itself was transformed into a legislative chamber. The driving force behind the triumvirate was its young secretary, Bernardino Rivadavia, a ruthless operator, bearer of pure liberal doctrine. He gave the new government a purpose and a programme, and sought to establish what he regarded as 'the limit to which its liberal principles ought to extend'.[26]

Rivadavia laid the foundations of a new education system, produced a liberal definition of civil rights and inaugurated an anti-slave trade policy. In the interests of enlightenment the government came down hard on its opponents. It abolished the Committee of Public Safety, now an instrument of reaction not of revolution; it brought back the victims of Saavedra's regime; and it dismissed Saavedra himself. When the junta threatened to become a rival pressure group representing provincial interests, it too was suppressed and the provincial deputies were ordered back to their provinces. This was the reign of *porteño* centralism and liberalism, Rivadavia's 'oligarchy of intellectuals', the American version of enlightened despotism. This was San Martín's first sight of the May Revolution when he arrived in Buenos Aires on board the English frigate *George Canning* on 9 March 1812, fifty days out of London. The *Buenos Aires Gazette* obtained the latest news from Spain, 'the collapse of the army of Galicia, the state of utter anarchy in Cádiz helplessly split by a thousand political divisions.'[27] Not surprisingly, it was reported, people were emigrating in droves to England and even more to South America. The arrival of San Martín and others made a stir in the small political community of Buenos Aires, and Rivadavia observed the newcomer with a critical eye.[28]

San Martín in Buenos Aires

Argentina was not immediately attractive to new arrivals. The fastidious Lord Ponsonby, British minister from 1826 to 1828, was shocked by what he saw and never recovered from his first impressions: 'No eye ever saw so odious a country as Buenos Ayres is . . . I do not recollect having ever before disliked any place so much, but I really sigh when I think I may spend my days here . . .

this land of mud and putrid carcases.' Even Woodbine Parish, the first British consul, who strove hard to understand Argentina, described it as a 'disagreeable and disheartening place'.[29]

Buenos Aires was not yet one of the great cities of the Americas and still had a raw, unfinished look about it. The city centre had a minimum charm inherited from its colonial past, with regular, crudely cobbled streets crossing at right angles and spacious plazas relieving the monotony of the low buildings; but the approach roads were deep in dust in dry weather and mired in mud in the rainy season, the single-storey houses were unimposing and the skyline was enhanced by only a few towers and domes. The environment was insalubrious and there were few amenities: theatre productions and various coffee houses (men only) offered some relief from the prevailing tedium, but bullfights and cock fighting were the popular spectacles.[30] Numerous awkwardly shaped carts with creaking wheels of enormous circumference lurched through the streets, their animals urged on by brutal drivers. Happily the transition from town to country was abrupt, and after about ten miles the traveller approached the undulating ground around Quilmes, and could take refreshments at occasional *pulperías*, a combination of bar and general store, where riders could rest under the veranda and watch the gauchos, militia, peons, Indians and other denizens of the pampas. But the only food was very hard beef, cooked immediately after killing, from the toughest part of the beast.

San Martín's immediate impressions of Buenos Aires and its environs are not recorded. Was he disheartened by this anarchic and primitive society and by life at the limits of civilization? Did he compare it unfavourably with Bourbon Spain and the briefly observed England? Did he share the views of foreign visitors that the women were good-looking, with lovely faces and fine figures? He kept his thoughts to himself, and when he discovered the rest of this land its attractions became more obvious. Further south and west the traveller entered a paradise of natural parkland, the home of Indians, cattle, horses, ostriches and myriad wild birds. Much of the land was flat and treeless but endowed with a wild beauty. During the spring the plains were covered with flowers and the grass was a brilliant green; in winter they were inundated in great floods of water; and in summer, when the tall grass wilted and crumbled, they were arid and dusty in the burning heat. The pampas were vast grasslands, which W.H. Hudson recalled vividly from his childhood: 'a flat land, its horizon a perfect ring of misty blue colour where the crystal-blue dome of the sky rests on the level green world . . . there were no fences, and no trees excepting those which had been planted at the old estancia houses, and these being far apart the groves and plantations looked like small islands of trees, or mounds, blue in the distance, on the great plain or pampa.'[31]

There was nothing to see except the herds of cattle and horses, and an occasional rider galloping over the plain. The greatest enemy on the pampas was not the solitude nor the climate but the Indians. Much of the country that now forms the province of Buenos Aires was then controlled by Indians, unoccupied by white men and unprotected by the state. These and their neighbours further west towards the Andes were not the friendly Indians familiar to San Martín from his childhood among the Guaranís of Misiones, though he would seek their friendship within a few years when he was recruiting his great army.

Meanwhile in Buenos Aires, by the muddy waters of the River Plate, San Martín had a lot to live down, welcomed by some, suspected by others. He had spent most of his life in Spain and many years in the Spanish army, an officer of the colonial power. He noticed distinct reservations among the authorities: 'I arrived in Buenos Aires in early 1812 and had a mixed reception from the governing Junta of the time, one of its members being favourable, the other two decidedly distrustful. So, with very few family connections in my own country and my only asset a desire to be useful, I put up with this discrimination until circumstances enabled me to overcome all prejudice.'[32] There were rumours that he was a British spy and alternative reports that he was anti-British.[33] His possession of a sword he had bought in London, a curved and oriental type popularized by the English, drew suspicion that he was an agent not only of Spain but also of France and therefore an enemy of Britain. These absurd reports made their way to London where troublemakers in the Hispanic community conveyed them to the British Foreign Secretary, Lord Castlereagh, who passed them to the Spanish ambassador Fernán Núñez and he to the Spanish government. Much effort was wasted on nonsense of this kind at a time when Britain was an ally of Spain.[34]

With San Martín came other patriots, notably Carlos María de Alvear and Matías Zapiola, the first of whom in many eyes outshone San Martín in merit and lineage. Alvear at twenty-three was eleven years younger than San Martín but his superior in social rank and family fortune, which counted for a lot in the Río de la Plata. Ambitious and pushing, he returned to inherited wealth and prestige, accompanied by an attractive bride whom he had recently married in Cádiz. San Martín, of modest origin but cool and confident, was superior in military rank and experience; but at thirty-four he was unmarried and unknown in Buenos Aires, while his record was one of service to Spain and his only connections the comrades of the Lodge. Bartolomé Mitre describes the difference in language that exaggerates somewhat the lowly condition of San Martín: 'On return to his country San Martín was an unknown and powerless man, whose only asset was his sword and his only reputation that of a brave soldier and skilful tactician. His companion Alvear, on the other hand, rich and noble by reputation, bore a name distinguished in the Río de la Plata and belonged to a family already well established.'[35] San Martín was happy to accept the temporary hospitality and patronage of his companion, unperturbed by Alvear's blatant push for the top; he was confident that his own abilities would secure him a role in the revolution, which was not so rich in military talent that it could afford to ignore a ready-made recruit. A favourable reference, presumably from Alvear, gave him a helping hand: 'Don José de San Martín, who has emigrated from the army of Spain, having served as a commander in the Sagunto Dragoon Regiment [in fact in the less distinguished Bourbon Regiment] with the rank of lieutenant colonel, has presented himself in this capital offering his services in honour of the just cause of the patria. The unofficial news we have of this officer recommend him for appointment to a posting in which his professional qualifications can be employed to best effect.'[36] On the same date the triumvirate appointed him 'lieutenant colonel of cavalry with the salary of such and a squadron commander of the mounted grenadiers' and authorized him to apply the new French cavalry tactics, a detail evidently inspired by San Martín himself.[37]

In due course military promotion was accompanied by social success. Within six months of his arrival in Buenos Aires San Martín met his *novia*. She was María de los Remedios de Escalada, the attractive daughter of Antonio José de Escalada, a wealthy *porteño* who had held leading appointments in the royal *audiencia* and the *cabildo*, and his wife Tomasa de la Quintana who presided at the family *tertulias* held in their large house in the street of Santísima Trinidad (now San Martín). It was in these social gatherings where music and dancing offered relief from the gloom of Buenos Aires that the couple met and became close. A tall, pale girl, Remedios was only fourteen, twenty years younger than San Martín, an age difference not unusual at the time. And the match was pleasing to both. She gained a presentable officer, rising in a decent career, he a 'wife and friend', words he would eventually use in her memory. They were married on 12 September 1812 in the church of Our Lady of Ransom, with licence from the civil authorities and, 'being well informed in Christian doctrine,' with approval of the bishop. The Alvears were witnesses and the bride's family and a few friends were present. A larger veiling ceremony was held in the cathedral on 19 September, with nuptial mass and reception of Communion, and the covering of bride and bridegroom in the same white mantilla to celebrate their union.[38]

Were they virgin lovers? For Remedios the answer is yes; culture, religion, circumstances would permit no other answer, and she seemed to love her husband. For San Martín, his age and career mean that we deal in probability. He was not blind to attractive women but he was no womanizer. For him principles, not passion, were his guiding light, and Remedios was his first love.

But it was an affair of the head rather than the heart, and the lengthy separations imposed by army duties seemed not to trouble him unduly. This was a stage in his career, an alliance with the elite of Buenos Aires, a family with some influence in the revolution, who were snobbish enough to regard San Martín as plebeian, 'that soldier fellow' as his father-in-law called him. Her parents gave Remedios an expensive trousseau which, it was said, a touchy San Martín returned.[39]

Meanwhile he had to work hard to establish his military career. In the colonial period the profession of arms, like the bureaucracy, did not in itself qualify for elite status, which was dominated by landowners and merchants. But from the time of the British invasions and then more rapidly from the revolution onwards the military rose to greater prestige and to the upper ranks of society. At the same time the army outgrew the previous militia organization and became a professional career with a new organization. More specialist units were created. The triumvirate decided to create a squadron of cavalry, an arm hitherto neglected in the revolutionary forces. San Martín was the organizer and trainer of the new unit, which he conceived as an elite corps, trained in the latest strategic models he had learnt in Europe, and which produced a series of officers who would serve the revolution well as it expanded west and north. He personally directed drilling, dress, smartness of officers and men, insisting on the highest standards of style and discipline. The government ordered provinces to send mounted men to join the squadron, but San Martín selected the officer corps and was active in its formation. By August the first squadron consisting of two companies of seventy men each had been enrolled and begun training.

Yet the government kept a wary eye on San Martín, not trusting him completely nor satisfied with his assimilation. As they prepared to send an army across the river for operations against the Spaniards in the Banda Oriental, they were concerned about the new corps and demanded a greater sense of urgency from San Martín to justify the responsibility he had been given.[40] But he was not responsible for the shortage of arms, the difficulty of buying abroad and the lack of a domestic arms industry, basic problems that lay at the government's door. Nevertheless, recruitment continued and by the end of 1812 new recruits from San Luis and Corrientes were incorporated into San Martín's corps. He was authorized to recruit troops from his native land, the Guaraní villages in the region of Yapeyú, people on whom he had learnt to rely from his Father's experience in their active service against the *paulistas*. On 5 December the creation of the regiment of Granaderos a Caballo was decreed, and two days later its commander San Martín was promoted to the rank of colonel, Alvear to lieutenant colonel and Zapiola to sergeant major.

San Martín wrote a small manual, drawing on European sources and his own experience, and covering specific details of good soldiering. Words of command must be loud and clear and correct: 'It is not enough simply to hurl oneself bravely against the enemy, but it needs that grade of intelligence which ought to distinguish every officer according to his position and duties; nor can the soldiers ever fight with spirit unless they have confidence in the ability of their leaders.' The book included detailed instructions on combat preparation, tactical positions and movements, and modes of attack: 'The cavalry must in no circumstances wait to be attacked while halted; for in this case even if they are superior, their defeat will be inevitable. When a cavalry corps attacks another, the one under attack must receive it at full gallop'. The disciplinary rules for the Granaderos were severe and applied by a tribunal of honour. They were even more severe for the officers, who were expected to maintain high moral standards as well as combat excellence. Officers could be expelled from the corps for, among other things, cowardice in battle, dishonesty, injustice to the troops, associating with lower ranks, striking any woman, and also for appearing in public with women known to be prostitutes, and for drinking excessively.[41] This secret tribunal, which investigated, judged and sentenced on anything regarded as harmful to the honour of the regiment, was controversial and not universally popular in the army, but it reflected the hard edge of San Martín's military character.

The Politics of Revolution

In the early months of 1812 the triumvirate presented a pathetic spectacle, its actions extreme yet hesitant, oppressive to its friends yet reluctant to engage with its enemies. The muzzling of the press, the harassment of public meetings, and ambiguity towards absolute independence from Spain damaged its prestige and caused resentment against its authoritarian ways. It continued to declare loyalty to Ferdinand VII, a way of avoiding decisions. When the government of the United Provinces of the Río de la Plata granted citizenship to a British merchant, James Winton, a privilege regarded by some of his countrymen as 'not much coveted by those who had no immediate ties to the country', radical journalist Bernardo Monteagudo was scathing: 'How preposterous to grant citizenship in the name of the king. What a mask! As useless as it is odious to free men'.[42] In the Banda Oriental the revolution was hard pressed yet unresponsive; and while hostilities against Portugal and Spain were renewed, the results were meagre. San Martín observed the dissent and indecision and was not impressed.

Historians have assumed too readily that San Martín came to Buenos Aires as a soldier, not a politician, as though the one excluded the other. While in public he focused on his military duties, his thoughts were ranging widely over the problems of the revolution. He himself later explained that from the

beginning he had two objectives in mind for his public career. First, a determination not to participate in the Buenos Aires politics of the time; hence his
aloofness and subsequent absence from the capital. 'My second object was to
regard all the South American states which my forces entered as brothers in
the same holy cause.'[43] The politics he abjured were the provincial disputes of
Buenos Aires, because he had a wider vision of the revolution in which he
expected to play an active part. This included an unwavering political position
that was apparently common knowledge, as Juan Bautista Alberdi makes clear.
'In the year 1812, in a meeting of patriots in which San Martín, recently
arrived in the country, explained his ideas in favour of monarchy as the most
suitable form for the new patriot government, Rivadavia could not refrain
from throwing a bottle in his face for the sacrilege. "In that case why did you
come to the Republic?" he asked him. "To work for the independence of my
native land", he replied, "and as for the form of its government, it will get what
it requires in exercise of this same independence".'[44] Two years later Rivadavia
accepted a mission to seek a monarch for Argentina from within Europe.[45]

Meanwhile, Rivadavia's 'oligarchy of intellectuals' was losing support among
important sections of the people. New men were entering the revolution. In
addition to San Martín, Alvear, who had also seen military service in Spain,
added further strength to the reinforcements. Bernardo de Monteagudo, a man
of many principles and few scruples, attacked the triumvirate from the other
wing. As co-editor of the *Gaceta de Buenos Aires* he turned the newspaper into
an organ of radical views. In this phase of his turbulent career he was an advocate of extreme democracy; fanatically anti-Spanish, he exhorted his fellow
Americans to 'exterminate the tyrants'. The administration replied to criticism
by stifling the private press and allowing the publication only of official news.
It provided for a general assembly, but gave a majority of seats to Buenos Aires
and effective control to the central government. And when the assembly began
to claim more power as representative of the people and the provinces,
Rivadavia dissolved it and at the same time curbed the *cabildo*. At this point the
enemies of the triumvirate—the new revolutionaries, the assembly and the
provincials—began to fight back, and on 8 October 1812, with the slogans of
independence, constitution and democracy, 'a powerful army faction' led by
Alvear and San Martín overthrew Rivadavia's government and installed a
second triumvirate.[46]

San Martín joined those who wanted to remove the first triumvirate because
it was authoritarian, inefficient and reluctant to embrace independence. The
golpistas were a combination of more radical revolutionaries, the *morenistas*,
the Lodge and the new military. The leader was Alvear. From his elite power
base he could command and expect others to follow, a situation that San
Martín accepted, true to his own convictions. The second triumvirate was

above all an instrument of the Lodge; so too was the General Constituent Assembly operating in Buenos Aires from January 1813 as the first national congress, which gave the country, among other things, its flag and anthem. The coup of 8 October 1812 was justified as giving a new impetus to the revolution, ending a period of indecision and arbitrary rule; and more precisely it wanted to depose Rivadavia and Pueyrredón. The Lodge became the exclusive decider of policy, but policy itself was not well defined. The new leadership failed to declare essential goals, and soon Alvear and his allies were seen as merely another power-seeking faction. Nevertheless, San Martín gave the coup his military support, warning politicians in effect not to take the military for granted.[47] Observing *porteño* politics from the standpoint of the British naval station, Captain Peter Heywood considered that the new corps of cavalry commanded by Colonel San Martín 'will have more weight in an election than the whole city of Buenos Ayres *united*, if union could possibly happen.'[48]

In supporting direct action against the first triumvirate San Martín had to oppose Pueyrredón, a man of respectable revolutionary credentials and elite status, with whom he had no particular quarrel. While the troops were assembling in the square on the eve of the coup, a group of extremists threw stones at the house of Pueyrredón's brother, breaking windows and seeking to detain the triumvirate. But Pueyrredón and Rivadavia had gone into hiding. Once the coup was successful San Martín heard rumours that he had allowed a gang of extremists to roam the streets and throw their weight around, which angered him as being untrue and not in his style. Believing that Pueyrredón gave credence to the rumours, he promptly wrote to him to clear the air: 'Nothing is so regrettable to anyone as to be accused of something he has not done. . . . It is well known that when I arrived in the square the incident had already taken place and I disapproved of it. My honour and my discretion demand that I give this assurance to you and the rest of the people who believe otherwise, and this I do'. In his reply Pueyrredón assured San Martín that he was happy to receive his explanation, though from him it was not really necessary. The incident itself, he continued, did not surprise him; it was 'a common and unfortunately frequent event in our revolution', and without a constitution showing the way 'to those who rule and those who obey' there is bound to be anarchy. These letters reveal two *logistas* communicating confidentially with each other, though they are more interesting as showing an understanding among the elite, because above all Pueyrredón respected San Martín 'for the family you belong to' (the Escalada family).[49]

The role of the Lodge, a secret society of the revolutionary elite and its instrument of unity and control, has been placed by many historians at the centre of the October coup and the subsequent march of the revolution. Inspired mainly by the narrative of Mitre, they see San Martín, Alvear and

Zapiola, proselytes of *logista* methods from London, as founding members of the Buenos Aires Lodge, defined as an exclusive society providing the brains and the organization of the revolution, and a more disciplined creation than the Patriotic Society that preceded it.[50] Their first triumph was the overthrow of the triumvirate controlled by Rivadavia and Pueyrredón. Alvear seized the initiative and monopolized power, and his temporary fall meant the fall of the first Lodge. San Martín then undertook the organization of a second Lodge, in which good principles of politics and education would take precedent over ambition, and which would spread roots to Mendoza and Santiago, as an instrument of the Andean policy of the revolution.

There is a flaw at the heart of this theory: there is no firm documentary evidence for any of it. It is true that Mitre spoke to participants in the revolution, but the resulting information is hearsay and Mitre is a secondary source. Mitre was then followed by one derivative secondary source after another, each repeating and adding to speculation, playing down or playing up the Lodge's masonic character according to the ideology of the writer. The very secrecy of freemasonry guaranteed no other result. It provided perhaps the signs and codes of the Lodge, some of them preserved in the correspondence of San Martín, but not the substance, which was devoid of religious significance. William Miller, who had a long period of service in the Army of the Andes from Argentina to Chile and Peru, an experience that should have qualified him to elucidate the problem, discovered nothing of the secretive Lodge, except its baleful influence. Afterwards, preparing his memoirs, he wrote to San Martín to ask whether he could explain the ill effects of the Buenos Aires Lodge: had it tied his hands when he needed to be free to deal effectively with fractious chiefs enjoying its protection? San Martín replied, 'I do not think it is desirable that I should say the slightest thing to you about the Lodge in Buenos Aires; these are entirely private matters and although they have had and have a great influence on the events of the Revolution in that part of America, they cannot be revealed without my failing in a most sacred obligation.'[51] San Martín had suffered from the Lodge but would not open up about it. Alvear, not San Martín, was the leading *logista*; San Martín followed its directions when it was useful to do so, but he subsequently ignored it and indeed had the audacity to disobey its orders when it suited him. Miller knew nothing of its actions yet was able to rise in the Army of the Andes to the position of general and to able to publish a chronicle of the revolution without his ignorance being a handicap in any way, either to action or to events around him. The Lodge was too self-absorbed—self-important best describes it—to fully represent the revolution. As a secret society it abandoned recourse to democracy and 'public opinion' as a means of policy control in favour of more immediate instruments of purpose and power; this was especially so in the preparations for a liberating army and declaration of independence. Whether its existence affected the course of the revolution or its expansion is open to doubt.

The Battle of San Lorenzo

While the interior of the Río de la Plata challenged the unitary policy of Buenos Aires, the periphery provinces—the Banda Oriental, Paraguay and Upper Peru—came to reject any association with the new state and to seek their own solutions, leading eventually to the independence of Uruguay, Paraguay and Bolivia. In 1812, however, Buenos Aires recognized none of these pretensions and treated dissent as rebellion. To defend the revolution against Spain and against regional resistance the second triumvirate had two priorities. First it had to reinforce General Belgrano in the north and enforce its authority in Upper Peru as far as the Desaguadero. Second, it had to secure the Banda Oriental, not only against Spain and Portugal but also against local creoles, who sought freedom from Buenos Aires as well as from Spain, convinced that a new more proximate dependence was at hand.

These convictions were articulated by José Gervasio Artigas, a gaucho caudillo born to a landowning and military family in Montevideo, who graduated from rustler to rural police and the royal service. In February 1811 he joined the independence movement in Buenos Aires, whose government gave him a small force to revolutionize the Banda Oriental. He soon moved beyond this position, and came to command the vanguard of the patriot forces that defeated the Spaniards but then found that Buenos Aires and Portuguese Brazil had rival designs on their country. His power base was the *estanciero* class but he also had a popular following, as he demonstrated in his leadership of what became known as the Exodus of the Oriental People, an exercise of provincial sovereignty asserting that the Banda Oriental would serve neither Spain nor Buenos Aires.[52] When the second triumvirate summoned the people to elect delegates to a general constituent assembly, Artigas instructed his deputies to demand an immediate declaration of independence and the establishment of a federal system of government in which each province would retain its sovereignty. Other delegates, representing a more centralist outlook, prevented the *artiguistas* from being admitted to the assembly. So the congress which opened its sessions on 31 January 1813 contained irreconcilable groups, each of which put forward opposing constitutional plans. The result was that the Constituent Assembly of the United Provinces of La Plata produced neither unity nor a constitution.

Meanwhile, the Spaniards were still occupying Montevideo and from there making aggressive forays up the Paraná river. San Martín was ordered to lead a company of Granaderos a Caballo to protect the people and their cattle from enemy attacks along the river banks from Zárate in the south to Santa Fe in the north. Anxious to strike quickly, he lost no time in assembling his force, but was furious to find his progress checked, not by the enemy but by disorganized planning. As he explained rather edgily to the chief of the general staff, he was held up at Santos Lugares by the misdirection of his guide and a shortage of horses; it was an embarrassing experience, for the delay revived the defamatory rumours that he was a Spanish spy and taking the first opportunity of betraying the forces entrusted to him. Now on 29 January he was still stuck in the same place, and the most he could do was to order an officer forward along the route to make sure the necessary horses were available in future. Intelligence reached San Martín on 31 January that Spanish ships were anchored off San Lorenzo, over halfway between Zárate and Santa Fe, and had disembarked 100 marines. To make up for his initial delay, conscious that this engagement could make or break his revolutionary career, he drove his cavalry forward, reaching San Pedro on 1 February, having covered 420 kilometres in five days in the heat of summer and across tracts of giant thistles.[53] Discarding his uniform and disguised as a peasant in straw hat and poncho, he went forward with another officer to reconnoitre the position and observed the enemy squadron anchored opposite the monastery of San Lorenzo.[54] He then returned to head his column of cavalry of 150 men and and at ten o'clock at night reached the staging post of San Lorenzo, about 5 kilometres from the monastery.

There he encountered a young Scottish merchant, John Parish Robertson, halted in his journey from Buenos Aires to Paraguay by the presence of the enemy and the requisitioning of his horses. He was sleeping in his carriage when the trampling of horses, the rattle of swords and loud voices woke him, and rough soldiers whom he took to be Spanish marines peered in the windows and ordered him out:

At this moment there came up to the window a person whose features I could not in the dark recognise, but whose voice I was sure I knew, as he said to the men, 'Don't be rude; it is no enemy, but only, as the post-master informs me, an English gentleman travelling to Paraguay.' The men retired, and the officer came close up to the window. Dimly as I could then discern his fine prominent features, yet combining the outlines of them with his voice, I said, 'Surely you are Colonel San Martin, and if it be so, behold here is your friend Mr. Robertson.' The recognition was instant, mutual, and cordial, and he got a hearty laugh when I described to him the fright into which I had been thrown, by taking his troops for a body of Marinos. The colonel then informed me the government had got positive information that it was the intention of the Spanish Marine force to land that very morning; to pillage the adjoining country; and especially to sack the Monastery of San Lorenzo.

San Martín added that he had travelled from Buenos Aires with 150 grenadiers, to confront double that number, 'but I don't think for all that, they will have the best of the day.' Robertson got his wine out and they all had a stirrup cup. He persuaded San Martín to let him accompany him to the monastery. 'Only mind', said he, 'that it is neither your duty nor your business *to fight*. I will give you a good horse, and if you see the day going against us, be off at your speed. You know sailors are no horsemen.'[55]

San Martín positioned his troops behind the deserted monastery, screened from the observation of the marines coming up from the river. He ordered silence while he climbed the monastery tower to observe the enemy through night glasses, as they prepared to disembark from seven vessels. He placed his militia with their firearms in the interior of the building to defend the main gate and cover the cavalry when they attacked. If the cavalry were resisted then the infantry could give them covering fire in their retreat. At about 5.30 in the morning of 3 February San Martín ascended the tower a second time and watched 220 Spanish sailors and marines landing at the foot of the cliff and marching up the long winding path towards the monastery, their flags flying, and their drums and fifes playing a quick march apparently unaware of what awaited them. He came down and said to Robertson, 'within two minutes we'll be at them with our swords'. Then drawing his sabre he gave orders to his soldiers, forbidding them to open fire but to attack with lances in the vanguard and the rest with swords, and demanding action from officers and men worthy of the regiment. He would lead the attack in the centre and Captain Justo Bermúdez on the right flank to the enemy's left flank.

The enemy were two hundred metres from the monastery, a good distance for San Martín to launch a sudden charge with a surprise element, and demonstrate the lessons he had taught for non-stop impact; this prevented the full effect of the enemy fire, and once the cavalry had taken the first burst of fire they would have the advantage and could continue with swords against rifles. They broke the enemy ranks and in fifteen minutes the ground was strewn with wounded and slain. In leading the charge San Martín had his horse shot from under him and his right leg pinned to the ground. He took a glancing blow on the left cheek as a Spanish marine slashed at his head with a sword. Another enemy soldier ran up to bayonet him but a grenadier saved his colonel with a lance thrust. Another grenadier, *correntino* Juan Bautista Cabral, dismounted to pull him free, before being himself killed by two shots. The grenadiers launched a second charge and drove the Spaniards to the riverbank, from where they managed to escape to their boats, aided by the high and precipitous banks of the Paraná at that point and by covering fire from the boats. Robertson took his leave. 'I begged of San Martín to take my wine and provisions for the benefit of the wounded men of both parties; and, bidding him a hearty adieu, I quitted the scene of action, with regret for the slaughter, but admiration of his coolness and intrepidity.'[56]

San Martín was aware that he had not prevented the enemy's retreat and escape, though they suffered many casualties, 40 dead, 14 prisoners and 12 wounded, as against 26 of his own men, 6 of them dead, the rest wounded. He attributed this to the failure of his right flank to clear their front and get back quickly enough, making an unnecessarily long circuit to the left. Captain Bermúdez was conscious of blame, though he had fought bravely and been badly wounded; when his leg was amputated he pulled off the tourniquet and bled to death. San Martín reported about San Lorenzo: 'On 3 February in their first combat the grenadiers under my command have added a new triumph to the country's arms. The bravery and daring of my grenadiers on this day would surely have brought to an end in a single blow the enemy invasions of the shores of the Paraná, had they not taken advantage of the proximity of the slopes to assist their flight, but I dare to predict without fear that this will be a warning to the enemy not to return to harass these peaceful people.'[57] He also gave due credit to the priest Julián Navarro, who ministered earnestly to the troops at San Lorenzo. If the victory was incomplete, it was also profitable to an impecunious army; useful arms were captured from the enemy, 41 rifles, 1 cannon, 8 swords, 8 bayonets and 8 pistols.

San Martín had to dictate his reports, a practice that never appealed to him, for he was incapacitated in the aftermath of battle. His wounds comprised the slash across the left cheek, a sprained arm and bruised leg. His action had been that of an experienced officer, brave but not rash. To lead from the front was necessary on this occasion to demonstrate and give example in the first active service of the grenadiers. The enemy artillery captain, the Basque Juan Antonio Zavala, returned to the scene of battle seeking to buy fresh meat for the wounded. San Martín readily agreed, on a word of honour that it would only be used for this purpose. Zavala also wanted to greet the grenadiers and meet their commander. He was given a hearty creole breakfast with wine supplied by the monastery, allowed to arrange an exchange of prisoners, and departed with a lasting admiration for San Martín.

The Revolution Fades

San Martín received no favours for his achievements at San Lorenzo. It was Alvear who was promoted to full colonel and given command of the 2nd Infantry Regiment, though he had no active service to his credit. San Martín was made commander-in-chief of all forces for the defence of the capital

(4 June 1813), but he was not impressed by the appointment, preferring to remain at the head of his cavalry regiment, then stationed outside the capital. But he was forced to accept, so he made the best of it, and employed his organizing talents in improving the defences of Buenos Aires. Even in this role his status was inferior to that of Alvear, who denied him reinforcements for his cavalry, while the second triumvirate gave priority to Alvear's infantry. San Martín had no influence in the triumvirate, which was becoming a mere instrument of Alvear's faction. After three months San Martín, disillusioned with the capital, tried again to disengage from his defence post and return to the Grenadiers, where he was confident he could give the greatest service to his country. On 8 September the triumvirate decided to divide responsibility for organizing the defence of the capital between San Martín as commander of cavalry and Alvear in command of infantry.

The second triumvirate had started promisingly: in the Banda Oriental the military victory of San Martín at San Lorenzo and in the north Belgrano's success at Salta confirmed its wider credentials. At home its liberal programme advanced its political reputation and justified the position of the Constituent Assembly, presided over by Alvear and inspired by the Patriotic Society and the Lodge. A series of reforms read like a model of contemporary liberalism and enhanced the government's revolutionary reputation: the gradual abolition of slavery; the suppression of Indian tribute, the *mita*, the *encomienda* and all forms of personal service; the ending of titles of nobility and of entail; the abolition of the Inquisition; reform of the administration of justice; and new laws on trade, agriculture and industry. But as the regime's early impulse died, so its intolerance of opposition grew and the preference of *porteño* leaders for absolute power reasserted itself. As for a declaration of independence and a new constitution, these were as remote as ever. Power was in the hands of Alvear, 'the real director of the whole political machine', and policy came from the second Lodge.[58] Where did San Martín stand? He had gained a foothold in the army and in society but nothing more, and politically he was stationed well behind Alvear, whose faction also prevailed in the Lodge. Given the structure of power in Buenos Aires, where elite colonial families still dominated, San Martín was not a big player and his preference for a declaration of independence was ignored.

Meanwhile storm clouds were gathering from abroad and people were alarmed by news that a Spanish force was preparing to leave Cádiz for Montevideo. Soon the triumvirate was further demoralized by setbacks on the fighting fronts. In September 1813 royalist reinforcements reached Montevideo from Spain; on 14 November Belgrano was defeated at Ayohuma in the north and his rabble army swept ignominiously out of Upper Peru with the loss of three thousand men and the desertion of many others; in Europe the prospects of Spain and her allies were showing distinct improvement. These reverses reduced the government in Buenos Aires to despair and in the subsequent panic there were many who advocated accommodation with Spain; even Alvear, who had returned to the Río de la Plata 'full of ideas of liberty and independence', subscribed to these defeatist views.[59]

The sequence of hope and despair was a political constant in Buenos Aires. The panic was no more than temporary, if only because the Spaniards themselves were the worst enemies of reconciliation: they refused to offer suitable terms to the insurgents or to speak of anything but an unconditional return to colonial status. From Montevideo they 'make no secret of the exemplary punishment they mean to inflict on Buenos Aires whenever they can reconquer it'.[60] Moreover, the defeatists were challenged from within the revolution by a hard core who advocated absolute independence and who on this issue at least followed Monteagudo and Artigas. Gradually, the government began to recover its nerve. The unwieldy second triumvirate was abolished, and central government was consolidated in the hands of a single executive, Gervasio Antonio Posadas, the uncle of Alvear and a seasoned politician who held office from 31 January 1814.

Meanwhile the prospects of San Martín had at last improved and he had now been appointed to the stricken Army of the North. On 2 December 1813 news reached Buenos Aires of the costly defeat at Ayohuma. On 3 December Colonel San Martín was appointed chief of the expedition to reinforce Belgrano, consisting of 250 mounted grenadiers, 100 artillery gunners and 800 infantry troops from Battalion No. 7. It was more or less what he wanted, an honourable route out of Buenos Aires, though a stony one. While he went to a defeated army and a difficult campaign in the north, Alvear continued his rise at the centre of power, military commander and manipulator of politics. He accompanied San Martín out of Buenos Aires, seeing off his rival on 18 December 1813 as he began his long journey across the pampas. To what? Was San Martín marginalized yet again, or was he elevated to his rightful station at the frontier of the American revolution? Belgrano thought it was excellent news: 'Fly, as quickly as possible', he wrote, 'our country needs exceptional endeavours.'[61]

San Martín's fate now lay in his own hands: the appointment would be what he made it. He had come to Buenos Aires to serve a wider cause than the provincial policies of the Río de la Plata, convinced that military power should serve an American purpose and not a mere local interest. He had played a modest role in advancing the revolution and defending its territory, but these were minor achievements. His main assets were his commanding presence, his leadership qualities and his military experience. With these he now had the chance to fulfil his greater mission, to define the revolution anew, to expand horizons from country to continent and to establish a new base for the war of independence.

CHAPTER 3

A Continental Strategy

To the North

As San Martín made his way northwest from the capital in the fiercely hot summer of 1813–14, crossing the Puente de Marques, he travelled an historic route of trade and silver linking Buenos Aires, Santa Fe, Santiago del Estero, Tucumán, Salta and Potosí. He commanded a long convoy of men and supplies, arms, equipment, artillery, cattle and water carriers, and he faced a month's journey. The roads were everywhere primitive and potholed as they forced a way through an Argentina of many landscapes, from the dusty tracks of the pampas to the rugged hills of the midwest and the blue range of the sierra de Córdoba on their left; then they got their first sight of the looming mountains of the north, their peaks covered in snow, seemingly belonging to a different world.

San Martín's thoughts too passed through a variety of places and problems. The recent defeats of the revolutionary army in Upper Peru opened the way for the royalist forces of General Joaquín de la Pezuela to move south against the patriots, and the first duty of San Martín was to contain this offensive. The government in Buenos Aires would then be able to focus its resources on the Banda Oriental, which was seen as a potential bridgehead for a Spanish expedition from the peninsula; and if such an offensive could join up with the royalist campaign from the north, the revolution would be in real trouble. The northern front was regarded as less urgent and more remote than the southern, but if San Martín's rivals for leadership in Buenos Aires thought they had marginalized him, they misread the signs. This was the beginning of his American mission, a hard beginning, but one that gave meaning to his life.

The years 1814–16 were years of depression for the Spanish American revolution. The end of the Peninsular War and the restoration of Ferdinand VII in

1814 enabled Spain to turn its sights on America. In the north a large Spanish army under General Pablo Morillo, veteran of Spain's own war of independence, crushed the Venezuelans and New Granadans in 1815–16. In Upper Peru the royalists threw back the *porteño* armies of liberation in 1813–15 and threatened Tucumán. In Chile the patriots, divided among themselves, were crushed by the forces of the counter-revolution in 1814 and were reeling from a reign of terror. By 1816, as a British naval observer noted: 'it was impossible for appearances to be more unfavourable to the revolutionary cause.'[1] San Martín referred to the risk of utter ruin in 1816: 'I fear this not from the Spaniards but from domestic discord and our own lack of education and judgement.'[2] On the ruins of the first revolution the liberators would create a second movement of independence, and in 1814 San Martín's thoughts were already considering the wider strategies of such a task. But more immediately, caught between the politicians in Buenos Aires and the faltering campaign in the north, he was facing a painful predicament. The government plan was to demote Belgrano and place San Martín in command of the northern front.

Even before meeting Belgrano he felt for the man, a civilian in a general's uniform, an intellectual forced to be a soldier, who frankly confessed his anxieties of not being up to the task. 'My friend', he had written, 'what opinion have you formed of me? By chance, or God's will, I find myself a general, without knowing where I am, for this has not been my career and I am forced to try and learn just to get by . . . I was completely beaten in the pampas of Ayohuma when I thought I was on the point of victory.'[3] San Martín had sent the beleaguered commander some advice about firearms and the preferred use of sabre and lance by the cavalry, and promised to send him a book on tactics. He also had to defend him against the politicians of Buenos Aires who were demanding his replacement, though the basic problem was the lack of competent and experienced senior officers. Belgrano was desperate to meet him: 'America is not yet ready to receive the great benefits of freedom and independence. I am only waiting for you, a companion who can enlighten me, assist me and recognize my straightforward ways and honest intentions.' And he warned San Martín that he would see the difficulties for himself as he marched north: 'You will see the poverty of our countries and the difficulties presented by their great distances, the sparse populations and the resulting lack of resources to enable us to operate with due speed.'[4] It was a good summary of the problems of the revolution: immense spaces, poor lines of communication, the poverty of people and provisions.

San Martín reached Tucumán on 11 January 1814, and as he approached his destination he was still being urged by Buenos Aires to take command of the Army of the North, or the Army of Peru as it was also called, and he was appointed its general in chief on 18 January. Such was his respect for the senior statesman that San Martín could not bring himself to accept the appointment. But the decision to replace Belgrano had already been taken in the Lodge. The two met on 17 January near the village of Algarrobos, a few miles south of the River Juramento, and San Martín took over command of the stricken army on 29 January.[5] On the next day he warned them of the need to save the country 'from the imminent danger of perishing.' And from the people of Tucumán he asked for solidarity: 'Be resolute, stay united, people of Tucumán, and we shall be invincible. . . . If my army and you hold together, our country need have no fear.' He took command of an army which, as he explained to the government, 'after four long years of sacrifices has exhausted its physical resources and retains only its moral strength.'[6] His own military training was that of an officer in the Spanish army, fighting Moors in North Africa and the French in the Iberian Peninsula. Now he was looking towards Upper Peru, a mountainous region stretching northwards from Salta to the River Desaguadero, between the Pacific to the west and the Chaco to the east, among people whose customs and culture were new to him. He proceeded cautiously, his priorities clear, first to clothe 'the naked army', then to pay it and finally to train it, and in securing the defences of the northwest he began to show that organizing ability which became the hallmark of his military success. He got his troops to build their own garrison, the *ciudadela*, a forti-fied camp outside Tucumán, setting the ultimate line of defence against a royalist invasion from the north, and giving his formless army a new sense of identity and structure.

He started with leadership, for he was convinced that the great defect of the army in its present state was the poor quality of its officers, inferior, ill-educated and weak on discipline. He set up a military commission to judge officers, and to improve standards he demanded proof of candidates' *curriculum vitae*; he dismissed those whom he regarded as lacking officer qualities and took steps to improve the training of others. When General Belgrano, with typical modesty, also took his place in the training course he was sneered at by Colonel Manuel Dorrego, who had been under his command in Upper Peru. San Martín took severe exception, banged the table with a candlestick, brought Dorrego to order and exiled him to Santiago del Estero.[7] He also sought to raise the moral tone of the officer corps. In his own Grenadiers he had introduced a tribunal of honour, but this was resisted in the north. There was also resistance to his efforts to encourage the duel as a defence of honour, in contrast to Belgrano who punished duelling severely and warned San Martín to tread carefully and not arouse the susceptibilities of the people. Other officers had reservations, feeling 'it could become a terrible abuse, especially among young people in a country whose civilization is not well advanced.'[8] In his care for the troops, however, San Martín showed a surer touch and displayed his distinctive style.

He had to start from scratch, taking over an army scarred by failure. In Tucumán he found 'only a few sad groups of a defeated army. A hospital without medicines, men lying on the floor. Troops so naked that it offends decency to see a defender of our country clothed like a beggar. Officers ashamed to appear in public, having lost their uniforms in the last actions of the campaign. And everyone shouting for their pay.' He requested three thousand uniforms in time for winter, for 'the recruits cannot go out of their barracks, ashamed of their nakedness.'[9] One of his first steps was to pay the soldiers a proper wage, no matter where the money came from or what the government said. He ordered that they should be paid four reales a week and receive a regular ration of spirits. Caught between obeying the government and sustaining the army, he diverted money from the treasury in Potosí to Tucumán instead of sending it to Buenos Aires as the government was demanding: 'This province is not providing the resources to sustain the army; the country will be lost and the army destroyed if the government does not support it. These are the pressing reasons which have caused me to *obey and not fulfil* the government commands and to explain to you the absolute necessity of this money for the preservation of the army.'[10] Posadas' agreement came with a rebuke. 'Let us overlook for now the *obey but not comply*, for if obeying means leaving you in trouble, the not complying leaves me looking like a stupid swine here.'[11]

For San Martín to take control and exert his own will not only raised hackles in Buenos Aires, but also alarmed these conservative societies in the northwest, who wondered whether this man from Spain and Buenos Aires understood them. This was the reason for Belgrano's advice, once San Martín began to make an impact. He warned his colleague to tread carefully and not to offend popular culture or arouse religious susceptibilities. Duelling was an issue over which Belgrano had found consternation among local people. But his concern ranged wider than duelling and was expressed in terms that contained perhaps a trace of irony:

> The people are very respectable in their concerns, especially those who trust in things religious, no matter how little; I am sure you will take account of this and decide the best way to prevent this attitude increasing and particularly not engaging the attention of the peoples of the interior. There you have to wage war not only with arms but also with principles, always holding fast to moral, Christian and religious virtues, for our enemies have been calling us heretics and with this argument alone have recruited uncultured people, telling them that we were attacking religion. Perhaps some will laugh at my idea, but you should not be taken in by exotic opinions nor by men who do not know the country they are treading in; moreover in this

way you will keep the army under control, for after all it is composed of people educated in the Catholic religion which we all profess, and whose doctrines are indispensable for the maintenance of order. I am sure that the peoples of Peru lack the slightest virtue and that all classes reduce religion to mere externals. I speak in general. But they are so committed to these that there is nothing further to say and I can assure you that it will be noticed if there is the slightest departure from them in your army and from the judgements of the popes. Look after the flag I gave you and raise it whenever the whole army parades; do not cease to pray to Our Lady of Ransom, always naming her our General and do not forget the scapulars for the troops. Don't worry if you are laughed at; the results will compensate you for the laughter of the idiots who view things superficially. Remember you are a Christian general, Apostolic and Roman; make sure that in no way, not even in the most trivial conversations, you lack respect in anything pertaining to our holy religion.[12]

Belgrano seems to have feared that San Martín came to the conservative societies of the interior trailing Enlightenment ideas and encountered military mentalities that did not appreciate his European assumptions; and in Upper Peru he would have to persuade as well as conquer, for the local population was suspicious of the liberal intentions of Buenos Aires. It is not precisely known how San Martín responded to the advice. It was serious and relevant for him, because he himself knew that there was a problem with inferior officers and commanders who were arrogant, their minds closed to new tactics; there was hostility too between officers who had served long in the interior and those coming out raw from Buenos Aires and expecting rapid promotion. He continued to support Belgrano, in spite of the government's prejudice against him for the defeat of Ayohuma; he remained at San Martín's side with his advice and moral support against turbulent officers, and with the benefit of his experience in the north. San Martín dragged his feet over government orders to dismiss him and send him south to Córdoba, knowing that Belgrano had a lot of support in the interior. But the central government was stubborn and instructed San Martín to toe the line, warning him 'in future not to delay in complying with the orders that emanate from this government.'[13] San Martín had no alternative. Belgrano was ousted and marginalized, and at the end of May 1814 was ordered to return to Buenos Aires. For the commander of the Army of the North it was another round in his running battle with the central government and the irksome meddlers in the Lodge. Meanwhile he had to guard his own watch.

Relations with the enemy were a daily concern. What was the appropriate level of response and was it right to shoot prisoners? Antonio Landivar, a

Spanish colonel taken prisoner at Santa Cruz de la Sierra, was known as one of the cruellest agents of a royalist policy of executing prisoners and displaying their bodies along roadsides to intimidate the patriots. He was shot for war crimes, a punishment decided in a war council held in San Martín's house, when it was decided to give an exemplary sentence as a warning to royalists. Landivar was sentenced 'not for having fought for the enemy against our system but for the deaths, robberies, looting, violence, extortions and other excesses committed against the laws of war.' San Martín authorized the death sentence on 15 January 1814 and ordered his execution without previously consulting the government. He justified his action, which he acknowledged to be extreme, as essential for morale and to demonstrate effect: 'The enemy think they are authorized to exterminate the very race of the revolutionaries, for no other crime than that of claiming the rights which they regard as usurped. They make war on us without respecting our sacred human rights and they are not concerned about shedding torrents of blood of the unfortunate Americans.' To treat a criminal like Landivar with indulgence would be to encourage the royalists to regard San Martín's moderation as weakness.[14]

San Martín's position on the execution of Landivar as a war criminal was consistent with his determination to establish the rights of Americans as regular soldiers, protected by the normal rules of war. He was also anxious to end the perception of creole compliance and inferiority as an unacceptable heritage of the colonial mentality. In an *estancia* outside Córdoba in 1814, condemned to inaction by a bout of ill health, he brooded on the stagnation of the revolution: 'this is a revolution of sheep, not of men.' A *peon* came to complain that the Spanish overseer of his *estancia* had beaten him. San Martín was indignant. 'What do you think? After three years of revolution, a *maturrango* (Spaniard) dares to raise his hand against an American!' He repeated, 'this is a revolution of sheep, not of men', and encouraged the *peon* to reject such treatment.[15]

The overwhelming question facing commanders in the north was, how should the Spaniards be fought? By a conventional army or by irregular forces? Inspired by Belgrano and advised by Dorrego, both of whom had experience in the north, San Martín's preferred strategy at this stage was to support the *guerra gaucha* waged by local warlords and their gaucho followers. As these were already in place and in action, he preferred to reinforce them with men and supplies rather than commit the Army of the North to yet another wasteful campaign. Service in the Spanish army had familiarized him with the concept and conduct of guerrilla warfare, and the Peninsular War had given him many examples, some of them anarchic, some successful. Now he was in territory made for such a strategy, divided as it was between the mountains and valleys of the *altiplano* and the tropical plains of Santa Cruz and the Choco, terrain where a large army would find it difficult to manoeuvre but smaller units could come and go at will.[16]

Among the leaders San Martín identified the 'valiant' Martín Güemes, caudillo of Salta, as his most reliable ally and his forces as the most effective means of waging a *guerra de recursos*, or guerrilla war, on the royalist army. Güemes was a creole officer and landowner in Salta, and came from a family whose background in land and public office enabled him to mobilize the province and tap its reserves of men, agriculture and livestock. He accompanied San Martín from Buenos Aires, was promoted to lieutenant colonel and began irregular operations against the royalists in the woods, hills and valleys south of Salta to deprive them of resources and drive them back. According to San Martín, 'The gauchos, peasant patriots, on their own are waging a terrible war of resources on the enemy.'[17] He backed this war as a matter of policy, rewarding Güemes for his success on the frontier by promoting him to general command of this front, and reinforcing him with officers and troops; it was they who halted the advance of Pezuela southwards from Jujuy.

For over five years from 1815 Güemes governed Salta with a large measure of autonomy from Buenos Aires and the support of the popular sectors as well as of San Martín. As the region continued to be a theatre of war against royalist forces in Upper Peru, part of the gaucho population was permanently mobilized into rural militias. These preyed upon local *estancias* and rich merchants, seizing crops, cattle and other property, while Güemes himself issued decrees requisitioning cattle, confiscating goods and levying compulsory donations to the war effort. How did this system of government manage to survive? In the first place it had the support of the central government. Once the campaign against Upper Peru was abandoned as unfeasible, Güemes undertook the defence of the frontier at minimum expense by making the Salta aristocracy pay for it. The conservative governments in Buenos Aires, therefore, were prepared to tolerate his autonomist leanings and populist policies as a necessary defence of the revolution.[18] In the second place Güemes was the representative of a powerful group of Salta families related by kinship and interest.[19] These, of course, were exempt from his plunder, and ultimately participated in the actions of their caudillo until his death in action in 1821. Thus the new commander of the Army of the North began to understand the interior provinces and adapt to the kinship culture of the northwest.

San Martín had clear and distinct ideas on guerrillas, and applied his ideas on the northern front. At their best guerrillas denied the enemy stability and resources. 'Guerrilla war is the most punishing war from which we can gain great advantage, especially with new and only partially trained troops whom we will never risk in a full-scale action, only in partial attacks which multiply and give equal results.' Guerrillas depend on popular support for subsistence, supplies, communications and espionage, and they in turn most protect local people. 'One of the first obligations of justice they have to ensure is to provide absolute protection to the friends of American liberty.'[20] They were also expected to incite insurrection among the Indians of Peru, though it was recognized that not all of these were friendly and could well be a danger to isolated groups.[21] San Martín was learning the ways of Argentine caudillos and guerrillas. He could see that they were a cheaper form of waging war. Regular armies had to be clothed, fed and paid, in default of which desertion was likely. Caudillos did not have to clothe their followers; they fed them off the land, and they promised them payment in loot.

The revolution was full of dilemmas, and San Martín now experienced one of the hardest. What should take priority, the eastern or the northern front? And in the north what route should the revolution take, westwards across the Andes or north into Upper Peru? His status was not supreme, as he knew, and decisions were not in his hands. Buenos Aires was more concerned with the Banda Oriental than with distant Tucumán, and San Martín was kept short of funds and provisions for his army, which by April 1814 was still not in a position to go on the offensive. Guerrilla warfare was his holding position while he manoeuvred for more distant goals. Belgrano warned him against the temptation to go for the enemy too soon, and ill-prepared, the mistake that he himself had made: 'If you are not convinced that you have the army well trained and under control, then don't make the slightest move. Remain on the defensive.'[22] Belgrano saw the problem not only as one of materials but also of morale; both needed to be strengthened under the guiding hand of San Martín.

Decision-making was complicated by the state of his health. From the beginning of 1814 he was not fully fit.[23] At the end of April he suffered a chest infection, was vomiting blood and troubled by stomach pains. He was residing in La Ramada, a hacienda thirty-six kilometres from Tucumán, where he began to recuperate, although still suffering pains in his chest. But asthma was troubling him and medical advice was that he should move south to Córdoba for a drier climate. On 6 May the government gave him leave to go, replacing him in command by José Rondeau, a second-rate retainer of the revolution, and at the end of the month San Martín decided to leave; he took up residence further south in a country house in the hills around Saldán. He was suffering not from tuberculosis, as has often been supposed, but from asthma, and the vomiting of blood was not from the chest but from his stomach, indicating a gastric or duodenal ulcer.

Reports and rumours of San Martín's illness stirred the politicians in Buenos Aires and produced contradictory reactions. Posadas was reassuring to the patient but alarmist to others, describing his illness as 'fatal' and 'mortal', requiring alternative arrangements and probably demotion. Calculating or not,

Alvear, nephew of Posadas, profited from the occasion in focusing policy and resources on the eastern front where he dominated. He assured San Martín that priority for Montevideo was not a rival strategy but a necessary move, and once Montevideo was taken then men and resources would be released for the northern campaign.

Alvear, of course, had his own agenda and hoped to advance it through the infirmity of his rival. With command of the sea won by the *porteño* flotilla and fresh troops provided by his uncle Posadas, he had the field to himself in the Banda Oriental for a dramatic victory over the royalists. On 22 June he entered Montevideo in triumph and received its surrender on 23 June. At the same time he overthrew Artigas's deputy, Fernando Otorgués, and was sharp enough to avoid any accommodation between the *orientales* and the royalists. Posadas, having already appointed Rondeau to the north, now reassured San Martín: 'Take heart. Montevideo has capitulated and is ours. Carlos has his troops inside and the naval squadron has taken the port. . . . Get better and beat the wretched illness in order the better to resist Pezuela if he approaches Tucumán, as you tell me.'[24] The victory of Alvear, he continued, released resources, and now Posadas ordered reinforcements for the Army of the North. So his partiality for his nephew did not revoke his responsibility towards San Martín.

Posadas never dealt in certainties and San Martín had to take his fate in his own hands. He had already decided to relinquish his command of the Army of the North, invoking his health as explanation. His illness was not simulated, as was suggested by General José María Paz, in order to withdraw from a command that he no longer desired and in which his own future was not assured.[25] Nor was San Martín inclined to respond to Posadas' invitation to surrender to his ill health and return to Buenos Aires. His intention is revealed in his actions. When he left Saldán it was not to take the trail to Buenos Aires, which he was content to let Alvear dominate, but to head west for Mendoza, where as part of a wider plan he wished to become leader of the new government of Cuyo. On 10 August 1814, at his own request, he was appointed governor intendant of Cuyo, to the *alvearistas* an obscure posting to an insignificant province, which raised no alarm. But this was a province on the march. Detached from Chile in 1776 to become part of the new viceroyalty of the Río de la Plata, it used the revolutionary years from 1810 to prise itself from the intendancy of Córdoba and become an intendancy in its own right. San Martín inherited a government confident in its status and ready to defend the revolution. This was his place of choice, exactly where he wanted to be to develop his strategic ideas, without alerting his enemies or exciting his friends.

The taking of Montevideo was Alvear's greatest glory to date. Could he resist going for new triumphs in the north, where San Martín was sick and his army inert? He could not resist boasting to San Martín of his victory and his booty: 'Fortune has favoured me admirably in all my endeavours. May she be equally favourable to yours ... I have increased my army prodigiously not only with the prisoners who have changed sides but also with the great number of recruits which I have enrolled in the campaign, and now stands at almost 7,000 men. My regards to our friends and to you, from your true and fervent friend.'[26] No words for others; there was only one victor. San Martín wrote laconically in the margin, 'Not even Napoleon.' It was time to move on.

Plan Continental

A new conviction began to dominate San Martín's thinking. How long these ideas had been germinating in his mind is unknown. His concept of liberation had always been wider than that of Buenos Aires and its provinces. It would not be surprising if his observation and experience of strategy on a grand scale in Europe, of French and British military planning, had already set him thinking of applying big ideas to South America.[27] He came to see—as other experienced soldiers and advisers saw—that the northern strategy of the revolution, the attempt to carry independence from Buenos Aires to Lima by way of Upper Peru, was fatally flawed.

Westward was the way of the future and Cuyo the key to the west. In this belief San Martín had requested and received from the authorities in Buenos Aires the governorship of Cuyo, and at the beginning of September 1814 he set up his headquarters in Mendoza. He was determined not to lead any expedition into Upper Peru; as for the defence of Argentina against Spanish attacks from the north, the 'valiant gauchos of Salta' could keep them at bay. He had greater priorities: he had left the Army of the North; now he had to create the Army of the Andes. His strategy was based on the thesis that the South American revolution could not be secure until the heart of Spanish power in Peru had been destroyed; that the northern route to Peru was 'not the true strategical line of the South American revolution', closed as it was by the terrain, the altitude, the extreme temperatures, the lack of resources and the hostility of the local population, all of which made Upper Peru a barrier not an opening to Lima, a barrier that was finally locked by the narrow passes of the Desaguadero, where the Spaniards needed only a small garrison to close Peru. There was only one way ahead—a gigantic flanking movement across the Andes to Chile, then up the Pacific in a seaborne invasion of Peru.[28] After the defeat of the Chilean patriots at Rancagua just south of the capital Santiago in October 1814 and the subsequent revival of Spanish power, this presupposed that Chile too would first have to be liberated. In 1815 San Martín estimated that he would need an expeditionary force of 4,000. These plans coincided with the interests of the Chilean revolution and they appealed to its leader, Bernardo O'Higgins, and to most of the Chilean émigrés.

San Martín's *Plan Continental*, like many problems in Argentine history, was an object of dispute in his own day, of rival claims in subsequent generations accompanied by the inevitable apocryphal documents, and of active controversy in recent years.[29] The first question is: who was the author of the plan? At the time San Martín had to use all his powers of persuasion on his political chiefs in Buenos Aires to introduce and to preserve his plan. In this sense he was certainly the author. After his death his supporters had to fend off other candidates—Enrique Paillardelle, Bernardo Vera, Tomás Guido—whose plans pointed in the same direction but lacked the precision and the scope of the final project. Paillardelle, a colonel in the Army of the North, argued in December 1813 for a naval expedition from Chile to Peru: Argentine and Chilean forces would leave by sea from Valparáiso near Santiago and disembark in Arica in the north for an offensive against Lima further north still, simultaneously with the advance of a reorganized auxiliary army through Upper Peru.[30] In the same year Bernardo Vera y Pintado, an Argentine deputy to the government of Chile, had sketched, though without details, the idea of a joint expedition landing in Arica or Pisco for advance on Lima, and submitted it to the second triumvirate. But these plans were not identical with San Martín's thinking. Tomás Guido, a young veteran of the revolution and now a senior official in the war ministry, a friend and collaborator of San Martín who stayed close to him during his illness in 1814, focused on the occupation of Chile as the 'principal object', not Lima.[31] But at least these were Argentine rivals for authorship.

More recently Rodolfo Terragno has astonished nationalist historians by uncovering a British author of the plan, Sir Thomas Maitland, M.P., a Scottish military officer of high rank and colonial experience in India and the West Indies, who submitted to the British government a plan of attack on the Spanish empire, a plan that was received by Henry Dundas, secretary of war, in mid-1800 but was shelved when the government of William Pitt fell from office in the following year. Maitland's plan, discovered by Terragno in the Scottish Record Office, proposed an expedition 5,500 strong (British of course) to capture Buenos Aires, establish a base in Mendoza, cross the Andes, defeat the Spaniards in Chile and then dispatch a further expedition to emancipate Peru, 'the end of our enterprise'. Maitland planned a crossing of the Andes in five or six days with a force that would be augmented in Chile with further British troops from across the Pacific for the final attack on Peru.[32]

Terragno refers to the 'extraordinary similarity' between Maitland's plan and San Martín's actual campaign, fifteen to twenty years later, and further argues that it is 'probable' that San Martín knew of the plan from his contact with British officers in the Peninsular War, including officers who had participated in the failed invasion of Buenos Aires.[33] There were, in fact, many plans at this time and the subject was hardly a secret; Spanish American projects became a popular genre among British strategists, who produced numerous proposals for expeditions for conquest and even for liberation, most of them highly unrealistic.[34] The thesis presented by Terragno is reasonable. It can be inferred that San Martín knew of Maitland's paper, though whether this made any difference to developments and decisions in the combat zone is open to discussion. He had an army, not of 8,900 regular soldiers (the optimum planned by Maitland), but of fewer than 5,000 creole volunteers. He did not have a powerful naval squadron waiting in support on the other side of the Andes, as Maitland wanted, and he was confined to an attack from one side only. As for crossing the Andes, that was to take much longer than Maitland's five or six days. And the whole operation took not three months, as he and Maitland thought, but three years. Yet San Martín's campaign proved that Maitland's plan, conceived two decades before and without direct knowledge of South America, was feasible and effective.

In 1814 San Martín's own views were strengthened by direct observation in northwest Argentina and the advice of experienced colleagues, including Belgrano and Güemes as well as Guido, and starkly demonstrated by the successive defeats suffered by patriot armies at Huaqui in 1811 and Ayohuma in 1813, soon confirmed by the defeat of a third expedition at Sipe Sipe on 29 November 1815. By February 1816 his plans were approaching final form: 'Chile is the country, if skilfully managed, that is capable of determining the fate of the revolution. . . . Its occupation is the highest priority. Once that is secured Peru will be free, and the legions of our soldiers will advance with greater success. Lima will fall, starved of supplies.' But Chile would have to be secured not by minor expeditions, as had been suggested, but in one decisive blow by a powerful force; he himself could do it next October, leading an army of four thousand across the cordillera.[35]

By May 1816, speaking of Lima as 'the scourge of liberty . . . the fortress of tyranny', San Martín was more specific:

> Let us not think small as we have up to now but on a large scale, and if we lose at least it will be with honour . . . Peru cannot be taken without first making sure of Chile: that country can be totally conquered by the end of April next year with 4,000 to 4,500 men. These troops should embark immediately and in eight days disembark at Arequipa. By the end of August this province will have 2,600 men available. If the rest are forthcoming I will answer to the nation for the success of the venture.[36]

While San Martín in Mendoza applied his mind to the strategy and logistics of the enterprise, in Buenos Aires Guido was drafting and communicating the plan to the government. His *Memoria* addressed to the director, Pueyrredón, integrated all the data San Martín had given him and was the first comprehensive proposal for a total campaign, an '*expedición general*', beginning with the occupation of Chile. This was the weakest flank of the enemy, and offered the shortest and surest route for the liberation of Upper Peru.[37]

Yet it was still not San Martín's final plan, for it did not include his ultimate objective, the conquest of Lima. This was spelt out by San Martín himself, the true author of the plan, the professional soldier and experienced campaigner, who designed the project from first to last. He had already staked his own career when he requested, and received, the governorship of Cuyo in August 1814. Now he declared against partial efforts which had plagued the revolution for too long: 'We need to think big; it is our own fault if we don't . . . Chile is ours for a little effort, and that country will enable us to take Peru, without which all our efforts are in vain: time will tell.'[38] To think big, in other words, was to replace a national objective by a continental one.

The Enemy Within

A continental planner could not afford to ignore the regional details. The Chilean dimension was not straightforward. The revolution in Chile had recently suffered a severe reversal. The royalists won a decisive victory at the battle of Rancagua (1–2 October 1814), where in spite of the heroic efforts of O'Higgins, the revolutionaries were beaten and lost the majority of their forces.[39]

Remote from the major shipping routes and rival empires, Chile had been a neglected colony, its role to occupy imperial space and keep at bay hostile Indians and intrusive foreigners. Yet this did not prevent the growth of regional identity, creole patriotism, consciousness of wrongs. Grievances were heightened in the second half of the eighteenth century when a modest restructuring of administrative and fiscal institutions still left Chile behind in the priorities of the Spanish empire, while across the Andes Buenos Aires and its hinterland were promoted to higher roles. Colonial monopoly was relaxed under the later Bourbons; access to international markets was easier and foreign manufactures were in greater supply. Chile's difficulty was to earn a surplus to pay for expanding imports, and at the close of empire Chileans believed that their economy needed freedom to control its own growth, to develop resources neglected by the metropolis and to earn more by producing more. These were the arguments used in 1810 when Chile took its first halting steps towards liberation, an open *cabildo* was summoned and a governing junta established. There were some who wanted more, the end of colonial rule in any form and the complete independence of Chile. Among these was Bernardo O'Higgins.

Bernardo was the son of Ambrosio O'Higgins, an Irishman in the Spanish colonial service who became governor of Chile and viceroy of Peru. The young man received much of his education in England, where under the influence of Miranda he was converted to the cause of independence and became 'nourished in the liberal principles and love of liberty which at that time burned fiercely in the hearts of European youth'.[40] He returned to Chile to take over the hacienda he inherited from his father and to live the life of a rich landowner. Politics did not immediately attract him, but he saw no alternative to revolution. Rule by Spain meant rule by Peru, the base of Spanish power in South America and an alien and traditionally hostile neighbour. And Spain closed all doors to compromise; neither liberals nor absolutists had any policy for America other than unconditional surrender to imperial authority. So O'Higgins joined the revolution and reluctantly, after much vacillation, accepted appointment as commander-in-chief of the patriot forces, an inexperienced soldier against hardened professionals. He soon found that there were enemies on his own side. A rival entrant to the revolutionary scene, José Miguel Carrera, twenty-six-year-old veteran of the Peninsular War, had returned to Chile convinced that 'the age of American independence has arrived and no one can prevent it'. He was backed by a powerful landed and military family who regarded Chile almost as a private domain, and he was fired with ambition for personal power. In a sense Carrera answered to the revolution's need of a military caudillo; he was able to control the patriot army and give the cause of independence the military leadership and organization it needed. But he had no time for rivals and clashed with the forces following O'Higgins. Meanwhile the Spaniards, reinforced from Peru and united under General Mariano Osorio, struck at the divided forces of the revolutionaries. O'Higgins and Carrera were unable to integrate their rival units in time to confront the royalists, and they lost the battle of Rancagua.

The patriot leaders fled across the Andes to Mendoza in October 1814, while behind them the royalists began to terrorize their supporters. So San Martín's plans for the reconquest of Chile coincided with the interests of the Chilean revolutionaries, and appealed to O'Higgins and most of the Chilean *émigrés*. But there were problems for San Martín. The defeat of Chilean independence left his Andean flank open to invasion by the royalist victors. And the mass of Chilean exiles flooding into Cuyo had to be regulated and supplied with food and transport. Security was now a major concern and in October 1814 he went to the Andean valley of Uspallata to study the situation and decide on his defences. The Chileans included the forces commanded by

José Miguel Carrera, who had already been a problem for O'Higgins and, with his two brothers, Juan José and Luis, was to become a bigger problem for San Martín. Carrera, no less arrogant in Argentina than in Chile, demanded the support and authority that he regarded as his due.

San Martín made it clear that while Carrera was chief of the Chilean troops he was under the authority of the chief of the province, and he, San Martin, did not wish to be taught his duties towards the exiles.[41] Those Chileans opposed to the Carreras petitioned San Martín to detain and confiscate the goods of the Carrera brothers and their followers. He was not prepared to go as far as this but made it clear to the Carrera faction that he was consulting the government in Buenos Aires and prepared to take measures for the tranquillity of the province. Carrera rejected his stance and added insult to injury, asserting the 'rights of man' and the 'rights of my country', and insisting on his independent command and determination to place his troops under the orders of the Buenos Aires authorities.[42] Threatening language and defiance of his authority outraged San Martín because he lacked the material strength to control the troublemakers and had to suffer further ignominy, while he awaited orders and reinforcements from Buenos Aires. Meanwhile in the interests of security and conscious of the proximity of Spanish forces ready to exploit these divisions, he appeared to compromise and suspend all measures against the Carreras.

He requested additional forces from Buenos Aires and meanwhile prepared his own response. On 30 October, recruiting Argentine auxiliaries, local militia and Chilean troops loyal to O'Higgins, he surrounded the barracks where the Carreras were quartered, pointed two pieces of artillery at the gate, ordered the surrender of troops, and arrested Juan José and José Miguel Carrera and other Chilean leaders, who promptly complained of conditions and insults to their honour. Banished to San Luis to the east, they were later freed by the Buenos Aires government and allowed to proceed to the capital if they wished; in fact the Carrera troops did not wish to enlist in the Argentine army. San Martín also made his own dispositions for defence of the province against unruly Chileans and the royalist army; he reordered the local militia and put patriotic pressure on the local population to join up, integrating with these the small force sent by Buenos Aires. But the tirade of accusations and insults continued from Juan José Carrera, to the fury of San Martín; the Chileans were lucky his hands were tied.[43] In due course, and beyond the jurisdiction of San Martín, the Carrera brothers were dealt revolutionary justice; meanwhile they were a thorn in his flesh. With Bernardo O'Higgins, on the other hand, a genial and uncomplicated character, he established an instant rapport, eventually giving him a role in Cuyo and a command in the Army of the Andes; and the two became personal friends and political allies for the rest of their careers.

Rethinking the Revolution

While keeping his eye on the big picture, San Martín also had to watch his back against Alvear and the politicians in Buenos Aires, and the possible influence of the malign Carrera in these circles. Posadas was styled Supreme Director of the United Provinces of the Río de la Plata, though the provinces were not united and Posadas did not govern them. He had little authority outside Buenos Aires, and even within the capital effective power lay with his nephew Alvear, commander-in-chief of the military forces in the area. Local caudillos and municipal authorities defied Buenos Aires and claimed autonomous or federative status for their provinces, a situation that astonished foreign observers. 'Buenos Aires has always repelled these pretensions by force and treated those who advanced them as rebels and traitors, [so] she has been considered by the inhabitants of the interior as unjustly usurping a dominion to which nothing entitles her, and her authority has been resisted by arms whenever a fair opportunity offered.'[44]

Buenos Aires in fact was an object of revulsion, not attraction. In January 1815 Posadas resigned, overcome by sterile disputes with provincial caudillos and insubordinate military. Into his place stepped the ambitious Alvear, and for four months he maintained a precarious hold in the capital. Alvear was appointed Supreme Director in January 1815 and while promoting San Martín to brigadier-general he also placed him in direct dependence on himself when he reorganized the army into three corps: the first under the command of Alvear and comprising the garrison forces of Buenos Aires, the littoral provinces, Córdoba and Cuyo; the second the forces of the north under Rondeau; and the third the Banda Oriental under Miguel Estanislao Soler. San Martín was on his guard against Alvear, feeling that he was at last on firm ground in Cuyo and in a position to move the revolution forward and outward. He had the respect and support of the people, while the effective political and military power he had established gave him a regional power base for the promotion of his plans; he did not intend to surrender easily. But Alvear had overreached himself and his power rested on shaky foundations. In 1815 San Martín began subtle tactics to thwart him. He asked for temporary leave in Rosario for health reasons, which Alvear promptly granted, sending a replacement. This was a trap, for it provoked an uproar in Cuyo, spreading from the streets to an open *cabildo*, supported by militias; it was made clear that Cuyo wanted no replacement for San Martín and his appointment should be made permanent. Alvear was wrong-footed and had to agree.[45] San Martín thus consolidated his regional power and henceforth remained the immovable governor of Cuyo. Alvear, however, was not immovable. In the course of 1815 Santa Fe and Córdoba announced their independence of Buenos Aires. In the Banda Oriental Artigas ruled without reference to Alvear and headed a loose federation of Uruguay and its riverine neighbours. In April 1815 troops who had been sent against Artigas mutinied and fraternized with the enemy, while in the capital the *cabildo* led an uprising against the supreme director. Alvear resigned on 17 April and sailed with his wife and three children into exile in Brazil aboard an English ship. A provisional government succeeded him.[46]

Instability in Buenos Aires had its effect on the plans of San Martín. The capital was still incapable of imposing its will on the southern cone and providing support for the revolution in Chile. It could do no more than maintain the status quo in Cuyo, lacking resources for offensive action westwards, while San Martín was specifically forbidden to intervene in Chile. Yet Buenos Aires still gave priority to mobilizing a third expedition to Upper Peru under the command of General José Rondeau, whose weak personality and military incompetence guaranteed a third catastrophe.[47] San Martín saw his project constantly relegated in importance and Upper Peru still favoured in the minds of the distant policy-makers. He was told in effect to remain on the defensive in Cuyo, with no prospect of further resources until a result was obtained in Upper Peru. San Martín knew that the only result there would be further defeat. Had they learnt no lessons?

San Martín was teaching a new lesson, original in design and skilful in execution. His trans-Andean strategy needed a powerful engine of movement and a new approach to resources. Argentina, in suspended animation between colony and nation, did not yet exist as a unitary state capable of firing continental liberation. This mosaic of countries, variously called Buenos Aires, the Río de la Plata, the United Provinces, and ruled by a mixture of directors and caudillos, was incapable of fusing policy, resources and personnel into a single project reaching beyond its own boundaries. In status and title San Martín was not the ranking leader of the revolution and had to take orders from superiors whose knowledge and ability were inferior to his. The solution was to create his own mini-state and his own authority, giving the revolution a new power base from which to launch his project. Cuyo became the cornerstone of continental independence, and Mendoza its capital. There an army was assembled and an economy nurtured to sustain it, and the lives of the people were taken over by the demands of war. In the shadow of the Andes San Martín was creating a dedicated base for a second front, a model of warfare unique in the Spanish American revolution.

CHAPTER 4

Power Base of Revolution

Cuyo: Cradle of Resistance and Resurgence

As he approached his fortieth year, San Martín left a vivid impression on his English friend, Commodore William Bowles, commander of the South American naval station, an officer with service in the Napoleonic war behind him and a distinguished naval career ahead. Bowles mistook his age but in other respects judged him well:

> General San Martin is now about forty-five; tall, strongly-formed, with a dark complexion and marked countenance. He is perfectly well-bred, and extremely pleasing in his manner and conversation. His way of living is in the highest degree simple and abstemious, and he rarely even sits down to table, dining in a few minutes on any dish which happens to be ready when he feels hungry. . . . He disregards money, and is, I believe, very little richer than when he came to this country, although if his views had been inter-ested or personal he might have easily amassed a large fortune since his entry into Chile. He is well-educated, reads a great deal, and possesses much general information. His system of policy is enlarged and liberal, and particularly so with regard to commerce, which he understands well.
>
> His health is bad, and he is subject to violent haemorrhages of the lungs—the consequence of a fall from his horse some years since.[1]

Bowles was much struck by San Martín's fanatical devotion to work; no detail escaped him. To his troops he was a hard disciplinarian, but he earned their allegiance through his concern for their welfare. The Englishman was fasci-nated by the policy as well as the personality of San Martín; he noted with approval his determination to restore peace as soon as possible, once independence was gained, his aloofness from politicians and what he regarded as their endemic corruption, his liberal views, especially on trade, and his evident partiality towards Britain. Bowles's views of San Martín apparently influenced other British observers, including Henry Chamberlain, the British consul general at Rio de Janeiro who informed the foreign secretary, Viscount Castlereagh, that 'his moral character stands higher than that of any other person of the independent party; his military abilities are evidently of the first class.'[2] Here was a soldier without personal ambition or avarice, a loving, if distant husband and a caring father. His taciturn manner masked a well-informed mind, and his notorious caution was accompanied by an ability to take decisive action when it was needed.

As a soldier San Martín had two great qualities, the ability to think and plan on a large scale, and an unfailing talent for organization. He now needed all his resources of mind and will, for he had to prepare his trans-Andean expedition in the face of two great obstacles—the creeping anarchy that threatened to engulf the whole of the Río de la Plata, and the complete lack of financial resources. Many observers, impressed by the magnitude of the task and the strength of Spanish defences in Chile, doubted the capacity of the general to obtain his objective: the reports of Bowles, supportive though he was, were sceptical about the outcome.[3] Yet from late 1814 San Martín began to translate his vision into reality, converting Mendoza into a military as well as a civilian headquarters, and making Cuyo in effect into a separate province isolated from the anarchy surrounding it and geared economically and psychologically to the demands of war.

He arrived in Mendoza in September 1814 as the new governor and he needed a family home as well as a power base. At first he declined the offer of a house prepared by the *cabildo*, preferring to obtain one himself. But the *cabildo* insisted and to avoid offence he gave way, persuaded that to begin a good relationship with the local government was vital for his project. Posadas gave him sound advice: 'The key to success is to establish good relations with the elected members of the cabildo, for these are related by family and kinship with the whole community, so if you are liked by them you are liked by all the people.'[4] San Martín began to worry about his wife Remedios and her delay in joining him, a delay for which she was not responsible. Posadas reassured him: 'Your lady has left at last, after a delay caused not by her but by her parents, according to what they themselves have told me, for they have not wanted her to go to a new country without all the attire appropriate for her age and birth.'[5]

His health began to improve and his domestic life to prosper. Remedios arrived accompanied by her niece Encarnación de María and her *mulata* servant Jesús; now he could face Cuyo and its people from his own domain and reassure them by his permanence. In Mendoza San Martín and his wife spent their longest time together, a mere two years, for his subsequent commitment to continental liberation restricted them to brief reunions. And when he decided to retire, first political obstacles, then the illness and death of Remedios in Buenos Aires on 3 August 1823, prevented a final reunion.

The setback involved in the loss of Chile to the royalists and the possibility of a royalist invasion persuaded San Martín in 1815 that the time had come to send Remedios back to Buenos Aires, but he delayed the decision in order not to alarm the people until Mendoza was made more secure. When that was done and the *cabildo* knew of his intention, they were alarmed and argued against it; they wanted him to take a full salary and support his family in a state appropriate to its leading position, for it gave respect and stability to his presence. It was he who had changed the face of the province: 'This people owes its rapid growth and its future existence to you alone. . . . It would feel insecure, dishonoured, and exposed unless you cancel the departure of your family.'[6] San Martín gave way, though he insisted on taking only half his salary. Remedios stayed, and on 29 August 1816 gave birth to their only child, their daughter Mercedes Tomasa, Merceditas as she was known, and San Martín was proud to call himself 'father of a Mendoza Infanta', a jibe at his detractors who were calling him 'King José', alluding to his supposed ambition for power and his known monarchism.[7]

Not all *cabildos* were as supportive as Mendoza. While in April 1815 Mendoza confirmed San Martín as governor intendant, San Juan and San Luis did not follow suit and showed signs of going their own way. The Argentine disease seemed to be spreading. San Juan succumbed to the separatist tendency and some dissidents wanted autonomy. San Martín saw federalism as one of the curses of political life and had no time for autonomy against central government, attributing it to 'lack of education and ignorance of public duty', which would have to be checked before it led to anarchy and the breakdown of law and order. He was ready to coerce San Juan to enforce obedience to authority, order and hierarchy; he scorned those who confused anarchy with liberty, and took steps to shore up existing regimes in Cuyo.

To his new army, the Army of the Andes, he applied his basic priorities: uniforms, pay, training. And he insisted, as he had done in Tucumán, on high qualifications for the officer corps. He established a security screen to prevent the infiltration of royalist spies, put out patrols in the cordillera and personally reconnoitred the mountain passes to test the routes his army would take. Training was non-stop. San Martín always insisted that blind heroism was not enough. He wanted soldiers who were disciplined, skilled in tactics and responsive to orders. He personally instructed and drilled his grenadiers and turned peasants into soldiers, raw recruits into men trained in manoeuvres. 'From elementary drill they moved to marching and turning, from the front and from the flank. Then to handling the shotgun, the lance, and the sabre (both attack and defence, which San Martín taught personally), explaining with patience and clarity the movements, the stances, the theory and the effects. . . . When he saw his soldiers sufficiently in command of the use of arms, he alternated periods of instruction with route marches and manoeuvres in squads and companies, in order not to bore them with the monotony of single movements.'[8]

San Martín led the way not only in the more obvious work of recruiting and training troops, assembling supplies and liaising with the Chileans, but also in the unpopular tasks of raising money.[9] The United Provinces had insufficient revenue even for ordinary expenditure, and its economic position was precarious until the 1820s. Cuyo itself, with a population of some 43,000 divided in numerical order between whites, mestizos, Indians and blacks, had a relatively healthy economy based on agriculture and livestock, with commercial production of wines and fruits. The challenge for San Martín and his officials was to transform this regional economy into a continental war machine.[10] Through their encouragement to farmers and ranchers and projects to expand irrigation, he increased the production of cereals and forage and the herds of cattle, horses and mules to the point where, with the addition of extra resources from the central government, they could sustain an army in training and on the move.

San Martín reformed the incidence and administration of taxation, drawing revenue by virtually any means—direct and indirect taxation, customs, sales tax, municipal dues, voluntary contributions, sequestration of the capital reserves of church organizations and finally forced loans.[11] Demands and yields reached a peak in 1816 and left the regional economy, already weakened by the severance of its trade with Chile, struggling to recover. Economic development was out of the question for some time to come. He was thinking of a total war economy of unparalleled austerity (comparable to that accepted by Britain during the Second World War). So he instituted rationing, wage cuts, taxation, confiscations, conscription, everyone being forced to live minimally and the women to do civilian war work. Enormous sacrifices were demanded of Cuyo, and especially of Mendoza. After the battle of Rancagua in October 1814 and the loss of Chile, treasury income was reduced by half because of the closure of trade across the Andes and the loss of import and export duties. In June 1815 San Martín established an agency for collecting voluntary contributions and immediately volunteered half of his salary. Then, when the treasury could not meet the costs of troop maintenance, he was forced to impose a more drastic measure, an *único arbitrio*, or 'special levy', which meant a forced loan, something he acknowledged to be 'too painful' but inevitable: 'Either we have the special levy or the troops perish, there is no alternative.'[12] An income tax of four reales on one thousand pesos was in force for the second half of 1815 and all of 1816. The *alcabala* (sales) duty strictly enforced, voluntary charges on wines and brandies, a meat consumption charge, sale of public land, donations of jewellery and other valuables by the women of Mendoza led by San Martín's wife, work by female volunteers in textile workshops 'happy to cover the nakedness of the soldiers', these were some of the measures and gestures of total commitment, a spirit of common endeavour among the people as well as among the soldiers.[13] Frustrated by the persistent parsimony of Buenos Aires, the community began a process of self-help; sociability was encouraged by sacrifice. Cuyo in general and Mendoza in particular responded generously to their general's demands. In Mendoza project and people met in perfect unity. Without the participation of the citizens of the province the whole plan would have failed. San Martín himself inspired the popular response. Patrician though he was, he had the common touch.

Local skills and resources were brought into play to supply the need for arms, munitions and gunpowder. José Antonio Alvarez Condarco, an engineer and close collaborator of San Martín, arrived in Mendoza after experience of directing a gunpowder factory established in Córdoba by an Englishman, James Paroissien. Saltpetre was abundantly available in Cuyo, and the manufacture of gunpowder was now established in a house provided by Tomás Godoy Cruz, landowner and politician, and furnished with mortars, sieves and other tools of the trade. The results inspired confidence. San Martín appointed Fray Luis Beltrán to be commander of military ordnance and director of the arsenal. A *mendocino* brought up in Chile, he had returned to his native land in the recent emigration and now turned his skills to army workshops, converting church bells into cannons, ammunition and bayonets. A mathematician, physicist, carpenter, blacksmith and gunner, he could turn his hand to any ordnance task, including the manufacture of cartridges, grenades, horseshoes, backpacks, saddles and harness. On the eve of the army's departure for action in Chile Beltrán designed an extraordinary firework display in the plaza of Mendoza and launched a burning globe high into the sky.

San Martín had increased his troops in the course of 1815. To the four hundred men he had at the beginning of the year he added another seven hundred slaves conscripted under the decree ordering European Spaniards to surrender their slaves or pay a fine of five hundred pesos per slave.[14] In the first half of the year he received a new force of artillery, with one hundred more men and two cannons. He later incorporated squadrons 3 and 4 of the mounted grenadiers consisting of 207 men who arrived in Mendoza in July

1815, having travelled from Buenos Aires bearing equipment and arms for four hundred men. Out of the refugees from Chile he formed the Patriotic Legion of Chile. Methods in constant use were the conscription of vagrants and the recruitment of volunteers. There were never enough. Well might San Martín proclaim that he had 130 sabres lying neglected in the barracks of the mounted grenadiers for lack of men to wield them. He was also aware that there was a critical shortage of doctors to care for the troops.

He initiated a number of measures to improve the health of soldiers and civilians in Cuyo: compulsory vaccination against smallpox, military hospitals in Mendoza, San Juan and San Luis. And he acquired an English surgeon, James Paroissien, a young man from Barking in Essex who had gone to Montevideo in 1806 to seek his fortune in the wake of the British invasions and been obliged since then to adopt a life on the fringe of military and medical affairs. In September 1816 he was appointed by the Buenos Aires government as chief surgeon to the Army of the Andes, and from the time of his arrival in Mendoza in December he began a long association with San Martín. In Mendoza he took command of medical and hospital services, and established a military hospital. Resources were small, three doctors, five Bethlehemite monks and seven assistants for an army that by the end of 1816 consisted of 4,000 regular troops and an auxiliary militia of 1,400.[15] But patients in San Martín's army were no longer confined to hovels with a space on the floor.

San Martín became addicted to Mendoza, his terrain, power base and one of the few places where he was genuinely popular. In October 1816 he requested a small grant of land for his eventual retirement; farming was the only job he wanted after soldiering, and he did not have enough money to buy an estate for himself. The *cabildo* not only granted him the land in Los Barriales, but also awarded another grant of land to his infant daughter. San Martín tried to divert this, in the name of his daughter, to members of the army appointed to special services in the coming campaign. This was not allowed, but another grant was made for the same purpose. The *cabildo* had reason to be grateful to San Martín for his services to the community: apart from his medical reforms, his development of new irrigation and stimulus to agricultural expansion, and his promotion of trade and industry, he also established the first library in Mendoza, and initiated reforms in education. And future generations of *mendocinos* would enjoy their evening walks along the handsome *paseo de la Alameda*, four rows of high poplars in straight lines extended and embellished by their extraordinary patron.

The social life of Mendoza looked up. The general would mark special occasions with balls and festivities, and he himself liked to take a turn on the dance floor. He once asked his young regimental colleague, Manuel de Olazábal, to introduce him to a *cotorrana* (lady of a certain age) for a dance. The partner chosen for him turned out to be a much younger girl, and afterwards, when he had escorted her back to her seat, he wanted an explanation from Olazábal. 'I thought you would rather dance with a young girl than an older woman', was the reply. The girl in question later became the wife of Olazábal.[16]

The services of Cuyo and its people to the revolution were something special to San Martín, and he placed his views on record to the central government:

> How admirable that a country without a large population or public revenue, without extensive commerce or great merchants, deficient in wood, hides, wool, cattle, and other primary materials as well as imported goods, has been able to raise from its own ranks a force of 3,000 men, even depriving itself of the slaves and the labour for its agriculture. It has developed arsenals, gunpowder and arms workshops, an artillery depot, armouries, fulling mills, barracks and camps. It has provided more than three thousand horses, six thousand mules, and countless head of cattle. In short, these extraordinary services towards the creation, progress and support of the Army of the Andes have come not from Buenos Aires but from the people of this province, whose prime concern has been to contribute their own possessions to the common cause.[17]

In the Foothills

The months were passing and San Martín still awaited decisions from Buenos Aires. He was getting impatient: the politicians had not even bothered to ask him for a single plan. The Chileans too were getting restless, using their underground links to press for liberation.[18] Through Guido he told the government, still obsessed with Upper Peru, that the trans-Andean expedition was as vital as ever and needed detailed preparation in advance: 'I repeat that the expedition to Chile is more formidable than it seems; the crossing alone requires great deal of thought, but on top of this there are the material preparations, and the political hazards to overcome, not only over there but also among this frenzied crowd of émigrés. So it is a massive job.'[19] He was convinced that the moment had come to strike, and urged the Buenos Aires Directory to authorize an expedition into Chile for February 1816. Guido seems to have conveyed San Martín's worries to the Lodge, who had managed to get one of its leading members, Antonio González Balcarce, into the government. He promptly asked San Martín for a list of his requirements and a plan of campaign; and the government made available a monthly subsidy of four thousand pesos to support his army. But when at last things seemed to be turning in favour of San Martín's plans, he was told that they were inopportune and dangerous.

It was a time of blighted hopes. False information and flawed analysis led the politicians in Buenos Aires to launch a new campaign in Upper Peru. Command of the third expedition fell predictably to General José Rondeau, an ineffective soldier, ignorant of the routes in the Andes and something of a fool. He had no control over his troops; they plundered on a scale unprecedented even among the liberating expeditions, and when they were not looting they were drinking. Not surprisingly they had little credit or support among the local guerrillas. The Spanish General Pezuela outmanoeuvred Rondeau with effortless precision and, with the help of his Chilean reinforcements, annihilated the third auxiliary army on the plains of Sipe Sipe on 29 November 1815.[20] San Martín could have been forgiven a feeling of *schadenfreude*. Sipe Sipe proved his point. It was then that he invited his officers to a banquet and pronounced a famous toast: 'To the first shot discharged against the oppressors of Chile on the other side of the Andes.'[21]

Frustratingly it was soon after this, in January 1816, that his illness returned. 'A severe attack of bleeding and resulting weakness have left me prostrate in bed for the past nineteen days; the setbacks I subsequently experienced have forced me to confine myself increasingly to my office; the danger from the enemy and my preparations to confront them have caused me to neglect my friends.'[22] During these painful weeks he could hardly sleep, even in short spells sitting in a chair, and it was now that he began heavy use of opium, a medicine recommended by his doctor, Juan Isidro Zapata, described by Mitre as a 'coloured person from Lima' who attended him on all his campaigns. In the next months the perverse priorities of the government weighed heavily on his mind and the option for Upper Peru became one of his worst demons, to the point when he would have accepted the dismemberment of the United Provinces if that would rid them of Upper Peru. 'There isn't a more obvious truth than the one you tell me', he wrote to Godoy Cruz, 'that Upper Peru should be detached from these provinces. I have known this ever since I have been in command of this army: the interests of these provinces have nothing to do with those of above.'[23]

While the government in Buenos Aires was inert and apparently uninterested, San Martín's restless mind was exploring other means of waging war. In 1815 he unleashed a *guerra de zapa*, an underground war of espionage and sabotage, with a network of spies in the mountain provinces reporting on the movements of the enemy, directing black propaganda across the Andes, keeping the cause alive and the resistance movement active in readiness for the invasion, while San Martín himself organized hit-and-run attacks on the enemy. And if he could not confront the enemy in Chile, perhaps he could lure them to Cuyo and fight them there. The idea was to spread news via his intelligence channels that he was evacuating Mendoza in order to reinforce the beleaguered Army of the North. The new royalist commander in Chile, Casimiro Marcó del Pont, appeared to take the bait and royalist troops began to mobilize on the other side of the Andes. In turn Buenos Aires was prompted to send San Martín rapid reinforcements of arms and supplies: three hundred rifles, two hundred cavalry sabres, two hundred sword belts, three hundred infantry cartridge belts.[24] He prepared his tactics, to surprise and overcome an enemy already split into various sites of occupation in Chile and now exhausted by a march over the Andes against a unified mass of San Martín's forces. He was confident, though not credulous: 'If they come I hope to have a successful day, but you know I am not gullible.'[25] A moot question. As he was not in a position to risk an offensive, was it feasible to rely upon the movements of the enemy? They had numerical superiority against San Martín's 1,500 men, and his plan really depended on their tribulations in crossing the Andes and improvising their deployment. At the end of January 1816 San Martín's plan of conquering Chile on the plains of Mendoza was unravelling. A delay held back the royalist army; its motive to attack depended on the belief that San Martín's force was leaving for Peru, but as he explained, 'a treacherous Chilean betrayed my plan to the enemy and ruined the whole thing.'[26] He was incandescent. Another opportunity lost! Between abandonment by Buenos Aires and unpredictability in Chile, his predicament was painful. How could he keep faith with his adherents? How could he explain another year of inaction to his army, and to the people of Cuyo, from whom he was demanding so much?

Towards the government in Buenos Aires his bitterness mounted. They seemed to have abandoned him and his cause, keeping him waiting without instructions, without resources and without encouragement. In fact they took away such resources as he had and sent them to Buenos Aires and the Army of the North, while leaving him responsible for all the infrastructure expenses in Cuyo. Two squadrons of his own regiment were obliged to join the Army of the North, from which they returned to Mendoza in November 1816 more dead than alive. He traced his treatment not only to the nature of his demands but to the enmity of politicians in Buenos Aires and his lack of support in the country:

> They have abandoned and compromised me in the most outrageous way. I well knew that as long as I commanded these troops not only would there be no expedition to Chile but I would even be denied basic assistance. That is why I have repeatedly sought to resign not so much because of poor health as for these reasons . . . San Martín will always be a man suspect in his own country and so my decision is made: I only want the cordillera to close in so that I may bury myself in a corner where no one will know of my

existence; and I will only emerge to head a party of gauchos if the devils invade us.'[27]

He continued to press for resources from a government not convinced of the trans-Andean strategy. He rejected a compromise proposal from Buenos Aires for a mini-expedition to Chile. They did not realize the magnitude of the task or the value of Chile to the revolution. Any partial effort would be doomed. 'It needs an outstanding force to avoid bloodshed and give us complete occupation in the space of three or four months. Otherwise the enemy will dispute the ground inch by inch. Chile is a natural castle. The war could be interminable.'[28]

Instead of the government's pathetic plan San Martín proposed another—to cross the cordillera next October and meanwhile to press on with the *guerra de zapa*, which would need a subsidy of fourteen thousand pesos. To take the war to the enemy across the Andes required 1,800 men added to the 2,200 they had in Cuyo, 3,000 extra rifles, 800 swords and 4 cannons. There would have to be a subsidy of sixty thousand pesos, for it was not acceptable to take funds from an impoverished country like Chile as the enemy oppressors had done. He also requested two warships operating along the coasts of Chile to stop the enemy escaping and confiscate any treasure they had seized. He would be ready to move as soon as he had the resources. He received the usual reply; the government agreed in principle but did not have the resources to back the plan. Undeterred, he continued to prepare for a war his masters denied him. His engineers surveyed roads and passes across the cordillera, and he constructed defensive batteries in the passes of Los Patos, Uspallata and Portillo, for as he explained, 'Let it not be said that in taking the war to a foreign country we neglect our own.'[29]

Then he intensified the *guerra de zapa*, subverting the enemy's war effort and sustaining morale at home. He established a security screen to prevent the infiltration of royalist spies, and counter-intelligence became so efficient that Fray Bernardo López, agent of Marcó del Pont, governor of Chile, hardly set foot in Cuyo before he was picked up and sentenced to be executed; he was only saved by confessing and handing over mail he was bringing to Spaniards in the lining of his hat. Normally San Martín was ruthless in dealing with enemy spies, for the Spaniards were desperate to discover the starting date, the strength and the route of his project. He organized his own intelligence service with a network of agents reporting on royalist plans in Chile, resources, troop numbers and movements. He was aware of the costs and the risks of espionage. Secret-service money was vital to keep spies on his payroll, otherwise they could be 'turned' by the enemy.[30] Chilean émigrés operating on the frontier informed him of the latest situation across the Andes; and there were agents in Concepción, Talcahuano and Santiago, a fifth column reporting on political trends, military opinions and the morale of the people. These sources concluded that the aristocracy were untrustworthy but needed to be coopted because of their influence, while the common people were the real patriots, along with many officials and officers. Public opinion of Marcó del Pont himself was contemptuous; he was a *maricón de cazoleta*, a sinister figure, surveying the streets from within his coach, withdrawn from view but ever menacing.[31]

Amidst San Martín's frustration and failure hope gave way to indignation. But faith in his project survived every setback and kept his expedition on course. It was his willpower that sustained the war effort and lifted morale in Cuyo during the long months of inaction, government delay and chronic indecision. Reinforcements were never sent, funds never paid. He was of course frustrated. His nerves suffered and from the end of January 1816 ill health reappeared. On 9 March he requested leave to go to the hills of Córdoba for two months. The government refused but rumours promptly spread in Mendoza that he had resigned. The *cabildo* reacted strongly and reaffirmed the unwritten pact between them:

> The reputation of San Martín has kept the enemy of Chile within its borders. To his efforts, tactics and talents we owe the army that garrisons us, and the active preparations for the destruction of Chile's oppressors. To him too we owe the resources which the province itself would not have produced and which will disappear the moment their creator ceases to lead it. He gave his word that he would not abandon us and in turn the people have denied him no sacrifice and spared no effort in his support. This pact is sacred, the only safety for our hopes. . . . Today more than ever the person of San Martín is irreplaceable.'[32]

San Martín reassured the *cabildo* that he had no intention of leaving, but it wanted more reassurance and pressed the national congress in Tucumán for confirmation of his promotion to general of the Army of Mendoza as 'final and decisive', in recognition of the sacrifices made by the people for the support of troops and the provision of resources for the expedition.[33]

Towards the Verge

San Martín's ordeal was part of a greater crisis for his country. By 1816 the United Provinces seemed to be on the verge of dissolution. As he was struggling to assemble a united force to cross the Andes, behind him in Argentina itself Santa Fe, Córdoba, Salta, Santiago del Estero, all were in conflict with the central government and determined to go their own way. Were they a real nation, he wondered, or a mob of caudillos? This was the worst year since the revolution began. San Martín referred to the risk of utter ruin in 1816: 'I fear this not from the Spaniards, but from domestic discord and our lack of education and judgment. . . . It was a moral impossibility that we should organize ourselves properly; we are very young, and our stomachs are too weak to digest the food they need.'[34] A Portuguese army was advancing from Brazil to occupy the Banda Oriental, a prospect that San Martín preferred to Artigas, whom he saw as a source of federal dissension in Argentina. In Upper Peru a Spanish army was assembling to carry the war into Tucumán. To fortify the country in the midst of its agony, and to reassure the provinces, the government of Buenos Aires called a new congress, to meet in Tucumán in the interior, and delegates assembled in March 1816. But there was still no national union, with unitarists, federalists and monarchists striking discordant notes. The firmest line was imposed on the congress from without, by San Martín and Belgrano, who wanted a declaration of independence as an indispensable preliminary to renewing the war effort against Spain. 'Otherwise, the enemy will naturally treat us as insurgents, for we are still calling ourselves vassals.'[35] On 3 May 1816 the delegates elected Juan Martín de Pueyrredón the 'Supreme Director of the State', and on 9 July they declared 'the independence of the United Provinces of South America,' 'a masterly stroke', thought San Martín, though whether they thought of the South American revolution in the same ample terms as he did only the future would tell. The past was not reassuring.

Pueyrredón promptly informed San Martín that he would come in person to look at the state of the Army of Peru—the last thing San Martín wanted. He did not need any lesson from the politicans. He could see the problems of that army, the misgivings of the local guerrillas, especially of Güemes, and its need of a new commander after Rondeau. San Martín had no doubt that it should be Belgrano, well organized, endowed with integrity and natural talent, no Bonaparte but 'believe me, he is the best we have in South America.'[36] There was worse to come from Pueyrredón: congress wanted to reinforce the Army of the North to confront the royalists and a strength of six thousand was mooted. An incredulous San Martín argued vigorously against such a proposal: it was wasteful and useless and would take too long; and local gaucho guerrillas were quite capable of defending the northern front. The whole trend of government policy was wrong. It needed to move away from Upper Peru to Chile. Otherwise 'everything goes to hell'. And in mid-1816, in a letter to Godoy Cruz, he began to reveal the breadth and detail of his own policy:

In the end, my friend, we must grasp this truth, if the war continues two years more we do not have enough money to wage it effectively, and in that case we are undone. To avoid that, let us think big, with our heads held high. Let us not think small as we have up to now, and if we lose at least it will be with honour ... Peru cannot be taken without first making sure of Chile: that country can be totally conquered by the end of April next year with 4,000 to 4,500 men. These troops should then embark immediately and in eight days disembark in Arequipa. By the end of August this province will have 2,000 men available. If the rest are forthcoming I will answer to the nation for the success of the venture. ... While the army for conquering Chile will be occupied on that task, the army for Peru will be assembling for taking that kingdom; then both can turn effectively on Lima.[37]

The ultimate objective, therefore, was Lima. The rapid force deployment to Chile was simply the indispensable preliminary to the strike on Lima. He envisaged a very short time lapse between the conquest of Chile and the strike from Arequipa. In fact this gap would be three years. By mid-1816 San Martín was getting desperate for a decision, keeping up the pressure on the government and pressing for action. He needed to stop any new invasion of Upper Peru and activate one to Chile, to halt the time wasting on useless projects and focus effort on the vital plan. To bring the whole thing to a conclusion it was crucial to get to the new director, Pueyrredón, to turn his mind and win his approval. With this object San Martín's friend Tomás Guido, the secretary of war, assembled all the data that San Martín had given him, the definite facts and the precise numbers, wrote them up clearly and eloquently, and sent them to Pueyrredón.

This was the *Memoria* of 20 May 1816, sent to Pueyrredón on 31 May. Guido drew attention to the 'three key points' for the success of the operation: the forces at their disposal, the forces of the enemy and the most effective means of destroying them. The first step was to bring an end to the ineffective and ruinous offensive by the Army of Peru; next actively to frustrate the enemy project, otherwise there will be no time to avoid disaster; then to pursue the major target. 'The occupation of Chile is the main object the government ought to pursue at all costs, for various reasons: first, it is the weakest flank of the enemy; second, it is the shortest, easiest and surest way of liberating the provinces of Upper Peru; and third, restoring freedom in that country will consolidate the emancipation of America in a system that will induce further developments.'[38]

Cogent as it was, Guido's paper was not San Martín's final plan. Presumably Guido had not yet received this, for he saw Chile and Upper Peru as the ultimate destinations. The final objective, however, and the central piece of San Martín's thinking, was the conquest of Lima. So in spite of the impact of Guido's memorandum on Pueyrredón, the director obtained the first clear idea of

San Martín's project from San Martín himself as outlined in his letter to Godoy Cruz.

Pueyrredón had still not made up his mind and he arranged to meet San Martín in Córdoba in mid-July on his way back to Buenos Aires, 'to regulate precisely the plan of operations for the army under your command in order to adapt it to our circumstances and to the information you have given me.'[39] He then received Guido's *Memoria* and seems at last to have been persuaded: 'I am more than convinced of the absolute importance that such an expedition offers for the security and advantage of the state, I have definitely decided on it. Therefore I charge you to take in hand all the measures necessary to advance this enterprise.'[40]

Did this amount to an absolute decision? San Martín was now amplifying his grand strategy with the detailed tactics of the operation and making sure Pueyrredón understood them. It was not enough to determine the best route for his forces to cross into Chile; this would depend on the position taken by the enemy. They had to strike precisely where the enemy forces were massed, destroy them in the first action and take the capital, Santiago. It would be useless to attempt to take them piecemeal, for they would then be forced to win territory step by step and the war would be prolonged: 'our single combined force ought to engage the bulk of the enemy, destroy him in the first action and take the capital, and this will avoid the serious drawback of prolonging the war and fighting a series of battles, disputing the ground inch by inch in a wet climate and spending seven months of the year in winter quarters.'[41]

At last, after what seemed an eternity, San Martín and Pueyrredón met in Córdoba on 16 July and spent the two following days in discussions. San Martín regarded it as a meeting of minds and wills, and the matter was concluded. 'In two days and nights we have settled everything; now it only remains for us to get to work; the day after tomorrow we each leave for our destinations, determined to work for the great cause.'[42] Now he could proceed to the final preparations for his campaign, secure in the knowledge that there was nothing to stop him. Nothing except the critical points of his offensive, first to identify the right point of penetration where he would have a single target of the massed enemy on the plains on the other side of the cordillera; he was confident he could beat the enemy in combat but the second problem was more worrying, the actual crossing of the cordillera. 'My friend, what keeps me awake is not the resistance of the enemy, but the crossing of these enormous mountains.'[43] So it was more drilling, training, marching, a programme for discipline and stamina. He also wanted naval support, four to six vessels, which would have covered his Pacific front and protected the expedition to Lima. But Pueyrredón could not or would not supply it, and striking an Argentine attitude he expected Chile to do more.

The Army of the Andes

San Martín was appointed general in chief of the Army of the Andes on 1 August 1816, and to enable him to concentrate on military affairs he was relieved of administrative duties, the office of governor-intendant being assigned to Colonel Toribio Luzuriaga. Later the director and Congress confirmed on San Martín the appointment of captain general with the title of excellency, but this was not enough for the *cabildo* of Mendoza who pressed for him to be appointed to the rank of brigadier. San Martín was seriously embarrassed by the excessive attentions of the *cabildo* and felt obliged to disassociate himself from the move in a letter to the press, especially as some people were saying that it was all his own doing. 'I protest in the name of my country's independence never to accept any promotion beyond that which I now have, nor to obtain public office, and I will relinquish the military appointment I have the moment Americans cease to have enemies. Do not attribute this statement to any merit on my part but only to the desire to enjoy tranquillity for the rest of my days.'[44]

Lionized by the *cabildo*, he was resented by a group of officers jealous of his success. In reorganizing the army and its commanders in preparation for the coming campaign, he was convinced that Regiment 11 needed a new colonel better qualified than Juan Gregorio de Las Heras, who wanted the job but was not up to it. San Martín's decision soon leaked out and Las Heras and others affected by the changes conspired to depose, and even to attack, the commander-in-chief. San Martín got wind of the whole thing and on the eve of his departure for Córdoba confronted Lieutenant Colonel José María Rodríguez, the leading conspirator, with the words 'I know you are trying to depose me and you do not have a better opportunity than now that I am about to depart', which knowledge so shocked Rodríguez that he promptly took to his bed and spent the next day in hiding.[45] The conspiracy spread to San Juan, where Las Heras had cronies, and the battalion there seemed ready to support him and depose the general in favour of Marcos Balcarce. San Martín stayed cool and at the end of Sepember ordered the imprisonment of the ringleaders, sparing Las Heras out of insufficient evidence.

Recruitment for the Army of the Andes was now critical and urgent. San Martín needed reinforcements of veteran troops, for the rapid increase of the army had mainly been through younger recruits and volunteers. There were four infantry battalions, three cavalry regiments and one artillery battalion. Calculations of the army's size vary; there is some agreement that it totalled between the official 4,611 (excluding the Chilean battalions) and an informal figure of 5,000.[46] This was expected to face a royalist force in Chile of 7,613 regulars and 800 militia. The Army of the Andes was recruited primarily from creoles and mestizos. The cavalry consisted of mestizos and poor creoles, and its officers were from the creole elite. The Army of the Andes was joined by a number of British volunteers: a company of British light cavalry; James Paroissien, chief surgeon to the army; and subsequently William Miller, who had been commissioned in the Royal Artillery, seen active service in the Iberian Peninsula and North America, before becoming one of San Martín's most distinguished officers.

San Martín also wanted to recruit slaves.[47] A number had already been recruited in Buenos Aires and other provinces under legislation targeting the slaves of European Spaniards. But greater numbers were sought from all slave owners. The campaign to secure access to all slaves aged over twenty, the so-called *golpe de los esclavos*, met with resistance from reluctant proprietors, who relied on slave labour in the fruit farms, vineyards and livestock estates throughout Cuyo. By mid-1816 San Martín regarded the recruitment of slaves as essential and he exerted pressure on proprietors to release them for army service. He urged the measure on Godoy Cruz, who regarded it as extreme. 'There is no alternative, my good friend, we can only survive by putting every slave under arms. Moreover, while the Americans are best for the cavalry there is little doubt that they do not make the best infantry. Make no mistake, I have studied our soldiers and I know that only the blacks are really good infantry. Anyway, do what you think best.'[48] The problem was that the proposed conscription affected not only domestic-service slaves but also field slaves, including those from a religious community from whose plantations San Martín proposed to take three hundred or more slaves. Resistance was overcome and a sizeable proportion of slaves in Cuyo were secured for the army. Pueyrredón tried to do the same in Buenos Aires and was so resisted by 'an infernal clamour' that he had to give up.[49]

By the end of 1816, when the military preparations were complete, an army of about five thousand had been built around regular and auxiliary troops from the Río de la Plata, a vast quantity of equipment and supplies, and thousands of mules. Of the troops 1,554 were ex-slaves, constituting almost 40 per cent of the total.'[50] There were also female slaves, accompanying the soldiers in one capacity or another. One of them, María Demetria Escalada de Soler, was a slave of San Martín.

Multiracial armies were not to everyone's liking. General Belgrano had remarked of his Argentine army in Upper Peru that 'the Negroes and mulattos are a rabble, as cowardly as they are bloodthirsty . . . the only consolation is that white officers are on the way.' San Martín, on the other hand, was convinced that 'the best infantry soldiers we have are the Negroes and mulattos.'[51] William Miller, who became second-in-command of the 8th or 'Black' Battalion of Buenos Aires in San Martín's army, recorded:

The privates of the Battalion No. 8 were Creole Negroes, and had been for the most part in-door slaves, previously to the commencement of the revolution, when, by becoming soldiers they obtained their freedom. They were distinguished throughout the war for their valour, constancy and patriotism. . . . Many of them rose to be good non-commissioned officers.[52]

There was a price to pay for this kind of freedom. The black infantry of the patriot armies suffered heavy casualties, and conscription often led not to freedom but to death. If Argentine society in the nineteenth society was predominantly white, this was due in in no small measure to black losses in the war of independence.

While he had a high regard for the fighting qualities of the black soldiers, San Martín thought that it was inadvisable and impractical to mix whites and blacks in the same unit. 'Class differences have been embodied in the culture and customs of almost all nations in all centuries; it would be absurd to think that by an inconceivable break with the past a master would agree to parade in the same unit as his slave.'[53] His practice was to separate whites and blacks into different units. Without sacrificing his principles a general on campaign had to be a pragmatist.

Nothing escaped San Martín's strategic eye. Indian territory was a vital front and southern Indians invaluable allies for the Andean crossing. In September 1816 he went in person to the lands of the south to reach an understanding with the Pehuenche Indians for assistance in the passage of troops through the Planchón, opposite Curicó and Talca. In advance he sent abundant supplies of bridles, spurs and other presents, not forgetting wine and brandy. After eight days of carousing with the Indians, he signed an agreement with them to provide the army with cattle and even to take action against the enemy. A large group of Indian chiefs dressed in hides and smelling of horses sat on the ground in a circle while he addressed them seated on a chair in the middle. Through an interpreter, the Franciscan Friar Julian, he explained that the Spanish army was preparing to invade their lands from Chile to kill and rob their women and children. I myself am an Indian, he told them. He was going to cross the Andes with his army and guns (some of which were then giving a display of parading and firing) to finish off the Spaniards who had robbed their peoples of their land. But he needed their permission to pass through their territory. They replied with '*Vivas*' and acclamations, stirred by the liquor they had been drinking since breakfast, competing to embrace him, and swearing to help and follow him. He later had to change his uniform, joking 'What devils! These lice are going to feed on my friend Marcó del Pont, who always smells of scent'.[54] One of the *caciques*, Necuñán, betrayed the deal and sent messengers to the royalist camp revealing the route of the patriot army. San Martín soon got to know of this and, alerted or not, decided to advance by the most difficult and longer northern pass, Los Patos, so continuing to deceive the enemy. In any case, he was satisfied with the deal, as he told Guido. 'I have concluded my Great Parley with the Indians of the South, a happy conclusion. They will not only help me with cattle for the army but they undertake to play an active role against the enemy.'[55]

At the end of September 1816 San Martín moved his army to the camp of El Plumerillo, four kilometres northwest of Mendoza, 'an infernal place, where before digging a foot you come across water and the ground is always white with saltpetre. . . . Only our youthful vigour and patriotic fervour enabled us to resist such discomfort. The general could not find another camp to set us down.'[56] This was San Martín's base camp for the coming campaign, the final training ground for the endurance test that awaited them. The army was as fit as it would ever be. 'Its organization', wrote William Miller, 'reflects the highest credit upon the tact, talent and industry of San Martín. The discipline which he established showed that the experience he acquired in the peninsular war had given system and efficiency to these natural qualifications which fitted him so well for the task.'[57] He never gave up on discipline. He still had time, in September 1816, to issue a lengthy order on military crime and punishment, listing forty-one offences including blasphemy, sedition, desertion, malingering, troublemaking, the rape and robbery of women, all with drastic punishments intended to keep order in the ranks and an example before the eyes of the people.[58]

As the time approached, he assembled his final resources. He received a convoy of vital war materials and supplies from Buenos Aires, which had to run the gauntlet of bandits and guerrillas on the way. He needed still more supplies against the cold of the Andes crossing, warmer clothing, more uniforms, saddles and trappings. Troops deprived of basic clothes and equipment, he told Pueyrredón in Buenos Aires, became low in morale and he had to struggle to keep them warm and fighting fit.[59] Women were saving clothes and mending uniforms non-stop. He needed, he reckoned, 7,500 mules, 3,000 horses, mounts for the infantry and subsistence for twenty days. Pueyrredón thought he was never satisfied, though he retained a wry sense of humour. He was sending the clothes requested, blankets and ponchos; and if you need more you will have to beg for them around the houses; and quantities of jerked beef are on the way:

Here come 400 saddles and trappings. Here come by separate post in a box the only 2 bugles I could find. Here come 200 extra sabres, 200 tents, that is all there is. Here come the devil, the world, and the flesh. I don't know how I am going to get away with the debts I have incurred to pay for it all. I'll

just have to go bankrupt and cancel all the bills, and I'll have to come too
and feed on the jerked beef I'm sending you. Bloody hell, don't ask me for
anything more, otherwise you will hear that I have been found at dawn
hanging from a beam in the fort![60]

In mid-December San Martín sent José Antonio Alvarez Condarco, his
armourer, on a risky intelligence mission. He travelled to Chile by the Los
Patos pass, the longer northern route, on the pretext of delivering to Marcó del
Pont an official copy of the act of independence of the United Provinces,
assuming that the Spanish commander would send him packing by the
shortest route back, which was Uspallata further south. This would be the
opportunity for a final reconnoitre and mapping of the routes. The documents he carried bewildered Marcó, who ordered them to be burnt in the
main square by the public executioner. Alvarez was lucky to escape with his
life, for Marcó wanted to execute him, but he was saved by officers who were
masonic liberals and persuaded Marcó to expel him instead, which he did in
words that branded San Martín as a traitor: 'I sign with a white hand and not
like that of your general which is black.'[61]

Problems and pressures mounted as the final days approached. San Martín
was not afraid of the military challenge and did not doubt the outcome. But
there was a trace of nervousness in his political thinking and he was anxious
about the welcome that awaited him in Chile. Basically he did not trust the
Chileans, 'these villains' he called them, at least those outside the O'Higgins
party. The Carreras were a malign influence in the army and they had
followers among the émigrés; even his secretary José Ignacio Zenteno was
suspect and could not be trusted on Chilean matters.[62] So San Martín felt
vulnerable politically; this was why, time and again, he asked his friend Guido
in the defence ministry to leave Buenos Aires and accompany him for support
and expertise. But Pueyrredón would not release him, and San Martín was left
to manage the future on his own and judge Chilean affairs for himself. He had
to fight a campaign and at the same time establish political relations with
people he did not know, create another army, initiate postwar reforms and
finally launch his ultimate weapon, an expedition to Peru. It was a formidable
prospect in unknown territory. And it could no longer be delayed: he believed
that he had to take crucial decisions by the end of February 1817. He was on
his own now. His moment of truth had arrived.

CHAPTER 5

Across the Andes

The March

Mendoza raised the spirits of San Martín and his men, as it raised the spirits of all who travelled there, a welcome oasis between peaks and pampas. Across its fertile plain of vineyards and poplars the distant cordillera was in full view, the pure air in a clear blue sky a delight to the senses, and the great chain of mountains stretching north and south a challenge to inspire the invaders. In early January 1817 the Army of the Andes began to move westwards. After three years planning and training, San Martín did not intend his army to leave Mendoza in silent order. He knew the importance of spectacle and liturgy, and he owed it to the people of Cuyo and the soldiers under his command to mark their departure with a show worthy of the combat to come. In fine summer weather his troops left their camp at El Plumerillo, their uniforms smart, buttons shining, weapons gleaming, and as they marched through the streets of Mendoza the drums sounded and the fifes played and the crowds shouted. The first stop was the monastery of San Francisco, where the statue of Our Lady of Carmen, the Virgin General, whom San Martín had designated Patron of the army, was carried out to head the column with San Martín at its head. From there it made its way to the church to collect the blue and white flag made by the women of Mendoza and lying at the foot of the altar. The army chaplain celebrated mass and blessed the flag, which was then taken by San Martín to the porch of the church and shown to the crowd in the square outside: 'Soldiers! This is the first flag to have been raised in America. Swear to uphold it and to die in its defence, as I swear.' 'We swear' came the reply. There followed three days of feasting, drinking and dancing.

By all accounts the army was in good shape, but everyone agreed that crossing the Andes would be the greatest challenge. 'General San Martín's army', reported Commodore Bowles, 'has been increased to near 5,000 men and I am told by people who have seen them that they are in a very good state of discipline and extremely well-equipped and appointed. . . . The difficulty of passing the Cordilleras with so considerable a body of troops in the face of any enemy is generally considered as the greatest obstacle to San Martín's success.'[1] But the general had a plan and a drill for that too. The order of advance was staggered, starting on 9 January. Small, lighter detachments were sent in carefully timed departures to each flank over a front of 805 kilometres, to lure the enemy into splitting his force into parts to face what was thought to be a major attack. One detachment was sent to the northern flank to break through the pass of Guana into Coquimbo, another probe went further north through Come Caballos towards Copiapó. In the south a detachment cut through the Planchón pass towards Talca to liaise with the patriot cause in the south. Then, at intervals between 18 and 19 January the two major divisions of the army set off to penetrate the Andes by the two central passes, Uspallata and Los Patos one under Juan Gregorio de Las Heras, the other commanded by another *porteño* soldier, Miguel Estanislao de Soler. Behind him marched the centre division under O'Higgins and the reserve under San Martín.

Between Mendoza and Santiago lay four mountain ranges and two of the highest peaks of the Andes, Aconcagua and Tupungato. The route between these rises from the plain of Uspallata across the natural rock bridge, the Puente del Inca, up through the gorge of the Mendoza river to the wild Paso de la Cumbre at 12,600 feet, and then falls steeply to the mountain slopes of Chile, leading to the great ravine of the Aconcagua river. North of Aconcagua, a second route, the Los Patos pass, longer but equally difficult, also led to the valley of the Aconcagua. The long line of marchers extending in single file had to cross by narrow paths along the mountainside, clinging to the narrow *laderas*, or shelves, between rock and precipice, keeping close to the inside, though mules and their riders walked on the edge of the cliff for the rider knew that his cargo might strike the side of the mountain and throw them both off balance. The men marched over one ridge after another in endless ascents and descents, struggling against the intense cold and the draining altitude, either frozen stiff or slowed by the *soroche*, with the wind howling through the valleys far below. Heavy pieces of artillery were slung on poles between mules or dragged by ropes up and down the slopes. The extraordinary procession had its local witnesses, the condor floating almost movelessly above and the occasional *guanaco* watching from the side, while between earth and sky the snow-capped beauty of Aconcagua was always in view, a stark contrast to the misery around it. Out of 9,251 mules not more than 4,300 arrived in Chile, and out of 1,600 horses not more than 500. The cold, the *soroche* and sheer exhaustion accounted for most of the human losses, estimated at 300 on the crossing.[2]

The first division under Las Heras left Mendoza on 18 January for the shorter crossing from Uspallata leading into the Valley of Aconcagua after a march of 340 kilometres covered in ten days. It encountered some royalist opposition, and in one action even its Dominican chaplain José Félix Aldao fought vigorously, killing two Spaniards: 'With his clothes, sword, and hands covered in blood he presented himself to Colonel Las Heras who severely rebuked him: "Father, such conduct is not your job; that is ours, yours is to read the breviary". Father Aldao, who had expected to be praised, withdrew furious, swearing to hang his habit from a tree, as he did later and made a career for himself in the Granaderos a Caballo.'[3]

The main army division started out on 19 January, consisting of the vanguard under Soler, the centre under O'Higgins and the reserve under San Martín. He was dressed in his blue grenadier uniform and a pointed bicorn hat with a chinstrap against the wind and lined with oilcloth; black boots with bronze spurs; and his curved sabre in his belt. He wore a cloak against the mountain cold and a tunic of otter skin, and rode a mule with wooden stirrups for a secure footing. Ascending the slope of Valle Hermoso, he was conversing with guides about the routes across to meet up with Las Heras, when a fierce hailstorm from the mountains forced the division to a halt. San Martín dismounted and spent the night in a cutting (*trinchera*) in temperatures below zero. In the morning he got his servant to bring out the brandy, lit a cigarette and ordered the band to play the Argentine national anthem, the music echoing high through the mountains. The spot preserved the name *Trinchera de San Martín*.[4] As he shrewdly remarked, the troops having experienced the terrible obstacles getting to the top, some 12,000 feet, there was no danger of their wanting to pull back, or as Miller put it, 'Every step the patriots took convinced the least reflecting that the obstacles already overcome were of a nature that left not a ray of hope that a retreat would be practicable, if they were beaten in the field.'[5]

The Los Patos pass was sixty-seven kilometres north of Uspallata and the army's march was planned to take the bridge of Aconcagua, open communications with Las Heras and then march directly to Chacabuco. The Spaniards were alerted to the danger of a junction of the two divisions, which they could prevent by dominating one of the passes and so stop the Army of the Andes from occupying the plain. San Martín was aware of the threat and sent in a unit of twenty-five mounted grenadiers, whose epic charge on 4 February— the first of a series—put to flight the Spanish detachment, taking their stores and equipment.[6] With the occupation of the exit of this pass the campaign was saved and the patriots were able to overcome pockets of resistance on the way to the plains. On 10 February, having set out in three divisions eighteen days previously and negotiated the passes of Los Patos and Uspallata, San Martín's men united on the Chilean side as planned, truly a miracle of timing. They took up position on the heights overlooking the hill of Chacabuco, which blocked the north end of the central valley of Chile and was the key to the advance on Santiago.

The Spaniards, about four thousand of them, were stationed at their head-quarters on the Chacabuco estate, awaiting reinforcements from Santiago. The patriots had just endured an excruciating march across the Andes, and their artillery and spare horses had not yet arrived. Yet San Martín had confidence in their training and stamina, and wanted to strike before the Spanish forces were ready. This was the critical moment of the campaign, the ultimate test of his leadership. His actions were clear and decisive, balancing the capability of the Army of the Andes, still recovering from its march, against the depleted Spanish forces, short of their full strength. He explained his decision coolly at a meeting with his senior officers and gave them their battle plans. On the night before the battle he was emerging from his tent when he saw one of his officers, Manuel de Olazábal from his grenadiers escort: 'When he saw me he said, "Well then, how are we doing for tomorrow?" "As always, sir, perfectly". "Good! The devils are still stamping around, so hit them hard over their heads with the swords." '[7]

It was daybreak on the 12 February when San Martín ordered the advance and the patriots approached the summit. The main body under Soler made an oblique movement, a favourite tactic of San Martín, and took a route to the right, towards Cuesta Nueva; they had to cross twisting gorges in order to attack the royalists on their left flank and in the rear. The Spanish commander seeing his retreat endangered fell back towards the Chacabuco estate, where his unit joined the rest of the royalist army. In the centre, towards the Cuesta Vieja, the column led by O'Higgins had instructions to threaten the front of the enemy without committing themselves to a direct attack, pending the arrival of Soler's forces, when they would mount a joint offensive. These, however, were held up by their lengthy detour and difficult terrain, and the impatient O'Higgins, disobeying orders, threw his men in alone against the Spaniards, shouting, 'Soldiers! Live with honour or die with glory! Columns, charge!' Argentine opinion was critical of O'Higgins: 'It has always been said that it was imprudent of General O'Higgins to advance so rapidly without taking account of the time needed by the Soler division. General O'Higgins was a brave general; but his excessive zeal led him to lengths that could have been disastrous for the patriot army, though he has insisted that he never doubted victory for he had full confidence in his troops.'[8] This one impulsive act threatened the whole strategy of San Martín, who had always planned a single massive attack on the Spanish forces. The patriots suffered over an hour's battering from the enemy's superior firepower and had to retreat in disorder, leaving on the field 'a heap of poor negroes', in San Martín's words.

When San Martín saw the danger, he raised his arm towards the Cuesta Nueva (a gesture immortalized in an equestrian statue) ordering Alvarez Condarco to hasten to Soler and urge him to attack the enemy flank, while he ordered Matías Zapiola to lead his three grenadier squadrons and attack from the front. He himself intervened decisively: 'The general in chief with two squadrons of mounted grenadiers charged the right of the enemy and routed them,' thus encouraging O'Higgins's infantry to renew their attack with a fierce bayonet charge, which overcame the Spanish infantry.[9] Simultaneously the advance force of Soler's division, 'which he led from the right with such skill and judgement in spite of coming over a rugged and difficult peak that the royalists did not realise they were there, attacked the enemy and threatened their left flank.'[10] The royalists were astonished to find themselves in a classic pincer movement, caught between O'Higgins's infantry and the main body of Soler's division, which cut off their retreat, and though they resisted spiritedly they were forced to surrender. Two charges of the grenadiers were decisive, reported Manuel Pueyrredón, or as San Martín remarked with typical brevity 'the battle of Chacabuco can be described as the work of the squadrons of the mounted grenadiers.'[11] The Spaniards too fought hard and their heavy casualties proved it: 600 dead and many captives, against the 12 dead and 120 wounded of the Army of the Andes. 'Chile is ours', claimed San Martín. One of the historic exaggerations of the war.

Chacabuco, a Victory Squandered

In the shadow of the great cordillera, Santiago was a mass of green in the centre of a bare plain, its buildings and churches surrounded by olive and fig trees, mimosas and carobs; the houses, single-storey against earthquakes, were enclosed by walls shut to the outside world with rooms facing into an inner patio. The city was exposed to looting and mayhem, once Marcó del Pont ordered its evacuation. San Martín sent an advance squadron of grenadiers to restore order, and on 14 February he himself led the liberators into the capital. He reported to his English friend, Commodore Bowles:

At last the expedition against this country has attained the most happy results: they have lost everything and, what is still worse, they have not even saved their honour: these advantages you must not attribute to my abilities but to the faults which the enemy committed and of which I had the good fortune to avail myself.

Good order (which the flight of the enemy and the abandonment of the capital on the night of the 12th had disturbed) was re-established on the morning of the 13th by the arrival here of the vanguard of this army and by punishing a few of the lower class who had already begun to pillage; however, not a single life was lost, which was what I most feared.

The country is wholly ours excepting Concepción, which only contains five hundred discontented troops who by this time are dispersed.[12]

The remarks of a happy warrior, overcome by victory. The royalists who escaped from the battle and others who had not taken part went south, while the patriots were slow in pursuing them, and they were able to dig in and reinforce. Las Heras led a force of one thousand southwards but took forty days to arrive and found the enemy reassembled. Distracted by the next stage of his continental strategy and by the immediate problems of governing Chile, San Martín took his eye off the royalists and eventually paid the price. For the moment, however, he had his hands full. Victory had made him master of Chile, but he preferred to make Chileans sovereigns of their own land. He was determined that O'Higgins should head the government of Chile upon liberation, partly because O'Higgins was a national and liberal leader, two political touchstones for San Martín, partly because he himself was dedicated to an American role and wished to remain free for the invasion of Peru, his greatest ambition. He convoked an assembly of notables, which then tried to give him full powers, but he refused these and convoked a new assembly which on 16 February appointed O'Higgins Supreme Director, as San Martín had agreed before the campaign. He only reserved for himself military command as general in chief of the united Argentine-Chilean army.

Not everyone liked O'Higgins. Some thought him despotic, others that he was too easy-going. And the Argentine commander Soler, still indignant over the Chilean's impetuosity at Chacabuco, had to be sent away from Santiago because of the bad feeling. But San Martín had long known that O'Higgins had a good political record and justified the trust he placed in him. He was easy to work with and his political thinking mirrored San Martín's own instinct for conservatism tempered with liberal values. His regime from 1817 was one of enlightened despotism, but his social policies made him vulnerable and he did not have enough influence, or ruthlessness, to survive the hostility of the Chilean elite. He was forced to abdicate in 1823, to spend the rest of his life in Peru. 'His errors of judgement', wrote William Miller, 'are forgotten in the recollection of the goodness of his heart.'[13] And for San Martín there had always been a decisive factor in his favour, his commitment to the continental strategy.

A victory ball was held, where wine flowed, dancing proceeded into the night, and the blue and white of Argentina was the colour of choice among the women. San Martín rose and gave a patriotic toast, before smashing his glass, signifying that it could not be used to toast any other cause; everyone followed suit and soon the floor was covered in glass. He joined in singing the Argentine national anthem, while two black trumpeters sounded the music.

The spirit of victory and celebration continued in Santiago for many months. When the English traveller Samuel Haigh arrived there in October 1817, he was invited to a grand reception and ball given by San Martín in the town hall in honour of Commodore Bowles, whose frigate the *Amphion* was then lying in the bay of Valparaíso. Haigh was introduced to San Martín, 'this Hannibal of the Andes':

He is tall and well formed, and his whole appearance is highly military: his countenance is very expressive; his complexion is deep olive; his hair is black, and he wore large whiskers without mustachios; his eyes were large and black, and possess a fire and animation which would be remarkable under any circumstances. He is very gentlemanly in his deportment, and, when I saw him, he was conversing with the greatest ease and affability to the company around; he received me with much cordiality, for he is very partial to the English nation. The assembly was most brilliant, consisting of all the inhabitants of the first rank in Santiago, as well as of all the chief military officers; hundreds were performing the mazy waltz, and general satisfaction was depicted in every face. . . . During the supper which was laid out in a very splendid and sumptuous manner, many patriotic and complimentary toasts were exchanged between the chief officers, both civil and military, and our own naval commander.[14]

Meanwhile, as the victors rejoiced, the vanquished either escaped south-wards or were taken into captivity. When Captain General Marcó del Pont was brought before him, San Martín referred ironically to the latter's previous insult: 'Let me shake that white hand, señor don Francisco Marcó'.[15] His thoughts on Marcó, whom he undertook to treat correctly, he revealed to his friend Commodore Bowles; his conduct was despicable, his language disgusting, and he had even 'pledged himself to hang me in the event of my being taken.'[16]

Between reorganizing the army and keeping his eye on Chilean politics, San Martín's days following Chacabuco left little time for rest, but he suddenly told his Irish aide, John O'Brien, to get ready, they were going to Buenos Aires, and they left on 11 March. He declined a gift of ten thousand pesos from the *cabildo* of Santiago for his travel costs and diverted them to the public library of Santiago. He could not avoid all expressions of gratitude. After a pause at Uspallata with chest pains, he had to stop in Mendoza, where he was the subject of extravagant festivities. He reached Buenos Aires on 30 March and though his prime object was to raise resources for the next stage of his strategy, in spite of himself he was caught up in regional politics, the problem of the Banda Oriental, and the hostilities of the Carrera brothers. These details had little interest for him now, except in so far as they hindered his search for resources, and he distanced himself from the Buenos Aires government. His position in Chile gave him some independence, and he was impatient with what he regarded as an obsession with regional politics and Argentina's conflict with Brazil over Uruguay. Negotiations with Britain were more important.

Commodore Bowles was absent in Rio de Janeiro, but San Martín sought out the British consul Robert Staples and made his views and needs known to the government in London. He would appreciate, he explained, the views of the British government on his future operations in Chile and Peru. He needed warships and officers; and he advocated a British naval presence on the Pacific coast to protect commerce from Spanish aggression. He appreciated that he could not expect any direct assistance from Britain, and he did not require it, but he relied upon British neutrality and influence against intervention by the reactionary powers of Europe. He offered Britain implicitly a special relationship with the liberated countries, and expressed a preference for monarchy over republicanism, though excluding any branch of the Bourbons.[17] He was disappointed he had not been able to see Bowles, 'the main object' of his journey, but he left a letter for him and referred him to Staples for the details he had wished to confide to him personally.

Bowles had already made it clear to the admiralty that he had a high regard for 'this very distinguished officer, whose views are, I firmly believe, entirely divested of all personal ambition and tend solely to the pacification and happiness of his country.' Now, having spoken to Staples, he reported the general's latest views: it was clear that San Martín considered he had a complete ascendancy in Chile and was so independent of the Buenos Aires government as to take his own measures on all important subjects without consulting it. Chile must in future be treated as an independent state over which Buenos Aires can claim no authority. He sought, for himself and for O'Higgins, an indication of the wishes and views of the British government, and expressed his own readiness to listen to them. 'He does not request assistance of any sort, either pecuniary or otherwise.' His arguments were all in favour of a monarchical government, as the only one suited to these countries, but ruled out any deal with the Bourbons.[18] San Martín warmly recommended his friend and former armourer José Antonio Alvarez Condarco, who was on his way to England to purchase equipment, books 'and some other things required by the state of Chile'. The other things amounted in fact to the purchase of a navy.

Bowles's remarks on the independence of San Martín from Buenos Aires were prescient. For the moment, however, the general had no problems with Pueyrredón, who agreed that Chile should form a naval squadron and in April 1817 appointed Tomás Guido '*diputado de este gobierno*' to the Chilean government with instructions to establish good relations based on mutual interests.[19] In fact Guido was more like the personal agent of San Martín than a representative of the Argentine government. They both left for Chile on 20 April, passing Alvarez Condarco in Mendoza on his way to Buenos Aires and England. They reached Santiago on 11 May and from now San Martín occupied the episcopal palace in the Plaza de Armas, which had been sumptuously prepared as his official residence. This he could not refuse, nor the six thousand pesos a year as a general of the Chilean army.

Maipú, Victory Reclaimed

In the wars of independence fame was cheap, and a hero one day was a villain the next. The months following his return from Buenos Aires were not good for San Martín. His Chilean ally, O'Higgins, was in the south, challenging the Spanish presence. In San Martín's absence Chilean hostility to the Argentine liberators and their subsequent promotion increased, and from Argentina the Carreras and their friends pulled strings of resentment and cultivated allies in Chile. A specific conspiracy to overthrow O'Higgins and try San Martín was discovered and stopped in its tracks, but San Martín felt the unpopularity and pressure that he had always feared, and it affected his health. His chief medical officer reported to Guido, 'I can foresee an early end to the esteemed life of our general if he does not divest himself of the responsibilities which daily afflict him, at least for the time needed to repair his health, now affected in the nervous system.' The illness was attacking his weakest points, his chest and stomach, and he was vomiting blood and suffering from chronic insomnia. Guido reported to Pueyrredón on the depraved state of the Chilean administration and the lack of support for San Martín from the elite, still affected by a colonial mentality; their attitude 'adds to the problems of the general and reduces his strength to the point where his important life is at risk'. He needed to be relieved of administrative and political duties, and take a rest in the country.[20]

San Martín himself laid the blame less on his work than on Chilean hostility and intrigues. His forebodings were coming true, and he saw himself struggling with three types of Chileans, 'the dissidents, the half-hearted, and the agitators.'[21] Among many Chileans it was a sore point that they owed their liberation to a foreigner, who whatever his office behaved as though he ruled the country. Moreover, some of them believed he was now using Chile for his own purposes, as a supply base and a springboard for the invasion of Peru, which was not necessarily in Chile's interests. He believed they were badly mistaken, that there was no security for the independence of any of the Pacific countries of South America unless Spanish military and naval power on the Pacific coast was destroyed. To his friend Godoy Cruz he confided, 'The state of my health continues to be pretty bad. I know the remedy, four to six months peace and quiet, but an extraordinary situation makes me the unfortunate victim of circumstances ... you cannot imagine the violence I do to myself by staying in this country: in the midst of its delightful attractions everything about it fills me with loathing; the men in particular are of a character that does not conform with my principles and so, you see, I have this continual repugnance that corrodes my miserable existence: two months tranquillity in the estimable town of Mendoza would give me a new life.'[22]

But there was no instant health cure; he contracted a throat condition and suffered from rheumatism, though some called it gout, and as if this were not enough he had to endure periodic attacks of painful haemorrhoids.[23] His friends rallied round and he eventually found his way to the thermal springs of Cauquenes and took the cure in the River Tunuyán, which seemed to help him. But it was the 'plague of dissidents' that most disturbed him: 'You know that these devils would have ruined the cause, if America did not have the good fortune or more likely the good luck to have men in charge of its affairs whose exemplary conduct rescued it from the clutches of these villains. This is one of the reasons, as you know, why I have had to demand so insistently a form of government decisive, stable, and permanently established that would curb the violent passions and not be subject to the indecisions which are so common in times of revolution.'[24]

From the other side of the Andes he had always dreaded this encounter, not the battle but the subsequent politics. The shock of moving from popularity and respect in Mendoza to resentment and criticism in Chile lowered his resistance to political turmoil. The formation of a new government on 7 September 1817 brought temporary relief. But the Carreras were still out there, part of the problem, conspiring in Argentina for action in Chile. O'Higgins' insistence that their death was the essential solution was hardly reassuring. In due course Juan José and Luis Carrera met their nemesis at the hands of Argentine justice and were executed in Mendoza on 8 April 1818 for the crime of conspiracy. San Martín deliberately distanced himself from the case, and when José Miguel Carrera launched a violent denunciation of him, and of O'Higgins and Pueyrredón, for the 'assassination' of his brothers, he publicly denied any part in the executions and published documents proving it.

San Martín had virtually no family life in these years. At the start of the Chilean campaign he had sent his wife and baby daughter to Buenos Aires;

after the battle of Maipú and his journey to Buenos Aires he would bring them back to Mendoza. There Remedios suffered a miscarriage in October 1818. In anticipation of the Peruvian campaign, she returned to Buenos Aires on 25 March 1819. 'On the day of the departure of this distinguished lady the General invited to his table the army chiefs who were in Mendoza and they kept her company until she entered the carriage that was waiting at the door. He said fond goodbyes to her and his young daughter, with all the affection of a loving husband and father.'[25] This was a fond farewell; he was preoccupied for her health and for her safety on the journey to Buenos Aires, a route frequented by bandits and guerrillas, and he asked Belgrano to provide security for her passage.[26] They had been together in Mendoza in the years 1815–16, a happy time, when their daughter Mercedes was born, and then briefly in 1818–19. The lengthy separations of the distinguished couple did not go unremarked among the gossips of the time. Evidence of infidelity there was none, and the rumours concerning the attractive mulatto girl, Jesús, who had accompanied her mistress to Mendoza, were based on nothing more than scurrility and scandalmongering.[27] According to this, the general had a son by the girl, remarkably like him in appearance and commented on in Lima, where much of the slander continued. As for Remedios she lived her last years in Buenos Aires, distant from San Martín and withdrawn from social gatherings by the absence of her husband and death of her father, a patient young woman, frail in health and forbearing in the cause of independence.

Whatever he thought of Chileans San Martín needed them. Argentina and its most famous general were going separate ways, in fact if not in principle. San Martín continued in his continental quest while Buenos Aires reverted to localism, and he was forced to seek the collaboration of Chile to contribute to the cost of the next phase of the war, ships for the invasion of Peru and subsidy for the armed forces. He believed he had a right to this in payment for Chile's liberation. His political alliances changed, towards closer ties with O'Higgins and more distant relations with Pueyrredón. He had made it clear in his conversation with Staples that Buenos Aires had no authority over Chile.[28] Pueyrredón refused to subsidize a naval force in the Pacific and expected Chile to pay for it; in effect he delegated to Chile responsibility for the war in the Pacific, while Buenos Aires concentrated on the Banda Oriental.

Sea power was essential for the invasion of Peru, and for this San Martín was forced to rely on Chile. 'Domination of the Pacific', he wrote to Belgrano, 'will allow an expedition of 6,000 men to sail and disembark in Lima. My object is to attack the focal point of their resources, and if the capital falls the rest will suffer the same fate. I hope that we shall be ready for next March. Let me know what you think.'[29] A great strategist, San Martín could make mistakes of detail; perfect for the big picture, he was not infallible in the design. His letter to

Belgrano is revealing on two counts. In 1821 San Martín would clash with Admiral Cochrane in refusing to go immediately for Lima, preferring a more cautious route. And in the larger framework, he has been criticized for supposing that the core of Spanish power lay in Lima rather than the sierra, though we can assume that he was not so ignorant of Peru as to make this mistake. Belgrano was still a faithful supporter and encouraged San Martín not to be downcast by the forces of inertia, because the country recognized what he had done and his reputation was high. He agreed with his plan—attack Lima directly, for once the capital was subdued the job was finished—but he advised San Martín that he would need two thousand more troops over the six thousand he advocated. Meanwhile, he should look after his health so as to take the project to its conclusion. 'You no longer belong to yourself; you belong to the great cause which only you can bring to its final close.'[30]

But first he had to conclude the war in Chile. There the royalists still had troops and allies in the south, and were receiving reinforcements from Peru. The royalist General Manuel Osorio, with a naval power that San Martín did not possess, was able to land forces in Talcahuano in the south, less than a year after the supposedly decisive victory of Chacabuco. The forces were not very impressive; according to Commodore Bowles who saw them assembling in Callao, they were mutinous and augmented with 'prisoners, negroes, and recruits of the worst description. . . . A very bad spirit pervades the whole corps: the Europeans are dissatisfied and disaffected . . . and many of the officers in all the regiments are Americans, whose conduct and expressions leave little doubt as to their intentions of joining their countrymen whenever an opportunity offers.'[31] The campaign in Chile evidently was not such an opportunity. Effectively the *Plan Continental* had gone into reverse and needed a new start. Chile had to be re-won. San Martín had to disengage still further from Buenos Aires and make his own judgements and decisions independently. On the eve of crossing the Andes, San Martín had received instructions from the government of the United Provinces: speaking with characteristic imprecision of 'a form of General Government which would make of all America, united in identity of cause, interests and objective, one single Nation', they instructed him to seek the unity of the two countries either as a single nation or through a federal alliance.[32] Such a bizarre idea, coming from a government that could not even establish unity with its own provinces, had little impact in Chile and little influence with San Martín himself, who while making verbal gestures to a 'constitutional alliance' of the South American states, also made it clear to his British friends that Argentina had no political authority in Chile. A further rebuff for Buenos Aires was the Declaration of Chilean Independence on 12 February 1818, the anniversary of Chacabuco, independence not only from Spain but also from Argentina, an affirmation of

Chilean identity over which Argentina was not consulted but presented with a *fait accompli.*

The royalist forces had been allowed to entrench themselves in the south in Talcahuano and for six months successfully resisted the besieging patriots. Upon news of the Spanish expedition under Osorio, Viceroy Pezuela's son-in-law, O'Higgins was forced to raise the siege in January 1818 and make a strategic retreat northwards, taking with him men, supplies and cattle, and leaving a blank space for the Spaniards to occupy. Once Osorio had landed he had a force of 4,600 men which he used effectively to surprise and disperse the joint army of 8,000 and 43 pieces of artillery that in February 1818 San Martín and O'Higgins had assembled at Cancha Rayada, halfway between Concepción and Santiago. Here was a classic example of underestimating the enemy. San Martín decided on a tactical retreat but was slow to pull out, and this allowed the Spaniards to attack quickly. He then made a mistake in adopting a cavalry charge on poor ground with poor coordination and authorized a second charge with no more success than the first. On 19 March 1818 the forces of O'Higgins were routed and O'Higgins himself wounded. Fortunately for the patriots the troops under Las Heras, 3,500 in all, retreated and escaped in good order, and managed to emerge ready for the next round. The losses from Cancha Rayada were not so great and the disorder was not so damaging as pessimists claimed, but morale was affected and needed reviving.

There was panic in Santiago, rumours of total disaster and retribution, and a dramatic exodus of the well-to-do towards Mendoza. San Martín acted quickly. He entered the capital on 25 March and exerted all his personal authority to restore order, belief and morale. The enemy too had suffered losses and was unable to conquer Santiago. Belgrano's advice to his friend injected a note of realism: don't worry, these things happen, and it makes no difference to you whether they speak well or ill of you: 'Cheer up and take heart and tell yourself that in spite of everything there is not a soldier anywhere who does not hold you in high regard and does not realize that the result of your actions was beyond your control.'[33]

And so it was. San Martín picked himself up and came back fighting, determined to guide his army to a better day. He was more decisive than his colleagues. In a pre-campaign discussion with army chiefs there were some who preferred not to make a stand in front of the capital but to relocate. San Martín, who favoured fighting on the plain of Maipú, closed the argument by asking his captain friar, Luis Beltrán, 'How are we for ammunition?' 'Up to the roof!' he replied, raising his hands high. San Martín knew this was untrue but declared 'That's it then, we defend the capital.' He was ready to take on the royalist army, as it advanced slowly from the south, crossed the Maipo river, and with drums beating and flags waving moved towards the Valparaíso road.

San Martín was watching with his aide O'Brien: 'How stupid these Spaniards are! Osorio is even slower witted than I thought. Victory is ours today. The sun is our witness!'[34] The sun rising over the Andes on Sunday 5 April heralded a calm day in a cloudless sky and soon the guns could be heard in the capital.

'This battle is going to decide the fate of all America' were San Martín's final words to his troops, as he briskly brought the enemy to action. Using his favoured tactics of oblique attack, he sent his right to overcome the Spanish left, with his reserves attacking in the rear. A series of brilliant charges from the mounted grenadiers crushed the Spanish left, but their right put up a stouter resistance. The Burgos Regiment inflicted heavy casualties on the patriot left, which was composed chiefly of black infantry, and it required a vigorous response from San Martín to recover the initiative. A combination of artillery fire and San Martín's decision to order his reserve to charge won the day, as he later recalled. 'Success was due to the reserve, composed of battalions 7 and 3 commanded by Colonel Quintana; they were ordered by the general in chief to charge the right of the enemy who were advancing strongly on our left, and whom they confronted and threw into confusion. The attack was carried out vigorously and proved decisive in gaining this victory and enabling the war to be carried to Peru.'[35] The Spaniards were surrounded and taken right, left and in the rear, and in a final brave stand their infantry troops were massacred. 'Nothing could exceed the savage fury of the Black soldiers in the patriot army,' wrote Samuel Haigh, who was present at the battle. 'They had born the brunt of the action against the finest Spanish regiment, and had lost the principal part of their forces; they were delighted with the idea of shooting their prisoners. I saw an old Negro actually crying with rage when he perceived the officers protected from his fury.'[36] The royalists lost two thousand dead and as many prisoners, as against one thousand patriots between dead and wounded. 'The entire royal army is either dead or prisoner in our hands,' reported San Martín, who was impressed above all by the bravery and determination of his forces, 'the brilliant and outstanding actions of this day both by entire units and by individual commanders and soldiers.'[37] The war in Chile was won and its independence secured. With his usual brevity, the victor summed it up to Paroissien, 'The country is free.' Paroissien himself had had a good battle, toiling in his makeshift hospital; his services were recognized by San Martín in dispatches and he was promoted to colonel, awarded the Gold Medal of Maipú and granted a landed estate near Mendoza.[38] O'Higgins, his right arm in a sling, rode up to San Martín and hailed him, 'Glory to the saviour of Chile!' a scene made for a war artist. San Martín gave command of the united army to Balcarce, while he prepared to leave for Buenos Aires to raise support and resources for the next surge forward. He was away for six months.

He arrived incognito in Buenos Aires on 12 May, cheating the triumphal arches. A few days later the elusive hero was caught. According to the diarist Juan Manuel Beruti, Congress honoured him with a ceremonial reception and he was led to the palace through decorated streets and cheering crowds accompanied by military bands, attention that he endured until four richly dressed young women crowned him with a floral tribute; this he promptly removed, unwilling to be seen walking through the streets of Buenos Aires with flowers on his head.[39] In the following days the celebrations for San Martín, for the victory in Chile, and for the anniversary of the May Revolution, all merged to make May 1818 a memorable month in Buenos Aires.

Historic Disobedience

While Buenos Aires rejoiced, San Martín faced a discouraging future. The years 1818–20 were difficult years for the Liberator, when his momentum seemed to stop and his strategy to falter. For a time in late 1818 his life was at risk from a conspiracy to assassinate him and O'Higgins orchestrated by José Miguel Carrera, to be carried out by a group of French killers. But his real enemies were the royalists and towards Spain his policy was as implacable as ever. Indeed the bloody Spanish counter-revolution and the violent response from Lima towards the southern movement of independence filled him with loathing, and he saw no possibility of reconciliation between Americans and Spaniards. This was a deep-seated conviction and he prepared for further war. His preferred model was a war of ideas backed by arms. But the means were open to development, and it was now more than ever that he looked to Great Britain. But first he had to test the ground in Peru. The workings of his mind can be read in a letter to his friend James Duff, where he speaks of the disastrous yet positive effects of war and its salutary lessons: 'The events of a wasteful revolution and a ruinous war have cooled the passions incident to all political changes, and men's minds, by this time more settled, aspire solely to an emancipation from Spain, and the establishment of some solid form of Government ... democratical notions have lost ninety per cent among the leading men.'[40]

In this mood he made a reasoned and moderate approach to Viceroy Pezuela in Peru to stop the bloodshed.

> Your Excellency must be aware that war is a grievous scourge, a cause of destruction wherever it has occurred in America, and that the outcome of battle has turned in favour of the claims of the southern part of the New World. Your Excellency has also been able to discover in the last seven years that the United Provinces and Chile desire no more than a liberal constitution

and a moderate liberty, and that the inhabitants of the viceroyalty of Lima who have had to shed their blood against their brothers would wish to take hold of their political destiny and raise themselves from colonial subjection to the dignity of the two neighbouring nations. None of these aspirations is opposed to friendship, security, and good relations with the Spanish metropolis; none of these claims is a crime; on the contrary in the present century they are a true reflection of the enlightened values of civilized Europe. To try to hold back with the bayonet the surge of opinion in America is to try to enslave nature. Take an impartial look at the result of Spanish efforts for so many years and, ignoring a few fleeting victories of the royal arms, you will discover their impotence against the spirit of LIBERTY.'[41]

He also proposed a general congress in which the peoples of Peru could decide their own destiny instead of trial by battle. Pezuela rejected the whole approach as the insolence of an insubordinate soldier, encouraged by a temporary victory.

It was now too that San Martín made another effort to interest Britain in his cause. In October 1817 Commodore Bowles had arrived in Valparaíso on board the frigate *Amphion* and proceeded to Callao in early November, returning to Valparaíso on 10 January 1818, where on the following day San Martín went to meet him, carrying a letter from the Supreme Director of Chile to the Prince Regent. He backed the request from O'Higgins to the Prince Regent for British mediation in favour of the American revolution against Spain.[42] In a conversation with Bowles, from which the commodore took notes, reading them back to him afterwards, San Martín outlined an idea for dividing liberated America among a number of European princes; this, he thought, would satisfy all the major powers, and he sought the good offices of the British government and its participation in the scheme. He emphasized the great danger from internal dissensions and civil contentions: weak governments concede too much to popular opinion, 'the lower orders have thus obtained an undue preponderance and are beginning to manifest a revolutionary disposition dangerous in any country but more particularly in this, where want of education and general information is so strongly felt.'[43]

The overtures to the viceroy of Peru and to Britain, made from a base in Chile and independently of Argentina, invite speculation concerning the Liberator's thinking in the years 1817–18. In the first place, was San Martín completely confident that he could overcome Spanish power in Peru by military action alone? And even if he could, was he convinced that the liberated countries of South America could emerge from a prolonged war as working states with their institutions and economies intact? Second, was Argentina itself a problem? Was British support a possible substitute for wavering commitment in Buenos Aires? There was always a British assumption in favour of San Martín, though short of actual commitment. Henry Chamberlain, British consul-general at Rio de Janeiro, recommended his moral character and military abilities, and noted that 'Commodore Bowles, whose judgement on such points may be implicitly depended upon, speaks of him in the highest terms of commendation as an honest, honourable and correct man.' 'The victory of Maipú has strengthened rather than diminished his wishes on this point [the mediation of Britain]. . . . He is avowedly a friend to a monarchical form of Government and says that none other can suit the people of Buenos Ayres and of Chile, or their habits.'[44]

On 11 April 1818, only a few days after the victory of Maipú, San Martín wrote to Castlereagh renewing a previous request for British mediation. He argued that the victory of Maipú was absolute and in effect 'decided the fate of South America'. The military power of the patriots ruled out any need to sue for peace, but the interests of the new states had been damaged and their prosperity impaired by the prolonged war. Therefore he sought British mediation to reach an accommodation with Spain and so put an end 'to the sufferings of the South Americans by contributing to the consolidation of their political liberty.' The mediation he sought at this stage of the war was not between equals but between victor and vanquished in the interests of peace. And in the final analysis he insisted that 'South America is resolved to be buried under her ruins, rather than submit to her former yoke.'[45] The British government was non-committal. The times were not propitious for intervention, and British ministers had never envisaged mediation of this kind. Between a world power and a remote country beyond the Andes there was no dialogue, and San Martín received no response to his overtures.

Armed struggle was the only way, and that meant first a search for resources. The grand strategy remained in place, though San Martín's political tactics in 1818–19 are difficult to fathom and the details of his thinking are elusive. The historian must telescope the action or lose the track of the Liberator's overall project in a maze of false signs and dead ends. He had to make three arduous journeys across the Andes back to Argentina in search of money and support, to endure constant frustrations, changes of plans and postponement of policies from a crumbling government. In a sequence of curious confrontations known in Argentina as the *repaso de los Andes*, subsidies were offered and withdrawn, the Army of the Andes was ordered back to Buenos Aires and then halted, messages were exchanged and ignored, reports were neither wholly false nor wholly true. The central government wanted San Martín's continental forces for local conflicts in the littoral. He refused even to consider it and resigned four times in less than a year.[46] The excruciating inaction was almost unbearable. Since 1814 he had been kept waiting three years for the invasion of Chile. Now he was held back another three years for the invasion of Peru. His requests for men and money for the Army of the Andes were ignored, and he received 'not a single *real*'. 'Nothing has been done and there is not the remotest hope that it will be done. . . . In short, the conduct of this government is perfectly clear: its intention is not only to disavow the projected expedition but also to get rid of the Army of the Andes.'[47] The Chilean government was also difficult, short of money and sometimes of support, though O'Higgins remained a loyal ally. These events confirmed San Martín's worst suspicions of *porteño* politicians and reinforced his determination to stay aloof from Argentine politics, a signal that his biographers can usefully follow.

The experience demanded extraordinary reserves of patience and perseverance. Inner strength rather than rational calculation enabled San Martín to keep alive his plan of campaign amidst setbacks and doubts that would have defeated a lesser man. Did he break under the strain? Appearances are deceptive. It is true that his health suffered in these years. Samuel Haigh visited him in Mendoza. 'I found the hero of Maypo stretched upon a sick bed, and looking so wan and emaciated that, but for the lustre of his eyes, I should hardly have recognized him: he received me with a faint smile, and stretched out his hand to welcome me. Upon delivering my letters he was raised on his bed to read them; the contents appeared to give him great pleasure . . . I was requested to call again before I left Mendoza.'[48] But San Martín's mind was clear and his will firm. He 'resigned' not from his continental project but from his Argentine appointments to 'give my services instead to the Chilean state.'[49] And he remained in command.

Yet he still had to resolve the dilemma of two loyalties. A break was inevitable, given the local priorities of Buenos Aires and the continental commitment of San Martín. Distancing himself from his colleagues' preoccupations with Spain, Uruguay and provincial *montoneros*, he set his sights on a different route, and he sacrificed his loyalty to Argentina in favour of his greater loyalty to America. In an act of 'historic disobedience', as it has been called, he ignored orders to return with the Army of the Andes to Buenos Aires and committed himself completely to the liberation of America.[50] 'A terrible responsibility is about to fall on me, but if we don't undertake the expedition to Peru the whole thing goes to hell.'[51] But on whose authority did San Martín take the Army of the Andes out of Argentina into Peru?

Authority was in short supply in Buenos Aires. Since 1816 and the declaration of the independence of the United Provinces of South America, a number of small republics had emerged, their independent governments sustained by local economic interests. Provincial caudillos and their guerrilla followers proclaimed their independence of Buenos Aires and of each other. As unity collapsed, the instinct of the unitarians was to fight back. José Rondeau, successor of Pueyrredón as Supreme Director, 'a weak and timid man, governed entirely by his secretaries', sought assistance from the forces of San Martín and Belgrano.[52] This he was denied, and the military impotence of the unitarians was now starkly exposed. Rondeau marched with inadequate forces against the *montoneros* of Estanislao López, caudillo of Santa Fe, and Francisco Ramírez of Entre Ríos, and was comprehensively defeated at the battle of Cepeda (1 February 1820). Backed by his gaucho cavalry, Ramírez scattered the directorate, the congress and every vestige of central authority. All that remained was the government of Buenos Aires province, and in the course of this fateful year government changed hands on an average once a fortnight.

The fall of the central government of the Río de la Plata was not followed by the appointment of a replacement, and no volunteers hastened to assume national authority. This enabled San Martín to move independently and to argue that in the absence of legitimate government in Buenos Aires the Army itself conferred authority upon him. He sent to General Las Heras, his second in command, a sealed document which was taken to Rancagua, eighty-two kilometres south of Santiago, where the expeditionary army was garrisoned, and read to the assembly of officers on 2 April 1820. The message is clear: as the government from which San Martín holds his commission as commander-in-chief is dissolved, he tends his resignation to the officers of the army and authorizes them to elect by ballot a successor. By the so-called Act of Rancagua the commander in effect consults his officers and the officers choose their commander:

> The congress and the supreme director of the United Provinces no longer exist: from these authorities derived my own as general in chief of the Army of the Andes. Consequently I believe that it is my duty and obligation to explain these facts to the officer corps of the Army of the Andes, so that they themselves by the exercise of their own will may nominate a general in chief as their commander.[53]

The officer corps, 'all the chiefs and officers of the Army of the Andes', unanimously re-elected San Martín and confirmed him in all the authority he already enjoyed to make war on the Spaniards and advance the interests of the country. An instant solution but a future liability. Bartolomé Mitre described this as 'a revolutionary act'. 'It was an act of double insubordination, which compromised both discipline and authority, and meant that from then onwards the general only gave orders to his subordinates on the basis of consent and comradeship, for he was obliged to consult the will of each and all.'[54] Only leadership could make this work, another task, another test, for San

Martín. But it was not an immediate test, for everyone knew that he was the supreme leader and no one his equal. His enemies in the Río de la Plata denounced him as a traitor to the cause, but their cause was the road to disaster. On the eve of his departure for Peru he rejected the calumnies poured upon him and warned his compatriots beyond the Andes of the disastrous course they were following. 'An evil genius has inspired in you the madness of federalism. This word is death, signifying nothing but ruin and devastation.' He refused to commit his army to the anarchy and disorder to which Argentina had been reduced, and to worsen the conflict by spilling more blood in its resolution. Independence was his ruling cause, as he would prove in Peru.[55]

Lord Cochrane, Master and Commander in the Pacific

In 1820 San Martín was ready to embark upon the last stage of his grand strategy. It was a costly strategy, and from Chile in particular it demanded great sacrifices. To clear the South Pacific of Spanish sea power, an indispensable preliminary, Chile had to create an instant navy, to buy ships and equipment, to recruit personnel, to find an admiral. The ships and crews were obtained in Britain and the United States. Negotiations in the United States were hindered by lack of funds and concern over neutrality laws, but two frigates were planned and eventually joined the Chilean navy.[56] In London San Martín's friend and agent, Alvarez Condarco, was busy with $100,000 to spend and authority to negotiate additional credit. First he sent the *Windham*, an ex-East Indiaman of 820 tons, built in 1801, and mounting 34 guns. The purchase price of $180,000 was to be paid in Chile, where the vessel arrived in March 1818. O'Higgins struggled to raise the money from the treasury and from private individuals. The ship carried an English captain and officers, and a mixed crew of Englishmen and Chileans, and was quickly in action as the *Lautaro* and the winner of prize money that almost paid for its cost. This was followed in May by a second East Indiaman, the *Cumberland*, 1,200 tons and built in 1802; mounting sixty-four guns it was the most powerful warship in the Pacific, and was soon in action as the *San Martín*.[57] Two other vessels, the *Chacabuco*, twenty guns, and the *Araucano*, eighteen guns, were of American provenance, and all were officered and manned by Britons, Americans and Chileans. In October 1818 these four captured the 1,200-ton Spanish frigate, *María Isabel*, promptly renamed the *O'Higgins*, together with a number of troopships on route from Spain to Peru. Where four ships had left Valparaíso in October, thirteen returned in November.[58] Other additions to the Chilean navy were the *Intrépido*, contributed from Buenos Aires, and the *Galvarino*, a former British sloop of war, brought out from England by two British naval

1 Goya's unforgettable picture of the popular response to the French invasion became a metaphor for Spain's war of independence.

Nada prefirió mas que la
Libertad de su Patria.

2 This portrait of San Martín as liberator of Chile by José Gil de Castro, the Peruvian mulatto artist, brings out the reserve and austerity in his character. The curved sword and silver inkstand were the conventional symbols of leadership.

3 San Martín's portrait of choice. The Belgian artist Navez painted him during his exile at the age of 50, capturing the cool and steady demeanour of the liberator and suggesting a trace of a warmer nature.

4 Buenos Aires, primitive outpost of empire and setting for stirrings of independence, was a city of few amenities and many politicians. These gave San Martín a 'mixed reception', as he recalled.

5 As the sun rose over the Andes on Sunday 5 April 1818, San Martín gazed on the landscape before him and planned the deployment of his army. He was about to win one of his great victories over a determined enemy who fought as bravely as his own troops.

6 Valparaiso was the home base of the Chilean navy, the port from which in 1820 San Martín led his forces to Peru full of hope and to which he returned alone and disillusioned two years later.

7 Lima, the City of the Kings, which San Martín hoped to make the capital of a new monarchy, was the key to his continental project and the backdrop to his political and social reforms.

8 'And now, my lads', joked Cochrane to his boarding party, 'we shall give them such a Gunpowder Plot as they will not forget in a hurry.' The action was admired even by his critics in the Royal Navy as 'a most brilliant affair'.

9 Controversial in Britain and a hero in Chile, Cochrane was the bête noire of San Martín, who described him as a money-making lord, and disagreed with virtually every aspect of his strategy.

10 Among all the liberators O'Higgins was San Martín's closest political ally and friend. His genial and honest nature immediately appealed and his political thinking mirrored San Martín's own instinct for conservatism tempered with liberal values.

11 San Martín described Remedios as his friend as well as his wife. She was faithful to her modest role and endured his lengthy absences with a forbearance which makes her a conspicuous heroine of independence.

12 San Martín at the age of 70, thoughtful and serious to the end. His triumphs in South America were now a distant memory, and the discord and disappointment of leadership long past. He ended his days quietly with his family in Boulogne-sur-Mer.

officers; other ships were acquired in 1819, notably the *Independencia*, an American-built corvette, commissioned from the United States, and the *Montezuma*, a merchant prize.[59] There was rivalry among the English officers to command the Chilean Navy, and many Chileans wanted one of their own, Manuel Blanco Encalada, a young officer who had experience in the Spanish navy, to lead them. The argument was soon resolved.

In London Alvarez Condarco was spending lavishly on ships and supplies on behalf of the Chilean government. He also recruited a commander, Thomas Cochrane, future Earl of Dundonald, the most celebrated naval officer in Britain after Nelson. The meeting is not documented but there was urgency on both sides. Chile needed an admiral with leadership qualities, Cochrane needed an income and a new life following his break with the British government at the age of forty-one. Both sides regarded the deal as opportune. Cochrane arrived in Valparaíso in November 1818 after a voyage around Cape Horn to assume command of the new navy, seven warships in all, with the rank of vice admiral and pay the equivalent of £1,200 a year.[60] He brought his wife and two young children with him, and Lady Cochrane was soon a leading attraction at the parties and balls that greeted their arrival, young, fascinating, 'a flattering specimen of the beauty of England', as William Miller describes her, while Samuel Haigh ungallantly remarks that Chileans were so accustomed to seeing plain English wives that they were astonished to meet a pretty one. Cochrane himself regarded the incessant round of parties as 'a waste of time', and 'I had to remind His Excellency [O'Higgins] that our purpose was rather fighting than feasting.'[61]

Cochrane had pursued Kate Barnes from his uncle's house in Portman Square, London, in 1812 when she was a teenage schoolgirl, an orphan twenty years his junior; they eloped to Scotland, came back married, and she soon charmed London society with her fetching ringlets and winning ways. Now from her delightful country house at Quillota just north of Santiago, where she coolly survived an attempted mugging, she won over Chileans. She studied Spanish and within a few weeks was writing to a bemused San Martín, who courteously congratulated her on her Spanish: 'I am vain enough to call myself your friend, and offer my services with sentiments of affection, friendship, and respect.'[62] And he lent Cochrane five thousand pesos to finance a journey she had to make back to England in 1821. Did the thought cross San Martín's mind that while he kept his wife secluded in Buenos Aires, Cochrane brought his round Cape Horn to Chile?

Cochrane could be described as a superior mercenary, but he was also a professional sailor whose hallmarks of valour, panache and originality had earned him a reputation during the Napoleonic wars of a master and commander who could win actions by deception and effrontery as well as by naval skill. He had never commanded a fleet or fought in a major sea battle but he had won public acclaim and enemy respect for many decisive actions, of which the capture of the Spanish frigate *El Gamo* in 1801 by his smaller sloop *Speedy* made his name in naval history.[63] He had had a noisy political career, partial to radicalism but also accident-prone. He had been dismissed by the Admiralty, expelled from parliament, accused of a stock exchange scam and marked down by the government as a persistent troublemaker. Historians differ on his involvement in the stock exchange fraud, though most agree that he was 'money-getting', as another British admiral described him.[64]

It was cruel luck for San Martín that of all the naval talent in Britain he had been sent not someone like his Royal Navy friend, Commodore Bowles, supremely correct and competent, but a sailor who was an expensive nuisance in port, an incomparable leader at sea, and whose liberal sentiments were accompanied by a notorious interest in money and status. Yet he was probably the only available commander whose personality and prowess could instantly organize a disparate collection of ships and crews into a fighting navy. His reputation had preceded him, and while he enjoyed the confidence of O'Higgins he was suspect to some in the Chilean administration and resented for taking precedence over their own heroes. British naval opinion, of course, was well aware of Cochrane, and Commodore Bowles had his eye on him from the start, warning the Admiralty that his threats to the Spanish squadron in Callao might compromise British interests: 'I have no doubt that his insolence will be intolerable. His squadron now consists of the two Indiamen mounting 60 and 50 guns, the prize frigate Maria Ysabel and four corvettes and brigs. I am told they are well armed and equipped, and that great numbers of English merchant seamen have deserted and joined him.'[65] Bowles subsequently modified his views and came to expect better of Cochrane.

Although Cochrane did not work well with San Martín this was not obvious from the beginning. The general stood by Cochrane when necessary and the admiral looked to San Martín for support. There were some misunderstandings and early strains over the terms Cochrane was willing to accept, but San Martín begged him not to resign: 'Never mind, my lord, I am general of the army, and you shall be admiral of the squadron.'[66] And he could not ignore the fact that Cochrane, from his flagship the *O'Higgins*, a captured Spanish warship, leading a squadron that he considered a credit to independence, delivered victories as well as prestige to the revolutionary cause. In two expeditions in 1819 Cochrane made his presence felt as far north as Guayaquil and menaced Callao harbour near Lima. In February 1820, without consulting the Chilean government, he captured Valdivia in southern Chile, Spain's strongest naval base in the Pacific. His tactics were a perfect demonstration of combined operations. He personally reconnoitred the harbour, a large sheltered bay with a narrow entrance, to find that the garrison was dispersed and the guns positioned to face attack by sea. Chilean forces under the command of William Miller landed at night and took the Spanish garrisons one by one. A land attack guarded by naval power was a tactic of which Cochrane was a past master, but on this occasion he excelled himself, bluffing the Spaniards into fleeing on the appearance of the *O'Higgins*, when in fact it was badly holed and had to be beached. On 6 February he received the surrender of the outmanoeuvred and outfought Spanish forces, and Miller was subsequently promoted by San Martín to lieutenant colonel.[67] The operation reassured the Chileans and Cochrane went on to establish such a powerful command of the sea that the Chilean squadron was able to intercept reinforcements from Spain, to destroy Spanish trade in the South Pacific and to impose a blockade on the Peruvian coast. San Martín was impressed. On the departure of the expedition from Valparaíso, he assured Cochrane, 'We have a common cause, and your fate shall be the same as mine.'[68]

The liberation of Peru could give Chile long-term gains—political security and a new market. In the meantime it was a crippling burden on a primitive economy. To provide an army was expensive enough. But to create and sustain sea power was one of the costliest operations any state could undertake. In February 1819 Chile and Argentina, putting differences aside and uniting in the war against the common enemy, Spain, signed a treaty of alliance in which each undertook to contribute half the forces and finances needed to invade Peru. But Argentina, which had borne the main burden of the trans-Andean expedition, could not repeat this effort in the Pacific; financial disputes strained relations between the two countries to breaking point, and eventually Buenos Aires managed to send not the 500,000 pesos promised but about 300,000 and the rest in war materials.[69] Chile had to dig deep into its meagre resources. Ordinary revenue—taxes on agriculture, mining production and trade—was not sufficient, nor was it sufficiently augmented by extraordinary devices such as confiscation of royalist property and forced loans; and O'Higgins got virtually no help from a parsimonious senate, representing the landed aristocracy, whose vision was as narrow as the map of Chile. The root difficulty was the stagnant economy, after eight years of war and revolution with consequent loss of labour and capital. On the other hand freedom of trade from 1811 had attracted a number of foreign merchants to the ports, and many of these were now making good profits from trade with royalist Peru. Yet the Chilean government's attempt to raise a forced loan of 300,000 pesos met with much resistance; British merchants in particular refused to pay. Lacking resources of its own, the government was forced to rely on private enterprise. The cost of the naval operation alone would be 700,000 pesos; this could only be raised by costly contracts with foreign merchants for loans against the customs revenue and in return for a share of the prize money which the warships could earn. And the contract to transport the liberating army to Peru was consigned exclusively to a private company.[70]

By August 1820 the contractors had assembled sixteen transports, most of them prizes taken by privateers. Cochrane's navy was ready to escort and to fight. San Martín's army was assembling to embark. And San Martín himself, impatient for action, his prize at last within his grasp, toured the bay of Valparaíso in a launch taking the cheers of his men, before boarding the *San Martín*. His message was inspiring. 'The moment is approaching when I am going to undertake the great work of giving liberty to Peru. I am going to open the most memorable campaign of our revolution, while the world waits to declare us rebels if we are defeated, or to recognize our rights if we triumph.'[71]

CHAPTER 6

Peru, the Carthage of San Martín

Peru was inhabited by diverse races split by latent antagonism; even the whites were divided, according to whether they were Europeans or Americans. Peru was also the heart of the royalist reaction, and for fifteen years she held the revolution in check. Peru was the Carthage of San Martín and had to be destroyed. So it was that in 1820 the liberating armies from the north and from the south converged upon her.[1]

Terra Incognita

As San Martín looked towards the Pacific, did he really know what awaited him? How extensive was his knowledge of Peru? How deeply did he understand his next challenge? Argentina he knew and had served. Chile he had liberated and confronted. But Peru? He had intelligence contacts and received confidential reports on the political and military resources of the enemy.[2] But a true appreciation of this complex society was more elusive and he had few close acquaintances there. Peru would not be easy to conquer, if conquest he had in mind. Given its history, it would be equally difficult to persuade. This was a colonial society, perhaps the most colonial of all Spain's possessions in South America, its institutions, mentalities and resources all linked firmly to Spanish interests and conditioned by Spanish power. The experience of Argentine expeditions to Upper Peru had taught him some of these things, but did he yet appreciate convictions in regions beyond the Desaguadero? What evidence did he have that Peruvians wanted liberation? His appeal to Viceroy Pezuela after the battle of Maipú had contained an unproven claim that Peruvians were ready to assume their political destiny and rise from colonial subjection to the dignity of a state. This assumption had still to be tested.

On the eve of the revolution Peru had a population of just over 1.1 million.[3] The Indians (58 per cent of the total) and mestizos (22 per cent) were concentrated in the Andean region, where they practised subsistence agriculture and provided labour for mines, *obrajes* and haciendas. Black slaves formed some 4 per cent of the population, and free coloureds about the same. But in Lima and the coastal valleys, where commercial agriculture and a plantation economy demanded a more mobile labour force, blacks and *pardos* predominated among the non-Spanish population. The whites totalled less than 13 per cent of the whole and were to be found chiefly on the coast, with a sizeable concentration also in Cuzco. But race was not the only determinant of status. Peru was split too by deep social and economic divisions. The ruling elite, of course, Spaniards and creoles alike, were inevitably white. But not all the Indians were culturally Indian. As the author of *El Lazarillo de ciegos caminantes* pointed out, it was sufficient for an Indian to wash, cut his hair, wear a clean shirt and get a useful job to pass for a *cholo*: 'If he serves his Spanish master well, the latter dresses him and puts him in shoes, and in two months he is known as a mestizo.'[4] The mestizos themselves were not a single social group; depending on their education, work, way of life, they could approximate to whites or to Indians. The mulattos and other castes suffered even worse discrimination than the mestizos: they were forbidden to dress as whites, to live in white districts, to marry whites, and they had their own churches and burial grounds.[5] But even the coloured people were not immutably classified by race; economic advancement could secure them white status either by 'passing' or by purchase of a certificate of whiteness. So there were cultural as well as racial determinants, though this did not lessen the divisions in Peruvian society or dilute its seigneurial values. It was precisely in the social fragmentation and the clash of interests—between an educated elite and Andean peasants, between blacks and Indians, between slaves and free workers—that Spanish rulers found mechanisms of social control and a guarantee of stability.

Absolute independence had never been the prime concern of Peruvians. The Peruvian aristocracy—an aristocracy of land, office and trade—clung fanatically to their power and privilege. In recent decades new waves of immigration reshaped the local ruling class into one dominated by newly arrived *peninsulares* who quickly came to control commerce, forge links with the bureaucracy, acquire titles of nobility and constitute for Spain a basis of loyal support. Their conservatism was induced not only by pride in present status but also by fear of future disorder, in a society where whites were outnumbered by Indians, castes and blacks.[6] The propertied classes of Lima were terrified by 'the licentiousness of the populace and the coloured people of this city and its environs, who exceed the whites by a third or a fifth and who are arrogant, insubordinate and lawless.'[7] The elite preferred security to change and were not prepared to risk their social predominance for the sake of independence. They were inspired less by loyalism than by fear of social upheaval and the collapse of law and order. Even Peruvian liberals sought reform, not revolution. Intellectuals like José Baquijano, Toribio Rodríguez de Mendoza, Hipólito Unanue, and the writers of the *Mercurio Peruano*, who imbibed the thought of the eighteenth-century Enlightenment, condemned the obscurantism and intolerance of the old regime, and advocated liberty and equality, did so within the existing order.[8] The growing sense of *peruanidad*, of Peruvian identity, was also limited by an innate caution. In fact Peruvian liberals held conflicting ideas of *patria*. A few believed that it could be fulfilled only in independent nationality. But the majority saw it as compatible with the ideal of imperial unity: 'Uniformity of religion and language, similarity of customs and the ties of blood, these are and always will be the guarantees of the indissoluble union of both Spains.'[9] And in spite of disillusion with the idea of reform within the empire, this union was regarded as the safest guarantee against anarchy. In the eyes of the Lima elite the Spanish cause was also regarded as the best defence against the growing challenge from the interior and southern provinces, where sporadic armed rebellion from 1811 pointed to creole dissatisfaction with rule from Lima and Indian resentment of historic grievances.

The Peruvian liberals, therefore, did not produce an independence movement. Prisoners of their society, they demanded no more than political reform and equality for creoles within the colonial framework. Their spokesmen were the *cabildos*, drawn suddenly into the limelight in 1808 by the collapse of imperial government. In 1809, responding to the decision of the central junta that they should assist in the election of a deputy to be sent to Spain, the *cabildos* of Peru chose an elderly conservative, José de Silva y Olave, rector of the University of San Marcos. His instructions were issued by the *cabildo* of Lima and they summarized the demands of the creoles at that moment, demands that revealed as much conservatism as liberalism.[10] They criticized the intendants for abuse of power and oppression of the *cabildos*; and they sought the restoration not only of the *corregidores* but also of the infamous *repartimientos* (forced sale of goods to the Indians), arguing that the suppliers of the *corregidores* had been deprived of a market. They demanded the abolition of monopolies, a lowering of taxes and freedom of trade. Finally they expressed resentment of the meagre career prospects of creoles—'farmers, clerics or lawyers'—and they insisted that Americans should be given at least half a share of the government of America.

This manifesto revealed the acute concern of the creoles over their living standards and a criticism of the Bourbon policy of *comercio libre*, a criticism that was not entirely justified. No doubt the economy had suffered from the need to adjust to the loss of the silver provinces of Upper Peru to Buenos Aires in 1776, and the new competition from the economies of the Río de la Plata stimulated by their access to the transatlantic trade. But foreign trade was sustained by silver exports, and Lower Peru increased its silver output in the late eighteenth century.[11] The merchants of Cádiz continued to be attracted to the silver-rich Peruvian market. And Peru's mining-based economy continued to stimulate overseas and internal trade, and even to sustain viable manufacturing and agricultural sectors in the last fifty years of Bourbon rule.[12]

Nevertheless the very success of Peru in exporting silver and defending its trade helped to damage its economic prospects. For Peru's role as a royalist stronghold had to be paid for, and Viceroy José Fernando de Abascal (1806–16), Spain's proconsul and gendarme in South America, raised his tax demands to the point where they really hurt. At the same time Abascal was horrified by demands for freedom of trade: 'It would be tantamount to decreeing the separation of these Dominions from the Mother Country, since, once direct trade with foreigners was established on the wide basis which they demand, the fate of European Spain would matter little to them.'[13] Meanwhile Peru's leadership in defending Spanish authority throughout South America and resisting subversion in Upper Peru, Chile and Quito involved ever greater increases in military expenditure and heavier demands on Peruvian taxpayers, culminating in Viceroy Pezuela's imposition of forced loans on the eve of San Martín's invasion. Yet economic arguments were no more decisive than political ones. Peruvians were still not convinced that the hour of revolution had come. They still sought reform, not independence, from Spain, and from 1808 they were encouraged in their expectations by the emergence of a liberal regime in the peninsula.

The creoles were the key to the situation in Peru as elsewhere in Spanish America; with their numerical superiority over the Spaniards, they could promote or prevent political change. In Peru, it is true, the Spanish presence both in the bureaucracy and in the private sector was more powerful than in the Río de la Plata or Chile. 'Lima has been the refuge for most of the Old Spaniards driven from Buenos Aires and Chile, and, independent of this, Peru, from being considered the principal viceroyalty, has many more natives of Spain in proportion to the other provinces.'[14] But without creole support, and the allegiance of the creole militia, Viceroy Abascal could not have held Peru, much less launched the counter-revolution against neighbouring provinces. Abascal himself was at once an asset and a liability to Spain. His leadership and vigour made him a staunch defender of empire, but his contempt for Americans did great moral damage to the Spanish cause. His decree re-annexing Upper Peru to Lima (13 July 1810) spoke of Americans as 'men born to vegetate in obscurity and abasement.'[15]

The greatest threat to Abascal's policy came not from Peru but from Spain, where successive regimes in the years 1808–13 hopefully exported liberalism—of a kind—to America. In 1810 the council of regency summoned a cortes for 24 September, and the Peruvian *cabildos* were called upon to elect deputies. But the Spanish liberals did not support equality of representation in the cortes: this would have enabled Americans, superior in numbers, to outvote the *peninsulares*. The seven Peruvian deputies to the cortes of Cádiz supported the American demand for greater representation, but cautiously, lest the franchise be extended to Indians, mestizos and castes. Spaniards in the cortes were able to play upon the racial prejudice of Americans in order to exclude the great mass of the castes from citizenship and franchise, and thus to diminish American representation. And they had the support of the Peruvian deputies who, in addition to taking a position of total loyalty to the metropolis and to union with the Spanish monarchy, also sought to ensure that the Indians could neither elect nor be elected, citing 'the grave disadvantages which equality of this sort would have, notably in Peru.'[16] This was the true voice of Peruvian liberalism.

Creole mentalities were also conditioned by fear of social revolution and Indian violence, especially the memory of the great rebellion of Tupac Amaru in 1780 and the experience of more recent Indian unrest in the southern Andes. The Peruvian whites, 140,890 in a population of 1,115,207 (1795), were always conscious of the superior numbers of Indians and mestizos, and of the volcano in their midst. Two rebellions, in 1780 and 1814, fuelled by classical Indian grievances—excessive demands for taxes and labour—shook the colony to its foundations. Creole supporters of rebellion withdrew once the violence intensified, and the movements demonstrated a truth that the Spaniards always believed, that most creoles preferred Spanish rule and imperial security to Indian rebellion backed by creole protest. The memory of Indian rebellion haunted the creoles for many years to come. Indian pressure, therefore, far from hastening independence, brought out the latent conservatism of the creoles and persuaded them to accept Spanish rule until a more favourable opportunity occurred.

For the next five years Peru remained a royalist base, internally secure but subject to increasing pressure as the American revolution approached its borders. In mid-1816 Abascal retired from office and left the viceroyalty in the hands of Joaquín de la Pezuela, an Aragonese officer who had organized the counter-revolution in Upper Peru. The new viceroy shared Abascal's conservative principles but lacked his clarity of mind and singleness of purpose. Within a year of taking office he allowed himself to be outmanoeuvred at great distance by San Martín; failing to keep pace with the military thinking of his adversary, he continued to concentrate his forces in Upper Peru and did not anticipate the greater threat to the royalist position in Chile. His judgement was soon challenged by his own colleagues, particularly by a group of new officers released for service in Peru at the end of the Napoleonic wars—General José de la Serna, commander of Upper Peru from November 1816, Colonel Jerónimo Valdés, chief-of-staff and the Frenchman General José Canterac who brought further reinforcements to Upper Peru in 1818. These veterans of the Peninsular War represented a new and younger school of political and military thinking. They were not absolutists but constitutionalists who believed that the American revolution was a consequence of Spanish intransigence, that the colonies could only be held by a more flexible policy and that the vehicle of this should be the Constitution of 1812. Above all, as experienced professional soldiers they despised Pezuela's irresolution and defective tactics.[17] Spanish unity in Peru was beginning to crack, and San Martín's great opportunity was approaching.

Pezuela's preoccupations grew in the course of 1817–18. San Martín's victory in Chile pushed back the royalist frontier in the south, and even sparked a conspiratorial movement in Lima itself, ineffectual but a sign of growing patriot strength. The viceroy found it difficult to increase the royalist forces; he lacked revenue and the *cabildos* refused to cooperate. In 1818 he was pessimistic, though he probably overstated the problem: 'Loyalists are apathetic; the cholos and Indians are not favourably disposed to the king; and the mass of the slaves are without exception supporters of the rebels, from whom they hope to obtain their freedom.'[18] San Martín's victory at Maipú caused heavy casualties among the Peruvian expeditionary force and much concern in Peru itself. Pezuela's political position was further weakened in 1820 when the Spanish army at Cádiz mutinied and forced Ferdinand VII to restore the Constitution of 1812. In due course Pezuela was instructed by the Spanish government to apply the constitution in Peru, to restore the elected *cabildos* and to implement yet another version of Spanish liberalism. Confusion followed: the Peruvian aristocracy were alienated; the people were not impressed; Pezuela dragged his feet; and the *cabildo* of Lima constitutionalized itself. The only pattern was instability, which was the last thing Pezuela wanted in his own camp. San Martín was poised to invade.

The War for Peru

The liberating army to Peru assembled at Valparaíso on 19 August 1820, embarked on 19 and 20 August, and sailed on the 21st in 18 transports escorted by 7 warships manned by 1,600 seamen; the latter included about 600 foreigners, mainly British and Chilean, and the captains were either British or American. The army, comprising the Division of the Andes and the Division of Chile, totalled 4,500 troops between infantry, cavalry and artillery (with their 35 field guns); of these 2,313 were Argentines and 1,968 Chileans. Not more than 10 officers and 90 other ranks of the original force survived to fight at Ayacucho (1824), the last battle for Peru, the rest having become the casualties of war or been displaced by politics.[19] No such fears marred those fine August days in 1820. People of the capital and the country poured into Valparaíso to cheer off the troops, as bands played and flags waved. Among those weeping were many women who had followed their men in previous campaigns and were now left behind with their children. As the ships sailed from the bay, Lord Cochrane in the *O'Higgins* had his work cut out to keep the convoy together.

San Martín had the advantage of surprise and the option of various landing points. Viceroy Pezuela, with a long coastline to defend, had no intelligence on the enemy's destination and no prospect of reinforcements from Spain after the army revolt in Cádiz in January 1820. But the liberators too had their problems. O'Higgins had given clear instructions to Cochrane that General San Martín had 'exclusive control of the operations of this great enterprise, and you are to act strictly in accordance with the plan which he will provide.'[20] The instructions were soon tested. Looking out towards the coast of southern Peru the invaders saw a dismal desert of sand and scrub, interspersed with ridges of black rock, until they navigated towards Pisco, south of Lima, where fertile inland valleys of grapes planted by the early Spanish colonists yielded high-quality wines and brandies. Inland, successive ranges of mountains attracted the eye, and on a clear day a glimpse of the distant summits of the cordillera might be had. Cochrane wanted to continue north to Callao and Lima, engage the royalists immediately and occupy the capital. But San Martín would have none of it. He disembarked his army at Pisco, 100 miles south of Callao, 'to my great chagrin', reported Cochrane, and there he remained in an 'excess of caution' for six weeks, his troops largely inactive.[21] An advance party under Las Heras, carrying saddles and harness on their shoulders, secured the area and procured horses and cattle, rum and fresh meat for the troops, before the main landing on 11 September. The troops were under strict instructions not to plunder, and to conduct themselves as liberators, not oppressors. 'You come to liberate peoples not to make conquests' was a mission statement that reverberates among invaders throughout history.[22]

These and subsequent differences between San Martín and Cochrane were born not only of personal incompatibility, the cautious general versus the audacious admiral, the calculating politician versus the impulsive Scot, but also of conflicting strategic concepts. Cochrane maintained that it was both necessary and possible to destroy Spanish power. He knew, moreover, that to keep a fleet inactive for any length of time was an extremely expensive proposition, that what was possible for the army was bad for the navy. San Martín had other priorities. He too sought an absolute victory in Peru: 'to destroy for ever Spanish rule in Peru and place its peoples in the moderate exercise of their rights, this is the essential object of the liberating expedition.'[23] But the methods that he envisaged were more complex than those of Cochrane; they were subtle and possibly unique in the American revolution. San Martín believed that a foreign liberating expedition could not in fact liberate Peru on its own, that liberation depended upon the cooperation of Peruvians and should be completed if possible by Peruvians, with the minimum of violence to their country and its institutions. 'He has always expressed the greatest anxiety to prevent if possible any revolution in Lima which might occasion bloodshed and calamity,' reported Commodore Bowles.[24] And San Martín himself declared: 'My soul would never be satisfied with a victory obtained at the cost of spilling American blood: I desire a peaceful victory, fruit of irresistible necessity.'[25] To the intendant of Trujillo in northern Peru, the marquis of Torre Tagle, he wrote: 'Public opinion hardens and declares itself more openly, for it sees that I scrupulously fulfil my promises to respect the rights, offices and property of those who are not enemies of the cause which I am charged to sustain and promote', and he called on Torre Tagle to join the cause of independence. Would it be prudent and just, he asked, 'to struggle against the torrent of events and the demands of justice, against the will of the people and the dictates of necessity?'[26]

San Martín was a true liberator, the most scrupulous in all the Americas. If his own words meant anything, he went to Peru to wage a war not of conquest but of ideas, a war for the minds and hearts of Peruvians. Rather than engage the enemy immediately, he preferred to wait for the Peruvian patriots to join his cause. He has been criticized for expecting too much of Peruvians and overestimating popular support for independence. But he had his reasons. In the years of inaction he had been thinking hard and deeply about Peru, its social structure, its balance of races and the reasons that kept this hierarchical society loyal to Spain. And behind the high-minded ideals, there lay a reserve of realism.

He saw a society deeply divided between Spaniards and creoles, between whites, mestizos, blacks and Indians, and he came to appreciate that Spain held Peru by more than military means alone. The Peruvian whites were always aware of the superior numbers of Indians and mestizos, and of the demon in their midst. Outnumbered as they were, they were reluctant to disavow the colonial state, while Spain for its part knew that Spanish defences against Indian rebellion depended on creole cooperation. For these reasons the creoles were conscious of some bargaining power, and when, in the years after 1810, the possibility arose of political reform from the Spanish constitutionalists— reform that would reduce the absolute power of viceregal government and give the creoles a greater share in decision-making—the creoles, at least in the Andean south, were ready to move, though not necessarily in the direction of absolute independence. The colonial state benefited not only from divisions between creoles and Indians but also from disunity within Indian ranks; even during recent Indian rebellions, many *caciques*, driven in part by personal, community and ethnic rivalry, kept their people loyal to the Crown. The slaves lived outside this society, though not unaware of it. Although there were no more than forty thousand in all Peru, the great majority of slaves lived on the central coast, where they formed a plantation labour force, and ten thousand of them lived in Lima, where they made up 16 per cent of the urban population and were regarded as indispensable in trades and domestic work.[27] Spain held Peru on the principle of 'divide and rule', well informed on the size of the ethnic divisions and adept in manipulating them.

While he was aware of the social problems facing the invaders, San Martín's strategy could also be justified on military as well as political and social grounds. Basically it was a question of power. His own army was not large, fewer than five thousand, and it faced royalist forces which, including contingents from Cuzco and Upper Peru, militia as well as regular units, totalled about twenty-three thousand, though only some nine thousand of these were readily available.[28] Viceroy Pezuela could not immediately exploit his military superiority, for he was tied by instructions from the new liberal regime in Spain to seek pacification. San Martín responded promptly to his overtures; he sent commissioners, civilians Tomás Guido and Juan García del Río, to a peace conference at Miraflores (25 September 1820) and agreed to an eight-days armistice.[29] But there was no basis for a settlement; while the royalists were reassured by San Martín's conservatism, they could not accept his insistence on independence, even in the form of an independent Spanish monarchy in Peru. Yet San Martín had spotted a possible opening that he kept in mind for the future. The revolt of the constitutionalists in Spain ended the possibility of military reinforcements for the royalists in America, and the royal army in Peru was now on its own. At the same time the tension between absolutists and liberals in the Iberian Peninsula was mirrored in Peru where some of these ideologies were brought across even by the military. So some officers, called '*blancos*' or '*constitucionales*', favoured peace, while the '*negros*' or '*serviles*' insisted on continuing the war at all costs. San Martín had hopes of dealing with the moderates in the army, if moderate was the right word for anyone in the Spanish high command, and kept the possibility in mind for the future, not to be nullified by all-out war. The Liberator then prepared to put his military plan into operation. It was a daring strategy, and a risky one.

A flying column of 1,200 men under General Juan Antonio Alvarez de Arenales was sent inland to Ica, near Pisco, with orders to advance into the sierra, revolutionize the Indians and move northwards along the Jauja valley parallel to the coast with the intention of cutting Lima off from the interior. Arenales was a peninsular Spaniard by birth and had served in the royalist army in the Río de la Plata until disillusionment with the colonial regime caused him to join the revolution. A veteran of campaigns in Upper Peru, he was an expert in irregular as well as regular warfare. He had joined San Martín in Chile and came to occupy a special place in the service of the Liberator, who appointed him general of division and always addressed him as *compañero*. In the course of December his campaign made significant military gains and he was able to establish communications with the coast. San Martín, therefore, now had a foothold in Peru, a revolutionary presence in the sierra and else-where an audience for his intentions. So on 23 October he re-embarked and took the main force beyond Lima, first to Ancón, a miserable village to the north, then on 9 November to the small port of Huacho, seventy miles north of Callao and commanding entry to the fertile Huaura valley, thus interposing his army between the capital to the south and the agricultural region of northern Peru on which the royalists relied for food supplies. He established his headquarters in Huaura for the next six months. His intention was to blockade Lima by land and sea, and thus to avoid the need of direct assault.

This cautious strategy was deeply resented by many of San Martín's officers, not least by Admiral Cochrane, who controlled the seas and provided the naval cover for the move to Ancón. In spite of their differences the two men had collaborated routinely since August. Letters between them in September and October show frank exchange of information and ideas. San Martín writes, 'Let us go on after Pisco and work with the patience previously adopted, for there is no other way to conduct this enterprise', and referring to the method of re-embarking the army he adopted Cochrane's plans: 'without your tireless activity I would not be able to rely on the speed of preparations necessary for this operation.'[30]

Yet Cochrane was impatient. To the outrage of British naval opinion he was enforcing a blockade of the Peruvian coast to deter neutral vessels, including those of English merchants, from supplying the royalists. But he wanted more action. Naval forces were too expensive to keep inactive; and he was deter-mined to destroy the remnants of Spanish naval power in Callao and simulta-neously to attack Lima. This was the mindset that had brought him fame and success in the Atlantic and Mediterranean, and he had no reason to doubt its message in the Pacific. He was incapable of influencing San Martín's policy by land, but at sea he was master. On the night of 5 November 1820 in a striking naval action brilliantly organized and bravely executed, he cut out the *Esmeralda*, a forty-four-gun Spanish frigate anchored in the port of Callao. The flawless manoeuvre was based on meticulous preparation. He personally reconnoitred the opposition, took soundings in the bay of Callao, selected and trained his men. 'And now, my lads,' he joked, 'we shall give them such a Gunpowder Plot as they will not forget in a hurry.' Approaching the vessel silently with muffled oars, amidst enemy ships and under the very batteries of

Callao, two heavily armed boarding parties, one commanded personally by Cochrane, took the crew by surprise and after a fierce struggle in which Cochrane was wounded, forced their surrender, cut the frigate's cable and sailed her out, thus capturing the best Spanish warship in the Pacific, 'a death blow to the Spanish naval force in that quarter of the world.'[31] Cochrane's force had suffered 41 casualties, the Spanish 160. The *Esmeralda* was not the first Spanish frigate captured by Cochrane, whose action against the *El Gamo* off Barcelona in 1801 had helped to establish his reputation in the Royal Navy. But such audacity was new in South America. San Martín approved the action and wrote effusively to O'Higgins, recommending the admiral, his officers and men. Even the Royal Navy had to admire it: 'On the morning of the 6th instant about 12.30 a.m. a most brilliant affair took place between the boats of the above ships and the *Esmeralda* (Spanish frigate), commanded by Lord Cochrane in person, which he carried, together with a gunboat, from under the batteries and out of their line of defence, and in less than half-an-hour had her under sail. This was done so quick and in so masterly a style, that I had scarcely time to get out of the line of fire.'[32]

Yet San Martín persisted in his own war of waiting. To encircle the enemy by sea and land, to blockade him, starve him, harass him and stifle him, this was the strategy, but it took time and patience. It was a trying experience and tested his own policy to the limit, and his health, as he became one of the hundreds suffering from waves of epidemics during these endless days in a noxious climate. 'My health is very low', he told O'Higgins, 'and if it continues like this I am convinced I shall soon be for the grave.' But his spirit was strong and his military instincts were still vigorous. 'It is he', commented a Peruvian witness, 'who props up the corpse of his army, fast disappearing under the scourge of the climate until there are not even enough troops to relieve his forward positions.'

Misery was relieved by the arrival of Lady Cochrane with her children on the British vessel *Andromaque* that sailed into Callao in January 1821. She made her way inland, where she had a stunning effect on William Miller's troops in Huacho:

The sudden appearance of youth and beauty, on a fiery horse, managed with skill and elegance, absolutely electrified the men, who had never before seen an English lady: *que hermosa! que graciosa! que linda! que guapa! que airosa! Es un ángel del cielo!* were exclamations that escaped from one end of the line to the other. This is our *generala*. Her ladyship turned her sparkling eyes towards the line, and bowed graciously. The troops could no longer confine their expressions of admiration to half-suppressed interjections; loud *vivas* burst from officers as well as men. Lady Cochrane smiled her acknowledgments and cantered off the ground with the grace of a fairy.[33]

San Martín could not postpone action indefinitely. An attempt to take the offensive in January 1821, advancing south towards the royalist stronghold of Aznapuquio and hoping for a reinforcing link-up from the flank as Arenales descended from the sierra, failed to take effect. San Martín was unable to synchronize the operation and when threatened by the royalists was forced to retire to Huaura. It was an unfortunate mistake that weakened his highland front without any gains for his coastal position. In bringing down Arenales and his forces in a fruitless operation on the coast and then consigning them to his main army, San Martín had vacated the sierra and abandoned a model operation, the most promising so far and one which had demonstrated that a flying column of a thousand men could take the revolution into the interior and disconcert the enemy by placing a combat force within their midst. The Indians were not really convinced by one side or the other, but royalist commanders were not concerned with niceties when they reconquered the sierra and took bloody reprisals against abandoned Indian communities.

San Martín continued to expect the enemy forces to collapse and the Peruvian patriots to rise. He believed that his mere presence had a disturbing effect on the royalists, that patriot recruits were swelling his forces while the viceregal army suffered desertion and demoralization. Observers differed on the size of the royalist army but they agreed that its ranks were filled by a majority of Peruvians. Sir Thomas Hardy, the most famous of Nelson's captains, who had succeeded Bowles as commander-in-chief of the South American squadron, reported the view from his station that 'out of the royal army of 6 or 7,000 men, not more than 2,500 are Europeans.'[34] San Martín's spies presumably kept him informed of these facts, a disturbing test for his thesis. But loss of nerve was not in his nature. On 25 June 1821 in a long interview on the deck of his schooner with the British naval captain, Basil Hall, he insisted that he could take Lima immediately, but what would be the point if the inhabitants were politically hostile? This was a war of opinion in which his task was to be the liberator, not the conqueror, of Peru, and he asked, 'How could the cause of independence be advanced by my holding Lima, or even the whole of the country, in military possession? Far different are my views. I wish to have all men thinking with me, and do not choose to advance a step beyond the gradual march of public opinion.'[35] Was he right?

José de la Riva Agüero, pride of the colonial aristocracy, warned San Martín of the dangers of expecting too much of Peruvians:

> Those of the upper class who want independence will not make the slightest move to achieve it or to support it, because as their fathers are officials, or they are eldest sons or hacendados, they are not very keen to change the prevailing regime, which enables them to live comfortably under the present

government. Those of the numerous middle class will not take action either, until the liberators arrive and actually place weapons in their hands; meanwhile their patriotism will only go as far as to spread news, distribute papers of the independists, make proclamations and so on, and spread lies, which annoys the government but nothing more. The lower class of this country is useless and incapable of any revolution. In short, there is no hope of any movement to support the protecting army in this capital.[36]

A supercilious intervention from one of the colonial elite who, like the rest of his class, was primarily concerned neither with the survival of Spanish rule nor with the winning of independence but with the degree of power and control that they would have in any regime. And his realism was not entirely accurate.

The proximity of the liberating expedition and the consequent reaction of the royalists caused many Peruvians to rethink their position. San Martín's appeals were not unrewarded. A number of leading creoles, among them Agustín Gamarra, Andrés Santa Cruz and Ramón Castilla, who were later to play leading roles in the republican life of Peru and Bolivia, deserted the king to join the ranks of the liberators. A growing number of municipalities declared independence, first Supe in April 1819, then in the following year Ica, Tarma and Lambayeque. Torre Tagle, a creole aristocrat, was not a convinced believer in independence, and he would have preferred autonomy within a Spanish framework. But reassured by San Martín's political moderation and bias towards monarchy, he led the *cabildo* of Trujillo in northern Peru in a declaration of independence on 29 December 1820, delivering not only an example but also valuable reinforcements of recruits and supplies. The example was soon followed by Piura and other towns of the north. The greatest prize, however, was Guayaquil, a major northern port and centre of a shipbuilding industry, which had joined the revolution in October. By May 1821 the whole of northern Peru had declared for independence, and under the leadership of the creole elite began to supply men and money to San Martín at a time when he badly needed both.

In the south he authorized an expedition to Intermedios in March 1821, commanded by Cochrane with discretion to act as required. The English officer William Miller commanded the land forces, which served the dual purpose of spreading the revolution and diverting enemy forces from central Peru; Arica on the coast was occupied and Miller penetrated successfully as far inland as Tacna and Moquegua, and drew off royalist forces from elsewhere, before eventually coming to a halt for lack of troops and arms. None of this was conquest, but it kept the enemy at full stretch, without risking a pitched battle. And in the interior a second expedition by Arenales defeated a royalist detachment at Pasco, and in May advanced as far as Tarma. At that point

Arenales proposed to San Martín a plan of transferring the entire military operation to the sierra, leaving Lima to the efforts of the navy and the guerrillas, but none of this was accepted and when Arenales reached Jauja he received news that another ceasefire had been negotiated.

As San Martín tightened his hold on Lima and Cochrane controlled the sea, tension in the Spanish ranks added further credibility to his thesis of revolution without war. Desertions multiplied, and in December 1820, following its defeat by Arenales at Pasco, the veteran *Numancia* battalion, about 650 strong and composed mostly of Spanish Americans recruited in Venezuela and New Granada, passed over to the liberating expedition. Pezuela's conduct of the war, his vacillation, loss of Chile and defeats in Peru drew angry criticism from his own army and led to a palace revolt, when a group of higher officers at Aznapuquio deposed the viceroy (29 January 1821) and replaced him by General José de la Serna. This military *golpe*, although condoned by Madrid, impaired Spanish legitimacy in Peru without earning military dividends. Peruvians were having a hard time, as Captain Basil Hall of the Royal Navy, who visited Lima in February, observed. People of all classes were suffering the effects of deprivation as the colonial state lost its way. The poor were starved of basic needs, the middle sectors of society were deprived of their usual comforts and the elites saw their tables empty of luxuries.[37] Taxation and shortages compounded the misery.

Lima, of course, was not Peru, and in the highlands the royalist position remained strong, seconded by historical regional resentments against Lima; and it remained unaffected by occasional expeditions from the coast, such as a second penetration by Arenales in April 1821. San Martín held back from Lima and remained inactive in Huaura, which was now a death trap for his army. There it was exposed to malaria, dysentery and other epidemics, causing grievous loss of troops. Of the five thousand soldiers who disembarked at Pisco three thousand fell ill, and the number of deaths varied between thirty and fifty a day. The rest were hardly fit enough to dig graves, much less to bear arms against the enemy.[38] And Cochrane was still impatient, convinced that Lima was ready to fall into the lap of the expedition. Only an 'insane jealousy' that saw the admiral as a rival, he later claimed, had prevented San Martín giving him a force capable of capturing the place for the expedition.[39] A typical Cochrane exaggeration, but one shared by his crew, and not lessened when San Martín authorized the admiral to provide naval cover for Miller's landing in the south. On the larger strategy he remained unmoved, convinced that he could starve Lima into surrender while he did not have an army large enough for a pitched battle.

La Serna and his colleagues failed to exploit their military superiority over San Martín, when they 'could have driven the inferior forces of San Martín into the sea', preferring instead indecisive negotiations which further confirmed the Liberator's argument.[40] Meanwhile, stuck in Huaura and immersed in the gloom of the present, San Martín's mind turned to the past and he gave a hint that his own history was always in his thoughts. One of the peace commissioners appointed by the constitutional government in Spain was the navy captain Manuel Abreu, who before his arrival had opened communications with San Martín, mentioning he had once seen his family in Málaga. 'Your letter', replied San Martín from Huaura, 'has taken me back to a time that I cannot recall without emotion. I am delighted that you have met my mother and sister in Málaga, a further reason why I look forward to your speedy arrival here.'[41] The royal envoy, a pitiful cripple in body, had his confidence boosted by his generous reception in San Martín's camp when he arrived on 25 March, in contrast to his frosty reception by La Serna and his officers, who resented that he had visited the enemy first. San Martín had confided in Abreu his military plan 'to take Lima by surrounding it, cutting off all supplies without risking engagement', keeping his troops for a more dangerous occasion in case of attack, 'because to destroy the forces in the capital would need the rising of the whole country.' His political project was even more interesting to the negotiator, who reported him as saying, 'If Spain insisted on continuing the war it would lead to the extermination of Peru. . . . He well recognized that America was incapable of erecting itself into an independent Republic because it lacked the necessary qualities and civilization, and as a last resort he had agreed with his army chiefs to crown a Spanish prince, the only way of avoiding the feelings of enmity and to reconcile once more families and interests; and in deference and respect to the peninsula, favourable commercial treaties would be made, and as for Buenos Aires [the following in cypher] *he would use his bayonets to compel them to accept this idea if they did not agree.*'[42] A military expression of a political position, if indeed San Martín used those words attributed to him by a loyal Spaniard.

Negotiations opened at Punchauca just north of Lima on 4 May 1821, a provisional armistice was signed on 23 May and on 2 June San Martín himself met Viceroy La Serna. Again it was San Martín's monarchism that attracted the interest of the royalists. He proposed first that Spain should recognize the independence of the Río de la Plata, Chile and Peru; second, that a governing junta should be formed, composed of a nominee of the viceroy, another of San Martín and a third of the Peruvians; third, that two commissioners should be sent to Spain to notify the king of the declaration of independence and to invite him to place a prince of the royal family on the throne of Peru, on condition that the new sovereign accept the constitution. Again, the Spaniards rejected independence, the talks ended in deadlock, the armistice expired and hostilities were resumed.[43] According to subsequent explanations, San Martín was aware that Madrid would never ratify such a treaty, and his real object was to compromise the royalist commanders, thus leaving them no alternative to uniting with him, and recognizing the independence of Peru.[44] But Punchauca taught a more significant lesson. It was another vindication of the revolutionaries, another sign that Spain, liberal or absolutist, had nothing to offer America. But in the short term the interlude also served La Serna, giving him breathing space for his next move.

The Fall of Lima

In Lima the position of the royalists was now insecure, blockaded as they were by sea and surrounded by an increasingly hostile public. On 6 July La Serna evacuated the capital—but not nearby Callao—and took his troops into the interior. It was a smart move: in Lima his army was starved of food and exposed to infection. The sierra had greater resources and a healthier climate. In spite of the urging of Cochrane, San Martín still made no move to destroy the viceroy's disorganized army, which was able to regroup in the sierra. San Martín had the same options as La Serna. Should he not shelter his troops from the pestilence of the coast and give his own casualties of the climate a chance to recover in the highlands, as those of Arenales had done?[45] He decided otherwise, preferring the political option of making the capital a focus of the revolution to the military advantages of the sierra. In the eyes of many citizens he chose well, delivering them not only from Indians and blacks but above all from hunger and disease.

On 5 July, before the entry of San Martín's troops into Lima, the city was without a garrison, and panic broke out, spreading from the aristocracy and the middle sectors of society. People were afraid not of outrages by the troops but of a great revolt of the urban slaves, who would take advantage of the absence of troops in a re-enactment of the risings in Haiti. Captain Basil Hall, a direct observer of these events, did not share the alarm: 'The slaves had never any leisure to plan such a scheme; their habits were not those of union or enterprise, for they were all domestic servants, and thinly scattered over an immense city, with very rare opportunities of confidential intercourse.'[46] On 10 July an advance guard of the liberating army under Colonel José Manuel Bogoño moved into the capital, and San Martín himself entered the city incognito, to see and assess. Basil Hall, who had come ashore to observe events, saw him in the streets and was greeted by him. Women threw themselves at the Liberator when he was recognized and he had to disengage himself courteously from their embraces, though he was not so dismissive of a younger woman, whom Hall does not name.[47]

On 12 July he entered Lima openly, and took up residence with his staff in the viceregal palace. In the following days further units of troops entered, amidst popular enthusiasm. Among them was a young *porteño* officer, Juan Isidro Quesada, recently a prisoner of war and freed under an exchange of prisoners with the royalists. He had now been posted to the 8th Battalion of the Army of the Andes, and after settling in Lima he made his way to the palace with other officers of his battalion to greet San Martín:

> After we were announced the General invited us into one of the assembly rooms, where he received us with all the kindness and courtesy that he always showed to army officers. When we were all there, he said 'I have brought down the 8th Battalion to the capital in order that the young among you may form opinion in this country, which is so impregnated with old habits of aristocracy, and that through your presence these will begin to be forgotten and those of our own democratic system prevail. I am confident, gentlemen, that you will not in any way damage the good name of the liberating army, much less that of the battalion you belong to. But if regrettably there is anyone who forgets the path of honour and virtue which distinguishes them, I will be inexorable in imposing the punishment which its failure deserves.'[48]

San Martín promised full protection of all inhabitants, who had asked him not to delay in coming to rescue the city from disorder. But the elite were faced with a painful dilemma:

> The Spaniards, who formed the wealthy class, were sadly perplexed: if they declined entering into San Martín's views, their property and their persons were liable to confiscation; if they acceded to his terms, they became committed to their own government, which, it was still possible, might return to visit them with equal vengeance. The natives, on the other hand, who had better reasons to be confident, were even more alarmed at the consequence of their present acts. Many questioned San Martín's sincerity, many doubted his power to fulfil his engagements.[49]

The answer to the dilemma was to sign up for independence or flee. On 15 July a *cabildo abierto* representing upper-class citizens declared for independence. This was officially proclaimed on 28 July in the Plaza Mayor. The large public square of Lima was a fitting venue for the scene that followed. One side was occupied by the viceroy's palace, now Government House, another by the cathedral and the remaining two by handsome houses two storeys high. The ceremony was attended by San Martín and his staff, smartly dressed and mounted, with the troops formed up and the crowd pressing forward. He declared 'From this moment Peru is free and independent by the

general will of the people and by the justice of its cause, which God defend.'
And unfurling the red-and-white flag he had designed in Pisco, he exclaimed
'Long live the patria, long live independence, long live Liberty'[50] Coins were
thrown to the crowd, eight thousand pesos in all; some of them rolled between
the legs of the troops on parade, who were disciplined enough not to break
ranks to collect them.

There was a solemn Te Deum in the cathedral the next day, though not all
the bishops supported independence. The bishop of Maynas encouraged the
faithful to resist 'these gangs of bandits and scoundrels', and the bishop of
Huamanga condemned the troops of Arenales 'who rob and kill without
mercy'.[51] A grand ball was held that night at the viceregal palace, with people
crowding to enter. Talking to his soldiers at the door about the checks on
admissions, San Martín wondered 'and what about this mob?' and was told
that there they were, along with their masters. 'In that case don't allow anyone
to enter who is not dressed for the ball, without distinction of sex.'[52] These
days in Lima saw a relaxed San Martín. Though never anything but strict and
formal in public affairs, he was human and amiable in his social contacts and
especially in his treatment of younger colleagues, whom he encouraged to
come to the *tertulias* and to meet Peruvian girls on the dance floor.

Patriotism was not the only explanation of these events. The transfer of
Lima from royal to revolutionary government was accompanied by incipient
social violence and by creole fear of massacre at the hands of the slaves.
Patriots and royalists alike looked to San Martín to protect them from social
disorder, and after the departure of the viceroy leading citizens invited the
Liberator to take over promptly in the interests of law and order. According to
Basil Hall, 'it was not only of the slaves and of the mob that people were afraid;
but with more reason, of the multitude of armed Indians surrounding the
city, who, although under the orders of San Martín's officers, were savage and
undisciplined troops, and were likely to enter the place in a body as soon as
the Spaniards had gone.'[53]

San Martín, therefore, came to the rescue of Lima, with the collaboration of
those who in the circumstances placed security above royalism. Not all
subscribed to this position and many suffered for their beliefs, either fleeing
and abandoning their homes and property, or remaining and taking their
punishment, subject now to curfew, forced exactions, and still in the end
unpardoned and ordered to leave the country. Many others hid their true
convictions, signing the declaration of independence out of fear or under
duress. The 3,504 signatures, therefore, were not a true gauge of Peruvian
opinion or a sure guide for San Martín. No doubt the fall of Lima vindicated
his strategy of non-violence. But only to a degree. For Lima did not represent
the whole of Peru, and there was no evidence that the interior, where there was

a royalist army, could be secured by similar methods, or that the royalist forces would retreat indefinitely. Yet he was still not prepared to engage them. Arenales was recalled without the opportunity of striking them in the interior.

San Martín brought decisive military action virtually to a halt and allowed the enemy to dominate the sierra. Arenales believed that the war could be won in the sierra and wanted to attack General José Canterac's army; he pursued the disordered enemy in forced marches but was then instructed by San Martín not to risk his forces but to withdraw towards Pasco or Lima. He protested that he was anxious to attack but ready to obey: 'My troops are fine, but ill-clothed and about a hundred infirm, though not seriously. Don't worry; eager though I am, I prefer security to risking this force. But if you happen to need it to take Callao or for any other operation, let me know and I will be ready to move quickly.'[54] So once again Arenales was reined in and forced to abandon a region, which he thought was conquerable and which the royalists then promptly occupied.

Arenales was a responsible officer and his innate sense of discipline held him back, but his impatience can be read in his despatches from the front. When he was already in Matucana, near the capital, he received orders dated 25 July 1821 to remain in the sierra but without risking an unfavourable action. His reply revealed his exasperation: 'I can only admire this advice . . . I repeatedly said, I say now, and will always say that if my force once leaves the centre of that province and the enemy managed to occupy it, we would be powerless to recover it; and I still remember that in one of your communications you told me that it matters little to lose the sierra compared to other measures under consideration.'[55] A few days later he added, 'It is obvious, sir, and you know better than I, that this cannot be proved without engaging the enemy; and between not fighting and not abandoning those positions there is no middle way.' At the same time, bewildered by the inaction of the general and anticipating what was in fact soon going to happen, he asked concerning Callao, 'What do we do, sir, if we don't attack that castle as soon as possible to deprive the enemy of all hope of returning to it? I assume that for this operation it is not necessary for the troops to remain long on the coast and on the contrary they can soon evacuate it and escape the effects of its climate.'[56]

Independence could not be secure as long as Callao remained in royalist hands. It would be difficult to take by force. But San Martín did not even prevent the royalists from reinforcing it. On 10 September a large Spanish corps of some 3,300 men from the interior under General Canterac marched past Lima unmolested: the two armies simply looked at each other, as though waiting to see who blinked first, until Canterac's army moved off to enter Callao. There it remained only a few days before shortage of provisions forced it to retire into the interior taking the town's treasure and almost five hundred of its defenders with it. Again San Martín declined to attack, allowing Canterac to retreat with impunity, arguing that 'the risks of a battle would not benefit the patriot cause.'[57] His judgement could be defended and reflected his lack of confidence in his army; further reduced by losses in Huaura and reinforced with raw troops recruited in the hills, it was not expected to win a pitched battle against veteran, disciplined soldiers. 'The slightest military reverse at that moment', wrote Hall, anxious to explain San Martín's tactics, 'must at once have turned the tide; the Spaniards would have retaken Lima; and the independence of the country might have been indefinitely retarded.' General Miller agreed: 'San Martín has been severely censured for not attacking the royalists upon this occasion: but when it is considered that many of his troops consisted of raw recruits, perhaps it may be allowed that he acted wisely.'[58]

But could victory be won by avoiding battles, allowing the enemy to come and go, and leaving intact the royalist forces? The answer was, probably not. Yet San Martín had a further compelling reason for restraint. Defeat in a pitched battle would have strengthened and encouraged the social groups hostile to independence, their numbers unquantifiable but menacing. Spaniards and their sympathizers had not been conquered, any more than their army had been defeated, and independence was still on a knife-edge. The possibility of counter-revolution was a nightmare for San Martín; against that a flawed army intact was better than a defeated one defenceless. Independence needed a higher military profile within Lima, and this explains the reliance on *pardo* units and the frantic efforts to recruit the common people into the '*cuerpos cívicos*' to defend the revolution.[59] The Protectorate was on high alert.

There was now a storm of criticism and protest, from his officers, from Cochrane, and from patriot opinion: 'His loss of popularity may be said to take its date from that hour.' And his popularity was not restored when the fortress of Callao, its creole commander General José de La Mar and its suffering garrison surrendered on 19 September, without San Martín risking the loss of his untried army in an engagement with veteran troops, while Canterac's forces arrived back in the highlands the worse for wear after a journey not entirely unchallenged. These events sparked disaffection in the army. It was no secret that the army was divided; rivalry between Argentines, Chileans and Peruvians blunted its fighting edge, and many of the Peruvian officers were unwilling to embark on active service, preferring, according to Miller, the pleasures of Lima to the hazards of the sierra.[60] Indiscipline of this kind remained unpunished and the Liberator was the victim of his own generosity. But the problem went deeper than this. San Martín's defensive tactics and what were seen as flawed military decisions cost him the support of senior officers of the Army of the Andes, who could now withdraw the consent they had given in the Act of Rancagua. The tactical ideas of San

Martín were not necessarily inferior to those of his critics and they were imposed with great conviction. But as Bartolomé Mitre, himself a soldier as well as a statesman and historian, pointed out, a general who prefers the shield to the sword encourages defeatism and risks losing the loyalty of his soldiers.[61] And discipline was deteriorating even among senior officers, especially from resentment among those who did not benefit from San Martín's distribution of the properties of royalists confiscated by the municipality of Lima. Las Heras, Enrique Martínez and Mariano Necochea were now giving notice of retirement from the army. And a more dramatic retirement was imminent.

Lord Cochrane's Lecture

The acquisition of Callao confirmed the patriots' dominance of the coast and opened their sector to foreign shipping. But conflict in the Pacific now entered a new phase, as relations between San Martín and Lord Cochrane reached breaking point. San Martín behaved as though the war was over. Cochrane was convinced that it had still to be fought. He was also convinced that the independence won so far owed more to him and his officers than to San Martín, who had assumed power in Peru without any consultation with the naval arm, much less with the people, in order to establish 'a despotic government'. Indeed it only proved that the army had been kept unused and intact 'for the purpose of preserving it entire to further the ambitious views of the General', a pretended Liberator but in reality a conqueror.[62] The general, moreover, was a tyrant not a liberal, and he persecuted Spaniards to reward his own politicians.

Writing to him as 'an honest man and a friend', Cochrane lectured San Martín on his duties. You could be the Napoleon of South America, he told him, but you also have the power to go your own way: 'No man had yet arisen, save yourself, capable of soaring aloft, and with eagle eye embracing the expanse of the political horizon. But if in your flight, like Icarus, you trust to waxen wings, your descent may crush the rising liberties of Peru and involve all South America in anarchy, civil war and political despotism.' He added, 'flatterers are more dangerous than the most venomous serpents, and next to them are men of knowledge, if they have not the integrity or courage to oppose bad measures, when formally discussed, or even when casually spoken of.'[63] This was fantasy, indulged after the events, but the fact remained that Cochrane had legitimate grievances. He had now lost two of his warships and had neither supplies nor pay for the rest. But his method of acquiring money was arbitrary and corrupt in the eyes of San Martín. He released blockade runners on purchase of a trading licence obtained by payment of a duty at 18 per cent of the cargo's value, to be paid in cash.[64] Commodore Hardy, speaking as the British station commander, complained to O'Higgins, who in turn complained to San Martín, but Cochrane was beyond control, an embarrassment who would not be stopped. And trading licences were not the end of it. Among other things, he charged Spanish refugees leaving the coast 2,500 pesos for a passport.

Meanwhile, arrears of pay due to his crews had not been met, and promises of bounty money remained unfulfilled. Before the departure of the expedition Cochrane's seamen had wanted an assurance on pay, which they did not get from the Chilean government. Instead they received assurance from a joint proclamation by San Martín and Cochrane: 'On my entry into Lima, I will punctually pay to all foreign seamen who will enlist into the Chilean service, the whole arrears of their pay, of which I will also add to each individual, according to his rank, one year's pay over and above his arrears, as a premium or reward for his services.'[65] Now this seemed to be forgotten.

General and admiral met in Government House on 5 August to resolve the issue of pay and supplies. It was a stormy meeting, with different versions coming from each side. San Martín's opening argument, 'I am Protector of Peru,' provoked Cochrane, who retorted, 'Then it becomes me, as senior officer of Chili, and consequently the representative of the nation, to request the fulfilment of all the promises made to Chili and the squadron.' 'Chili! Chili!' shouted San Martín dismissively, 'I will never pay a single real to Chili, and as to the squadron you may take it where you please, and go where you choose, a couple of schooners are quite enough for me.' He snapped his fingers in the face of the admiral, then paced the room; turning to Cochrane he caught his hand and said 'Forget, my lord, what is past!' 'I will when I can,' replied Cochrane and left the palace.[66] San Martín had made what Cochrane regarded as a 'dishonourable' offer: abandon the squadron to his interests and accept the higher grade of 'First Admirable of Peru,' which he declined. 'I will not accept either honours or rewards from a Government constituted in defiance of solemn pledges.'[67] San Martín argued that this was a Chilean navy and therefore a charge on Chile not Peru: 'The debt is due from Chili, whose government engaged the seamen.'[68] In the eyes of critics, this was virtually to dismiss the Chileans from the war of Peruvian liberation, and create a suspicion that the new government wanted to acquire the ships and seamen of the Chilean navy for itself. And it remained to be seen whether San Martín could instil a comparable sense of responsibility in the Peruvians themselves. As for solemn pledges, the Protector had broken none, and he would notice that he was not the only target of Cochrane's invective; two of the admiral's English officers who aroused his exaggerated suspicion of plots were courtmartialled and dismissed.

Before his squadron disintegrated for lack of pay, Cochrane took the law into his own hands. After this interview he tried to do a deal independently with the governor of Callao. When this failed there was a last meeting in September when he begged San Martín to attack Canterac's troops as they passed to Callao. Again he failed, then learning that a quantity of treasure belonging partly to the government of Peru and partly to private individuals had been placed for safe keeping on vessels at Ancón, Cochrane sailed there on 14 September and seized the funds to pay his crews. Of a total of 400,000 pesos Cochrane kept 285,000 pesos of state money and distributed it between expenses, pay and prize money, and returned the money on deposit from private individuals.[69] This was the end of collaboration between the two men. An angry San Martín ordered Cochrane to quit Callao. Twenty-three officers and a number of foreign seamen abandoned the fleet, leaving it half unmanned. Cochrane took his remaining force out of the Liberator's service in order to pursue his own campaign against Spanish shipping in the Pacific. San Martín proceeded to create a separate Peruvian navy and he managed to acquire a few small vessels, and later the Spanish frigates *Prueba* and *Venganza*. But Cochrane's Chilean seamen did not entirely desert him or volunteer for Peru.[70]

San Martín was bitter in his report of these events to O'Higgins. 'The money which this villain has stolen places us immediately in a critical situation, but this state is capable of making good the loss quickly. The trouble is that this devil is going to commit thousands of robberies which will severely compromise you and me.' And at the moment Cochrane's hostile presence in Peruvian waters prevented San Martín from sending an expedition to Pisco to join up with Miller and cut off the withdrawal of La Serna in the interior. 'I dare not embark the expedition in the troopships for fear that he will take it over and sack the coast, with the result that I can take no action as long as this scoundrel remains here and all my operations are thus paralized.'[71] The Protector's anger was further conveyed in accusations to the Chilean government, denouncing the 'enormous and inexcusable crimes perpetrated by Lord Cochrane, his negligence, calumnies, and acts of lawlessness.'[72] A pirate in San Martín's eyes, Cochrane was welcomed as a national hero when he returned to Chile and he retained an honourable place in Chilean history.

San Martín never forgave the '*metálico lord*', as he called Cochrane, and he bore the stains on his reputation for some time to come. But his endurance was not impaired. He remained imperturbable, and with his instinct for organization intact he prepared to continue the war and simultaneously to govern Peru. Institutions as well as strategies were now his concern.

CHAPTER 7

Monarchist in a World of Republics

The Protectorate

The independence of Peru was declared on 28 July 1821, and on 3 August San Martín became Protector with supreme civil and military power.[1] He explained his position in a proclamation that left no room for dissent and no ambiguity:

> Since my arrival in Pisco I announced that by the rule of circumstances I had been invested with supreme authority and was responsible to the patria for its exercise. Those circumstances have not changed, for there are still external enemies to fight in Peru; and therefore it is necessary that I continue to possess political and military authority.
>
> I hope that in taking this step my motives will be justly attributed not to ambition but only to concern for the public good. It is well known that all I want is tranquility and retirement after so agitated a life; but I have a moral responsibility to sacrifice my most fervent desires. The history of ten years of revolution in Venezuela, Cundinamarca, Chile, and the United Provinces of the Río de la Plata has convinced me of the evils occasioned by the untimely calling of congresses, while the enemies were still at large in those countries. The first step is to ensure independence, and then to think of establishing a stable liberty. The scrupulousness with which I have kept my word in the course of my public life entitles me to be believed; and I solemnly undertake to the peoples of Peru that at the very moment in which their territory is free, I will relinquish my command to make way for the government which they prefer to choose. When I have the satisfaction of resigning my command and giving an account of my administration to the representatives

of the people, I am sure that they will not find during my administration any of those marks of venality, despotism and corruption that have characterized the agents of Spanish government in America.[2]

For the next year San Martín ruled as Protector, in the belief that 'the rule of circumstances' gave him political and military authority, and that independence came before constitutions. He took up residence in Pezuela's former country house at La Magdalena about five miles from Lima; there he had his offices and transacted affairs of state, commuting when necessary to Government House in Lima; he received a salary of thirty thousand pesos. He appointed ministers to decide and administer policy under his direction. Juan García del Río became minister of foreign affairs, Bernardo Monteagudo defence minister and Hipólito Unanue minister of finance. Monteagudo, who revelled in controversy, gave the government a high profile. But Unanue was a more significant appointment, an enlightened official who abandoned royalism to serve the new state, moved by a genuine change of mind and a conviction perhaps that there was a vein of continuity between the viceroyalty and the republic. Unanue was the inclusive face of the Protectorate.[3] A new creation, the Supreme Court of Justice, exercised the judicial power, while a future Congress would consider laws and the preparation of the first constitution. Command of the liberating army was delegated to General Las Heras, who swore to obey the Protectorate government as long as it did not conflict with the obedience the soldiers owed to their own national governments.

García del Río was Colombian, Unanue Peruvian, Monteagudo was Argentine, as was Las Heras. So foreigners dominated San Martín's government, a reflection of his Americanism and relative indifference towards Peruvian nationalism. And he immediately launched a substantial reform programme in favour of slaves and Indians, with implications for the Peruvian elite.[4] San Martín had a project for Peru, derived not from a reactionary conservatism but from the enlightened reformism that imbued his political and social thinking. The framework for his project would be a strong constitution, the leaders would be an aristocracy of merit, and the beneficiaries the poor and dispossessed among those who had become the marginal peoples of Peru. And a Peruvian army and navy, the creation of which San Martín treated as his personal responsibility, guaranteed the power of the new state.

The reverse side of San Martín's proposals for Peruvians was his policy towards Spaniards, who had always had a substantial presence in Peru and whose fate at independence historians have seen as a stain on his government. He gave a reasonable explanation for the initial confinement of Spanish civilians in the La Merced convent in September 1821, when Canterac was drawing close to Lima: it was for their own safety and to prevent them collaborating with the enemy, and

he ordered their release on 18 September. The situation of the European
Spaniards in Lima was precarious, as Commodore Sir Thomas Hardy reported:

> The European Spaniards, about 1,300 in number, were shut up in La
> Merced convent, as much for their own safety as to prevent their forming
> any plans against the patriots. On Friday the 7th the royalists came within
> sight of the patriot army, and an action was expected every hour. The black
> population and lower orders assembled in the plaza and demanded the lives
> of the Spaniards confined in the convent, and it was with the greatest diffi-
> culty a few patriot officers prevented them carrying out their horrid design
> into execution. The city, the whole day, was in a most miserable state. The
> native clergy, even the women and everyone who could get a sword or a
> knife were swarming about the streets vowing vengeance against the
> European Spaniards.[5]

Later in 1821, however, the *Gaceta del Gobierno*, the government newspaper,
began justifying the use of force, and in the hands of Monteagudo the policy of
San Martín towards Spaniards was soon seen as persecution. But the policy was
regarded by the government as a vital defence measure against the large presence of Spaniards in Lima and the possibility of counter-revolution. The first
line of defence was popular mobilization, and there was a campaign to recruit
the urban populace and the slave population into militia units where they
would be given rudimentary training in the use of arms, and indoctrination in
revolutionary ideology. These *cuerpos cívicos* as they were called were described
as 'the shield of public liberty', and were regarded as a kind of home guard
defending the streets while the army fought the royalists in the trenches.[6]

The organization of popular militias was a sign of the government's nervousness and realization that independence was only half won. It was
Monteagudo's conviction that the Spaniards had to be eliminated and he made
no apologies for it:

> I employed all the means in my power to inflame hatred against the
> Spaniards: I prompted measures of severity, and I was always ready to
> support those who wanted to reduce their number and weaken their public
> and private influence. This was my system, and it was not simply prejudice.

There was no personal animosity, he claimed. After all he did not know them,
and Spaniards had eminent qualities that deserved respect. But it was necessary to reduce their numbers, from ten thousand to six thousand: 'This is to
make revolution, because to think that you can establish a new order of things
with the same elements that oppose it is fantasy.'[7]

This was the hard dilemma facing all revolutionaries throughout South America. History had shown that where the counter-revolution prevailed, in Venezuela, Colombia and Chile, royalists were not compassionate and Spaniards killed Americans, forcing them into conformity. In Peru the Protectorate forced its opponents out and into exile. In January 1822 all unmarried Spaniards were ordered to leave the country and to forfeit half their property; and within a few months this policy was extended to married Spaniards and confiscation to the full amount of property.[8] On the remainder a curfew was reimposed and other restrictions on movement and activities enforced. Even the Church was investigated in pursuit of counter-revolutionary clergy, and the campaign against the eighty-year-old Archbishop Bartolomé de Las Heras became notorious. Harassed by the government into resignation, he was ordered out of Lima to await transport to Spain.

Spaniards were thus forcibly expelled. 'The large number of peninsulares in this capital, at a time when the Spanish army is making efforts to invade it with their possible cooperation, obliges the government to order their expulsion to Chile.'[9] Restrictions on Spaniards were tightened further in April 1822 after the defeat of the patriot forces commanded by Domingo Tristan at Ica south of Lima, a clear demonstration of the influence of military weakness on security policy. On 2 May government troops surrounded the houses of the remaining Spaniards in Lima at 3 o'clock in the morning, ejected them from their beds, arrested some six hundred of the men, and herded them, stripped of their possessions, towards Callao, young and old, sick and infirm, for deportation to Chile.[10] As the refugees entered the squalid port of Callao they passed other victims of independence, corpses of troops killed in the recent fighting and left unburied to rot on the ground, picked at by attendant vultures. The Protectorate did not bring universal enlightenment to Peru. According to contemporary estimates, in a population fewer than eighty thousand, between ten and twelve thousand peninsular Spaniards were forced out of Peru in the years 1821–4.[11]

Contemporaries were not slow to attribute the hard line to the baleful influence of Monteagudo, the Protector's closest political associate and effectively prime minister. 'The whole of these arbitrary measures were carried into effect during the nominal administration of Torre Tagle; and it was generally believed, that their offensive and cruel execution originated with the prime minister, the Argentinian Monteagudo', whose extremist record and monarchist bias were driven by an urge to despotism.[12] This was the view of Basil Hall of the Royal Navy. Another English observer, Gilbert Mathison, who otherwise found Monteagudo civil, clever, fond of power and a speaker of good English, also reported that under the name of liberty and patriotism the government exercised despotic power and was obeyed more from fear than from respect. A complete espionage system was maintained, he added, and in place of talking freely about politics in a republican spirit the greatest caution and reserve were maintained everywhere, and liberty of thought and word which the patriots had proclaimed was observed only in name.[13] In spite of his political ability and intellectual qualities, Monteagudo became a liability to the patriot government and unpopular with Peruvians. While San Martín was in Guayaquil in July 1822 he delegated authority to Torre Tagle as his 'supreme delegate'. Torre Tagle, a Peruvian aristocrat who had administered Trujillo effectively now made his mark in Lima. He responded to public opinion and removed Monteagudo from office and from Lima. He rashly returned later and was assassinated in 1825.

San Martín himself, of course, was no friend of Spaniards. Basil Hall admitted that although the persecution of Spaniards was largely Monteagudo's responsibility, San Martín still had to bear the ultimate blame: 'It will not avail San Martín's friends to say they were the acts of another, for he was notoriously the main-spring of the whole government.'[14] San Martín's predicament was that the Peruvian elite, *peninsulares* and creoles alike had long been united by solidarity against the popular sectors and loyalty towards Spain. Society was dominated by linked groups of landed, merchant, municipal and bureaucratic oligarchies, in which *peninsulares* and creoles merged as a white ruling class.

In advance of his expedition San Martín, like many other liberators, assumed too readily that there was historic conflict of interest in Peru between Spaniards and Peruvians. But Peruvian creoles were just as committed to their own interests as were the royalists, and in some cases they saw these interests threatened not by Spain but by social change in the wake of the liberating army. Independence did not satisfy their immediate or long-term concerns. Gilbert Mathison saw the Lima elite in April and May 1822 as disaffected: 'Nearly all the inhabitants have been more or less injured in their fortunes, and it cannot appear a surprising fact that the government which occasioned their misfortunes and that was unable to alleviate, if not remove them, should be unpopular, or have lost the transient popularity acquired by the first burst of success.'[15] He noted that the number of those who had been financially ruined was high and included not only Spaniards but all those creoles who had been clients or dependents of the Spaniards, a fact that the government had not appreciated. There was no easy solution for San Martín, but he seems to have missed the opportunity to assimilate Spaniards who could have been useful to his regime; in the process he deprived himself of a vibrant commercial and financial community, and the Protectorate lost a vital economic infrastructure.

These were government decisions narrowly based, for San Martín's writ did not run in the interior, and outside of Lima and the coast the war had not been won. And he cultivated some ex-royalists, if he thought that their presence proved his concept of revolution by persuasion. In early 1822 he sent an expedition to the valley of Ica, commanded by upper-class Peruvians, General Domingo Tristán and Colonel Agustín Gamarra; their role was to hold ground at Ica against Canterac and at the same time Peruvianize the revolution, but they were incapable of doing either. Tristán in particular was well known for his incompetence and disloyalty in Upper Peru, and especially in Arequipa from where he came. In a rapid forced march of two hundred and fifty leagues Canterac moved his division of three thousand men from Jauja and at dawn on 7 April 1822 took Tristán by surprise in the hacienda of Macacona, winning a decisive victory and taking one thousand prisoners, four pieces of artillery, and a great number of horses and mules, and 'abusing their victory with their usual cruelties'.[16] Defeat at Ica was a blow to the morale as well as the resistance of the patriots, for this was a pitched battle, one of the first that San Martín's men had attempted, and it confirmed his suspicion that his army was inadequate for the task, at a time when the Colombian army under the leadership of the Bolivarian general, José Antonio de Sucre, was about to win a decisive victory at Pichincha (24 May 1822). It added to the criticism of the Liberator and doubts as to his judgement in appointing Tristan because he was a man of rank, and it caused a number of his officers to rethink their positions. 'The moral effect', wrote Miller, 'was to dispel the idea, which until then had been entertained, of the superiority of the patriots, and to throw a damp over the mass of the population. . . . Union was restored in the royalist council, whilst the patriots were distracted by dissensions, and weakened by insubordination.' Even Miller, normally supportive of San Martín, thought that he had abandoned his usual sense of judgement on this occasion, in 'the misplaced hope that promotion and commands bestowed on men of rank, who passed over to the patriot cause, would encourage other influential people to follow their example, and thus in the end attach all the country to the cause of independence, and settle the question *without bloodshed*; a benevolent motive, but the source of incalculable mischief.'[17]

It was clear that a final campaign was no nearer and Peru remained divided between the independists who held command in the north, the capital and part of the central zone, and the royalists who occupied all of the sierra, the south of the country and Upper Peru. La Serna established his headquarters in Cuzco and converted the former imperial capital of the Incas into the last viceregal capital of Peru. He enjoyed some support from the regional elite who had long aspired to free themselves from the authority of Lima. Otherwise, Cuzco paid dearly for its new status, as it was forced to provide money and soldiers for the royalist cause and its economy suffered from becoming a war zone, in which royal army and rebel insurgents fought intermittently for resources.[18] So a stalemate was established, costly to Peruvians, who saw independence and its

leaders as liabilities, unable to bring the war to an end. San Martín needed reinforcements, but could expect none from Chile or Argentina. He had already
begun to look north. In February 1822 a force of some one thousand men
under the command of Colonel Andrés Santa Cruz, a mestizo from Upper Peru
who had fought for Spain before he fought for independence, joined the army
of General Sucre, in his campaign towards Quito. This expeditionary force,
which played a significant role in the battle of Pichincha, was expected to earn
not only reward from the northern liberators but also respect for Peruvian
territorial claims to Guayaquil.

Guerrilla War in the Highlands

If San Martín was losing credit among Peruvians, the Spaniards too were
squandering their assets by their brutality and terrorism in the interior.
Patriots were shot and property was confiscated at the caprice of commanding
officers. The people of Ica had to endure the sadistic rule of Colonel Santalla,
whose circular order dated 19 July 1821 declared: 'The landed proprietors of
this valley will deliver up three hundred horses and mules at the house of the
Marques of Campo Ameno, within the peremptory and precise time of *four
hours*, taking them from any person who may have them, without any exception whatever; it being understood that, in failure herof within the said term,
the defaulters will be immediately shot, their houses pillaged and burned,
their estates ravaged, and their families put to the sword.'[19] The town of
Cangallo near Huamanga east of Ica was burnt to the ground; the viceroy
issued a decree (11 January 1822) that the walls of the houses should be
destroyed and that the name of Cangallo should henceforth disappear from
the map. Many other villages and estates in the vicinity of Tarma were victims
of Spanish incendiarism. Thus in Peru, as elsewhere, the Spaniards were
the worst enemies of the Spanish cause. Their savage and costly counter-
revolution increased the revulsion against imperial rule and strengthened the
case for the patriots. When these were able to impose sufficient power and
security, then property owners would openly declare themselves and thus
Peruvian resistance never died.

The *montoneros*, the guerrilla bands operating in central Peru between 1821
and 1824, were not Indian irregulars or populist forces. 'The montoneros of
central Peru represented a variety of interests. Popular causes? Up to a point.
Indians? In some cases. Independence? Perhaps.'[20] Some of the leaders were
creoles and mestizos of middle rank and modest fortune, whose property and
families had suffered at the hands of royalists and who then sought
vengeance.[21] Others were genuinely populist, seeking advantage for their
communities and their right to participate or not participate. Others were

Indian *kurakas*, moved by a mixture of personal and communal motives, and not normally friendly towards whites of any political persuasion. The *guerrilleros* were joined inevitably by vagrants and delinquents, by bandit chiefs and their followers such as those of the notorious Quirós, 'wearing long beards and dressed in the most grotesque manner', who used guerrilla operations as a means of personal plunder, murder and rape.[22] Guerrilla leaders sometimes imposed forced conscription in the zones of their command, partly to overcome the reluctance of *hacendados* to release their workers, partly to forestall recruitment by royalists. To conscript was not to disavow their popular base but rather another sign that both sides competed keenly for popular and Indian support.

In spite of their disparate composition and motives, the *montoneros* played a special part in the patriot war effort, when they could be persuaded to collaborate. Until mid-1821 they attacked communications between the interior and the coast, cutting supply lines into the capital. During the retreat of the royalists from Lima in July 1821 the *montoneros* were well placed to harass the enemy and cut off stragglers. It was San Martín's failure to second their efforts that perhaps lost him the chance to hasten the end of the war, as William Miller hinted:

> If the liberating army, instead of going, as it did, into cantonments in the dissipated city of Lima, had seconded the efforts of those armed patriotic bands, it can hardly be doubted that the war would have terminated in a very few weeks: whereas, for want of timely energy, unhappy Peru continued to suffer, and her capital and provinces were alternately in the hands of the friends and foes to freedom.[23]

Rather than directly criticize his hero, Colonel Miller preferred to spread the blame for inertia to the army as a whole. But San Martín cast a military eye on the guerrillas and decided, probably correctly, that they were a useful ally and valuable support for the army of the line but did not make a critical difference to his war effort. This is not to say that he discounted their contribution to his general strategy. He had always maintained that this was not an exclusively conventional war but was also a *guerra de recursos*, in which bands of irregular fighters under chiefs who knew the local terrain would harass the enemy, deny him resources and gather intelligence.[24] Beyond that there was a query over their commitment to the cause.

Operating in bands of fifty to a hundred each, most of them from a base in the town of Reyes (Huancavelica), the *montoneros* maintained guerrilla operations in the region between the central sierra and the coast, attacking and disappearing, preying on royalist communications and keeping the army under Canterac constantly on the alert. This was a Peruvian contribution to the war of independence, led by such men as Francisco Vidal, Ignacio Ninavilca, Gaspar Huavique and the Argentine officer Isidoro Villar, whom San Martín made commander-in-chief of the guerrillas of the sierra. But their contribution could not be decisive. They themselves lacked cohesion; interest and motivation differed widely between men and between groups. Ninavilca complained that 'all the commanders of guerrilla bands give themselves rank and recognize no superior chief', and the guerrillas themselves frequently complained of the lack of a single command for all the irregular forces.[25] Some communities in guerrilla territory refused to support the cause of independence. Many guerrillas were in the war solely for plunder. Others were forced into collaboration with the enemy in order to protect the lives of their families or neighbours. And dissension between guerrilla chiefs or between these and patriot officers often arose out of regional, racial and political rivalries. Some of the Argentine and Colombian military referred to the Peruvians contemptuously as *cholos, indios,* or *peruleros.* The fact remained that Indian suspicion of whites went too deep to transform popular guerrillas into instant patriots.[26]

Guerrillas as well as armies made demands on resources. The Peruvian economy could not be totally geared towards the war effort. Military operations damaged the economy of the central zone, at a time when the people had to provide recruits and supplies for the guerrillas and the patriot army. The destruction of the Spanish elite also damaged the economy; in punishing Spaniards and confiscating their businesses and haciendas, San Martín cut off some of his own resources. The revenue of the patriots at the beginning of the war was minute. When they entered Lima there was not a peso in the treasury. The mines were either occupied by the enemy or making a loss. Commerce and industrial activities had been hit by the siege imposed on the capital. So the government had recourse to forced loans, especially from Spaniards but also from foreign merchants. In 1822 a group of English merchants, including John Parish Robertson, were forced to make a loan of seventy-three thousand pesos, repayable on the customs but without interest.[27] Taxes, loans and confiscations gave the government a revenue of 2.8 million pesos in the period 1 August 1821 to 31 July 1822. But this fell far short of expenditure, and to some extent the patriot forces had to live off the land. Economic help from the towns and villages for the patriot cause began with the first expedition of General Arenales to the central sierra in 1820 and continued during the second expedition in 1821. But cooperation was not always forthcoming, and some areas resented the army's demands for cattle, foodstuffs and personnel, and communities caught in the ebb and flow of the campaign saw each army as alternative scourges on the people.

The *reglamento provisional de comercio* (28 September 1821) provided for freedom of trade and suppressed interior customs; but it placed a protective tariff (20 per cent) on imports in order to help local industries.[28] Notoriously the war dislocated trade and reduced production, while it also disrupted communications. The ranchers of Cajatambo, Huamalíes, Junín and other areas of the central sierra were ruined through lack of buyers; the farmers of Conchucas, Huánuco and Huaylas were deprived of transport (mules and muleteers) to take their products to the consumer markets, while demand itself was suffering. The mines had entered a period of rapid decline. Operations were disrupted by the flight of proprietors, technicians, labour and capital, by the shortage and cost of mercury, and by the devastation of the mining support regions. When the patriots took possession from the royalists they strove to increase output, and the silver mines of Cerro de Pasco northeast of Lima were one of the few sources of revenue that they possessed; but these were still vulnerable to royalist attack and plunder.

Economic disorder and the flight of private capital—exported sometimes with the collaboration of the British navy—led the minister of finance, Hipólito Unanue, to create a bank to issue paper money. The Banco Auxiliar was established in 1821 to provide finance for the war effort and for the new administration at a time when the patriots found it almost impossible to impose new taxes or increase old ones; a further function was to supply a circulating medium in paper money to compensate for lack of silver.[29] But the paper issue had no backing and was distrusted by the public, which was also coming to suspect San Martín's financial competence; the government itself, in a supreme understatement, admitted in the official *Gaceta del Gobierno* that paper money 'has given us some small discomfort, but we issue it willingly, for it is a means of destroying the Spaniards.'[30] In August 1822 the government ordered the withdrawal of the paper money. But this development could not disguise the fact that many Peruvians expected immediate returns from independence without investing in it, and that the Protectorate rested on fragile economic foundations.

The Lure of Monarchy

In spite of doubts, criticisms, desertions and betrayals, the Protector stuck to his course, determined to rule according to enlightened principles, to create a Peru free from conflict and free from crime. Although the Protectorate gave him military and political command, and with it legislative and executive power, he decided to subject himself to the Provisional Statute of 8 October 1821 to be effective until the whole of Peru declared for independence, when a general congress would be convoked.[31] He eschewed theory and discourse, and preferred a pragmatic approach to civil rights:

Convinced that to have a multiplicity of worthy principles is not the best
way of realizing them, I have preferred to limit myself to a number of practical ideas which can be more readily achieved. While enemies are still at
large in the country, and until the people are capable of forming the basic
ideas of government for themselves, I will administer the governing power
of the state, whose qualities, without being the same, are analogous to those
of the legislative and executive power. But I will refrain from ever inter-
fering with the solemn exercise of the judicial power, whose independence
is the only true safeguard for the liberty of the people.

The statute guaranteed some of the basic freedoms of the people, the press
and the municipalities, the latter being based on popular suffrage, as well as
trial by jury, and an independent judicial authority. San Martín also created a
council of state with a consultative function composed of twelve members,
including the three government ministers and four *títulos de Castilla,* now to
be called *del Perú.* This was, in short, a hierarchical and aristocratic corpora-
tion, appropriate for a monarchy, which San Martín was convinced would
appeal to many upper-class Peruvians who valued privilege and distinctions
above republican virtues. In fact the framework of traditional nobility was
maintained though it was accompanied by two pillars of what could be
regarded as a service nobility, more in keeping with a modern monarchy.

In October 1821 San Martín established a new honour, the Order of the
Sun, modelled upon the Legion of Honour in France, with pensions attached
to first-class membership. Commodore Hardy attended the installation at the
invitation of San Martín: 'The ceremony was exceedingly well-conducted and
appeared to have given general satisfaction.... There was nothing in the
whole proceeding indicative of a republican spirit . . . and it is most evident
that a monarchical government is best-suited to the habits and desires of these
people, of which I doubt not General San Martín will take advantage.'[32] Later,
on 21 January 1822, San Martín founded an honour for women who were
noted for their dedication to the cause of independence, the *Caballeresa del Sol*
(Dame of the Order of the Sun), awarded more as a courtesy than for actual
services, but it was valued by those who received it, 145 in all including the
good and the not so good; and their immediate families were favoured in
applications for official posts. Rosa Campusano was honoured and so was her
friend, Manuela Sáenz, soon to become Bolívar's mistress. The decree of
11 January announcing the order explained 'The most sensitive sex naturally
ought to be the most patriotic: the tender character of their social relations,
linking them closely to their country of birth, doubly predisposes all their
feelings towards it.'[33] Meanwhile, senior army officers were also rewarded. On
19 December 1821 property valued at five hundred thousand dollars was

granted to twenty general and field officers of the liberating army as a reward for past services, and was equally divided among them.[34]

The second pillar of a projected monarchy and further encouragement for an elite that should serve the state was the creation of the Sociedad Patriótica de Lima, a cultural institution, where the great and the good, or forty of them, could assemble and debate and glorify the regime.[35] They were given a wide agenda for discussion, 'all questions bearing directly or indirectly on the public good', and focusing first on the form of government that Peru should have: a constitutional monarchy or a republic? Monteagudo, leading those who argued for monarchy, based his case on the failure of republican experiments in South America and the capacity of monarchy to offer freedom and order, while respecting the division of powers between the executive (the monarch), the legislative and the judiciary. He insisted that such a monarchy would protect the liberties of the citizens against the abuses of the state and grant them free conditions for participating in politics, avoiding the arbitrary results of elections.

In the first years of his political career in Argentina, Monteagudo had been a radical firebrand, who had denounced what he called 'the crime of lenience', than which nothing was more prejudicial to the revolution.[36] He now claimed to have abandoned his early bias towards extreme democracy as a mental aberration. In fact his 'democracy' had never been so extreme as to include the popular sectors or those who were illiterate.[37] He still considered himself a liberal but one taught by experience of the need for limitations on liberty. He was dismissive of any 'general notions of the rights of man' and of absolute equality, concepts that few Americans understood. The social basis of his argument was that Peruvians, conditioned by the colonial system, could not aspire to democracy because of their hierarchical traditions, deference to authority, lack of education, maldistribution of wealth and social structure. Peru needed strong government to avoid anarchy and to provide guidance between extremes. The best form of government would be a constitutional monarchy, and the best example of this was the English Constitution because it preserved order as well as liberty.[38]

These ideas did not appeal to everyone and were challenged by republican intellectuals, who were just as conscious of the colonial legacy as Monteagudo but drew different conclusions. Although they were not well represented in the Patriotic Society they had an outlet in the periodical press and a public among liberal thinkers. José Faustino Sánchez Carrión, one of the leading theoreticians of independence and a future government minister, drawing inspiration from Locke and Rousseau, based his political ideas on republican foundations of popular sovereignty and representative government. He argued for liberty and equality, which he believed would be denied by monarchy and replaced by absolutism and inequality.[39] He insisted that the colonial mentality that still prevailed among many Peruvians would quickly reduce a new monarchy to an absolute monarchy.[40] Between them the Patriotic Society and the liberal press maintained an active political debate in Peru, even while royalist forces were still at large, and left a legacy of freedom of speech not usually associated with San Martín and the Protectorate.[41]

San Martín himself lived in a style appropriate to a head of state, dressed in a splendid new uniform embroidered in gold leaf, and surrounded in public by his Protector's guard as he moved through the streets of central Lima. At weekends a state coach transported him from La Magdalena to Lima, where he held receptions and parties and was a graceful presence on the dance floor. He was accompanied on occasion by Rosita Campusano, *guayaquileña* by birth and Peruvian by acclaim, nicknamed 'la Protectora' in popular talk, who was said to serve him from her salon as an informant and intelligence agent. Was she 'the beautiful young woman' whom Captain Basil Hall had noticed on the Liberator's entry into Lima pushing her way through the crowd and throwing herself into his arms murmuring *Oh, mi General!*, and whom San Martín had kissed before letting her go, overwhelmed by her hero?[42] Who knows? And who can decide whether she was really his lover or simply an excuse for scandal in this gossiping society? The historian Germán Leguía y Martínez, whose account of the Protectorate exudes Peruvian patriotism with little concession to San Martín, has no doubt that their relationship was serious, and that the Liberator, overcome by 'a mad passion for the Campusano', was a lucky man to gain the love of this Peruvian beauty, 'an irresistible woman, captivated by the leader from Yapeyú, who could inspire him with a lasting, deep, and fervent passion, at once sweet and harmful to the heart of the great liberator of the south.'[43] Yet little hard evidence for these romantic assertions emerges from the seven volumes of Leguía y Martínez, and the story looks suspiciously like folklore transmitted by the traditionalist Ricardo Palma and perpetuated by novelists who, amidst the paraphernalia of the revolution, create fables for want of documents.

San Martín did not change, though circumstances around him were changing. Did the style of the Protector lower his image and encourage speculation that he planned to make himself king of Peru? Only in the eyes of the envious and the minds of his political enemies. In reality, as William Miller declared, 'he never entertained the remotest idea of placing a crown upon his own head.'[44] He was rarely in robust health in these days, though observers describe a man who bore himself well. His English friends were invariably impressed. William Miller observed, 'The person of San Martín is tall and full-formed. He has a dark attractive countenance, with black, expressive, and penetrating eyes. His manners are dignified, easy, friendly, eminently frank, and prepossessing. His conversation is lively, and that of a man of the world.'[45]

Basil Hall, to whom San Martín revealed his political thinking on liberation, left a description of him on 25 June 1821. He received his guests on board his schooner, simply dressed in a loose coat and large fur cap, seated at a table made from wooden planks placed over some empty barrels. At first sight there was little that was striking about General San Martín's appearance, but when he stood up and began to speak his superiority was evident:

> He is a tall, erect, well proportioned, handsome man, with a large aquiline nose, thick black hair, and immense bushy dark whiskers extending from ear to ear under the chin; his complexion is deep olive, and his eyes, which are large, prominent, and piercing, are jet black; his whole appearance being highly military. He is thoroughly well bred and unaffectedly simple in his manners; exceedingly cordial and engaging and possessed evidently of great kindliness of disposition: in short, I have never seen any person the enchantment of whose address was more irresistible. In conversation he went at once to the strong points of the topic, disdaining, as it were, to trifle with its minor parts: he listened earnestly, and replied with distinctness and fairness, showing wonderful resources in argument.[46]

Both these descriptions are consistent with the portraits painted by contemporary artists such as Gil de Castro and Mariano Carrillo, who show him as an upright soldier with a steady gaze and calm demeanour, with his curved sabre at hand and an inkstand nearby, the two articles essential for a liberator and legislator.

The young Argentine officer, Juan Isidro Quesada, who caught up with the Army of the Andes in Peru, was enthralled by the sociability of San Martín outside the barracks, and his ability to pass from disciplinarian to companion when the occasion required. He was a guest at one of the Protector's dinners in the viceregal palace in Lima:

> There were twenty-five of us at the table, ministers, aides, officers, and others. . . . There seemed to be no distinctions of rank and we were all equal, with junior officers expressing their ideas as much as the General. Yet at the same time no one dared to exceed the limits of respect that we all owed to each other. . . . Everything written about the despotism of General San Martín is false. . . . I was only 19 when I served under him as lieutenant and captain, and I never noticed him cast a single intemperate word towards his subordinates. On the contrary he treated young officers with affection and respect.[47]

San Martín was a monarchist: that was one of his defining principles, a source of his revolutionary pride, not of shame. Monarchy would be the vehicle of his project for Peru. A contrast is often made between the monarchism of San Martín and the republicanism of Simón Bolívar. But the difference tends to be overstated. Although the political thought of the two liberators was expressed in different terms, there was a striking resemblance in their basic ideas. Both began with similar republican ideals. But these were eroded by circumstances. In the last years of his life Bolívar was haunted by the anarchy of the new states and obsessed by their need for strong government. His Bolivian Constitution, written some years after San Martín's reflections on monarchy, provided for a life president with the right to choose his successor, which he regarded as an essential antidote to chaos. San Martín had already learnt this lesson. His political thought was always finely poised between a preference for absolute power and a deference towards liberal ideals. Maria Graham, the English visitor to Chile who met him there in 1822 after his resignation as Protector of Peru, was not sensitive to the nuances and thought he was vacillating, unable to decide between liberty and despotism, between his reputation and his power.[48]

San Martín's political thought bore some traces of his origins and formation. He had grown up and served under an absolute monarchy; from it he learnt to respect continuity, stability and resistance to enemies. He had various objections to the Bourbon state but its record on law and order was not one of them. The mob appalled him and his instinct was to repress it, as he yearned to do in Cádiz in 1808 when his friend Solano was killed by rioters. In addition to experience, he also drew on his reading in the thought of the Enlightenment, and this could lead to a crossroads. Conservative or liberal? He had no time for absolute liberalism or federalism. From his library we can deduce that he had studied the history of the French Revolution and the Napoleonic age, and knew the hazards of the routes to democracy and dictatorship. A strong central state was his ideal but not one left to its own devices.

There is no evidence that San Martín owed his monarchical tendencies to his contacts with British sources and friends. The basic explanation of his monarchism stemmed more from American conditions than foreign influences. As he himself explained, his ideal was a republican government, but experience demonstrated that in Spanish America this was not feasible, because republicanism fostered anarchy, which in turn led to the despotism of a tyrant; moreover republicanism encouraged localist and divisive forces which would impede the war and damage the postwar settlement.[49] The lesson began soon after his return to Buenos Aires in 1812; his preference for monarchy was confirmed by the spectacle of anarchy in the Río de la Plata and by the hitherto fruitless search for unity and stability. He held a pessimistic view of human nature, its ignorance, its proneness to factionalism and violence unless restrained by strong rule, characteristics that were aggravated in the Americas by lack of any traditions of self-government and the ruthless search for power by the new politicians.[50]

The monarchy that San Martín sought, therefore, was not a decentralized or powerless figurehead, and was a 'constitutional monarchy' only in the sense that it existed alongside legislative and judicial powers which might restrain but not prevent the actions of the royal executive. His prime object was to concentrate authority and avoid disunion, the reverse of republicanism, which would encourage localist interests and forces opposed to the strenuous prosecution of the war and then of peace. San Martín's conversion to monarchy began in Argentina. In 1816 he even gave his support to the exotic ideas presented by Belgrano at the Congress of Tucumán, to crown a descendant of the Incas to form a moderate monarchy. San Martín reacted favourably to the idea, as long as it was not a regency of a number of people. 'In effect we simply need to change the name of our director to Regent. This could be the route to our salvation.'[51] For San Martín, therefore, the form of government was secondary to concentration of authority, as long as it avoided a republic.

San Martín equated republicanism with popular government, which was anathema to him. He declared himself 'a republican American from principles and inclination, but one who sacrifices these in the interests of his country.' He went on to explain that 'Americans have had no other object in their revolution than emancipation from the iron rule of Spain and to become a nation.' How, he asked, can we be a republic when we have no arts, sciences, or agriculture, and when most of our territory is a desert without population? An uneducated and uncultivated people would welcome 'a purely popular system of government'. But this would be unprincipled and have a tendency to destroy our religion. Uncontrolled passion setting provinces against provinces, towns against towns and people against people cannot be said to constitute a nation. 'We have had six years of revolution and victorious enemies oppress us on all sides; lack of military leaders and our own disunion are the reasons. And they could be remedied!'[52] So a republic was not suitable for union, nor was the social state of the people appropriate for such a system of government. These were the convictions of San Martín, fruit of early exposure to Spanish culture and subsequent experience in the Americas. In the course of 1817–18 his ideas matured, and he concluded that Chile was more suited to a monarchical than a republican form of government. To his friend the earl of Fife he argued that revolution and war had induced a yearning for peace, stability and firm government, and democratic ideas had lost their appeal among 90 per cent of leading men in Chile and Argentina.[53] Yet there was scant evidence that monarchy appealed to majorities in these countries, least of all in the implausible persons of the European princes nominated by the Liberator.

Peru, on the other hand, appeared particularly suitable for monarchy, and San Martín was ready to negotiate with the royalists on that assumption. A gem of the Spanish monarchy, with a long viceregal history and a society to match, each rank in its social hierarchy defined by its role in the colonial state, Peru seemed ready for a new Crown. At Miraflores, in September 1820, according to James Paroissien, 'the general has proposed to the Viceroy to allow the Peruvians free and complete liberty to elect the form of Government they please, even if they should wish to crown a King of the Spanish Branch of the Bourbons.'[54] Freedom, however, was not in the viceroy's gift. In June 1821 at Punchauca, before he had won a decisive victory, San Martín again proposed that Peru should be erected into an independent and constitutional monarchy under a prince of the Spanish royal house; until the prince arrived a regency should rule under the presidency of the viceroy. Although the Spanish monarchy in the peninsula might itself succumb to absolutism, he argued, this was no reason why America should follow the same example: 'the liberals of the world are brothers everywhere.'[55] But the plan was unworkable as the viceroy could not guarantee independence and San Martín would accept nothing less. Years later he claimed that he knew Madrid would never accept these terms and he negotiated simply to lure the Spanish commanders into recognizing the independence of Peru. But the terms bear the stamp of San Martín's political thinking and his known preference for monarchy. Ironically for so convinced a monarchist, when San Martín became Protector of Peru uniting in his own person both civil and military powers, one of his models, at least in 'his good points', was another soldier turned Protector, Oliver Cromwell.[56]

Punchauca did not represent the end of San Martín's monarchism. In late 1821 he sent Juan García del Río and James Paroissien to Europe to secure recognition of Peruvian independence, alliance with a European power and a prince.[57] One of the names proposed as emperor of Peru was the duke of Sussex, son of George III. The two commissioners raised no interest or support in Santiago and Buenos Aires, and by the time they began negotiations in England in the summer of 1822 San Martín had already resigned. No doubt the monarchism of San Martín, which Leguía y Martínez describes as *monarco-manía*, was strengthened in Peru not only by political conditions and social structure in that divided country but also by the influence of his combative collaborator Monteagudo, who had undergone a dramatic conversion from advocate of extreme democracy to promoter of ideas of monarchy. 'Of course in this, as in other faults in his life and his record, hidden behind him is Monteagudo, sinister inspirer and satanic tempter.'[58] But San Martín's defence of monarchy outlived his experience in Peru, and nothing that he learnt of Latin America during years of exile changed his view, that the ideal form of government was a constitutional monarchy and a liberal administration. He seems not to have considered that monarchy usually came with a price attached: hereditary succession. This was something that republicans did not overlook. Yet in spite of all he was a liberator first, a monarchist second.

San Martín's political thinking was moved primarily by the desire to avoid social upheaval and a drift into anarchy. He was not alone in these forebodings. Bolívar too feared social conflict and the possibility of race war; his ideal ruler was really a king with the name of president. In his career through the revolution, San Martín was influenced first by the Río de la Plata; he hated the political anarchy of his own country which threatened the stability of independence. In his view too much liberty and liberalism were undermining the gains so far made, and the revolution needed a firm hand. What use are theories of liberty, individual security, liberty of the press and all the rest when the military leadership needed more money to enforce policy and pay soldiers? These political advantages are reserved for more advanced societies, not for those that do not even know how to read and write. He was convinced that even Cuyo, so vital to the advance of the revolution, would be in chaos were it not for him. These very conservative political views were the same as those adopted later by the Congress of Tucumán, which sanctioned a law suspending individual rights that conflicted with the law of the revolution and the need for order. His political principles remained consistent and he never abandoned his distrust of absolute liberalism. You know me, he wrote to his friend Tomás Guido:

> For the five years you were at my side you more than anyone must have been aware of my hatred of everything associated with wealth and distinctions, of everything in short that is aristocracy. By inclination and principles I love republican government, and no one more than me. But my personal preference has not prevented me from seeing that this form of government is not attainable in America, and can lead only to terrible anarchy, and experience shows that this leads to the tyranny of a despot.[59]

The same thinking made him hostile to the growing federalist tendency in Argentina, as the provinces claimed independence of the central government. This he regarded as 'anarchy':

> Federation, it kills me every time I hear the word. Would it not be more convenient simply to transfer the capital to some other place and thus remove the legitimate complaints of the provinces? But federation! And it is so obvious! If in a government of a civilized country, well populated and advanced in the arts, agriculture, and commerce (I speak of the North Americans), they have encountered in the late war against the English the difficulties of federation, what will happen to us who lack those advantages?

My friend, if with all our provinces and their resources we are still weak, what will happen to us if each of them is isolated from the others? Add to this the rivalry of communities and the conflicting interests of each, and you will conclude that they will resemble a lion's den, and the mediator who steps in will be the enemy.[60]

From San Martín's point of view, the revolution against Spain could only be sustained and won by a strong central government in a unified country, with the capital more centrally situated if that were necessary. As he said in his letter to Commodore Bowles, they risked utter ruin in 1816: 'I fear this not from the Spaniards, but from domestic discord and our lack of education and judgment.'[61] And he continued to maintain his stand against what he regarded as 'the delirium of federation.'

As reported by Commodore Bowles, San Martín was convinced that the early revolutionary governments in America were unduly dependent on popular opinion and conciliatory to popular forces: 'The lower orders have thus obtained an undue preponderance and are beginning to manifest a revolutionary disposition dangerous in any country but more particularly in this, where want of education and general information is so strongly felt.' The danger, he thought, was greatest in Peru, 'where the unenlightened part of the community are so numerous (particularly the slaves and Indians) and at the same time so formidable.'[62] The situation was rendered more explosive by the prevalence of irresponsible demagogues thrown up by the revolution: 'visionaries, agitators, adventurers . . . patriots, true, but more harmful than all the chapetones [Spaniards] together.'[63]

San Martín's advice to Peruvians amounted to a political sermon:

Liberty, therefore, must be bestowed in moderation. Every civilized people is entitled to be free; but the degree of freedom which any country can enjoy, must bear an exact proportion to the measure of its civilization: if the first exceed the last, no power can save them from anarchy; and if the reverse happen, namely, that the degree of civilization goes beyond the amount of freedom which the people possess, oppression is the consequence. If all Europe were suddenly to be put in possession of the liberty of England, the greater part of it would speedily present a complete chaos of anarchy; and if, instead of their present constitution, the English were to be subjected to the charter of Louis XVIII, they would consider themselves enslaved.

The celebrated Spanish Constitution of 1812, which many Peruvian liberals saw as an instrument of domination, was not a model for San Martín, for it changed the religious and political state of the peninsula too abruptly:

We, on the other hand, ought to avoid running into such mistakes, and to introduce gradually such improvements as the country is prepared to receive, and for which its people are so well adapted by their docility, and the tendency to improvement which mark their social character.[64]

San Martín Beleaguered

Signs of decline in San Martín and disillusion in those around him began to appear, and the tide of opinion that at first flowed strongly in his favour now receded. There was defiance within his own ranks. In the army there was a conspiracy against his authority and possibly against his life, which came to a head on 15 October 1821 when chiefs of the Army of the Andes conspired against him or were prepared to do so. San Martín was overtly less alarmed than others who knew of the conspiracy—'no hay cuidado' ('don't worry') he said—and he decided to swallow his pride, pacify the situation and cover up for the conspirators, instead of punishing them. Only Tomás Heres, chief of the Numancia battalion, who announced the conspiracy, was punished, by banishment to Guayaquil. The rest in effect were bought off. The conspiracy took place before, not after, the distribution of the five hundred thousand dollars' bounty, which was decided on 21 November and effected on 12 December: 'the distribution of the valuable bounty granted by the town council of Lima was after the conspiracy and not before', and in effect was a gesture to buy the support of the conspirators.[65] The conspiracy failed but was still, as Mitre admitted, 'a moral mutiny'.[66] It was a period of discontent in the army, and San Martín's old companion, Las Heras, together with Martínez resigned and left for Chile. Genuine disillusion? Or rats jumping from a sinking ship?

Sensing insecurity, San Martín looked abroad for support, to Santiago and Buenos Aires, and beyond them to Europe. He was accused, at home and abroad, of unfulfilled ambition, which would only be satisfied with a crown. He wanted a crown, but not for himself. He was convinced that a monarch was what Peru needed, and his ministers, García del Río, Monteagudo and Unanue shared his views. They could count on a measure of support from the Peruvian aristocracy, who were allowed to retain their Spanish titles of nobility rebranded as Peruvian. And in November San Martín decided to send Juan García del Río and James Paroissien to Europe, not only to secure European recognition of Peruvian independence, but to offer a crown to a European prince. On 24 December the instructions for the two envoys were drawn up by the Council of State, and on the last day of the year the two envoys set sail for Valparaíso.

The secret instructions they carried stated that to secure order at home and respect abroad Peru needed a strong government, the recognition of its independence and the alliance or protection of one of the principal powers of Europe. Britain and Russia were the prime candidates, the first because of its maritime strength, financial capacity, vast resources and the excellence of its political institutions, the second because of its political influence and power. Therefore, the envoys should accept as emperor of Peru either the prince of Saxe-Coburg (who had been married to the late Princess Charlotte and still lived in England) or, failing him, a member of the British royal house, preferably the duke of Sussex, a relatively respectable son of George III. The new emperor would be required to embrace the Roman Catholic faith and to swear to uphold the constitution which would be presented to him. If neither of these individuals were available, other possible candidates in Germany, Austria, France or Portugal were suggested. And as if this was not enough, the envoys were further authorized to enter into treaties of alliance, friendship and commerce, to raise a loan in Europe of six million dollars and to offer special privileges to mining companies. Finally, they were to proceed via Chile and the United Provinces, to whose governments they were given special missions.

San Martín held particular hopes of Chile, but in that country O'Higgins had his own problems. 'I detest aristocracy', he declared, and as an active reformer with egalitarian tendencies he provoked the elite and alerted the Church. Yet he had no power base from which to promote his liberal ideas, least of all in the landed aristocracy; his relations with the senate deteriorated, and opposing his preference for a strong executive the senate blocked him all the way. As he had ruefully written to San Martín in August 1821: 'When men who are selected and supposedly friends present so disagreable an aspect, what can one expect from those who are indifferent and elected by the unbridled multitude?'[67]

From this unpromising material the envoys were to secure the agreement of O'Higgins to San Martín's monarchical designs and to join in the search for a crowned head of state; they were to demand satisfaction for the conduct of Admiral Cochrane; and they were to seek Chilean recognition of Peruvian independence and further military collaboration. But San Martín was no longer a Chilean favourite, if he ever had been. Public opinion was hostile to the idea of a monarchy, sympathetic to Cochrane and unimpressed by San Martín's conduct of the war. Some of this feeling had rubbed off on O'Higgins, who was obviously uncomfortable. Yet San Martín was counting for support from his old friend and ally. In November he had written:

I am going through a cruel spell of suffering, which confines me to bed still; though it is getting somewhat better, it shows only too clearly that this machine needs a rest, if I want to preserve a few more days of life. So in case I do not survive or leave this office I have finally resolved to send García del

Río and Paroissien to negotiate not only recognition of this country's independence but also to establish the bases of the future government that ought to prevail. These two will travel to England and from there, depending on the outcome of the negotiations, they will proceed to the Peninsula. On their way through Chile they will inform you verbally of my wishes; if these agree with yours and the interests of Chile, the two envoys may be joined by two delegates from your country, for a joint approach will have more political weight and more promise for the future happiness of the two states. I am sure that my aims will meet with your approval, for I believe that you too will be convinced of the impossibility of constituting these countries as republics. In the end I want nothing else than the establishment of a government that is appropriate to the circumstances of the time, thus avoiding the horrors of anarchy. How happy I will be to see from my corner of the world America established on solid and stable foundations![68]

He used almost identical words in his decree of 27 December convoking a General Constituent Congress, the particular objects of its meeting being 'to establish the definite form of government and present the constitution which best suits Peru in accordance with the circumstances of its territory and people.'[69]

From Chile, however, came only further criticism, sneers and rejections, and hostility towards his envoys. García del Río told him frankly, 'Feelings here are resentful towards you and your advisers, and people take delight in the news of what Cochrane accomplished in Ancón.'[70] In a final meeting with O'Higgins on 19 March García del Río and Paroissien presented the monarchy question head-on and were firmly rebuffed. Perhaps a monarchy was suitable for Peru, he said, but not for Chile, much as he respected San Martín.[71] O'Higgins was aware that his own position was too precarious to risk being denounced as a monarchist. Nothing, therefore, came from the mission to Chile and the envoys made their way ruefully across the Andes on the long journey to Buenos Aires, disillusioned with Chile and irritated even with San Martín, whom they complained was ignoring them. After an arduous journey across mountains and pampas they reached Buenos Aires in the last week of April 1822.

Following its year of anarchy in 1820 and subsequent humiliation at the hands of provincial caudillos, Buenos Aires had recovered its poise and, instead of provoking the interior, begun to concentrate on itself and to create in its own province a viable economy and society. The administration was inspired by Bernardino Rivadavia, now forty-one years old and recently returned from abroad. An apostle of the Enlightenment and follower of Jeremy Bentham, whom he had met in London, Rivadavia began to implement a programme of reform: institutions, civil rights, public works and welfare, all these he believed could be improved by legislation, as his master taught. Rivadavia endeavoured to modernize Argentina, starting with Buenos Aires. He sought economic growth through free trade, foreign investment and immigration; such a policy would require liberal institutions and a new infrastructure. This was Rivadavia's project, enlightened, liberal and unitarian, and too far ahead of its time to succeed. The British minister Lord Ponsonby expressed a very supercilious view of Rivadavia when he described him as 'a man of whom I can say nothing good either as a statesman, or as the head of government, beyond the praise that might be due to a bustling mayor of a small town.'[72] William Miller took a different view:

> In Rivadavia there is an affectation of superiority, and a hauteur exceedingly repulsive; but these are counterbalanced by a strength and capaciousness of mind, combined with a high degree of political courage, which places him far above every other South American in the character of a statesman.[73]

An impatient and intolerant liberal, Rivadavia had an abrasive personality that was not of a kind to attract San Martín. But in the South American world of 1822 you took what you found and negotiated with those you could not avoid.

Rivadavia, like O'Higgins, was preoccupied with political problems nearer home and had little time for San Martín's concerns. The Protector was not highly regarded in Argentina, where many believed that he had abandoned his native country in its hour of need in search of glory in Peru. For his part he had no great opinion of Rivadavia or of those in his country taken in by 'the madness of that visionary', in the belief that they could reproduce European civilization in Buenos Aires.[74] Equally Rivadavia was not well disposed towards San Martín; he remembered his role in the overthrow of the government of which he was a member in 1812, and distrusted his conduct in Peru. He made it clear to the envoys that he had neither the desire nor the ability to send troops against the royalists in Upper Peru, one of San Martín's requests, and as for a monarchical form of government for South America, a subject on which the envoys judged it prudent to remain silent, he subsequently described the idea as an 'utter absurdity.'[75]

The envoys left Buenos Aires on 26 May with nothing to show for their pains, and anxious to reach in England the civilized life they sought for Peru. From Peru they still received encouragement, at least from Monteagudo, who had recently added the foreign ministry to his portfolio of power. He reported that with the arrival of an envoy from Colombia, Joaquín Mosquera, negotiations between Peru and Colombia were making progress towards 'the formation of a general alliance between the five sections of America— Peru, Colombia, Mexico, Chile and the Provinces of Buenos Aires', and in the establishment of an assembly with deputies from each. More particularly the governments of Peru and Colombia were agreed on the establishment of a constitutional monarchy in the countries of America, and the envoys should continue their mission in England, first to secure a loan, then to negotiate for a prince. This dispatch, however, 'which moved so easily from the realm of fact into that of fantasy', was a forlorn hope from a failing politician; soon afterwards Monteagudo was forced to resign and then to flee the country.[76] San Martín himself had only a short time left to him in Peru. His one exercise in diplomacy died with the end of negotiations in England in the course of 1823 and a halt in his envoys' search for a prince and recognition. Otherwise the envoys seemed to be enjoying life outside Peru: they opened the Peruvian legation at 21 Grosvenor Street, London, and negotiated a loan in the London money market, out of which they began to pay themselves.[77]

Meanwhile, within Peru political opposition to San Martín was growing. While his monarchism appealed to some, to Torre Tagle for example, it alienated many others. The liberal wing of Peruvian politics had done virtually nothing to win independence; but now it sought to impose its views on the independent state. Whereas previously the liberals had sought to reform though not to subvert the colony, now they worked to control the new Peru and destroy its creator. They saw San Martín as an obstacle who had to be removed. The new regime gave them greater freedom and opportunity to propagate liberal constitutionalism than the colony had done. Manuel Pérez de Tudela proclaimed republican principles. The priest Francisco Javier Luna Pizarro worked behind the scenes to undermine monarchical plans. And Sánchez Carrión returned to the fray, launching polemical tracts advocating liberalism and republicanism.

While they frustrated San Martín's political plans, the Peruvians also withheld the military help which he needed to end the war. In the vicinity of Lima San Martín had an army, but its effective strength was less that its reputed numbers and it lacked cohesion. Rivalry between various national components reduced its fighting potential, and many of the local officers regarded military life as a comfortable career rather than the defence of independence.[78] San Martín himself, starved of choice, made a number of inept appointments, and many military commands were given to upper-class creoles not because they were qualified but simply because they had declared for liberation. For these military zeal was not a priority. Meanwhile Lima became resentful of this unemployed army and of the financial burden that it imposed.[79] And the royalist forces remained intact, secure in the safety of the sierra.

Soldiers who wouldn't fight, politicians who couldn't agree, a people who didn't care, as his world crumbled San Martín refused to admit defeat. He still had work to do.

CHAPTER 8

Liberal in a
Conservative Society

Practical Ideas for a New Society

The grey mist over coastal Peru, *el clima de Lima*, was the backdrop to the opening months of the Protectorate. As his military campaign faltered and his political ideas lost their appeal, San Martín still marched on towards his project for Peru. Constitutional monarchy remained his political preference, but he was open to more liberal ideas in social policy.

Progress and enlightenment were his ideals, and reform was the aim of his government. These were the sentiments he expressed to Castlereagh when he contrasted the counter-revolutionary policy of Spain with the 'liberality, mental improvement and philanthropy' which were the hallmark of the age.[1] He launched a programme of reforms in Peru no less advanced than those of Bolívar in Colombia and no less enlightened than those of Rivadavia in Argentina. In the first months of the Protectorate, between August and December 1821, he issued a total of 154 decrees, on matters ranging from the administration of justice to the establishment of a national library.[2]

The focus on social policy was part of San Martín's Peruvian strategy. He came not to conquer or to fight but to pacify and persuade. He was, of course, a professional soldier, but while he created and commanded the Army of the Andes he did not lead it into battle in Peru; in contrast to his actions in Argentina and Chile, in Peru he did more governing than fighting. He regarded the army as an agent of last resort; it was the ultimate sanction of his project, not the leading edge. The Declaration of Independence and the establishment of the Protectorate were the consequences not of a decisive battle or a military victory but of strategic manoeuvre and political planning. The culmination of his project was social reform, crowned by a constitutional monarchy.

His advisers and collaborators in the government of the Protectorate were not the higher military but a group excelling in political and civil talents. Bernardo Monteagudo, intellectual, journalist and propagandist, with a strong will and dominating presence, animated the Protectorate and drove it forward, though he also damaged it by his excessive zeal and hatred of Spaniards, and even those who admired his mind deplored his morals. Juan García del Río, a finer spirit, more cultivated and sensitive in the art of government, had taken San Martín's message beyond Peru and given it a voice in Europe. The friend and confidant of San Martín, Tomás Guido, had come with him from Valparáiso, as had James Paroissien, general practitioner in government as well as medicine. And Peruvians too added their weight to the Protectorate: Hipólito Unanue, author of a work on the climate of Lima, and critic as well as minister of the regime; and the marquis of Torre Tagle, who brought the support of the north but proved to be only half attached to the revolution.

It is impossible to identify a specific ideology in the Protectorate of San Martín or any school of thought, other than that emanating from the Protector himself. His support for reform was pragmatic rather than theoretical, and his devotion to liberty and equality was a matter of faith rather than philosophy, and was always qualified by a determination to avoid anarchy, which he believed could be destructive of independence.

While there was a distinctly liberal thread running through the social legislation of San Martín, it was not the liberalism of the Enlightenment, which had little to offer colonial peoples or seekers after independence. Nationality as a historical force escaped the attention of European intellectuals and statesmen of the eighteenth century; they seemed to be unaware of the emergence of incipient nations and indifferent to rights of colonial independence. Rousseau, the leading intellectual defender of political freedom against despotic monarchies, never thought of applying his ideas to dependent peoples. Few of the eighteenth-century progressives took any interest in revolutions for independence, and it was left to Thomas Paine and the Abbé Raynal to argue a case for colonial rebellion. Neither Montesquieu nor Voltaire nor Diderot took the ultimate step of advocating revolution; even Rousseau stopped short of sanctioning violent political change. Jeremy Bentham was one of the few liberal thinkers of the time to apply his ideas to colonies, to advocate independence as a general principle, and to expose the contradiction inherent in regimes that professed liberalism at home and practised imperialism abroad. But Bentham was exceptional, and most liberals remained no less imperialist than conservatives. Liberal political ideas in Europe tended to appeal to the new bourgeoisie, who were often involved in industry and trade, and were ready to promote formal and informal empire in order to secure captive markets. This was the world seen by San Martín in Cádiz, the world of the Cortes and the Constitution, which, under the influence of the Spanish business community as well as of Enlightenment ideas, firmly rejected any idea of independence for Spanish America.

The Protector, therefore, could find little direct inspiration for ideas of liberty and equality either from European or from Hispanic sources. Yet there was a source, close to Peruvians, where the case for liberty and equality had already been argued with vision and eloquence. The Peruvian Jesuit Juan Pablo Viscardo y Guzmán, writing from exile, was an ardent advocate of independence, to the cause of which he bequeathed his *Lettre aux Espagnols Américains*, published in 1799 and disseminated in the Americas by Francisco de Miranda:

> The preservation of natural rights, and principally of liberty and security of persons and property, is undoubtedly the foundation stone of every human society, under whatever form of government it is constituted. Consequently it is an indispensable duty of every society, or of the government which represents it, not only to respect but to protect effectively these rights of every individual.[3]

The ideas, and the words, of Viscardo were voiced in the Peruvian press, and the views of San Martín did not disagree with his conclusions, least of all in the context of Spanish Peru.[4] But he himself declined to theorize about liberty. He shared the aversion of Edmund Burke to declarations of abstract rights divorced from existing circumstances and institutions. That was the road to anarchy. San Martín preferred to take practical steps:

> I could have recommended the liberality of my principles in the Provisional Statute by making magnificent declarations on rights and enlarging the ranks of government officials, in order to give a display of greater popularity to the actual forms. But convinced that to have a multiplicity of worthy principles is not the best way of realizing them, I have preferred to limit myself to a number of practical ideas that can be more readily achieved.[5]

These came to him as self-evident truths, which demanded action rather than theory, and, translated into social policy, followed the style of enlightened absolutism rather than post-enlightenment liberalism, and made some, though not a great, concession to modernity.

Titles were not important among his values, though he sanctioned some and accepted the world of social distinctions as he found it. Equality, however, was not an absolute right. He wanted to improve the conditions of people, not to level them:

> That the top people in a state are those of money, talent, and birth, has always been the case, is still the case, and always will be. These social barriers are just as pronounced in the United States as in England, which proves that man under whatever form of government is the same, that is subject to the same passions and weaknesses. In short, the best government is not the most liberal in its principles, but the one that makes for the happiness of those who obey it.[6]

His project, therefore, did not threaten to revolutionize the social structure of Peru. It proceeded cautiously and legislated prudently. 'Distinguished patricians', he reassured the elites, 'the voice of political revolution in this part of the new world and the military effort to achieve it have not been directed, nor can they be, against your rightful privileges.'[7]

Was this promise extended to Spaniards? Writing in the government newspaper he denied that independence necessarily entailed a disaster for the Spaniards: 'I don't have enemies to fight, only friends I can rely on.'[8] He conceded that there were good Spaniards in Peru. 'Justice obliges me to say that not all Spaniards conspire against our rights.' Some abhorred extremism, and 'these will be certainly protected in their life and properties'.[9] His policy statements undertook to respect the security and property of Spaniards as long as they accepted independence:

> I have promised to respect your lives and properties: this I have done and no one can now doubt my word. In spite of this, it is secretly complained and some maliciously spread the idea that my intention is to abuse your confidence. My reputation is now too well regarded for me to sully it by breaking my promises, even when it is thought that I fail them in particular cases. So I finally declare . . . [That] every Spaniard who trusts in the protection of my word and continues to work peacefully, swearing to the Independence of the country, and respecting the new government and the established laws, shall be protected in his life and property.[10]

It was a qualified assurance, but even limited tolerance of this kind was not the policy of Monteagudo, his virtual minister of the interior, whose policy, as he explained in his *Memoria política*, was deliberately oppressive and unsparing, and served to throw San Martín's words back at him.

The Protectorate, therefore, was not a liberal state and did not promise Peruvians a liberal government. Foreseeing a vacuum of power between the collapse of the viceroyalty and the establishment of a new regime, San Martín began with the basic essential: to avoid disorder and anarchy. His principles of action can be observed in the Regulations of Huaura (12 February 1821), the first statement of his intentions, issued while still on campaign: 'Between the reef of premature reform and the danger of abuses left intact there is a mean, whose extent will be measured by the circumstances of the time and the great law of necessity.'[11] The details were spelt out in the Declaration and Proclamation of Independence (15 and 28 July 1821) and the creation of the Protectorate (3 August 1821). He was determined to avoid a period of inertia in which a vacuum of power might prevail; it would be equally fatal to allow instant assemblies and premature reform, for this would be to invite anarchy. At the same time he was determined to institutionalize post-independence and thus avoid a surge of personalism and danger of caudillism.[12]

This was a wartime state, for the Spanish army had not been defeated, and therefore such state building as took place was provisional. Nevertheless San Martín projected it as a strong state, a 'vigorous' system as he called it, a government in transition that would guarantee security and win the war. The Protector was self-appointed, beholden to no group, elected by no assembly, chosen by no Peruvians. It was a pragmatic, not a principled policy, driven as always by his abhorrence of anarchy and by the agreement neither of his collaborators nor of the army, but by his personal authority. The Protector assumed plenitude of power, except for the judicial function, and he accepted no limitations on his power except the rule of circumstance and the progress of the war. Whether he abused his power he left to the judgement of Peruvians and the assessment of historians. This was a transition to the end of hostilities, when Peruvians could choose their own form of government. San Martín's preferred choice, as he had always made clear, was monarchy. This was the juncture when his reasoning would be tested. Would any monarch have all the virtues that San Martín claimed? Could monarchy prevail against the republican bias inherent in independence? Would Peruvians accept it anyway?

Authoritarian in its institutional power, the Protectorate was libertarian in many of its political, economic and social precepts. The colonial state denied two basic freedoms to Peruvians, both highly prized by their eighteenth-century advocates: free speech and free trade. Censorship and monopoly were among the first targets of the Protectorate. Freedom of speech was decreed and people were assured the right of publication without any prior censorship.[13] Freedom of the press was announced with a worthy attempt to provide a theoretical justification:

> Ever since the liberating art of printing was invented society has experienced a beneficial revolution; talents have been released, genius has come to

light, and not only has civilization of peoples grown and abuses been reformed but the destiny of nations and governments themselves has been marvellously affected. The government of Peru, which desires nothing so much as the prosperity of the country for which it is responsible, now sanctions the freedom of the press, because it recognises the right possessed by all men to think, speak and write, and because it is convinced that without this the finest talents are lost for the country and for the cause of reason and enlightenment. But at the same time as freedom to publicly express his opinion is granted to every individual, it is essential to prevent freedom becoming licence, and to avoid the abuse of freedom to convert it in the hands of seditious and perverse people into an instrument of disorder and vengeance.[14]

Platitudes perhaps, but not out of place in a state suddenly impressed by its own independence and engaged in the deconstruction of colonial thinking. The particular limitations specified were 'the Dogmas of the Catholic Religion, moral principles, public order, and the good name of a citizen.' In spite of the restrictions, freedom of the press allowed newspapers and other media to conduct a vigorous public debate on issues of the day, and the promises of the Protectorate survived.

In a war-ravaged, underdeveloped country like Peru it was impossible to build a liberal economy. The commercial legislation of the Protectorate established freedom of trade and suppressed interior customs; but it placed a protective tariff (20 per cent) on imports in order to help local industry. But the Peruvian economy was difficult to protect. Farms and plantations suffered from military destruction, diversion of labour and poor American markets. The traditional prop of the economy and Peru's major exportable assets, gold and silver, were also depressed; mining production was hit by disruption of communications and by severe shortage of labour, mercury, mules and capital. Scarcity of capital affected all sectors of the economy. Between 1819 and 1825 an estimated 26.9 million dollars were shipped from Lima in British ships, representing payments for imports—consumer good and war materials—and flight of capital to safer outlets.[15] Starved of exports and deprived of working capital, trade sank to a low level of depression, and there it was held by heavy taxes and diminished output of precious metals. Inevitably Peru could not earn enough to pay for imports of manufactured goods, at a time when excited British businessmen swarmed in to provide goods and services. Captain Basil Hall noticed the impact of recent changes when he dined in a Peruvian home in Huacho: 'A roll of English broad-cloth was resting on a French wine case, marked Medoc; on the table stood a bottle of champagne; the knives and forks were marked Sheffield, and the screen which divided the apartment was made of a piece of Glasgow printed cotton.'[16] Foreign borrowing temporarily bridged the trade gap. A loan of £1,200,000 was contracted in London in 1822 by García del Río, one of the agents originally dispatched to Europe by San Martín to find a king for Peru. Of this loan the Peruvian government would receive less than £900,000, after the underwriters and agents had taken their cut.[17] If the experience proved anything it was that in a world of economic liberalism Peru would have to protect its flanks.

Not Indians but Citizens of Peru

Promise and prejudice, such was the story of San Martín's Indian policy. The Indian population of Peru, which grew steadily in the second half of the eighteenth century and constituted almost 60 per cent of the 1.1 million total, suffered more than other Peruvians from the wars of independence.[18] As they toiled in haciendas and workshops, or were conscripted for public services, or simply worked on their community land in order to pay the royal tribute, the Indians expected little from the revolution, if they even noticed it. They were plundered by all the armies, and as the war swept back and forth before their eyes they were seized by one side as auxiliaries or beasts of burden, and then suffered reprisals if the other side came back:

> Every military detachment that halted there unavoidably destroyed the crops of lucern, and often stole away their oxen, sheep, goats, or poultry, whenever they could lay their hands upon them. In this way hundreds of villages and thousands of individuals have been robbed of their little all; but they were poor oppressed Indians, and humble misery seldom arrests the attention or engages the sympathies of the world.[19]

Both sides treated the Indians as serfs, labourers and miners, transforming the personal service demanded of them in peacetime into military service in time of war. General Miller observed that it was the practice of both royalists and patriots 'to lay hold of the first Indian they met in the street, and compel him to clean out their barracks, to fetch wood and water, and perform the most menial offices. Habit had familiarized the officers to the custom, and they seldom corrected the evil: what, too, is most remarkable, the Indian soldiers were the most tyrannical in exacting these degrading services from their brethren.'[20]

The guerrillas of central Peru relied on the cooperation of the Indians for intelligence and other services, but gave them nothing in return. The Indians were never integrated either into the regular patriot army or into the guerrilla units, because they were considered inferior. When their services were required as combatants they were mobilized into separate units as auxiliaries.

But the patriots had the disconcerting habit of recruiting Indians for particular operations and then passing on, leaving their allies to the mercy of incoming royalists. Sometimes collaboration was successful. In operations north of Arica in the vicinity of Moquegua in May 1821 the patriots engaged local Indians to round up royalist stragglers; they were paid in money or mules, and were allowed to keep the mules on condition that they delivered a Spanish prisoner and listened to patriot propaganda.[21] For the most part the guerrillas kept the Indians working the land as serfs and working in the mines as *mitayos*. In this phase of the war the patriots continued to deny Indian rights and to diminish the status of the Indians in the revolution, misleading them with promises that independence would bring them liberation from tyranny. But it was a habit of mind among the Peruvian whites to treat the Indians as inferior beings, and this could not be eradicated by legislation.

San Martín was concerned over Indian rights and in winning the good will of the native populations. He wanted the Indians to know their rights; that was why he insisted that Quechua translations of his decrees and proclamations be made and issued to Indian communities. He inaugurated new policies, insisting on justice for the Indians in the name of reason and law, freeing them from the 'moral degradation' to which they had been reduced by the Spanish government. In a resounding decree of 27 August 1821 he abolished the Indian tribute and ruled that 'in future the aborigines shall not be called Indians or natives; they are children and citizens of Peru, and they shall be known as Peruvians,' a name previously confined to those born of Spanish parents and their descendants. And on the following day he abolished the '*mitas, encomiendas, yanaconazgos*, and every kind of compulsory labour service to which the Indians had been subjected.'[22]

These policies were not original. They placed San Martín in a tradition of Spanish reformers originating in the viceroyalty. More recently Viceroy Abascal had been forced to implement a series of reforms designed by Spanish constitutionalism; these included the abolition of Indian tribute and *mita*. He also produced a plan to replace the tribute by a tax on land; this would be distributed to the Indians as individual freehold taken from land occupied by Indian communities, though this idea was never implemented.[23] San Martín's laws were frustrated by the opposition of vested interests who had long regarded Indian labour as part of their property rights. Abolition of the tribute was not a priority of the Indians themselves: the tribute helped to define their status and protect their land rights. As for identity, Indians were not necessarily attracted to the nomenclature of whites. Nor were they invariably attracted to the patriot cause. At the battle of Ayacucho (December 1824), decisive for Bolívar, royalist Indians who had already harassed the patriots now waited in the wings to cut them down in the event of their defeat and flight. Lieutenant Colonel Medina of the Colombian army was killed by the Indians of Huando on his way to Lima with Sucre's dispatch of the battle.[24]

The Indian legislation of the Protectorate has a certain theoretical interest. It reflected a growing tendency to define the Indians in social and cultural rather than racial terms, and this was undoubtedly correct, though it failed to distinguish between the Indians of community and those of more mobile groups. Otherwise the legislation had limited significance, for it made virtually no difference to Indian conditions. San Martín was not ignorant of Indians: in Argentina he had grown up among Indians and had once claimed rhetorically to be an Indian, and in Peru he saw them daily. But his laws earned no particular gratitude: the elites were alerted, and the Indians continued to follow their individual, or community, interests which rarely coincided with the cause of independence as understood by San Martín and his colleagues. San Martín offered liberation and citizenship to the Indians but the state he sought to establish, as prefigured in the Protectorate, was a creole state, while the Indians retained their own ideas about the meaning of independence and its relevance to their lives. Those Indians who joined patriot armies or guerrilla bands usually did so without ideological convictions, and they could change sides without compunction. They might act under duress, or from habit, or to acquire arms, but rarely on individual initiative. A guerrilla leader in Upper Peru admonished royalist Indians:

'The *patria* is the place where we live; the *patria* is the true cause which we ought to defend at all costs; for the *patria* we ought to sacrifice our interests and even our life.' Proclamations of this kind were issued on all sides, but for the moment we did not have a single Indian. We were speaking to thin air, as though it were a foreign country which we had to reconquer.

The Indians of Upper Peru were more aware of traditional and communal allegiances, and the guerrillas could make no impression on those who had taken the king's medal, the *amedallados*:

They said it was for their king and lord that they were going to die, and not as rebels, nor for the *patria*; they did not know what this *patria* was, nor what it meant, nor what it looked like; they said no one knew if the *patria* was a man or a woman. As for the king, they knew him, his government was well established, his laws were respected and duly observed. So they were put to death, all eleven of them.[25]

Upper Peru was on San Martín's agenda, a country still to be liberated. Did he know what awaited the armies of liberation?

A Great Act of Justice

For San Martín social policy consisted in balancing interest groups and finding a mean of some kind between inherited rights and demands for change. Even his protection of *jornaleros* during his Mendoza days was qualified by his defence of hacienda rights: 'No peon may change his master without having a certificate from him confirming that he leaves no debts.'[26] During his preparations for the invasion of Peru he gave some thought to his social strategies, naively expressed in his instructions to his secret agents but no doubt refined as he learnt more:

> The masses, and especially the slaves, cannot be mobilized unless their fears are magnified or their hopes encouraged. The first can easily be done by skilfully exposing the most atrocious deeds which mark the conduct of the Spaniards and to which they will resort again if they emerge victorious from this final struggle. But the second requires great judgement and skill. Promises should not be made that cannot or should not be fulfilled. The object of the Revolution is the happiness of everyone: a sudden emancipation of the slaves and an indiscriminate plunder of property would propel the country into the most frightful anarchy, and the masses and the slaves would themselves be the first victims of the complete breakdown of order. So everyone should believe that they will be gradually free, gradually wealthy, and gradually happy. These are advantages that they have not enjoyed, nor would ever enjoy, under the Spanish government; and they are the very advantages that a government formed by themselves would provide.[27]

Peru at the end of the eighteenth century in a population of over 1 million consisted of about 80,000 blacks, divided equally between 40,000 slave and 40,000 free. The slaves worked in plantations and domestic service; some escaped to live outside the law; and a few were even owned by Indian communities in the sierra. San Martín did not favour universal manumission but preferred to proceed as possibilities arose. In the early months of the war he advocated recruiting black slaves from royalist haciendas, and his commanders such as Arenales and Miller recruited on the march. William Miller wrote that on landing near the former Jesuit estate of Caucato (Ica) in the Chincha valley many of the estate's nine hundred slaves deserted to join the patriots. Former slaves were valued not only as fighting troops but also as guides and spies. San Martín declared that his intention was not to subvert the properties of slave owners, but simply to accept those slaves who volunteered to fight for the patriot cause.[28] He speculated that if the viceregal government continued recruiting slaves he would have to counter by granting freedom to all the people of colour, 'repugnant though this is to my reason and feelings.'[29] He continued to take slaves for the army; if few were forthcoming or they were needed for hacienda labour, then owners had to pay an indemnity to army funds. He had to balance military needs against civilian concerns and to protect the right of *hacendados* to retain their work force. The policy of granting manumission in return for army service did not extend to runaway slaves who did not enlist; these were ordered (edict of 23 July 1821) to return to their owners, if they could be lured from the guerrilla or bandit groups they had sometimes joined. In general, slaves were not quick to exchange the hacienda for the army; not all of them saw the war of independence as their war, and self-interest might well be served by staying with a master they knew rather than face a violent future.[30] On the other hand General Miller remained convinced of the good quality of blacks in the patriot army: 'I believe that the blacks who have served in our armies deserve the highest praise for their constancy and valour. A proof of their patriotism is that the Spaniards have never been able to form a corps from their ranks, in spite of their efforts to do so.'[31]

Abolition of slavery was a distant prospect. In a decree of 12 August 1821 San Martín denounced the criminal traffic of human beings and the degradation of families by the sale of their members. His words of outrage were more resounding than the policies prescribed:

> When humanity has been so greatly abused and its rights violated for so long, a singular act of justice is needed, if not to compensate them entirely, at least to take the first steps in complying with the holiest of all obligations. A substantial portion of our race has until today been looked on as an exchangeable asset, subject to the calculations of a criminal tariff; men have bought men and have not been ashamed of debasing the family to which they belong, selling one person to others. I shall not try to attack this ancient abuse with a single blow: it needs time itself to destroy it, as time has sanctioned it. But I would not be responsible to my public conscience and to my private feelings were I not to prepare for the future with this merciful reform, reconciling for the present the interests of the proprietors with the vote of reason and nature.[32]

He confirmed the abolition of the slave trade, which he described as 'an ancient abuse', and as for slavery itself he declared that the children of slaves born from 28 July 1821, the date of independence, including those in royalist-held territory, were free and at the age of twenty-one would gain full rights of citizenship. These *libertos* (freedman), however, were to remain for some years under the control of the mother's owner, who by decree of 24 November was obliged to provide for their education and training.

San Martín ordered that each year a certain number of older slaves should be manumitted by means of state compensation to their owners. And on various occasions manumission was offered in return for military service. On 2 September 1821 as part of a recruiting campaign San Martín declared that every slave who fought against the enemy and conducted himself bravely would be free. A decree of 25 October threatened any owner who lured recruits back into his service with confiscation of property or exile, and those who denounced such a crime were rewarded with confiscations from the guilty party's possessions and with freedom if they were slaves. On 17 November, declaring that 'one of the duties of government is to promote the freedom of those who have inhumanely suffered until today the usurpation of that inalienable right', the Protector freed all the slaves belonging to Spaniards and enemy creoles. Those aged fifteen to fifty were to present themselves for military service; women and males who could not bear arms would receive their freedom papers from the departmental authorities.[33]

This was probably the only effective manumission, if manumission it was, for San Martín's other decrees were not uniformly applied. These measures he regarded as 'a great act of justice', but slave owners opposed even this moderate programme, protested against loss of slaves to the patriot cause and used every possible manoeuvre to avoid it. The policy was complicated by the simultaneous practice of confiscating royalist estates, which encouraged many slaves to flee both from military service and from work. Slavery survived independence virtually intact.[34] The Constitution of 1823 declared that no one could be born a slave in Peru and prohibited the slave trade into Peru. But slave owners opposed all these measures and although the trade was discontinued, slavery itself survived in coastal agriculture and domestic service, and was not abolished until 1854.

Meanwhile, slaves had to devise their own tactics to mitigate or escape from their condition, and a process of self-manumission and passive resistance emerged. The Church too became an agent in the demise of slavery, as it began to intervene more actively in the relationship between slaves and masters. To defend the integrity of slave marriages, the Church opposed the break-up of slave families. Slaves were able to exploit this concession which thus became an instrument of greater freedom. The intervention of the Church rather than the state limited the legal ability of slave owners to block slave marriages. Moreover, masters who attempted to sell married slaves outside the city of Lima, or who sexually abused their female slaves, might find themselves attacked not only by their slaves but also by the Church.[35] These developments continued irrespective of the government in power.

San Martín, therefore, did not abolish slavery. His policy sprang from a liberal mind and a humanitarian spirit, and if he stopped short of a total abolition of slavery, this was evidence of the constraints operating in a society dominated by a landowning elite. In the loyalist press the elite left him in no doubt as to their views: 'If he came to Peru to establish independence with the least possible sacrifice from its inhabitants, as he himself said, then he ought to maintain without any alteration the system of slavery, because it is an important resource for various reasons, and no one has ever abused it in the course of the war.'[36] He was also led by his usual search, in common with other liberators, for a middle way between two conflicting principles, personal liberty and rights of property, and by his own typical adherence to gradualism. The mentality of the liberators was of their time. Slaves did not have a right to freedom outside a creole-given right; it was not a natural right, and it was certainly not equality. This was the model of the revolution throughout Spanish America.

A Christian General

The political and social policies of San Martín were secular, not religious, in inspiration. Like most of the liberators, he was a Catholic by default rather than decision, but his convictions sprang from more than mere convenience. His membership of the Lodge, an essentially political body for meddlers among the elite, did not make him a freemason or seeker after alternative beliefs, and it eventually became an irritable and disposable constraint on his freedom of action.

San Martín believed in religious toleration and freedom of worship, considered them an extension of independence, and deplored any departure from these principles. Among the advice written for his daughter in 1825 he recommended her to have 'feelings of toleration towards all religions.'[37] He followed the fate of religious tolerance in Argentina with some concern and in 1833 asked Guido how it was faring. 'Very badly', replied his friend. 'We have had burning of books, marriages between protestants and catholics undone, and thousands of other sensations.' The government had agreed to the establishment of another presbyterian church, but 'you can't drain the sea with a shell'.[38]

Defence of toleration had not diluted San Martín's public commitment to Catholicism as the religion of the state. While the royalist press denounced the Liberator and his colleagues as heretics and freemasons, the record of the Protectorate was totally orthodox, and the patriot periodical *El Consolador* echoed San Martín's own words in extolling the providential character of independence, 'I am an instrument used by the God of the Armies to carry out the supreme plans of his adorable providence.'[39] The Provisional Statute of 8 October 1821, signed by San Martín and the ministers of the Protectorate, left no doubt that official religion was exclusive and orthodox: 'The Catholic,

Apostolic, and Roman religion is the religion of the State: the government recognises as one of its first duties its maintenance and preservation by all the means humanly possible.' It made clear that attacks on doctrine would be severely punished and that Catholicism was a prerequisite for government officials. It also allowed other Christians to practise their religion with the government's permission.[40] San Martín's commitment to the established religion of the Protectorate lasted throughout his administration. In the weeks before his departure from Peru in August 1822 he provided for public masses and ceremonies in honour of St Rose of Lima, others to mark the anniversary of the independence of Chile and a mass of the Holy Spirit to mark the opening of Congress.

In matters of faith a distinction was acknowledged by liberators throughout Spanish America between religion and Church policy, and especially between personal belief and the policy of Rome. During the period of San Martín's campaign and the Protectorate, the official policy of the Church regarded allegiance to Spain, obedience to the monarchy and repudiation of revolution as moral imperatives, and their denial as a sin. Yet the Church in America did not speak with a single voice.[41] The majority of the bishops rejected the revolution and remained loyal to Spain. They owed their appointments to the Crown, they had sworn allegiance to the king, and they were under immediate pressure to conform and deliver to the king a docile people. Bishops were urged 'to cooperate by their example and their doctrine in preserving the rights of legitimate sovereignty which belongs to the king our lord.' The clergy were divided, in Peru as elsewhere, but many, especially among the lower clergy who were predominantly creole, supported the cause of independence and the actions both of San Martín's army and of the *montoneros* in the sierra. From one guerrilla chief it was reported, 'The priests of these villages have been alongside me since I reached their *doctrinas* (Indian parishes), encouraging the soldiers as far as they could and determined to fight in order to give an example to the rest, in response to the outrages that have affected their churches.'[42] Some priests played leading roles in the struggle, many more were activists in the rebel ranks and numerous volunteers served as chaplains in the armies of liberation.

The crunch came for the Church in 1820, when a liberal revolution in Spain forced the king to renounce absolutism and accept the Constitution of 1812. The new regime promptly exported itself to the colonies, where it had immediate significance for the Church. Spanish liberals were just as imperialist as Spanish conservatives and offered no concessions to independence. They were also aggressively anticlerical, attacking the Church, its privileges and its property. Finally they forced the Crown to ask the pope not to recognize any Spanish American country and to appoint bishops faithful only to Madrid. The combination of radical liberalism and renewed imperialism was too much even for the royalist bishops in America, many of whom now lost their confidence in the king, and began to question the basis of their allegiance. San Martín's victories in Chile and Peru opened a new opportunity for the Church, and with it the eyes of the prelates. Some bishops in Peru were incorrigibly hostile to the patriots. But the upper clergy in Lima signed the Declaration of Independence. Archbishop Las Heras, the dean and most of the cathedral chapter also signed. The archbishop, an elderly Spaniard, had spent many years in America and was happy to identify with Peru; he refused to accompany La Serna and the royal army into the sierra, and preferred to remain with his flock. The majority of the Lima chapter were Americans, and a substantial proportion of them were Peruvians and *limeños*; it was not difficult for them to change sides. Of the 3,500 signatures to the act of independence a third belonged to clerics, most of them from religious orders.

During this time of crisis the Church in America received little help from Rome. Ignorant of the meaning of colonial grievance and creole nationalism, the popes judged the movements of independence in Spanish America as an extension of the revolutionary upheaval they observed in Europe, and they gave their support to the Spanish Crown. Papal encyclicals in 1816 and 1824 exhorted the bishops to defend religion and legitimate power against the forces of revolution, and thus made support for the Bourbon monarchy and Spanish rule a matter of conscience.[43] Rome's policy was known to San Martín, as it was to all the liberators, and this was the reason, not his aversion to religion, why he was subsequently angry at the attempts of the Argentine government to resume relations with the Vatican.

The anticlerical policies of Monteagudo seem to have been unrestrained by San Martín and leave a question mark not over his orthodoxy but over his authority. How much control did he have over his minister? A number of bishops were forced out; the bishops of Trujillo, Huamanga and Mainas all left Peru. Archbishop Las Heras, however, had a mixed reception from the Protectorate. San Martín himself had cultivated good relations with the prelate. Already before his entry into Lima he had assured him:

It will be a matter of great satisfaction to me to offer my respects personally to the oldest and most venerable prelate of Peru; and if to this I can add the pleasure of seeing established a government that guarantees order and prosperity, on principles directly opposed to the extremist ideas unfortunately diffused throughout the world since the revolution of 1792 [the French Revolution], I will retire from the public scene to enjoy the happiness of my fellows and to bless Providence for the benefits bestowed on the country to which I belong.[44]

But the details of ecclesiastical policy were left to Monteagudo, who among other things was determined to close a number of religious retreat houses on the grounds that they were potential centres of a royalist reaction. The archbishop resisted the move and made it clear that he would leave his office rather than concede the point. In early September 1821 the government accepted his resignation, and ordered him to leave for Chancay on the coast within forty-eight hours for transport back to Spain. The archbishop seems to have blamed Monteagudo, not San Martín, and his letter of farewell to 'his esteemed friend', who had done him a service 'in relieving me of a burden beyond my abilities', was affectionate and grateful for the expressions of 'consideration whenever we have met'. A possible exercise in irony. The archbishop, who tended to see sin in every street and crime at every corner, both before and after independence, blew hot and cold. When he returned to Spain his tone was different. He reported to Rome adversely on the moral and political state of Peru, the immorality encouraged by independence, the licentious behaviour and books allowed by the Protectorate, and its exercise of ecclesiastical patronage. He further deplored the influence of Monteagudo, 'an immoral and irreligious man', on San Martín, and blamed the responsibility of the Protector for the spread of ideas harmful to religion, morals and doctrine, and his commitment to toleration and freedom of religion, a deviation from orthodoxy in Las Heras's eyes.[45] The accusation concerning toleration was certainly correct. There was also some truth in the charge of regalism, a Bourbon tradition perpetuated by the Protector. He did not hesitate to exercise ecclesiastical patronage when it suited the government, and monastic vows also came under scrutiny, being prohibited before the age of thirty for men and twenty-five for women.

In September 1821 the Junta de Purificación was established to investigate the political conduct of the clergy towards the new government and to expose those who did not support the revolution. All priests were invited to present sworn declarations demonstrating their support for the republic. Although many did so—usually in effusive terms, 'my patriotism is notorious', 'these papers prove my patriotism', 'I am addicted to the cause of the *patria*', 'I suffered for the crime of insurgency'—their testimony has little value as a test of commitment, for independence was already an established fact in coastal Peru.[46] Many priests published proclamations exhorting the faithful to support the patriotic cause, and as good Americans to support the cause of religion, liberty and independence. These probably represented majority opinion among the lower clergy, some of whom went further; the Franciscan José María Blanco, persecuted by the royalists because he favoured independence, joined the army of Arenales in Jauja and was appointed chaplain of the Numancia regiment by San Martín. It has been estimated that between 1805

and 1824, about 390 priests and religious participated actively in the independence movement, 77 as conspirators, 48 as propagandists, 143 as collaborators and 122 as insurgents. Among the delegates to the first Constituent
Congress, convoked by San Martín in September 1822, 26 were priests and the
first president was the liberal priest Luna Pizarro. Many of the clerical delegates were among the liberal wing of the assembly.[47] Liberal though it was, the
first constitution established the primacy of the Catholic Church. Not all
liberals agreed and some argued that a confessional state was incompatible
with toleration.[48] But the constitution was clear: 'The Religion of Peru is
Catholic, apostolic, Roman, excluding any other.'

While San Martín's public profession of faith was correct for a soldier and
statesman, and his aversion to Rome's policies continued the traditions of the
Spanish Bourbons, his personal beliefs are more difficult to identify. As the
child of a Spanish family his upbringing and education were Catholic, and in
America he respected the Catholic ritual of the time and the expressions of
popular religion. In Buenos Aires he had a traditional Catholic wedding
according to the nuptial rites of the Church. In the Regiment of Mounted
Grenadiers he prescribed morning prayers, evening rosary and mass on
Sundays; it was his practice to have a chaplain always available for the troops,
and for those priests who were brave in combat he had special words of praise.
His initiation into revolutionary groups in Cádiz and London may have introduced him to new and foreign influences, but his thoughts on this are
unknown to us. The Lodge was a political rather than a masonic society, an
unaccountable elite, which far from being a support for him became an irri-
tant and obstruction. His hero Belgrano defended Catholic traditions against
the secular influences of the time and set before San Martín the model of a
'Christian, apostolic and Roman general', ideals which seem to have been well
received by the Liberator.

San Martín respected the Church for its public presence and social role, and
in Peru he encouraged religious observance in his army, joining in the liturgy
on military occasions as was expected of a commanding officer. Cochrane
used to say that San Martín professed religion in order to deceive the public
and in fact he was not religious at all. According to Maria Graham, who
suspected he was an unbeliever, he was 'not content with a decent acquies-
cence in the rites of which he was necessarily present', but distinguished
himself in Peru by his religious zeal and 'excessive veneration' for Saint Rose
of Lima, simply to create a good impression.[49] In the event he impressed yet
did not impress the archbishop of Lima, who seems to have chosen his words
to match the occasion and the audience. Argentine historians have differed on
these questions, between those who believe that San Martín was a deist, a
liberal Christian and a fervent Catholic.

What did San Martín himself say? His private views, or some of them, can be inferred from a letter to Tomás Guido, at a time when he did not have to think of public susceptibilities or reactions. Commenting on the Argentine decision to establish relations with Rome in 1830, he feared for the upsurge of fanaticism in his 'ill-fated country' and displayed a sardonic attitude towards the institutional Church, though not necessarily towards religion.[50] In his policies towards Indians and slaves the values he espoused were essentially those of secular liberalism, not those comparable to the friars' earlier struggle for justice. For San Martín the final arbiter was conscience rather than dogma: 'Conscience is the best and most impartial judge a good man can have.'[51] Whether his religious faith survived his role as a Liberator remained to be seen. On one thing he had a clear conscience. He had left the Church in liberated Peru independent of Bourbon control, yet free to preach its traditional faith and morals. It was a creole Church and its message was directed by creole clergy towards creole parishioners. In the sierra the Church was still a viceregal institution, and most of the Indian *doctrinas* remained faithful to the religion traditionally taught them, indifferent towards independence.

Order and Progress

The daily life of Peruvians before independence had not been closed to culture and an educated class had helped to subvert as well as support the colonial state. Intellectuals like José Baquíjano, Hipólito Unanue and the writers in the journal of the Academic Society, the *Mercurio Peruano* (1791–5), who had imbibed the thought of the Enlightenment, condemned the obscurantism and intolerance of the old regime, though they stopped short of advocating modern freedoms. San Martín went further and took freedom of speech beyond colonial constraints. He saw an intellectual elite as a necessary adjunct to his projected monarchy, but he also envisaged the spread of education to a wider public and in the midst of war kept in mind the benefits of popular culture. The creation and improvement of primary and secondary schools, and encouragement of the Lancasterian System (named after the English educationalist Joseph Lancaster, 1778–1838) were examples of modernizing policies. He commissioned a Presbyterian minister, James Thomson, to establish Lancaster schools of education, with the active collaboration of José Francisco Navarrete, parish priest of San Lázaro.

San Martín believed that Peru's emergence from colonial status opened the way to cultural freedom:

The large always has its origins in the small, and the institutions that most immortalize human power once existed as embryos of the ideas that brought them into being. Amidst the clamour of war and still under the powerful pressures of revolution the government at least seeks the distinction of opening the door to the present generation in order that it may begin to share in the progress which human reason has made in recent centuries. The establishment of a national library is one of the most effective ways of promoting intellectual values and ensuring that people of all ages share in the secrets that can be discovered in the heart of nature.[52]

In the first weeks of independence San Martín was personally responsible for the creation of the National Library (28 August 1821), 'an enlightened undertaking more powerful than our armies in preserving independence.' Its first acquisitions were six hundred books from his own collection, of which few now survive, most of them lamentably lost over the years and in the disastrous fire of 11 May 1943. The National Library was dear to the heart of San Martín, a gateway to science and the arts in Peru, an agent of toleration and enlightenment 'promising great benefits to the cause of America.'[53] The San Martín collection was testimony to the intellectual interests of a reader alive to the thought of the Enlightenment. Books on military and naval history and strategy were predictably included, but the collection also abounded in works by Montesquieu, Voltaire, Rousseau, Diderot, Beaumarchais and other encyclopedists, with an evident preference for French works and an interest in the French Revolution; classics of the ancient world were also represented. If a person can be judged by his library, San Martín was a man of the modern age, not of the old regime.[54]

A puritanical streak runs through some of the Protectorate's policies, others anticipate modern practices. Smoking in the theatre was deplored, at the same time as the theatre's educational value was praised and the acting profession liberated from archaic prejudices. A decree declared that 'gambling is a crime that subverts public morals and ruins families' and established prison sentences for owners of casinos. The abolition of cockfighting was announced, and the ringing of church bells restricted. Masters were prohibited under pain of a fine from forcing servants to work on holidays. There were edicts that sought to improve the services of markets, and others that took steps to prevent usury, so harmful to 'the needy classes'.[55] The government also looked at its own practices. Ministers imposed a seven-hour working day in government offices, arguing that government ought to be less expensive, as it was in the United States and as Adam Smith advocated. On the installation of the Supreme Court the Protectorate advocated swifter, less expensive and more transparent justice, and insisted that 'in cases of doubt it is better to release a guilty person than to condemn an innocent one.'[56]

Crime and punishment came under review. Reforms in the prison system and the treatment of delinquents were made, reflecting the Protector's own disquiet over existing practice as well as the liberal thought of the age. In October 1821 he personally visited the prisons, spoke to the prisoners, took account of their views and revised a number of sentences. He abolished all forms of torture. A decree of 3 January 1822 declared 'the abolition in Peru of the penalty of the gallows, and those unfortunate enough to incur the death penalty shall all be executed by firing squad.' The penalty of *azotes* (the lash) was abolished, and judges, schoolteachers and anyone applying this punishment would themselves be subject to severe punishment as enemies of the *patria*. This decree referred specifically to free persons, but the beating of slaves was also restricted and subject to control by a judge on pain of losing the slave.[57]

Enlightened despotism was the style of the Protectorate. The reforming legislation that it enacted seemed to come out in a rush, in contrast to the performance of its armies. San Martín was aware that he was under critical scrutiny and that he was expected to destroy the viceroyalty as well as replace it. But while he designed new policies for Peruvians and their institutions, these applied to a narrow political framework and in the sierra they did not apply at all. More was expected of him. He needed greater power than was provided by his limp army and supine support base. Could he cross the threshold of revolution? Could he conquer the whole of Peru for independence?

CHAPTER 9

Last Chance in Guayaquil

The War for Peru: Testing the Strategy

The year 1822 was San Martín's time of trial, when his thesis was tested and his strategy challenged, and a cloud of uncertainty hovered over his every move. The two essentials for a Liberator, a powerful army and personal power, for long evaded San Martín. He sought them in Peru, but where could he find them? The question troubled him and by 1822 he still did not have the answer. Peru remained a destination without a route.

The expedition to Peru, brilliant in concept, was flawed in practice, lacking as it did cohesion in composition, objectives and tactics. San Martín led a disjointed operation from first launch to final closure. The expeditionary force itself was not a coherent entity. The army and the navy were fighting different wars, San Martín's strategic ideas being totally at odds with those of Cochrane. The military command was also divided, in its composition and its concepts. Argentines, Chileans, foreigners were difficult to unite and unify, and from the beginning senior officers had too much independence over tactics and objectives. The defeat at Talca in Chile (19 March 1818), which still rankled, had destroyed the general's confidence in some of his senior officers. As for the troops, the 'animosities' between the Argentines and Chileans were clear enough for outsiders to notice, and the army never really bonded.[1]

Peru itself was a byword for division. Spaniards ruled it successfully for three centuries by the principle of divide and rule, with different rules for different sectors of society. It was a traditional and hierarchical society almost born to differ. Creole aristocracy, incipient middle class, *cholo* workers on the coast, Indian peasants in the highlands, slaves on plantations, and beyond the law groups of escaped slaves, delinquents and vagrants—this was a mosaic of problems lying in wait to confuse any invader who wanted to govern and command. San Martín never secured a power base among Peruvian interests. A fractured society, an unstable army, the problems were compounded by perplexity in San Martín's own mind, turning on three major issues: the Lima-sierra alternative; the quality of his military resources; and the concept of revolution without war.

The Liberator has been frequently criticized for giving priority to Lima over the sierra and for imagining that conquest of the capital was virtually conquest of the country. He was not so naïve. He was aware that the two were different places with distinct assets and significance. But there is no evidence that San Martín viewed them as mutually exclusive; both would have to be conquered for the revolution. Lima was the primary target because it was the seat of Spanish power and the location of the Spanish army. There was no way of avoiding that target; it had to be defeated. Lima was also the priority of Cochrane and of military planners and advisers such as Belgrano. Arenales exceptionally favoured the sierra as a battleground, but the operations of a flying column in the highlands, a tactical idea originating with San Martín, was not the same as placing the bulk of the army there. La Serna did precisely that with his army, and he too was then trapped in a stalemate.

The withdrawal of Arenales from the sierra was not due to tactical error by San Martín. He subsequently explained to William Miller:

The division of Arenales withdrew from the sierra because of a mistaken order given by Colonel Alvarado, who was in Palpa with the cavalry; when the General in Chief [San Martín] learnt of this order he ordered General Arenales to suspend his march, but he had already crossed the cordillera and his division was in a bad state from campaign fatigue and from sickness, which made it impossible for the general to return across the cordillera.[2]

The ideas that San Martín expressed to Captain Basil Hall were not the same as those he had developed in the *Plan Continental* and subsequent statements in Mendoza. These were for a military build-up sufficient to bring decisive force to bear on Spanish power in Peru. In the *Plan Continental* San Martín spoke of the *military conquest* of Peru. In the years of waiting, 1817–20, he was still speaking of an orthodox strategy of attack, victory and liberation. This would require, he argued, six thousand troops; Belgrano, with his experience of fighting royalist armies in Upper Peru, suggested eight thousand. These quantities were never reached and the expedition sailed seriously underpowered, with only 4,500 troops more or less ready for fighting. After exhaustive recruiting drives in Cuyo and Chile, and pressure on landowners for slaves, these were the final forces available, and the optimum strength was never reached. San Martín's preferred tactics had always focused on a pitched battle in which his maximum force faced and crushed the massed ranks of the royalists in a single engagement. Winning battles was his talent. Prolonged campaigns, he argued, led only to loss of power and recovery by the enemy. This is precisely the outcome he risked in Peru, when his estimate of the relative strengths of the two armies recognized the superiority of the royalists. No one was sure of exact numbers; royalist estimates had to take account of a number of armies and varied wildly according to the emergency of the moment, but the totals for Lima, Arequipa and Upper Peru amounted to eleven thousand for 1818–19, while estimates by outside observers varied between seven and ten thousand.[3] Having experienced the fighting qualities of Spanish troops at Maipú, (5 April 1818) San Martín was left in no doubt that this would be a difficult campaign.

Military weakness, therefore, explains San Martín's change to new concepts and new language, his increasing resort to the 'minds and hearts' theory of war, which he explained clearly in his conversations with Basil Hall. That had not always been his language, in Buenos Aires, Mendoza and Santiago. Three years of blighted hopes before he even set sail, three years of cutting back the *Plan Continental*, not least in his own mind, had changed the entire strategy. There was no question of postponing the invasion until army numbers and training had improved. Where would the reinforcements come from? Who would pay for more arms? He had drained the reserves, and his credit, in Argentina and Chile. He personally could not face further delay, and endless waiting would only destroy the credibility of the whole enterprise. This was too defeatist to contemplate.

So there was a strategic shift in his Peruvian thinking, from force to reason. It is true that he had always abhorred violent change. 'He has always expressed the greatest anxiety to prevent if possible any revolution in Lima which might occasion bloodshed and calamity. I really believe that he has avoided all attempts to work upon the black population in that country from this very motive.'[4] But 'revolution' in this sense means the overturn of the existing social structure and the release of the underdogs to terrorize their masters. San Martín had never subscribed to such a policy. Up to 1817 he was speaking of the conquest of Spanish Peru by an invading army. In 1820 the project is no longer the conquest of Lima, much less of Spanish Peru, but the conquest of minds and hearts. This was clear from his first proclamation to his troops in Peru: 'You come to liberate peoples, not to make conquests', a popular claim often made and violated by invaders. In San Martín's case it was only too true.

The hard fact was that he did not have the power to conquer Peru. He had no power base among Peruvians on which he could draw; his only strength was his own army. He knew this and he did not have confidence enough in that army, either in its officers, its soldiers, or its morale, to defeat the Spaniards. The Act of Rancagua (2 April 1820), making his legitimacy dependent on the Argentine military, left him exposed to unreliable colleagues who deserted him when the going got tough. While San Martín received enduring loyalty and affection from many junior officers, his senior officers were not so drawn. An obscure conspiracy and the abrupt departure of leading officers prolonged his ordeal and set back his campaign. His thesis of liberation without war was tested to the limit. But he won the battle of wills and his patient tactics prevailed. He never doubted that they were right. As he later explained to General Miller, 'Let me tell you that if I had had the good fortune to have in the army under my command only six chiefs who possessed your qualities and experience, I am sure that the war in Peru would have ended two years before it did.'[5]

Was there any way to salvage his project? Bolívar could be the model. He saw that he had first to create an army large enough to conquer Peru and impose itself on Spaniards and creoles, on royalists and patriots, and force them into independence. San Martín came to the same conclusion, but when he tried to reinforce his army with the help of Bolívar, he was rebuffed. Yet he proved his point; he demonstrated in spite of himself that a small army and the force of ideas were not enough, and that Peruvians would not volunteer for independence.

Conference in Guayaquil

Accepting his limited options, San Martín decided in June 1822 to go to Guayaquil to confer with the great Liberator of the north. They had already encountered each other at a distance and knew of their rival claims and achievements. Different in origins, career and character, they agreed on only one thing: Spain would have to be defeated in Peru. But which of them would achieve that victory? They approached each other warily. Bolívar hated the idea of risking his glory by coming second. 'I do not intend to throw away the achievement of eleven years with a humiliation, nor do I want San Martín to see me in any other role than that of the *chosen son*.'[6] He was also determined to claim Quito and Guayaquil for Colombia against any claims by Peru. Beneath polite phrases there was tension. The Venezuelans resented San Martín's retention of the Colombian Numancia battalion that had defected from the Spanish army and tried in vain to reclaim it. Bolívar's commander Antonio José de Sucre thanked San Martín for his military support in Quito but was convinced that this was a pretext for preempting the province. In October 1821 he wrote a long and prolix letter to San Martín, commiserating on the casualties suffered by his army through sickness and the less than brilliant outcome of his campaign, and describing the help that the 'Liberator of Colombia', recently triumphant in Venezuela, wished to give his comrade in the south. In the course of the letter he seemed to change his mind and suddenly asked a series of questions. Did the war in Peru really require Colombian troops? If not, could San Martín provide transports for the movement of Colombian troops to 'another place' in the war to liberate America? The reason was that Bolívar 'intended to postpone the Quito campaign in favour of that in Peru and that our massed forces should go to Peru, because the two states being free the small countries in between will be insignificant.'[7]

By now, if he understood any of this confusing speculation, San Martín should have been suspicious of his allies in the north and aware that they had their own agenda; this did not place the Protector of Peru above the Liberator of Colombia or the claims of San Martín above the determination of Bolívar to take the whole province of Quito, including Guayaquil, for Colombia. Moreover, their military plans could change rapidly, as they did when Colonel Andrés Santa Cruz arrived with his Peruvian expedition and Sucre launched his campaign northwards to Quito; reinforced by the Peruvian allies, Sucre's army defeated the Spaniards at the battle of Pichincha on 24 May 1822. On 17 June Bolívar wrote to San Martín and assured him of:

> the gratitude with which the people and government of Colombia have welcomed the distinguished liberators of Peru, who have come bearing their victorious arms to give their powerful support to the campaign which has already liberated three provinces in the south of Colombia.... This is not simply a tribute of gratitude to the government and army of Peru but the expression of our fervent desire to give similar and even stronger assistance to the government of Peru, unless by this time the liberating army of the South has not already successfully ended its present campaign. The war in Colombia has now ended and its army is ready to march wherever it is needed, and particularly to the land of our neighbours in the South.[8]

At the same time Bolívar was writing to Francisco de Paula Santander, vice-president of Colombia, in more calculating language and with a rather different message:

> If Guayaquil submits I shall send a couple of battalions to Peru. 1. so that our neighbours are not more generous than we are; 2. to help Peru before disaster strikes; 3. for reasons of economy, for we lack the means to keep so many troops here; 4. to begin to fulfil the offers of mutual aid; 5, 6 and 7, because I think it advisable that they send us three battalions from Peru to replace them once the war is over.[9]

Guayaquil was the gem of the Spanish Pacific. Situated on the west bank of the Guayas, upriver from the gulf of Guayaquil, it was a naval base, a ship-building centre and a major port. Strategically and commercially it was indis-pensable to the revolution and both liberators wanted it. From the beginning of 1822 Bolívar had made it clear that he regarded Guayaquil as part of the territory of Colombia. Now he took steps to make it so, whether Peruvians or locals liked it or not. He detained the division of Santa Cruz at Quito 'under specious pretences' in case it intervened on behalf of Peru, and ordered a Colombian division to march on the port without delay.[10] On 13 July he decreed the formal incorporation of Guayaquil into Colombia, subsequently confirmed by 'vote' of the *guayaquileños*. Soon Bolívar was a fixture in Guayaquil, with a Colombian army and a local girlfriend, Joaquina Garaycoa, whom he called his *amable loca*.

San Martín was not so sharp. In fact he had been slow to pick up the clues, and cautious in formulating his Guayaquil policy. On 13 July he still thought Bolívar was in Quito:

Peru is the only remaining battlefield in America, and it is there that those who wish to claim the honours of the final victory will have to join against those who have been defeated throughout the continent. I accept the offer you have generously made me in your letter of 17 June, and Peru will welcome with gratitude all the troops that you can make available in order to accelerate the campaign and leave nothing to fortune. I hope Colombia will have the satisfaction of seeing its arms contribute powerfully to bringing an end to the war in Peru, just as those of Peru have contributed to planting the flag of the Republic in the south of your vast territory.

Before the 18th I shall sail from Callao and no sooner landed in Guayaquil than I shall move to greet you in Quito. My soul fills with thoughts and joy when I contemplate that moment; we shall meet and I foresee that America will not forget the day we embrace each other.[11]

As San Martín reached Guayaquil waters and communicated with Bolívar through aides, he became more wary and, as he learned of his rival's coup, more distrustful. Bolívar expressed surprise but satisfaction at the visit, and regretted that he had not been warned and given enough time to prepare an adequate reception. San Martín suggested a meeting on board his ship, but Bolívar would have none of it. The Protector would have to see and learn and show himself in the city. 'I shall feel it as keenly as if I had been defeated in many battles if you do not come to this city; but no, you will not frustrate my desire to embrace the first friend of my heart and my country.'[12] When the ship approached the harbour on the morning of 26 July, Bolívar went on board and embraced his fellow Liberator. It was the beginning of two days of public friendship and private talks from which Bolívar expected to contribute 'to the good of South America'.

Bolívar was approaching the peak of his public career: he too had liberated more than his native land and, while not without problems, he had recent victories and a successful army behind him. San Martín, on the other hand, was conscious that his position in Peru was weak. He had not won sufficient territory, his forces seemed to be losing the war and the Spaniards had turned stubborn over negotiations. He could count on no further support from the Chileans, and the leadership in Buenos Aires was frankly hostile. With few bargaining points, he approached the meeting in Guayaquil with three needs in mind: the annexation of Guayaquil to Peru (though he insisted above all that it had the right to decide its own destiny); the assistance of Colombian troops to reinforce his own army and defeat the Spaniards; and support for his plans of monarchical constitutions for the new states.

The meetings were held on 26 and 27 July in private, behind closed doors and there was no third party present.[13] So the Bolivarian version of the interview came from Bolívar himself, particularly from the account he dictated to José Gabriel Pérez, his long-serving secretary general, for transmission to the Colombian government.[14] The other account is contained in a letter written by San Martín to Bolívar on 29 August, about a month after the meetings, a letter whose authenticity is challenged by Venezuelan historians, though not normally by their Argentine colleagues. The letter cannot be 'authentic', for it is not the original, nor a copy, but a French translation of a document of uncertain provenance published in 1844 by a French traveller, Gabriel Lafond de Lurcy, and known to San Martín, who neither confirmed nor denied it.[15] This was the Protector's normal reaction to controversy, especially concerning Bolívar: 'no comment'. If the Lafond letter is not authentic, however, that does not mean it is untrue. It raises a critical issue not recorded in Bolívar's account. Did San Martín request major assistance from Bolívar?

The Bolivarian version insisted that discussion was confined to political matters, that San Martín did not make an issue of the status of Guayaquil or request military aid, and that he did not procure Bolívar's agreement for a monarchy in Peru. The Protector complained about his military comrades who had deserted him in Lima, expressed his anxiety to renounce the Protectorate and retire to Mendoza even before the end of the war in Peru, though not before he had laid firm foundations of government. It should not be a democratic government, which was unsuitable for Peru, but a monarchy with an independent prince brought from Europe. Bolívar opposed the idea of a monarchy and the accession of a European or any other prince in the Americas. The Protector made it clear that he had no ambition to occupy such a throne, and he spoke of the problems inherent in leadership. He applauded the idea of a federal union between Colombia and Peru, and spoke enthusiastically of the exchange of military recruits between the two countries. And meanwhile he would agree to anything Bolívar requested of Peru. Yes, yes, yes were his words, and he hoped that Colombia would reciprocate. Apart from the question of monarchy Bolívar seemed well satisfied with the interview, though he noticed in passing that San Martín's language was occasionally coarse and vulgar. Bolívar's version of the interview is also given in a similar though shorter account to Sucre, in which it is stated that the Protector had no ulterior purpose in his visit to Bolívar, either political or military, expressed little interest in Guayaquil, and appeared convinced that the enemy was weaker than he; he made no reference to the troops that Colombia was about to send to Peru.[16]

The Bolivarian account of the interview is a frank analysis of what took place, though selective and partial. According to the Lafond letter of 1844, the Protector needed and requested the support of Bolívar's army to complete the destruction of royalist power in Peru, and to procure this he offered to serve under Bolívar's command. A letter of San Martín in April 1827 to General William Miller, who contacted him from time to time after the war when he was preparing his memoirs, confirms that he went to Guayaquil to request auxiliary forces from Bolívar:

> As for my journey to Guayaquil, the only object was to claim from General Bolívar the forces he could provide to end the war in Peru, forces that (quite apart from the general interests of America) justice demanded in recompense for those that Peru had generously provided to liberate the territory of Colombia. I was all the more confident in a good result in that after the battle of Pichincha the army of Colombia had been increased by the prisoners and numbered 9,600 soldiers. But my hopes were dashed when in our first conference the Liberator told me that, with all his possible efforts, he could spare only three battalions, with a total of 1,070 troops. These forces did not seem to me to be sufficient to finish the war, for I was convinced that success depended on the effective cooperation of all the Colombian forces.[17]

San Martín was deeply disappointed that Bolívar had preempted the status of Guayaquil, but realist enough to see that nothing could be done to reverse the Colombian occupation. Bolívar also made it clear that there could be no European monarchy in America. So San Martín's basic aim in Guayaquil was reduced to securing Bolívar's military support, in the form either of a large military force or of an army under Bolívar himself. But Bolívar rejected these proposals. He was ready to commit reinforcements but not his whole army, which he then needed for internal security in Colombia. He claimed to have offered San Martín four thousand men, but he also knew that he could not find them. So he regarded the offer and the request as excessive, and he had serious doubts whether San Martín could deliver his side of the proposal. Would San Martín really take orders from a younger man and would San Martín's army accept such an arrangement? Moreover, he was not impressed by San Martín's conduct of the war in Peru and regarded his military policy as impractical and irresolute. So the interview was fruitless. There was reason in Bolívar's position, yet the suspicion will always remain that he did not wish to share the glory of Peru with San Martín and preferred to go it alone to his own inevitable triumph.

At the end of the meetings the town council of Guayaquil gave a ball for San Martín. While Bolívar was showing his prowess on the dance floor, San Martín remained aloof, with nothing to celebrate, conscious that his career in Peru was finished. He left at about two in the morning, not in disgust as is sometimes implied but to board his ship which had to catch the tide. Bolívar accompanied him and gave him a portrait of himself, 'a memento of his sincere friendship'.[18] The Protector had been only forty hours in Guayaquil.

The Guayaquil conference became a byword for Bolívar's confidence, San Martín's frustration, and endless speculation. San Martín was now clear in his mind that, without a large army, he could not complete his project in Peru and he had no alternative but to abandon it. He had no fall-back position. After the conference he told Bolívar that he would call Congress in the following month, and the day of its installation would be his last day in Peru, adding 'now a new field of glory awaits you in which you will place the final seal of American freedom.' Bolívar took a more sanguine view of the meeting, and simply dismissed from his mind things he did not want to know. He summarized the encounter to Santander rather airily as nothing more than 'compliments, talk, and goodbye'. San Martín 'did not mention any special purpose in coming, and he made no demands of Colombia.' He was not a democrat but favoured a monarchy imported from Europe. He himself was not a candidate; in fact he was tired of the supreme command and of being a target for his enemies. 'He impresses me as being very military in character, and he appears to be energetic, quick, and by no means dull. He has the type of correct ideas that would please you; but he did not strike me as being subtle enough to rise to the sublime either in ideas or in action.' Bolívar was satisfied with his success. 'There is now nothing more for me to do, my dear general, except to store in a safe place the treasure of my success, hiding it out of sight where no one can take it from me.' The remarks are a guide to both liberators.[19]

Critical Days in Lima

Behind the courtesies, San Martín left Guayaquil on 28 July disillusioned, convinced that Bolívar either doubted the sincerity of his offer to serve with his forces under his command or was embarrassed by his presence in the revolution.[20] He believed that Bolívar was superficial, vain and ambitious, dominated by a '*pasión de mando*'.[21] San Martín also had the honesty to recognize that this was the man to win the war, a man who would crush anyone in his way, not only the Spaniards but if necessary San Martín himself. He was convinced that his own presence was the only obstacle that prevented Bolívar from coming to Peru with his army.

The leader of the southern revolution decided to withdraw and leave the way open for Bolívar to conquer Peru for independence. There were closer threats to his position than Bolívar. When he returned to Peru he found his standing eroded, his influence among the Peruvian ruling class weakened and his authority over his own army fading. Peru was crumbling into chaos, teetering on the brink of civil war. But he kept a cool head, pretending that the political situation was calm. During his absence a number of leading citizens led by Riva Agüero had presented a request to the *cabildo* for Monteagudo's removal. Amidst some popular commotion in support of the request, the *cabildo* approved the petitioners and restrained the army from intervening against them. Torre Tagle, sensing the mood, removed the unpopular minister of war and foreign affairs from office and ushered him away from Lima on 30 July. San Martín reported that his return (20 August) had quietened the commotion after the dismissal of Monteagudo. The fact was that others had taken awkward decisions for San Martín. 'On my return here I found that Monteagudo had been removed. His character has brought this on. I would have removed him to an appointment to a legation, but Torre Tagle frequently asked me to leave it, for there was no one to replace him.'[22]

If his control over events seemed to be slipping, he kept his eyes fixed on his traditional objectives right to the end. Military priorities still concerned him. A Spanish army of five thousand was threatening to descend down the Cuzco road, and it was reported that the Peruvian division from Quito together with Colombian reinforcements were on their way to join the army of independence.[23] San Martín had a plan of campaign for the sierra: two of his commanders, Alvarez de Arenales and Rudecindo Alvarado were to take the offensive against Cuzco and the power base of La Serna. He had promised Bolívar that he would open his campaign with an expedition to Intermedios in the south and a frontal attack on the enemy from Lima. He now activated these two fronts. Alvarado was instructed to penetrate the sierra from Arica via Arequipa and to attack Cuzco. This attack was seconded by Arenales from Lima to Huancayo, thus completing the encirclement of La Serna.

At the same time as he was finalizing these projects, San Martín was also planning to take the provinces of Upper Peru and re-annex them to the Río de la Plata, acting like an Argentine rather than a Peruvian. In May he had sent the Peruvian officer Antonio Gutiérrez de la Fuente on a mission to seek the help of the provinces of the Río de la Plata in assembling resources and troops for a campaign in Upper Peru; the object was to renew the war against the Spanish occupying forces, 'in the interests of the general cause of America'. The interior provinces were willing to collaborate, but Buenos Aires was not interested. Rivadavia, his eyes always focused on Buenos Aires, suspicious of the provinces and blind to a wider America, was never in sympathy with San Martín's projects. But San Martín continued to plan for Upper Peru. Alvarado was instructed 'to preserve the integrity of all the territory within its known boundaries belonging to the United Provinces', though the Protector also left open the possibility of Upper Peru declaring itself an autonomous state through making provision for a general congress after the war.[24]

But policies were taken out of San Martín's hands. The Constitution of 1823 defined Peru's territory as including Upper Peru and Lower Peru. A Junta Gubernativa headed by José de la Mar succeeded San Martín and it was this government that activated the expedition to Intermedios planned by the Protector. In the event the plans came to nothing, for Alvarado's forces, inadequate from the start, were crushingly defeated by Canterac at Torata and Moquegua in January 1823. The collapse of the army was the prelude to a period of serious anarchy in Peru, with interest groups and their leaders struggling for dominance, a fate that San Martín had always feared. This was a problem for his successors. His own ordeal had arrived earlier.

Thoughts of resignation, always lurking, came to the front of his mind in Guayaquil, as he made clear to Bolívar. This was not the first indication that a time would arrive for his retirement from office. Monteagudo claimed that when the invading army first reached Pisco in 1820 the leaders pleaded with San Martín to head the administration when they occupied Lima, though he was a man of war and averse to government office: 'He agreed reluctantly and only for a limited time'.[25] To Basil Hall he had insisted in July 1821 that once Peru was independent he would consider that he had done enough and leave.[26] And in the same month, when the Spaniards left Lima, San Martín told O'Higgins, 'I can now foresee the end of my public career; I am going to prepare to hand over this heavy burden to secure hands, retire to a corner and live like a man.'[27] On his return to Lima from Guayaquil in August 1822 he wrote to O'Higgins in terms similar to those he had used to Bolívar, 'I am sick of being called a tyrant who wants to become king, emperor, and even the devil. At the same time my health is very impaired: the climate of this country is the death of me. My youth was sacrificed in the service of Spain and my middle age in that of my country. I think I have a right to own my old age.' He would call Congress and immediately leave the country, which he had long wished to do, and if possible go to see his daughter in Buenos Aires.[28] Asthma took its hold, complicated by gastric problems and gout. His doctors prescribed opium, which he took in increasing quantities; the result was pain, not pleasure, as euphoria alternated with depression. Exhaustion and lethargy were not the best conditions for taking critical decisions.[29] He took refuge when he could in his country house, La Magdalena. But events continued to press on him.

He had always promised to refer government to Peruvians themselves, and now he convoked the first Congress of independent Peru. It met on 20 September 1822. Only the liberated provinces, Lima, Tarma, Huaylas, Trujillo and the Coast were able to send representatives, while the rest, occupied by the army of La Serna, were represented by delegates who resided in Lima. Of the eighty-one deputies, twenty-six were clerics, twenty-eight lawyers, five military, eight medical doctors, nine merchants and five landowners. Among these fourteen came from other American countries: nine Colombians, three Argentines, one Bolivian and one Chilean.[30] The Protector opened the sessions in person and formally resigned his office, before retiring to La Magdalena, his occupation gone.

A Terrible Example

The invasion, the war, the victory in Lima and the Protectorate, each gain had followed in regular succession, but now the momentum had been lost. San Martín's Peruvian project remained incomplete, his universe shattered. His coolness did not desert him, but he could not escape the facts. Quite simply, Peru had become an impossible place for the Protector. Others could see this. A letter from one of his most trusted colleagues back in March, García del Río, a man of judgement and integrity, told him the truth: 'I am convinced that it is absolutely indispensable that when you return from your journey [to Guayaquil] you solemnly resume your command. Proceed immediately to the opening of Congress and there resign your political office, without giving anyone the excuse to torment you and the idea that this step has been forced on you. This is my opinion. You will decide what best to do.'[31]

As García del Río implied, the situation was insoluble by San Martín's standards. He had managed to contain the chaos but not to dominate it. While the Protectorate was not exactly a democracy, nor was it a dictatorship beyond the law. In the Provisional Statute the Protector had fettered himself with the rule of law, which prevented him from imposing a dictatorship. His legalism was a constraint, an obstacle to peace and order. Only a despotism could rule in Peru, but he refused this road. There was no solution on his own terms and by his own standards; a fatal preference for the rule of law gave him legality but not force. The time had come for critical decisions, which he took calmly but beset by inner turmoil and external pressures. On his journey to Guayaquil he knew that Peru was in crisis and civil war not impossible, and he was powerless to avoid it. Effectively he was helpless, a general without an army, a Protector without power.

Bolívar saw things more clearly and acted more decisively. He had made a profession of dictatorships, imposing and receiving them in equal measure throughout his political career. On more than one occasion he invoked 'the terrible example' of San Martín to remind recalcitrant colleagues of the reactions of leaders when they were frustrated too far. In 1822–3, poised on the border of Peru, Bolívar had the plan and the army to re-enact his familiar procedure, yet Peru would not be easy even for him to conquer and he found what he had always suspected, that ideas and reason were not enough in Peru. He believed San Martín was too moderate. He later advised Sucre in Upper Peru not to fall into the 'moderation' of San Martín, who had believed that ideas would prevail:

> You have a very rare type of moderation. You are reluctant to exercise the authority of a general, which is yours as de facto ruler of the country occupied by your troops, and yet you wish to pursue a course of action which is legislative in nature. I am sorry if the comparison seems odious, but it is like the situation of San Martín in Peru. He thought that his authority as general and liberator was too great, and hence he undertook to apply a provisional statute, for which he had no authority.[32]

So Bolívar's assessment of San Martín's predicament in Peru was that he was too tolerant and his enemies took advantage of his moderation. Bolívar had no doubt that Peru needed 'a terrible remedy' to overcome its endemic anarchy. In February 1824 he declared to the sovereign Congress of Peru, 'Let me give you some salutary advice, the final proof of my dedication to your cause, perhaps the greatest service I can do for Peru amidst the frightful circumstances that engulf it. I believe that the sovereign authority of the nation ought to create a dictator with absolute and unlimited power, and that this dictator should declare martial law in the republic with such qualifications as his wisdom judges necessary. Only this dictator can offer a ray of hope for the welfare of the republic.'[33] And in Peru he became the dictator, a ray of hope that faded in the end. In a paper on the state of Spanish America in 1829, Bolívar singled out an ungrateful Peru for special execration, 'complicit with its tyrants during the war of independence, destroyer of the gallant General San Martín, whose services it desperately needed', home of divisive caudillos who were always ready to betray each other or sell out to the Spaniards. 'There is no good faith in America, nor among the nations of America. Treaties are scraps of paper; constitutions, mere books; elections, battles, freedom, anarchy; and life, a torment.'[34]

San Martín's old comrade in arms, Arenales, reported that the situation had deteriorated since he left, politics in chaos, the war disastrous; the government he had left in charge in Lima was 'useless for its task, and Congress too has been a great obstacle to the conduct of war.' The message of Arenales was clear: after you the storm. He himself could take no more and left.[35] After San Martín, Peru tore itself apart. A makeshift junta fell to the military; their government consisted of former royalists headed by José de la Riva Agüero; within months he was replaced by Torre Tagle; and when Bolívar arrived in Lima on 1 September 1823 he was faced with divided patriot forces, a large royalist army, a Congress and two presidents, while he himself was a dictator in waiting. He had to wait until 10 February 1824 when Congress suspended the Constitution and appointed him dictator.

Two preconditions were necessary for victory in Peru: a powerful army, which San Martín did not have, and an absolute dictatorship, which he denied himself. Bolívar was the only leader who could fulfil these conditions, leading the army and imposing a dictatorship. These conditions were bound inextricably together, and the one could not be resolved without the other. The Protector could not defeat his political enemies as long as they could appeal to, or threaten to bring in, the royal army. The royalist presence in the sierra meant not only that the war was not won militarily but also that there was a destabilizing element in the midst of the revolution with which dissidents could ally. San Martín was not even ruthless enough with the army. Facing the hostility of his own officers, which was a factor in his resignation, he admitted he should have dealt more firmly with them. There was hesitation, too, politically, as Bolívar noticed, and as he himself admitted. San Martín's government was not strong enough to confront his Peruvian enemies. During his exile, he agreed with García del Río that he should have applied a strong stick in Peru; the stick fell from my hands, he said, for want of knowing how to handle it. Others also noticed his reluctance to embrace absolutism. His political thought was always finely balanced between a need for strong government and a preference for liberal values. Maria Graham, much travelled widow of a British naval officer, met San Martín in Chile after his resignation, was not impressed and thought he was vacillating: 'There seems a timidity of intellect, which prevents the daring to give freedom and the daring to be despotic alike. The wish to enjoy the reputation of a liberator and the will to be a tyrant are strangely contrasted in his discourse'[36] In this analysis there was no room for nuances, only a choice between two absolutes.

San Martín insisted on using the term *regreso* and not *retirada* to describe his departure from Peru. Whatever the word, the time had arrived. He was resigned to his fate and he now resigned from office, being determined, as a British observer reported 'to retire from a country where his presence would be considered by many as a restraint upon the Congress, and where his acts were exposed to continual misrepresentation'.[37] The day of 20 September 1822 was a desolate one for San Martín, the end of his Peruvian project: he formally relinquished his command to Congress and returned to La Magdalena. There he went to his desk and wrote his farewell Proclamation and a letter to General Alvarado with instructions for his next campaign. The Proclamation was pure San Martín, straight and unadorned:

> My promises to the peoples for whom I have fought are fulfilled: to secure their independence and leave them to elect their own governments. The presence of a fortunate soldier, however disinterested he may be, is dangerous to newly constituted states. At the same time I am tired of hearing it said that I wish to become sovereign, though I will always be ready to sacrifice my life for the liberty of the country, simply as a private individual.
>
> As for my political conduct, fellow countrymen, you will differ in your opinions, as is usually the case. Your children will give the final verdict. Peruvians, I leave you a national assembly; place your confidence in this and you will triumph; do otherwise and anarchy will destroy you. May success crown your destiny and may this be one of happiness and peace.[38]

At nine o'clock in the evening he came out of his office and asked Guido, his friend and political ally, to come in for a drink of *mate*. After a short silence he suddenly told him that he was leaving; he had his horses ready to take him to Ancón, where he would embark in the brig *Belgrano* waiting to take him to Chile. Guido was astonished:

You are joking?

I'm serious.

But how can you leave with your work unfinished, a campaign that hasn't yet begun, the state in anarchy, your comrades abandoned who have followed you from the Plate and Chile? Who will replace you? I don't believe it.

I have thought deeply about this, I am conscious of my obligations and the interests of America, and of my comrades in arms. But I cannot remain here a day longer, I'm leaving. I am convinced that Peru would be worse off if I stayed than if I left now. Be assured that for many reasons I cannot any longer remain in my post under conditions absolutely contrary to my deepest feelings and convictions. Let me tell you frankly that one of them is the unavoidable obligation that to save the honour and discipline of the army I should shoot a number of commanders, and I lack the courage to do this to companions in arms who have followed me in good times and bad.

In and above all of this there is a major difficulty, one that I have not explained to anyone, not even to my loyal and noble friend, General O'Higgins, a difficulty which is impossible to overcome without sacrificing the good of the state and my own credit. There is not enough room in Peru for Bolívar and me. And Bolívar is anxious and determined to come here. I have come to appreciate his aims and intentions, and to understand the humiliation he would suffer because of the glory that could fall to me at the conclusion of the campaign. He will not forego any means, whatever they might be, to intervene in the affairs of Peru, to become its arbiter, and to be the one who achieves a successful conclusion.[39]

He said goodbye to Guido, promptly left La Magdalena, a favourite place soon to be despoiled by his successors, and made for the *Belgrano*, anchored at Ancón. There he wrote a note to Guido. 'My friend, you accompanied me from Buenos Aires, joining your fortune to mine. We have worked together all this time doing what we could for the country. Now I leave you, but with gratitude, not only for the help you have given me in the difficult tasks I have entrusted to you but also for your friendship and personal affection, which have smoothed the bitter passages and made my public life more tolerable. Thank you, thank you, and again my gratitude. Your San Martín.'[40]

He sailed for Chile the next morning. The route was one of the slower stretches of the Pacific coast, beating against the southerly winds, and it was 12 October before he disembarked in Valparaíso. He was warmly received by the governor, José Ignacio Zenteno, his old secretary in the Army of the Andes, whom he had never really trusted. The partisans of Admiral Cochrane, still a hero in Chile, mounted a campaign to discredit him, and Cochrane himself who was in Valparaíso at the time sought to bring charges against him for his actions in Peru.[41] The slander was already beginning. Guido ruefully warned San Martín that this was what he could expect, now that he had hung up his sword and left himself exposed to old jealousies and ambitions.[42] But this did not diminish the respect he received from the Chilean government, still headed by O'Higgins, who gave him a handsome escort to Santiago and placed the hospitable villa of Conventillo at his disposal. There San Martín attempted to restore his health, much reduced by his recent ordeal, and alleviated by a visit to the waters of Cauquenes. In Chile he could not completely abandon his Peruvian project and he still had illusions of liberating Upper

Peru, as he tried to hold on to the various threads of attack. But he could only watch from the sidelines as his former commanders marched into disaster.[43]

In Santiago he called on Maria Graham, whose admiration of Lord Cochrane seems to have influenced her views on San Martín. She did not like or approve of her visitor, but appreciated his ability:

> His whole manner was most courteous: I could not but observe, that his movements as well as his person are graceful; and I can well believe what I have heard, that in a ball-room he has few superiors. . . . His views are narrow, and I think selfish. He certainly has no genius, but he has some talents, with no learning and little general knowledge. . . . His fine person, his air of superiority, and that suavity of manner which so long enabled him to lead others, give him very decided advantages. He understands English and speaks French tolerably.[44]

A testing occasion for a general who has just relinquished his dearest ambition.

When he left Peru San Martín had not planned his ultimate destination. His decision to leave South America for Europe developed in stages, one step at a time in response to events and pressures. After a brief pause in Chile, his next stop was Mendoza where he had a house and an estate and a possible life. This was the closest he had come to planning his future.

Farewell the Big Wars

San Martín crossed the Andes for the last time and made his way to Mendoza, which he had long said was the haven he sought and the home of friends. The journey was hard, and for him evocative, as he travelled on a mule across the soaring landscape, accompanied by a captain and a train of assistants. On the ascent he caught sight of a young friend from the Mounted Grenadiers, Colonel Manuel de Olazábal, whom he had known on campaign and had once given his rosary. Olazábal was then stationed in Mendoza and hearing that San Martín was crossing the Andes had come to meet him. He found his general wearing a wide-brimmed Guayaquil straw hat, a Chilean poncho, blue jacket and trousers, and yellow gloves. He thought he looked much weakened from the crossing. It was an emotional meeting, amidst the peaks and memories of Andean glories, but the general was not for nostalgia; after stopping for a hot drink he moved on with the words, 'We had better descend from this height where in other times I gazed upon America.'[45] On the way down to Mendoza they spent a night in a tent that they improvised out of ponchos.

One of San Martín's first tasks in Mendoza in February 1823 was to write to his friend O'Higgins, who had just resigned from the presidency of Chile, something San Martín had been advising him to do: 'millions of congratulations on your resignation ... now my friend is the time to enjoy peace and tranquillity without having to encounter troubles every day.'[46] That ended an epoch of collaboration and ended too any influence San Martín had in Chile, and with it his attempts to pull together the strings of action in Upper Peru. Moreover, he now had to endure hysterical attacks from the extreme republican wing in Peru and personal insults from his enemies. He had stuck to his resolution not to reply to the attacks of his critics, though in private he recorded that 'the name of General San Martín has been more respected by the enemies of independence than by many Americans whom he has rescued from their vile chains.' And he confided his disillusion to O'Higgins: 'they will miss us before long.'[47]

San Martín stayed a year in Mendoza, in spite of the fact that his wife Remedios was ill in Buenos Aires. What went through his mind in these months? The historian can only speculate. Peru was not closed completely; there was still a crack in the door. He had resigned from his office of Protector but not as a general, and it may be that while his wife was waiting for him in Buenos Aires he was waiting on events in Peru. He kept in touch with the course of action there and followed the fate of the revolution, just in case there was a call for his assistance. The military plans he had made to defeat the Spanish in Upper Peru and to recover the provinces for Argentina had come to nothing; the Peruvian objectives of his successors were not his, and the expedition of Colonel Santa Cruz in 1823 disappeared into the thin air of the *altiplano*.[48] When it was clear that Bolívar had secured the revolution against its Peruvian enemies, if not yet against the Spaniards, and there was no crisis call for San Martín's return, he moved on rather than risk rebuff. 'Let us be clear, my friend', he wrote to Guido, 'could General San Martín appear in a country where he has been treated with less consideration than the enemy have shown him and where there has not been a single person capable of coming to his defence?' His equanimity seems to have deserted him for the moment, because he continues 'At the moment I am not in charge of myself and I cannot accept that a man who has had the fate of rich countries in his hands can see himself reduced to 31,000 pesos in capital ... accused of theft!'[49]

As he struggled to make sense of the various signs around him, he was not stuck in the past. He welcomed the initiative from Spain to negotiate peace and offered to go to Spain on behalf of Peru if that would be useful. He approved of the negotiations of Rivadavia with the Spanish peace commissioners, and was disappointed when the talks failed on the fall of the constitutionalists in Spain. He offered to work with the new government of Riva Agüero in Lima if he wanted him, but received no reply. He gave up on Riva Agüero, a Peruvian aristocrat, with whom he had nothing in common. San Martín turned on him scathingly when Riva Agüero had the temerity to request his intervention in Peru's factional conflict, a rare glimpse of pure rage from San Martín, reflecting perhaps his deep resentment still of the conditions that had brought him down in Peru. 'You must have forgotten that you were writing to a general who bears the title of Founder of the Liberty of the country.... Your crass insolence in proposing that I use my sword in a civil war is incomprehensible! Criminal! Don't you know that this sword has never been stained with American blood?'[50]

Life in Mendoza was agreeable if not demanding. Robert Proctor, British agent for the Peruvian loan, was travelling towards Lima in 1823 and met San Martín a number of times. He thought he detected 'a restlessness of spirit in his eye', though he was lively enough. 'He was leading a very tranquil life, residing chiefly at an estate eight leagues from the city, which he was rapidly improving. He seemed as much attached to Mendoza as the inhabitants were to him ... he often joined our party without ceremony in the evening, and amused us much by a number of interesting anecdotes, which he has a happy method of relating, set off by his strongly expressive countenance.'[51]

Yet in Buenos Aires his wife was dying of tuberculosis. Towards the end of July he received news that her condition was serious, and he decided to go to Buenos Aires to collect his daughter, Mercedes. Remedios died on 3 August, but Guido pressed him to delay his journey: as he had not gone immediately on arrival in Mendoza it would be prudent to delay it a little longer. The fact was he had created a bad impression with the Escalada family when he did not hasten to his wife's deathbed. San Martín agreed with Guido, saying he would only go to Buenos Aires for long enough to arrange his journey to Europe. The delay no longer depended primarily on events in Peru but also on the malicious rumours that he intended to overturn the Buenos Aires government of Rivadavia, now arousing the hostility of conservative dissidents. He had always spoken airily of cultivating his garden in Mendoza and looking after his estate; but once there he was isolated, an easy target for malice, no longer protected as in the days of his military command in Cuyo.[52] It was a lost world.

Could a Liberator be a dedicated husband? In a memorable confession Bolívar, who had married young out of passionate love, once asked whether his life would have been different had he not been widowed? 'I would not be General Bolívar, nor the Liberator, and I was not made to be the mayor of San Mateo. The death of my wife propelled me early on the road to politics.'[53] San Martín married and remained married throughout his life as a Liberator, but he embraced his public role at the expense of his married life and presumably the feelings of his long-suffering wife. Did he love his wife? Perhaps he did once, but distance and time had cooled his ardour or turned it exclusively towards continental liberation, and fond memory seems to have brought no light to his middle years. It is possible to explain his indifference but difficult to understand his final priorities. Rumour had it that he was unfaithful in Peru, but it has never been proved, and knowing his character there is a presumption against it. A decent reticence always prevented him from speaking of his emotional life.

There were now other rumours of a different kind, that he had political ambitions in Argentina, that he wanted to be governor of Buenos Aires; and reports that the authorities were ready to have him stopped on the way strengthened his decision to leave his native land.[54] In other words, the same hostility that he had received from Peru was now being re-enacted from Buenos Aires. The pro-government newspapers, the *Argos* and *Centinela*, unable to deny his great achievements were also incapable of generosity; the *Argos* reported on him in terms that San Martín considered hostile, and the *Centinela* attributed to him illusions of grandeur and absolutism.[55] Spies reported his every action; there was one within his own household; and his mail was intercepted. He was conscious of the hostile gaze of Rivadavia all the time he was in Argentina, though it was in his nature to give credit where it was due, even if only fleeting: 'You know that Rivadavia is no friend of mine', he wrote to Guido, 'but only an out-and-out scoundrel could fail to be satisfied with his administration, which is the best there has ever been in America.'[56] Good government or not, he just had to get out. 'I have figured too much in the revolution to be left in peace.'[57] It was impossible to live a tranquil life while the passions of the revolution were still alive; also, if the truth be told, perhaps life was just a little dull in Mendoza, while great events beyond his reach were taking place elsewhere:

> Confined to my hacienda in Mendoza, my only contacts a few neighbours who came to visit me, even this was not enough to satisfy the suspicious administration in Buenos Aires; they surrounded me with spies, brazenly opened my mail, and the official papers spoke of a plan to form a military government directed by a successful soldier, etc. etc. In short, I could clearly see that it was impossible to live quietly in my own country while passions were still alive, and it was this misgiving that made me decide to leave for Europe.[58]

The law of circumstance, which had so often ruled San Martín's life, now brought another stage to a close and he prepared to move on. Peru now had an answer to the anarchy that had tormented it and he could leave his watchtower in Mendoza with an easier mind: 'I see what you tell me of the state of anarchy in that unhappy country', he wrote to Guido. 'Fortunately I have seen in the mail which arrived yesterday from Chile news of the arrival of the

Liberator. He alone can stop the rot, but with an iron fist, for if he compromises then everything will go to hell.'[59] Before leaving Mendoza he received a communication from Estanislao López, the caudillo of Santa Fe, that the government of Buenos Aires was ready to arrest and judge him for having disobeyed orders in 1817, but López was ready with his forces to escort him in triumph into Buenos Aires. He only had to say the word. The word of course was no thank you, I will go alone.[60] He did not need further embarrassment and compromise. Years later he told Guido, 'On my return to Buenos Aires to take ship to Europe, López in Rosario warned me off entering the Argentine capital, another Don Quixote! I believed that I was honour bound not to retreat, and the risk I took stood me in good stead for I was not mixed up with this poor sacristan.'

Silent Hero

San Martín arrived quietly in Buenos Aires on 4 December 1823 and went to stay with the Escalada family observing the conventions but keeping a low profile throughout his brief time in the capital. He twice visited Monsignor Gian Muzi who was leading a papal mission to the Río de la Plata and Chile and who was impressed by his attentions; the mission included Gian Maria Mastai Ferretti, future Pius IX, who described the anticlerical Rivadavia as 'a minister from hell', and in contrast San Martín, dressed in civilian clothes, as 'displaying much courtesy'.[61] And he paid his respects to the governor and ministers but remained aloof from the politics and politicians of the capital and its provinces, and immune from the manoeuvres that still followed him.

He visited Rivadavia—how could he not, given their history and positions?— but there is no sure account of their conversation. Rivadavia later spoke at length to Woodbine Parish, the British consul-general, who arrived in Buenos Aires shortly after San Martín had left. Rivadavia's account of San Martín had the character of a warning rather than an appraisal and was a skilful exercise in disparagement. San Martín's achievements for independence will earn him great credit with the British government, he said, but it should be advised that his views carry little weight with the Argentine government. His great ambition had been to maintain himself as Protector of Peru, but 'his own arbitrary conduct very soon raised so strong and violent a faction against him, not only amongst the Peruvians, but amongst his own officers, that he found himself obliged to resign the Protectorship and hastily quit that part of America.' His journey to Europe, ostensibly to arrange for his daughter's education, had greater objects in view, which he had confidentially disclosed to Rivadavia as an old friend. He was convinced that monarchy and the establishment of a new dynasty in South America was the only form of government suitable for these states. Rivadavia slyly attributed these views not to political principles but to 'the difficulties he had met with in Chile and Peru, especially in the latter country, in which his own personal prospects had been foiled'. Rivadavia had disputed the arguments for monarchy as absurd, an abstract theory, with no chance of success here, and the general had given a solemn promise to take no step to alter the present constitution of these governments. Was this reconciliation? Woodbine Parish reported the exchange as one between friends, as Rivadavia intended him to, though it is also open to another reading.[62] In sending him his passport Rivadavia wished San Martín a good voyage. He had not heard the last of him.

San Martín could not avoid family tensions. There were financial matters to arrange and the legal details of his inheritance from his wife, forty-three thousand pesos. Reunion with his seven-year-old daughter Merceditas was painful for the grandmother who had been looking after her and now faced losing her; and his relations with the Escalada family were never cordial. He had a tombstone in white marble erected in the Recoleta cemetery with the inscription 'Here lies Remedios de Escalada, wife and friend of General San Martín'. Good words, in his own style, spoken with economy. Guido made a last effort to detain him: 'I would very much like to know your final decision about your journey. I think the moment of supreme crisis [in Peru] has arrived.'[63] It was too late for second thoughts. After two months in Buenos Aires, San Martín sailed for Europe on 10 February 1824 in the French ship *Le Bayonnais*, accompanied by his daughter. It was a journey he never wanted to repeat, seventy-two days in an inferior merchant ship with no comforts for the passengers, while his daughter, after being spoiled by an indulgent grandmother, probably did not take kindly in her cabin to the strict regime imposed by her father.[64] The reception in France was little better. The ship reached Le Havre on 23 April. A republican general and leader of revolution in Spanish America aroused the suspicions of officials in Bourbon France, whose government had recently sent an army into Spain to crush constitutionalism and restore autocracy. His luggage was searched; the Spanish embassy was informed, and the ministry of the interior ordered him to embark immediately for England, which he did on 4 May. Aboard the *Lady Wellington* he and his daughter arrived in Southampton and rested there a few days in the Star Inn.

His thoughts on the America he had left behind can only be imagined. The latest news from Peru was predictable: politics unstable, army disintegrating, life difficult. 'Peru is a chamber of horrors,' thought Bolívar. Ironically the only good news for San Martín was that Bolívar ruled by dictatorship.

CHAPTER 10

Exile

Return to London

San Martín's priority in London was to provide for the education of his daughter. He first left her in the care of Mrs Frances Heywood, wife of Captain Peter Heywood, a naval officer once court-martialled for his part in the mutiny on the *Bounty* and subsequently a senior officer on the South American station where he came to know the general.[1] San Martín eventually placed Mercedes in a girl's college in Hampstead. Next he got in touch with García del Río and Paroissien, his envoys and trusted friends from the Protectorate, still active in London and paying themselves handsomely from the Peruvian loan. His arrival in London was noticed in the press and soon *The Morning Chronicle* was reporting that he was fêted at a dinner at Grillons Hotel hosted by García del Río, Manuel José Hurtado, the Colombian envoy, and Luis López Méndez, Bolívar's agent.[2] Paroissien was staying at Carnfield Hall in Derbyshire, the home of his fiancée, and San Martín briefly visited him there, before returning to London to take up residence in a rented house at 12 Park Place, near Regent's Park, now 23 Park Road, NW1.[3] In London his old friend James Duff, fourth earl of Fife, welcomed him, invited him to his house in Banff, where on 19 August he had him made an honorary citizen. Meanwhile on 6 July, San Martín had made an exploratory visit to Brussels, accompanied by an old wartime colleague, Alvarez de Condarco, the hero who had reconnoitred the Andes crossing for him, but also the man who had brought Lord Cochrane into his life—and still a friend.[4]

Other Argentine contacts in London were less welcome. Carlos de Alvear, San Martín's nemesis from Buenos Aires, had arrived on a diplomatic mission to see Foreign Secretary George Canning. At a dinner given by John Parish

Robertson, the Scottish entrepreneur whom San Martín had met at the battle of San Lorenzo, a group of South Americans including San Martín, García del Río and Alvear were discussing the politics of the day. García del Río expressed the opinion that the new American states needed strong government, and if General San Martín had applied the stick more firmly he would not have been forced to leave Peru. San Martín agreed: 'It's true, I had to abandon government; the stick fell from my hands because I did not know how to handle it.'[5] At this point Alvear entered the discussion to rub salt in the wounds of the Liberator who had won more glory than he, and the discussion between the two rivals became animated. San Martín would never escape the envy and hatred of his Argentine enemies, and their efforts to discredit him before the British government and other audiences. Agustín de Iturbide, the failed Mexican emperor, was also in London in 1824 and seems to have tried to make contact with San Martín. But his visit coincided only briefly with that of the Argentine and there is no record of a meeting. This did not prevent Alvear from sending malicious letters to Buenos Aires accusing San Martín of conspiring with Iturbide to restore monarchy in South America. Worse was to come. In September 1824 Rivadavia arrived in London.

As envoy extraordinary and minister plenipotentiary, Rivadavia did not lack opportunities to subvert the reputation of his enemy in government and other circles, and to destroy his monarchism. To a colleague in Buenos Aires he wrote, 'I will treat this gentleman with the respect owed to all men in public life, myself included; but from what I have seen and felt with such regret in two conversations I have had with him and in which I have tried unsuccessfully to make him see reason, I am bound to advise you in government that our country is extremely fortunate that this general is far away from it. Over here he is losing credit every day, even among those most attached to him.'[6] Meanwhile the pro-government press in Buenos Aires continued to spread damaging rumours that San Martín aimed to establish a military government in South America.[7]

San Martín left London for Brussels on 11 September. Here he enjoyed a quiet life, walking and visiting theatres in a city whose low cost of living and liberal reputation attracted him as a base within visiting distance of London. He was still considering his options. 'I have decided to fix my residence here until my daughter finishes her education', he wrote to O'Higgins, 'then I will return to America to end my days on my farm, remote from all public duties and if possible from society.' He rented a country house outside the city, where he was joined by his brother Justo.[8] To his friend Guido he claimed to be happy in Europe, but he missed Mendoza: 'I prefer the life I lived on my farm there to all the advantages of cultivated Europe, including this country, which is liberal and cheap.'[9] Meanwhile in Mendoza they never forgot San Martín and he was the subject of much talk, including a rumour that he had married an English girl.[10]

He returned to London on 13 March 1825, where he visited Mercedes and renewed acquaintance with his South American and English friends. He was pleased with his daughter's progress and happy to see her losing what he regarded as the bad habits encouraged by her grandmother. His own influence can be found in his 'Rules for my daughter', a mixture of civic virtues and social morals, where love of truth, respect for others, toleration for all religions, discretion, restraint and precision in speech are urged, side by side with concern for the poor, fairness towards servants and the aged, and aversion to luxury, and all crowned with love of one's country and freedom.[11] The ideal daughter he had in mind was not 'a lady of great style' but a loving wife and mother.

In one of the social gatherings, on 22 March 1825, he crossed swords with Rivadavia in a heated argument over the appropriate form of government for South American states. Brooding upon the exchange the next day, San Martín reached breaking point in his relations with Rivadavia and called in his friend and collaborator, James Paroissien:

> I was call'd while at dinner by a note of S^n Martin to go instantly to him. I obeyed the summons and found it was to solicit me to be the bearer of a note of challenge to Rivadavia, whom S.M. thought fit to chastize for his brutal behaviour last night. I thought it was impolitic certainly, but everybody expects to receive such conduct from Rivadavia and dissuaded S.M. from so rash a step. Fortunately Garcia [del Río] soon came in and we succeeded in persuading him to drop this foolish thought altogether.[12]

It was in these years too that San Martín resumed communication with his friend and favourite general, William Miller, who returned to England after the conclusion of the war in Peru and his service in the army of Bolívar. He immediately got in touch with San Martín and promised to visit him in Brussels, for 'neither time nor political events have been able to efface from my memory all that I owe to the first general who honoured me and gave me his support in America.'[13] San Martín offered a soldier's welcome to the person who had given him 'so many proofs of friendship' and was the general he most admired in Peru.[14] A happy contact too for the historian of the war, for San Martín was ready to answer Miller's questions on events relevant to the Memoirs he was preparing; and in September 1828 Miller asked for a portrait of his hero to include in the Spanish edition of the work. Somewhat reluctant to sit for more portraits, San Martín agreed. The result, by Jean Baptiste Madou, was not entirely to his liking, and he preferred the portrait done by the Belgian artist François Joseph Navez, who had worked in the studio of the

French painter Jacques-Louis David. San Martín is seen in civilian dress, showing a high white shirt collar, black cravat, white waistcoat and a black frockcoat. He is a handsome man, some fifty years old, his hair, sideburns and eyebrows black, his mouth and nose regular, and a steady gaze looks out from dark eyes.[15]

Tomás Guido had also left the service of Peru, where his time had not been easy since the departure of San Martín. Unwelcome in Chile and without a living in Argentina, he had returned to Buenos Aires looking for an appointment in the administration. He had always been frank in his opinions, and now he bitterly compared the harsh treatment he had received after the years of their ascendancy with the life enjoyed by San Martín: 'I will never forgive your *retirada* [the word San Martín did not like] from Peru, and no doubt history will be written in words to justify this step. Think what you like about it, but that will always be my opinion. . . . What a terrible difference between those who suffer this fate and those who enjoy a life such as yours . . . I have to continue in government service and I still do not know what my future will be, while you live in peace.'[16] An unworthy sneer.

San Martín did not like being told that he was indifferent towards the fate of his friends. 'Now one has to believe (and only because you assure me) that all those who have not taken up the trumpet to discredit the ex general San Martín, have been persecuted by General Bolívar; I say one has to believe this because I have seen so much, so much, so much low and foul scandal-mongering that unfortunately is rife in our America that I have not wished to give credit to several anonymous letters written to me on this subject.' It is not worth bothering with such nonsense from stupid and wicked people; better to treat them with the silence of contempt, in the conviction that 'honourable people will do me the justice I deserve.' As for the state of the country there is little chance of it improving, 'until it is ruled without passions, something very difficult, with the education that we have received, and with the convictions that made the revolution.' And in words that reveal an enduring sense of destiny, he confesses, 'I have to accept the misfortune of being a public figure, yes, the misfortune my friend, because I am convinced that you are what you have to be, otherwise you are nothing.'[17] For San Martín, to be misunderstood was a fact of life.

Argentina: Attraction and Repulsion

The war of words between San Martín and Rivadavia did not end in London. The Argentine envoy returned to Buenos Aires, having failed to persuade Canning to support Argentina in its conflict with Brazil over the Banda Oriental. He then assumed the presidency and appointed Alvear his minister

of war. But it was internal politics that brought him down; he resigned from
the presidency on 27 June 1827, forced out by the combined forces of his
conservative enemies, a potent mixture of federalists and landowners. The
departure of Rivadavia might have encouraged San Martín to offer his services to Buenos Aires for its war with Brazil, but he had not made up his mind
on this step. He followed the course of the war, surprised that Brazil did not
take greater advantage of Argentina, weakened as it was by an impoverished
government and anarchic provinces.[18] But the moment for action came and
went, a characteristic predicament of San Martín, and he was content to await
the results of British diplomacy. He unburdened himself of his thoughts on
Rivadavia to his friend O'Higgins: 'His administration has been disastrous
and only served to divide opinions. He has waged a war of subversion on me
with the sole intention of undermining my views, alleging that my journey to
Europe had no other object than to establish governments in America. I have
had nothing but contempt for his gross slanders and his ignoble character.'[19]
And while Rivadavia lost no future opportunity to belittle his enemy, San
Martín continued to berate 'the madness of that visionary'.[20]

San Martín kept his distance from the war with Brazil, and when he decided
to return to Argentina it was for other reasons, partly to test conditions for
retirement and partly for financial purposes, but not for a political or military
role. He had various properties in South America and was becoming anxious
about their administration.[21] The legacy from his wife, in addition to the sum
of forty-three thousand pesos, also included a house in central Buenos Aires
shared with his brother-in-law Mariano. He had bought out his partner and
now drew an income from the rent. Another house, granted to him in 1819 by
Congress and Directory, had been sold by his attorney in 1825 for twenty
thousand pesos; and he owned the mortgage on an *estancia* which amounted
to thirty thousand pesos and was realized in 1833, when Gervasio Rosas
bought the property. San Martín also owned a farm in Mendoza, 'Los
Barriales', producing wheat and cattle, as well as property in town; and in
Chile another farm, 'La Chilena', in the Santiago region; in Peru he owned the
hacienda La Magdalena and a town house in Lima named 'Jesús María'. In
theory the sum of these properties should have made San Martín a relatively
wealthy man, but he had difficulty in realizing his income and in calling his
administrators to account.[22] In London he had invested twenty-one thousand
pesos in shares in the Peruvian loan, and when this ran into difficulties he had
been forced to sell his bonds at a loss, a fate suffered by many other specula-
tors. Even so the reduced dividends were important to sustain him and his
daughter. He had planned for an income from his property in Buenos Aires,
but Argentina's parlous economic situation—he blamed the circulation of
paper money and the war with Brazil—reduced the exchange rate in London

and left him with only a fraction of what he had expected. He was owed nine thousand pesos a year granted by the Congress of Peru, but this did not arrive and was now (1827) thirty-three thousand pesos in arrears. He asked O'Higgins, who then lived in Peru, if he would intervene with the government: 'I am aware of the situation of that Republic and it would show a lack of consideration on my part to demand my arrears; I would meet my needs with 4,000 pesos a year without troubling the government further if you find they are in difficulties.'[23]

He had to reduce his expenditure, moving at the end of 1827 from the country house outside Brussels to apartments in the Rue de la Fiancée. He was planning to return to the Río de la Plata to resolve his financial difficulties, but first he felt he ought to visit Paris: as he wrote to Miller, 'I am thinking of visiting Paris this winter because it would be shameful being so close to fail to see so interesting a country, especially before returning to America; it would look eccentric to do otherwise.'[24] In the first half of 1828 he toured France and visited Paris; by May he was back in Brussels, not in the best of health. Visits to Aix-la-Chapelle to take the waters brought him some relief, and he was now prepared to cross the Atlantic, waiting only for an end to the war or the lifting of the blockade of Buenos Aires.[25] At last he was prepared to go. Leaving Mercedes, now aged twelve, in the house of Miss Phelps, 'a respectable English lady', he crossed the channel once more. After visiting Miller's home in Canterbury, he sailed from Falmouth on 21 November 1828 in the *Countess of Chichester*, bound for Buenos Aires. He took his first precaution with an assumed name of José Matorras, adopting his mother's maiden name.

The news from Buenos Aires was not encouraging. In spite of his fanatical liberalism Rivadavia was essentially a man of peace; bowing to the opposition of provincial caudillos and *porteño* federalists, he stepped down from the presidency in July 1827 and retired to poverty and exile. He did not appreciate the changing pattern of power in Argentina. Did San Martín? The Rivadavia group consisted essentially of intellectuals, bureaucrats, professional politicians, 'career revolutionaries' as they have been called, who did not represent a particular economic interest or social group.[26] His enemies on the other hand possessed real power; the *estancieros* formed a strong political base, rooted in the country and the cattle industry, and they wanted their profits to remain in the province instead of being absorbed into a national economy. The *estancieros* were the new men of the revolution; they brought a military and economic power to the federal party and soon began to seek direct political power.[27] Manuel Dorrego, leader of the federalist politicians, was elected governor of Buenos Aires on 12 August 1827. In spite of his popularity he was overthrown on 1 December 1828 by the unitarians, when General Juan Lavalle led a coalition consisting of the military returned from the war with Brazil, professional politicians, merchants and intellectuals, all acting in the name of liberal principles against rural conservatism and caudillism. But Lavalle did not leave it at that: he ordered the execution of Dorrego, a man of peace and moderation, causing a popular revulsion against the unitarians and leaving the way open for Juan Manuel de Rosas to capture the federal party. Backed by his *estanciero* allies and his rural hordes, Rosas reconquered power from Lavalle and the unitarians, and was elected governor of Buenos Aires by a grateful assembly on 6 December 1829. It was no ordinary election, for the new governor was given dictatorial powers and a mandate to restore order. As Domingo F. Sarmiento remarked, 'the provinces had their revenge on Buenos Aires when they sent to her in Rosas the culmination of their own barbarism.'[28]

Such was the scenario San Martín observed when he arrived in the River Plate on 5 February 1829. His worst fears of anarchy seemed to be confirmed, and his determination to stay out of politics strengthened. He decided to disembark in Montevideo and wait upon events. Before he could do so, however, his ship continued to Buenos Aires. He refused to proceed beyond the buoys, and from the roadstead he requested an exit passport in a letter to the relevant minister, José Miguel Díaz Vélez. He explained that he had returned with the firm intention of ending his days in private retirement, counting on the tranquility he had expected to find. But in view of the state of the country, and as he did not belong to any of the parties in dispute, he had decided to proceed to Montevideo, 'from where I will earnestly hope for the prompt restoration of peace'.[29]

The mere presence of San Martín was enough to provoke fears and arouse hopes, and his subsequent actions did nothing to set minds at rest. Whatever he did could be badly construed. Was his stand-off an affront to the government or a criticism of the opposition in waiting? While his friends, Colonel Olazábal, Alvarez Condarco and Tomás Guido, came out to welcome him, other reactions were less friendly. Official circles regarded his withdrawal as a vote of no confidence in a government that had already established itself and objected to his talk of 'parties', giving equivalence to their enemies; on the other hand some were relieved that he stayed out, otherwise he could become a leader for the opposition. The pro-unitarian press criticized his decision to come yet not to come, giving an impression of pride and lack of patriotism. Guido advised him not to worry, for he had supporters to defend him. But when one such supporter came to his defence in the press, San Martín called him off in order to avoid a public polemic on his presence.[30]

A source of contention in Buenos Aires, San Martín was warmly received in Montevideo. A nation in the first steps of independence, looking for encouragement and advice, Uruguay had no inhibitions concerning the Liberator, only friendly expectations. Leaders applauded his good judgement in distancing himself from the two disputing parties in Buenos Aires, the military organized parades in his honour, the press treated him with respect, society ladies fêted him, the public regarded him as a popular hero and his friends crowded around. A Liberator of such celebrity was bound to attract attention. Who among the minor figures in the wars and politics of the Río de la Plata would want to miss this rare and sudden opportunity? So people called on him just to greet him, and he accepted it all with weary resignation. 'What do you want me to say', he wrote to Guido, 'that I am feeling good, bored, and concerned for the low state of our poor country'.[31]

There was only one direction for San Martín, to return to Europe, especially as he had at least accomplished one of the objectives of his journey. He thought hard about the administration of his properties and from Montevideo took the vital step: he appointed a new representative, his friend Goyo Gómez, with full powers of attorney over all his properties, possessions and interests in Buenos Aires and Mendoza, and in the event of his incapacity Vicente López y Planes.[32] As for his properties in Chile and Peru, he was relying on O'Higgins to look after his interests in these countries. Another personal interest that occupied his time in Montevideo was locating and collecting his papers and documents from his campaigns and administrations to take with him to Europe, papers that would eventually be formed into an archive propitious for publication.

Once he had made up his mind to return to Europe there was no turning back, in spite of the urgings of Guido and others:

> Are you not satisfied that your independence and personal peace and quiet are assured if you remain in Montevideo? Are you indifferent to the universal criticism that you would incur by again abandoning your country because you see it beset by conflicts? Can't you see that although you adopt the life of a hermit the hopes of your friends are bound to follow you everywhere, as well as the persecutions of your enemies?[33]

Yet even to remain in Montevideo would place San Martín at the heart of discord in Buenos Aires. Politicians in Argentina and Uruguay revelled in each other's conflicts. The state of Argentina and his own position there evidently preoccupied him; Guido's remarks, moreover, were close to sarcasm and caused him to think through his political beliefs. He evidently understood the pressures that would bring Juan Manuel de Rosas to power. In a long letter to Guido he argued that the insecurity caused by the revolution for independence and the many years of efforts to establish liberal governments had caused public opinion to seek an imagined solution, not by changing institutions, where the real trouble lay, but by imposing strong government, in other words a military dictatorship which would eliminate one of the two parties and restore order. 'In effect, they seek a saviour, one who combines a victorious reputation, respect for the other provinces, and above all a strong arm, who would save the country from the troubles that threaten it: public opinion presents a candidate for this, he is general San Martín, and I say so on the evidence of numerous letters I have received from people of judgement and of others who have spoken to me on this subject; and my own opinion rests on the circumstances of the day.' He went on to explain the reasons why he rejected any role for himself in this narrative:

> Starting from the principle that it is absolutely necessary to eliminate one of the contending parties, as the presence of both is incompatible with the public peace, would it be possible for me to be the one chosen to be the scourge of my fellow citizens and, like another Sulla, impose mass punishments on my country? No, never, never. I would a thousand times rather perish in the troubles that threaten it than become the instrument of such horrors. Moreover in view of the bloodthirsty character displayed by the parties, I would never be permitted by the victorious party to employ the clemency that is needed and I would be forced to be the agent of political extremism that consults no other principle than vengeance. My friend, let us be clear, the situation of our country is such that the man who rules it has no alternative than to base himself on one particular faction, or else to relinquish his rule. This last resort is mine.
>
> You have known me intimately for many years, and you know that I have never subscribed to any party, and that I have a poor head for politics and have relied on the trustworthy advice of my friends. No doubt there are those who will say that one's country has a right to demand of its sons every kind of sacrifice, but this has its limits: one may have to sacrifice life and interests, but not one's honour.

San Martín was nothing if not consistent: government needs to apply a strong arm, only don't ask me to do it. He foresaw the route to this solution in Argentina, the choice of an absolute dictator endowed with extraordinary power. After a great crisis, he argued, the first two years were crucial: it was then that the yearning for peace and security caused the people to surrrender power to their deliverer, and it was then that the victor eliminated the other side and took revenge. There was no place for him in this conflict: 'My presence in the country in these circumstances, far from being useful, would only be an embarrassment; for one side an object of continual distrust; for the other a source of vain hopes; and for me a future of endless trouble.' These were the thoughts that had also brought his career in Peru to a close, what he called his 'utter aversion to any political office', which he compared to 'the repugnance of a young girl for the embraces of a lascivious and dirty old man', and which revived in him the memory of being called thieving and ambitious by the very people, including his companions in arms, whom he had liberated.[34]

He was aware, of course, that some of his supporters thought he owed it to his country to return and provide a leadership it so badly needed, and suggestions of this kind pursued him back to Europe. To these he had a brisk reply: he would gladly sacrifice his life and tranquillity if he thought that it would achieve anything, but the root cause of instability in the Americas and the state of permanent revolution was 'not men but institutions', and until the problem of institutions was resolved there would be no peace.[35] Curiously San Martín's analysis of political conflict in Argentina ignored the social interpretation favoured by modern historians. He saw the division between unitarians and federalists as a war of ideas between liberals and conservatives, and not as a shift of social forces in which career revolutionaries yielded to landed interests and their caudillo leaders. He himself was not personally involved in these changes; he was a professional soldier, not a career politician, and although he owned land in Mendoza he was not a working *estanciero*. He stood outside the May Revolution: his destiny lay in the wider American revolution. His horizon was Independence.

For these reasons he was concerned yet personally indifferent to the agitation of 1829. Lavalle made an approach for support. His regime, threatened by rural hordes and their caudillo leaders, needed if not an alternative caudillo, at least a powerful general and protector who could defend it against the enemies of unitarian rule.[36] San Martín politely declined. He had no intention of playing the role of a Rosas, the saviour given absolute power to restore peace and security. A year later, back in Brussels, he continued to share his political ideas with Guido: the government ought to be inexorable with the individual who seeks to subvert the existing order:

> This does not mean that I advocate violent methods to maintain order, no my friend, far from it. What I want is for the government to follow a line of strict justice, to enforce respect for the laws ... I do not know Rosas, but I understand that he has a strong character and good intentions; this is enough, for lack of experience in government can be made good (in fact not a bad training for ruling this people), under the guidance of good ministers.[37]

Argentina was no place for San Martín, a hard lesson from a long journey. Whatever he might say about Rosas, the despotic rule of a rural caudillo was a total denial of the ideas that San Martín had hitherto espoused. As for the liberals, effectively marginalized after 1829, they too fell short of his political ideals; two months in the Río de la Plata were sufficient to convince him of

that truth. As San Martín recrossed the Atlantic in an English vessel bound for
Falmouth, his friend Guido could only ponder his final message, a rare show
of emotion, written on 27 April 1829 on the eve of his departure: 'I write to
you only to say Adios. I don't know whether it is the uncertainty I feel in
leaving the country and my few friends or other reasons I cannot fathom, but
the fact is my heart is heavy and weighs me down with greater turmoil than I
have ever felt.'[38]

On the journey from Falmouth to London, the mail coach he was travelling
in overturned and the glass from a broken window left him with a deep gash
in his left arm, though to avoid publicity he concealed his identity.[39] He was
confined to his house in Brussels with his wound for three months during one
of the worst European winters in living memory, the only consolation coming
from the attentions of his daughter. But the growing violence of the movement for Belgian independence and an encroaching cholera epidemic made
Brussels a risky place to live in, and in September 1830 father and daughter
left. After a stop at Aix-la-Chapelle for San Martín to take the waters, they
travelled to Paris, where he set up home in the rue de Provence and placed
Mercedes in a suitable college.

France had moved on since its coolness towards San Martín in 1824. Even so
the first years in France were not unalloyed joy. In the course of 1832 both he
and his daughter succumbed to cholera, followed in San Martín's case by a
gastro-intestinal illness which laid him low for some further months. After a
period of uncertainty financial remittances from his properties in Buenos Aires
and Peru became more regular and an army pension from Buenos Aires more
secure. During these months a young friend and carer in the person of
Mariano Balcarce, an attaché at the Argentine embassy in London, made a
welcome visit to offer help to the father and love to the daughter. For some time
San Martín had regarded the young man, son of a friend General Antonio
González Balcarce, as a suitable husband for Mercedes, and without actually
presiding over an arranged marriage he was an influence in its making.[40] The
happy pair were married in Paris on 13 December 1832—Mercedes was then
aged sixteen—and soon after the ceremony and the subsequent celebration at
the Chez Grignon restaurant, they left for Buenos Aires, he to promotion in the
Argentine foreign office and she to give birth to a daughter, María Mercedes, in
October 1833, a delight for San Martín in troubled times.

San Martín and Rosas

San Martín was not fit enough to accompany his family to Buenos Aires, nor
did he wish to return to a country tormented by the political convulsions of the
years 1833–4 when, in the interval between the first and second governments

of Rosas, federal politicians competed for control of the party and direction of policy. The resulting instability gave Rosas the opportunity to return to the governorship of Buenos Aires in 1835 with unlimited power; this he soon employed in imposing a hard-line regime backed by his rural power base and the systematic use of state terror. San Martín's friend, Tomás Guido, was not a blind admirer of the dictator but he was prepared to serve in his bureaucracy. And San Martín himself, at the age of fifty-five still disturbed by the country's endemic chaos, took his own political thinking, always balanced uneasily between authority and liberty, to a firmer position on the side of authority. What the people needed, he argued, was real liberty, not theoretical. In a private letter to Guido from 1834 he suggested that a government acquired its legitimacy not in any principles of liberalism but in its care for the welfare of the citizens; and he asked, what does liberty serve if a life's work is destroyed in revolution and one's family sacrificed to civil war? 'The man who establishes order in our country, whatever the means he employs, he alone deserves the noble title of its liberator.'[41]

San Martín now enjoyed better material prospects, as his income from Buenos Aires and Peru became more stable. In 1834 he was fortunate enough to move into a handsome country house in Grand Bourg, some twenty miles from Paris, and to look forward to healthier conditions; and in the following year he bought a house in Paris. He renewed his friendship with the wealthy Alejandro Aguado, an old Spanish comrade from the Murcia Regiment, who became a source of credit for San Martín's son-in-law, but not for San Martín himself, who always paid his own way, and as his will made clear, never owed anything to anyone.[42] But his life was not entirely untroubled. Personal irritation with his fellow countrymen was never far away. He discovered that the Argentine minister in London, Manuel Moreno, a *rosista* appointee and professional troublemaker, was spreading malicious and mendacious rumours that in order to gain influence in America San Martín had made a secret visit to Spain on a private diplomatic mission for which he was not authorized; and suspicions increased because he had stopped sending his mail to Argentina via the London embassy. He replied with a withering letter to the intriguer Moreno, condemning his crass conduct, which simply proved that 'either you are a complete scoundrel or have gone out of your mind.' As for avoiding the embassy mailbag, he had evidence that his letters were being opened.[43] And to Guido he confessed that he would really have liked to go to London and give Moreno a good thrashing.[44]

Concern for his health made San Martín anxious to have his daughter and her husband, who had lost his job in the foreign office, back in Europe. And in due course, in June 1836, they joined him in France, together with his granddaughter María Mercedes. He ruled out any possibility of returning to

Buenos Aires, even though the dictatorship of Rosas was re-establishing the conditions of order and security that he preferred, and would have enabled his family to live there. The dictatorship did not alarm him; on the contrary, he considered strong rule by an absolute government the only answer to Argentina's woes in 1835, in order to teach his compatriots to obey:

> I am convinced that when men refuse to obey the law, there is no alternative to force. Twenty-nine years in search of a liberty that has not existed have left the country with a legacy of oppression, personal insecurity, destruction of fortunes, indiscipline, venality, corruption, and civil war; these have been the only fruit of so many sacrifices. The time has come to put an end to these great evils, and to achieve so worthy an object I would approve as good and legal any government that establishes order and stability, and I am sure you think the same, as do all those who love their country.[45]

These thoughts were not a casual approval of the Rosas regime. A year later in 1836 he reaffirmed his support: 'I am pleased to see the progress our country continues to make. Let us not deceive ourselves; it will be many years before our countries can be ruled except by strong governments, frankly by despotic governments.'[46] This was the year in which Rosas had begun to consolidate his absolute government, promising that his policy would be to use his limitless power to bring swift judgement and death to the regime's enemies. The details would soon be made clear. To approve of Rosas, in many people's eyes, did not sit well with the image of San Martín, a fighter for the rule of law rather than the power of the state. What was moving him? Was it the influence of his friend Guido, a servant of the *rosista* state? There was a more likely explanation. To appreciate the enormity of Rosas, a person had to live under his rule and see at first-hand the 'outrages, confiscations, and throat-cuttings,' and the terrorist activities of the *mazorca* and other federal activists, as recorded by the diarist Beruti.[47] San Martín fell into the trap of looking only at the theoretical advantages of absolutism and ignoring the daily reality, the regimentation and the death squads, the kind of mistake that he had always condemned in his opponents' love of liberty. But he was not completely blind to injustice and he never ignored oppression, some of it directed at his own family and friends; Balcarce had to abandon his diplomatic career, the Escalada family were deprived of office and liberty, and his Irish friend O'Brien languished in prison. While accepting the regime, therefore, he condemned Rosas' repressive practices against his opponents, his persecution of good people and his violence in government. San Martín's views were not dissimilar to those of the British Foreign Secretary Lord Palmerston, who came to regard Rosas as a necessary evil, bringing order out of chaos and safeguarding the liberty and security of foreigners.[48]

San Martín was still an Argentine nationalist, sensitive to any slight on American independence and suspicious always of European motives towards his native land. This helps to explain his support for the dictator's foreign policy and his resistance to outside pressures, first from France in the blockade of 1838, imposed to improve the security of French citizens, then from the Anglo-French naval intervention in 1845, designed to assert free navigation up the River Paraná. In August 1838, writing from what was now enemy territory and wondering whether he was still regarded in Argentina as '*un hombre necesario*', he offered his services to Rosas in any war with France. Rosas thanked him effusively for his 'noble and generous offer', but adroitly turned it aside by playing down the impact of the blockade, which was in fact damaging the import and export trade of Buenos Aires.[49] It has been aptly remarked that Rosas wanted San Martín on his side but not at his side.

Yet the international respect for San Martín was something that Rosas could not ignore; he tried to recruit him for diplomatic tasks in Europe and Peru.[50] San Martín did not take the bait; he only wanted to collaborate 'as a simple soldier', and he had serious reservations about many aspects of the Rosas regime, as he confessed to his friend Gregorio Gómez: 'The state of our unfortunate country really troubles me and worse still I do not see the slightest chance of improvement. You know my feelings. I cannot approve the conduct of General Rosas when I see him persecuting the best men in our country; moreover, the assassination of Doctor Maza convinces me that the government of Buenos Aires rests only on violence. In spite of this I will never approve a native [of Argentina] supporting a foreign nation in order to humiliate his own country.'[51] San Martín's tendency to vacillate, to waver between the imperatives of freedom and authority, is nowhere seen more clearly than in his attitude to Rosas: approval in general, revulsion in detail, or in some of the detail. If this was the order the country needed, it came at a heavy price and, closing his eyes to inconvenient truths, San Martín was not prepared to say that the price was too high.

He continued to support the dictator's foreign policy and his defence of national interests, and he reacted angrily to the singular example of gunboat diplomacy in 1845, when Anglo-French naval forces imposed a blockade on Buenos Aires and a joint expedition forced its way up the River Paraná convoying a merchant fleet to inaugurate direct trade to the interior. He was travelling in the south of Italy when news reached him. He wrote to Rosas giving him his moral support, and in Europe he made clear his views to a wider audience.[52] He foresaw the intervention as doomed to failure, defeated by the fortitude of the country's leader, his command of its territory and his ability to rally the people against foreigners. The blockade would have only a limited impact, as the mass of the people lived on the country's own resources and did not need European imports.[53] These views were voiced in a public letter, published in the London *Morning Chronicle* (12 February 1846); they coincided with those of many opponents of the action in Britain, and became part of the anti-war campaign waged by commercial and political interests in parliament and in the country. In the course of 1846 the British government began to pull out and to take steps to improve relations with Argentina.[54]

When the blockade was lifted in 1848 San Martín wrote warmly to Rosas congratulating him on his triumphs 'in saving the national honour and presenting a model for all the new states of America to follow.'[55] 'I have done no more than imitate you', replied Rosas, a presumptuous comparison that seems to have been lost on the ageing San Martín, for he had further compliments to pay. In 1850 he wrote as 'an old friend', praising Rosas for 'the prosperity, the internal peace and order, and the honour recovered for our dear country, progress achieved in circumstances which few states will have experienced.'[56] And in his will he left his campaign sword to Rosas, who, he said, had sustained 'the honour of the republic against the foreigners who were seeking to humiliate it.'[57]

More important than the dubious friendship of Rosas was the restoration of San Martín's name in Chile. The rancour of the Cochrane years and the ambiguities of independence were things of the past. In Chile he had many true friends and his homes in Europe were rarely without Chilean visitors, anxious to meet the man who had belatedly become their national hero. In Chile remembrance of his great victories for independence was revived in these years, thanks in no small part to the eloquence of Domingo Faustino Sarmiento, liberal statesman and intellectual then in exile from the Rosas regime across the Andes, and in Chile he was offered a warm reception should he ever wish to retire there. He was moved by the grant of the rank and pay of a general by the Chilean Congress in 1842, and the death of his great friend O'Higgins in the same year affected him deeply.

Valedictory

San Martín approached old age surrounded by his family, now with another granddaughter, Josefa; in 1837 Mariano had to return to Buenos Aires in search of a new career, and the grandfather grew close to the little girls. He was reconciled to a life of exile. He had his books and his hobbies, cleaning his guns and busy with woodwork. There were visitors, too, trying on his nerves perhaps but reassuring. He was respected by new generations. The young Juan Bautista Alberdi visited him at home in 1843, waiting impatiently for him to come through the door:

At last he came in, with his hat in his hand, as modest and diffident as any other person. How different I found him from what I had been led to expect from the exaggerated descriptions I had heard from his admirers in America! I expected him to be taller, and he is only slightly taller than average. I thought he was an Indian, as I had so often been told, and he is simply a man with a dark complexion and a stern look. He has not put on much weight. He is lively, not solemn, in manner, and he speaks like any other man without affectation. I had heard that he suffers ill health, but he wears his age well and still has most of his hair, now almost entirely grey. He speaks Spanish with an American accent.[58]

Sarmiento visited San Martín a few years later, in May 1846, and recorded his impressions in somewhat exaggerated prose, writing for effect as a young journalist travelling in Europe rather than the statesman of later years. The political ideas of the two men had little in common but Sarmiento seeks to do justice to the hero, hidden in silent oblivion, and San Martín's recognizable preoccupations break through, though presented as ramblings. Sarmiento imagines the great days, the young general, the glory and now the silence:

The fantasy disappeared. San Martín was an old man, with human weaknesses and inner maladies acquired in old age; we had returned to the present, the age of Rosas and his system. That intelligence so clear in other times is now in decline; those eyes so penetrating when they made history were now clouded and in the distance they saw fantasies of foreigners, and all his ideas were confused, Spaniards, European powers, the patria, that old patria, and Rosas, independence, the colony restored; and thus bewitched the stone statue of the old hero of independence seemed to be standing on a tomb defending a threatened America.[59]

In France San Martín was regarded as a distinguished resident, and King Louis Philippe made a point of meeting him in the Tuileries Palace, where San Martín spoke with the king and other royals. He was happy in his country retreat with occasional visits to the sights of Paris, but the Revolution of 1848 caused him, in the interests of his family, to leave the environs of the capital for Boulogne-sur-Mer and a possible exit to England. The revolution drew from him, in a letter to Rosas, a rare social rather than political interpretation of contemporary history. 'The real conflict that divides the people is purely social: in a word, the have-nots seek to dispossess the haves. Think of the effect of this on the mass of the people, through the daily tirades of the clubs and the messages of thousands of pamphlets. If to these ideas is added the appalling misery of millions of proletarians, worsened at the moment by the paralysis of industry and flight of capital ... then you see the true state of France.'[60] A report on France or a warning for Rosas?

San Martín spent the last two years of his life in Boulogne, where he rented three storeys of a substantial house at 105 Grand Rue, surrounded by portraits and pictures of his life in America and keeping with him still a portrait of Bolívar and the standard of Pizarro, given him by a grateful city of Lima on its liberation. The later years of his life were shadowed by thoughts of death and his days became a time of melancholy, his mind still active and capable of recall and discussion of past and present, as his Argentine friend Félix Frías noted, but his body frail, wracked by pain and reliant on opium. A visit to Enghien-les-Bains in July 1850 offered him some respite and there were outings in the environs of Boulogne to relieve the tedium, but his days were often spent in silence. Religion seems not to have played a significant part in his life in these years, when the religious observances required by military tradition were no longer a duty. Once he had left public life, though he was concerned to obtain a Catholic education for his daughter in exile and he never completely abandoned the practice of religion, his religiosity was not obvious. His will was made 'in the name of Almighty God, whom I recognize as creator of the world', but made no reference to the Catholic Church, as would be normal for an earnest Catholic. He prohibited any funeral.

His friendships had always been selective. As he surveyed his Argentine contemporaries—Rivadavia uncouth, Alvear sly and Monteagudo erratic—few impressed him. In his professional circle he was a friend of Commodore Bowles, not of Cochrane, of O'Higgins, not of Bolívar, of Guido, not of Rivadavia. He appreciated messages of support from Argentina and Chile, and eventually from Peru, too, in a communication in 1848 from the Patriotic Society that had resolved to inscribe him as 'an ex officio founding member'[61] His reply was a form of closure: 'The greatest reward a public figure can desire is the approval of his actions by his contemporaries; so in spite of my old age, broken health, and impairment of sight, I have the consolation of receiving the esteem of the present governments of Peru, Chile, and the Argentine Confederation, which I regard as more than enough compensation for the brief services I rendered these republics in the war of our independence.'[62]

San Martín, the soldier who had crossed the pampas, climbed the Andes, fought in the highlands, navigated the Pacific and ruled from a palace in Lima, reached his journey's end in a house in Boulogne. His life ended in a sequence of pain and opium.[63] His years in Europe and America had been plagued by a series of medical conditions, principally asthma, duodenal ulcers and gout, but also a succession of temporary afflictions, including throat infections, dysentery, cholera, erysipelas, cataracts and battle wounds.[64] To have survived these conditions in the plains and mountains of America, in coastal camps and on campaign, was a triumph of fortitude and perseverence. But in the end willpower was not enough. His stomach pains seem to have been cancerous and his final agony came on Saturday, 17 August 1850; the slight improvement he had experienced in previous days was deceptive and his doctor was called. After a quiet morning sitting on a sofa, San Martín began to feel cold and asked to be taken to his daughter's bed. In her arms he murmured, 'Mercedes, this is the tiredness of death'. In the afternoon he felt sharp pains in the stomach; these subsided and were followed by a brief convulsion. He died at two o'clock in the presence of Mercedes, her husband and his granddaughters, with his doctor and the Chilean chargé d'affaires, Francisco Javier Rosales, in attendance. He was seventy-two. Félix Frías, who happened to call the next day, recorded:

In the morning of the 18th I had the satisfaction, sad though it was, of gazing at the mortal remains of the man whose life belongs to the most brilliant pages of American history. His face retained the distinguishing features of his stern and honourable character. He had a crucifix upon his breast and another on a table at the side between two lighted candles. Two sisters of charity prayed for his soul.[65]

In spite of his will, Mercedes arranged a modest funeral. The short cortège paused at the church of St. Nicholas for prayers for the dead, then proceeded to the cathedral of Notre-Dame, and he was buried in the crypt. Some years later, in 1880, his remains were transported to Buenos Aires; there they rest in an elaborate enclosure in the cathedral with a military guard.

Fallen Idol or Hero for all Time?

Peru was the memory that haunted San Martín, Peru the destiny of his Andean years, the graveyard of his ambition. He was deeply disappointed at the outcome, and although he kept his emotions under control at the time, his thoughts were troubled thereafter.[66] If a sense of fulfilment evaded him, however, this did not mean that he was a failed Liberator. He never disavowed his four certainties. He needed Bolívar's military support and asked for it; Bolívar did not send the forces he needed; he offered to serve under Bolívar's orders 'with all the forces I had'; when this was ignored it was obvious that there was not enough room in Peru for the two liberators and so he chose to go. He bound himself to 'absolute silence', but he was always conscious that his departure from Lima was a stain on his reputation, the more difficult to bear because he was convinced that with the united forces of Peru and Colombia the war of independence could have been won in 1823.[67] Guayaquil remained a horror from first to last; the very word a metaphor for his disillusion. He had hoped for better from Bolívar, but he would never countenance the more extreme slanders that were being hurled at the Liberator of the north: 'superficial in the extreme, inconsistent in his principles, and childishly vain, yes all this, but never deserving the slur of fraud, not fitting to apply to a man of his stature and eminence.'[68]

Contemporary criticism, echoed by modern historians, focused on San Martín's alleged failure of leadership in the conduct of the war in Peru; his persecution of Spaniards, who were forcibly expelled and deprived of their property; and his desertion of the revolution at its moment of greatest need, when the last bastion of Spanish power had still to be taken. To each of these charges there was an answer. San Martín showed great leadership in taking the campaign for independence to Peru, but the forces at his disposal were not adequate to the purpose. This was the root of his problem and the key to his strategy. Revolution by persuasion was a fall-back position, not his first choice, which was to destroy Spanish power. Knowing his weakness, he sought to revolutionize Peru, not to conquer it, and finally attempted to increase his forces by recruiting those of Bolívar, a lost battle.

His severity towards Spaniards was believed to be necessary in the interests of security, at a time when the royalist army was still in the field. Liberation movements in South America had seen too many examples of Spanish counter-revolution, usually accompanied by a reign of terror, to be indulgent towards a potential fifth column. And his retirement was realistic, for he had lost all influence in Peru and was convinced that his presence was the only obstacle preventing Bolívar from leading his army southwards. Inflexibility was never a mark of San Martín. It was time to quit the stage. To accept the dead-lock, conscious that his army was insufficient, his power base vanishing, his personal position fading and the Spaniards undefeated, was not failure of nerve. It took more courage to get out than to stay in. Bolívar himself, under-standably perhaps, never criticized San Martín for his premature retirement. In fact more than once he invoked the example of his fellow Liberator, 'a beautiful model', when threatening to resign his command.[69]

San Martín displayed classic qualities of leadership: his clarity of mind and strength of purpose were quickly recognized. His American objectives and determination to achieve them identified him as a supreme leader above the competence of his fellows and rivals. In planning for action and exercising the will to command he had no equal in the southern revolution. Yet his virtues were tested by events and did not always emerge intact. Calmness in a crisis, a leadership quality in San Martín, could transform into passivity. He had a habit of detachment from awkward situations—politics in Buenos Aires, reverses in southern Chile, Monteagudo's policies in Peru, mutinous army commanders, challenges to his authority.

Political judgement was not instinctive in San Martín. Politics was an unintelligible world. He needed advisers, well chosen in the case of Guido, less so with Monteagudo. A virtue in face of suffering in war and bloodshed on battlefields, coolness became a flaw in the heat of political crises; then his world of military command, orders, obedience and action metamorphosed into hesitancy in decisions and toleration of his inferiors. If San Martín had a weakness as a military leader it was loyalty. He admitted that in the interests of army discipline he should have shot some of his disloyal and mutinous commanders in Peru, and he lacked the courage to do so; another way of saying that his army failed him. In his farewell words to the people of Lima he recalled his promise to leave Peruvians to elect their own governments and suggested that the presence of a powerful soldier was dangerous to new states, wise advice for the future of Latin America but too diffident perhaps during an unfinished war and not exactly a fanfare for Bolívar. He was generous in defeat. He acknowledged that Peru could only be liberated by external aid, and that only Bolívar could do it. He could never satisfactorily explain, to himself or to others, the reasons for Bolívar's evasion in 1822. In 1826, when the liberation of Peru was complete, he acknowledged that Bolívar had always shown him a sincere friendship, and envy did not enter into it, for 'the successes that I have gained in the war of independence are really inferior to those which General Bolívar has won for the cause of America in general.'[70]

Not everyone would agree with San Martín's self-deprecation, and for the word 'inferior' the verdict of history might prefer 'different'. He had already secured the western provinces of the Río de la Plata, mounted a trans-Andean resistance movement and successfully reconquered Chile for the revolution. These conspicuous gains enabled him to invade and penetrate the viceroyalty of Peru, one of Spain's historic strongholds in the Americas. At this point in the narrative, historians begin to compare the alleged failure of San Martín in Peru and the success of Bolívar. But the comparison is not valid. General O'Leary, the aide, admirer and chronicler of Bolívar, contrasted the opportunity presented to San Martín and the difficulties faced by Bolívar. In an eloquent passage he wrote:

The situation of Peru when this decree [appointing Bolívar Dictator] was issued was very different from what it was when San Martín disembarked four years previously. At that time the support for independence was general throughout Peru, and enthusiasm for the liberators matched the resources placed at their disposal. San Martín had only to come, see and conquer; he came, he saw and he could have conquered. But the task was perhaps beyond him, or at least he believed so; he hesitated and finally abandoned it. When Congress entrusted to Bolívar the salvation of the republic, it handed him a corpse.[71]

O'Leary exaggerated the support and the resources that Peruvians offered San Martín, and he distorted the general's failure to exploit his opportunities. His estimate of the two liberators favoured Bolívar. 'It would be difficult to find two more opposite characters than those of Bolívar and San Martín. Bolívar was frank, candid, passionate in his friendships and generous to his enemies; San Martín was cold, guarded, and incapable of forgiving offences or of making a generous gesture that was disinterested. . . . Both were benefactors of their countries and both suffered the ingratitude and persecution of the peoples whom their genius and courage had freed.'[72]

It was premature to seek a constitutional solution. San Martín probably erred in trying to win the minds and hearts of Peruvians, before he had totally destroyed Spanish power. However, the basic reason for this was not faulty reasoning but inadequate resources; he invaded Peru with an army inferior in numbers and training to the Spanish army and not equal to the task of conquest. He then had to rely on the support of local elites and people, and he overestimated the commitment of Peruvians to independence at a time when they could see a familiar alternative in the royalist sierra. The Bolivarian model of liberation was more realistic: only power could persuade, Peru would have to be conquered before it could be liberated, and dictatorship was an essential prelude to democracy. But that lesson could not be learnt immediately. It needed San Martín's expedition to prove it, to test the ground.

San Martín had taken the first steps to subvert Spanish power in Peru; he had destabilized the viceroyalty and prepared the way for liberation. When Bolívar arrived, San Martín had already driven a wedge into Peru. General Miller, who served both liberators, expressed it succinctly: 'It was San Martín who first raised the standard of liberty in Peru, and then laid the groundwork of that great plan which was so gloriously accomplished at Ayacucho.'[73] Bolívar would have had an immeasurably more difficult task had he to face a Spanish Peru still intact behind its military and political defences. Of the two liberators San Martín was the trailblazer whose strategy and tactics were a necessary demonstration of what needed to be done. The two men represented two phases of the same war. For these reasons it is incorrect to place one above the other in the pantheon of liberators.

A further contrast is often made between the monarchism of San Martín and the republicanism of Bolívar. This too can be exaggerated. Although the political thought of the two liberators was expressed in different terms, there was a striking similarity in their basic ideas. Both began with similar republican ideals. Both saw these eroded by circumstances. In the last years of his life Bolívar was haunted by the anarchy of the new states and obsessed by their need for strong government. His Bolivian Constitution provided for a life president with the right to choose his successor, which he regarded as an essential antidote to chaos. San Martín had also travelled this route. His political thought was always finely balanced between a need for absolute power and a preference for liberal government. In San Martín's mind authority and liberty were indivisible, each a response to excess in the other.

Political ambivalence was rooted in his abhorrence of social upheaval and popular revolution. He was not alone in these forebodings. Bolívar too feared social conflict and race war; his ideal ruler was an autocrat, a president with absolute power. Both had reservations about democracy. Wealth and social distinctions were loathsome to San Martín: he insisted that by inclination and principle he loved republican government, but this did not blind him to the reality that this form of government was not possible in America without inviting total anarchy, and history taught that anarchy inevitably produced tyranny and despotism. His analysis was extreme but the product of actual situations in America. Why then did he hold back from personal dictatorship? A moot question. It was similar to the dilemma of Bolívar, who also prophesized a future of tyranny in the wake of anarchy, but who at least imposed a timely dictatorship whenever it was required. From exile San Martín followed the troubled career of his Venezuelan rival and he predicted, 'the man is marching rapidly towards the precipice'.[74]

San Martín and Bolívar can both be described as heirs of enlightened absolutism, who saw independence best served by strong government imposing social change against the inherited interests of landowners and lawyers. The experience of San Martín confirmed one of the great truisms of liberation, its inability to liberate Indians, blacks and slaves: Indians remained vulnerable, blacks remained poor and slaves remained slaves. San Martín probably proceeded even more cautiously along the reformist route and yielded even more to privilege than Bolívar. Both liberators were appalled by the political instability and party conflict in their own countries, and dismayed by the social history of the new states, in which conflicting demands from rival sectors became unanswerable and made stable government impossible. Both were victims of events and conditions bequeathed by the past, their ideals constrained by what San Martín called 'the law of circumstance.' Both left their native lands and headed for exile. In his later years horror of anarchy led San Martín astray from the path of liberation. His support for the dictator Rosas, who imposed state terrorism and calculated cruelty on a scale unknown in Argentina before that time, was a lapse of political judgement that only his distance from events can explain.

San Martín's very objectives in his heroic years left him in isolation without a political home or power base, and induced in him a sense of estrangement. The Continental Project and the grand American strategy marked him for life. Neither Buenos Aires, nor Santiago, nor Lima was his ultimate destination.

Return to Europe seemed the only route left. Europe had offered him little during the wars of liberation and Britain had not responded directly to his political overtures. But he recognized the critical importance of British sea power for the security of the Americas and for its effective guarantee of the international framework of independence. Britain was always his fail-safe option for the security of his family, even when it was not his first choice for exile. He did not plan a long exile, but he never found a compelling reason to end it. When in 1838 he offered to return to Argentina for service against France and then to retire there 'if my country offers me security and order', Rosas made it abundantly clear that he should stay in Europe; in a masterpiece of insincerity he exhorted him not to trouble himself or to undergo the travails of travel for a minor incident.[75]

San Martín's life was that of a migrant in a foreign land who returns home after a lengthy absence to find his house shuttered, the neighbours suspicious and the authorities wary. He moves on again. Argentine historians refer to San Martín's exile as his *ostracismo*, but it was a situation he willed and accepted. As Mitre said, with some insight: 'The great warrior, admired in Argentina and accepted as a necessity in Chile, was never loved or really popular in either country. . . . Without ceasing to be Argentine, he was American above all . . . a solitary soul, not inclined to close affections and condemned to a life without a home.' And he described him as 'the American man, the necessary man'[76] In her modern biography of San Martín, Patricia Pasquali argues that his strong sense of mission placed him in '*la soledad de la gloria*'. In spite of his displays of national pride there remains a strong suspicion that San Martín did not really love Argentina, or Argentina him, that he was always a man 'suspect in his own country'.[77]

Can the course of history be influenced or changed by individual leaders? The events of history, structures and their movement, continuity and change, these depend on human mind and will. Human action is focused by leadership, and in the South American revolution San Martín led with his ideas and his actions, taking the revolution outside national frontiers and beyond national interests and giving it an American identity. This was his mission and this was his glory. San Martín was rightly proud of his leadership and outraged by any suggestions that impugned his good faith or damaged his self-esteem. Like any world leader he could not be disinterested in his own fate. But he did not respond to any particular interest or pressure group; throughout his active career in America he was driven above all by political objectives and ideas. His only power base was the army that he himself created through his determination and organizing genius. He always maintained that the military objectives were more easily resolved than the political. He proclaimed a sombre verdict on post-colonial societies, as valid in the present

century as in the nineteenth, that the destruction of tyranny does not necessarily lead to democratic utopia but often to anarchy and a reversion to
tyrants. Thus he observed that America's great crisis would arrive not in
defence of independence, a relatively simple cause sustained by national pride,
but in the subsequent defence of freedom and civil rights in backward societies bereft of binding laws, and lacking citizens of sufficient education and
integrity to lead them into good government.[78]

San Martín's views are to be found not in discourse or treatise but in letters
to his friends and associates, written in a plain and vigorous style, his
authority unmistakable but unforced. His numerous decrees and proclamations say little beyond the immediate object. Even the trans-Andean project,
the signature of his American career, was presented as a series of practical
propositions: to cross the Andes, to reconquer Chile, to invade Peru. His
advice to 'think big' was strategic, not conceptual in its significance. So he used
Argentine resources to aid Chile, and Chilean–Argentine resources to invade
Peru, and beyond Peru he spoke of the 'general cause' of America. In this sense
his strategy was Americanist rather than nationalist in inspiration, because
American collaboration was the surest way to expand and complete the revolution for independence. These were strategies for war and revolution, not
concepts for the future direction of the continent. His Americanism was left
unadorned without a theoretical framework, or a comparative analysis. He
did not theorize about shared political traditions, or common cultural influences. He saw Argentina, Chile and Peru as distinct states with their own
national interests, and he learnt from experience that there was a limit to their
collaboration, once collaboration against Spain had achieved its purpose. San
Martín's American project did not envisage Latin American unity or regional
groupings or a common future; these were not subjects that engaged his attention. A vein of scepticism running through his political thinking restrained
any impulse he may have had towards postwar planning. To defend freedom
and preserve order were trials enough for the new American states.

A natural reserve, seen in his portraits, prevented him from theorizing
about his experiences in the world of revolution. He was conscious of the
problems of leadership, as his letters to Tomás Guido reveal. But he did not
philosophize about his own role or analyse the concept of glory, and in this
sense he belongs to Carlyle's 'great Empire of Silence' where the true heroes are
the strong, silent men of history, who do not need to adopt a declamatory
mode, display ambition or claim greatness.[79] That was the style of San Martín,
man of silence. Yet style was not the essence of San Martín. His life was
marked above all by decisive action at critical moments of Spanish American
independence and often against the flow of events: the decision to abandon
Spain for America in 1812, the insistence on the Continental Project in 1816

and the determination to quit the scene in 1822. In each case a difficult situation called for clear analysis and firm action amid discordant and often hostile voices. In each case the record shows that objectively he moved the revolution forward and secured positive gains for South America, preparing the way for total independence in the years to come. And in each case it was his innate sense of duty and power of leadership that drove him on. The Army of the Andes represented a continental cause, advancing beyond local boundaries and overcoming national interests. It was a hard call, and in answering it San Martín proved himself to be a man for America and a man for his time.

Notes

Abbreviations

CDIP   *Colección documental de la independencia del Perú*
DASM   *Documentos del Archivo de San Martín*
DGIRA   *Documentos referentes a la guerra de la independencia y emancipación política de la República Argentina*
DHL   *Documentos para la historia del Libertador general San Martín*
HAHR   *Hispanic American Historical Review*
JLAS   *Journal of Latin American Studies*
PCIS   *Primer Congreso Internacional Sanmartiniano*
PRO   Public Record Office, the National Archives, London
SMC   *San Martín: Su correspondencia, 1823–1850*

Chapter 1: Soldier of Spain

1. Patricia Pasquali, *San Martín: La fuerza de la misión y la soledad de la gloria* (3rd edn, Buenos Aires, 1999), 22.
2. Juan Bautista Alberdi, 'El general San Martín en 1843', *Obras completas*, 8 vols (Buenos Aires, 1886–7), II, 335.
3. José Luis Busaniche, *San Martín visto por sus contemporáneos* (Buenos Aires, 1942), 40–2.
4. Bartolomé Mitre, *Historia de San Martín y de la emancipación sudamericana*, 3 vols (Buenos Aires, 1950), I, 75–6, 449–50.
5. Bowles to Croker, *Amphion*, at sea, 14 February 1818, in Gerald S. Graham and R.A. Humphreys, eds, *The Navy and South America 1807–1823: Correspondence of the Commanders-in-Chief on the South American Station* (London, 1962), 227.
6. Revisionism moves into fantasy and makes him not only a mestizo but also the brother of Carlos de Alvear, his political associate and rival, whose father is alleged to have had an illegitimate child by a Guaraní woman and farmed him out to the San Martíns to bring up as their own; this was José Francisco de San Martín. The story is based on

nothing more than a 'tradition' in the Alvear family and popular rumour, and gets the dates of birth badly wrong. For the story and its refutation see *Desmemoria, Revista de Historia*, No. 26, 2° cuatrimestre 2000), 8–44.

7. Pedro Ignacio Galarza, 'La familia de San Martín', *Primer Congreso Internacional Sanmartiniano (PCIS)*, 8 vols (Buenos Aires, 1979), I, 279–306.

8. Demetrio Ramos Pérez, 'El solar de los San Martín', *PCIS*, II, 69–103; Eugenio Fontaneda Pérez, *Raíces castellanas de José de San Martín* (Madrid, 1980), 83–5, 99–137.

9. Quoted by Guillermo Céspedes del Castillo, *Lima y Buenos Aires: Repercusiones económicas y políticas de la creación del virreinato del Plata* (Seville, 1947), 123.

10. Príncipe de la Paz, *Memorias* 2 vols (Biblioteca de Autores Españoles, Madrid, 1956), I, 409.

11. Appointment by king, Aranjuez, 21 May 1785, Ministerio de Educación de la Nación, Instituto Nacional Sanmartiniano, Museo Histórico Nacional, *Documentos para la historia del Libertador general San Martín (DHL)*, 15 vols (Buenos Aires, 1953–79), I, 55–62.

12. Joseph Townsend, *A Journey through Spain in the Years 1786 and 1787*, 2 vols (3rd edn, Bath, 1814), II, 166, 169–70.

13. Charles Esdaile, *The Peninsular War: A New History* (London, 2002), 41–4.

14. Jean François Bourgoing, *Modern State of Spain*, 4 vols (London, 1808), II, 75–6.

15. Juan M. Zapatero, 'San Martín: Veintidós años en el ejército español', *Boletín de la Academia Nacional de la Historia*, 32 (1961), 104–14.

16. John Lynch, *Bourbon Spain 1700–1808* (Oxford, 1989), 393–4.

17. Julio Guillén and Jorge Juan Guillén, *Las campañas de San Martín en la fragata 'Santa Dorotea' cuando era subteniente del Regimiento de Murcia* (Madrid, 1966), 54–64.

18. Townsend, *A Journey through Spain*, II, 105–9, 109–11.

19. Lynch, *Bourbon Spain*, 369.

20. Cornelio de Saavedra, *Memoria autografa*, 1 January 1829, in *Biblioteca de Mayo*, 19 vols (Buenos Aires, 1960–8), II, 1040; see also Bartolomé Mitre, *Historia de Belgrano y de la independencia argentina*, 4 vols (6th edn, Buenos Aires, 1927), I, 155.

21. José Pacífico Otero, *Historia del Libertador don José de San Martín*, 4 vols (Buenos Aires, 1932), I, 100–5; Augusto Barcía Trelles, *José de San Martín en España, en América*, 5 vols (Buenos Aires, 1941–6), II, 166–79.

22. Alfredo G. Villegas, *San Martín en España* (Buenos Aires, 1976), 109–15; Pasquali, *San Martín*, 47–9.

23. 'Noticia del parte de combate de Arjonilla', 29 June 1808, *DHL*, I, 355–6.

24. *DHL*, I, 362–4, 367–9.

25. On the battle of Bailén see Esdaile, *The Peninsular War*, 77–84.

26. Ibid., 83.

27. Coupigny to San Martín, Madrid, 29 September 1808, *DHL*, I, 370.

28. Quoted by Esdaile, *The Peninsular War*, 86.

29. *DHL*, I, 384.

30. Esdaile, *The Peninsular War*, 335–6.

31. Quoted in Benjamín Vicuña MacKenna, *San Martín: La revolución de la independencia del Perú* (Santiago, 1938), 595.

32. Ricardo Piccirilli, *San Martín y la política de los pueblos* (Buenos Aires, 1957), 93–4.

33. Esdaile, *The Peninsular War*, 337–9, 342–9.

34. Ibid., 394–7.

35. Piccirilli, *San Martín y la política de los pueblos*, 118–19.

36. San Martín to Supreme Director, 31 June 1819, Ibid., 119.

37. San Martín to Ramón Castilla, Boulogne, 11 September 1848, Museo Histórico Nacional, *San Martín: Su correspondencia, 1823–1850 (SMC)* (3rd edn, Madrid, 1911), 296.

38. San Martín to Tomás Guido, Brussels, 18 December 1826, in Patricia Pasquali, ed., *San Martín confidencial: Correspondencia personal del Libertador con su amigo Tomás Guido (1816–1849)* (Buenos Aires, 2000), 210.

39. San Martín, Proclama, 22 July 1820, *DHL*, XVI, 99.

40. Informe, Real Isla, 26 August 1811, *DHL*, I, 393–4.

41. James Duff, in *Oxford Dictionary of National Biography*, 61 vols (Oxford, 2004), vol. 17; Rodolfo H. Terragno, *Maitland & San Martín* (Quilmes, 1998) 126–30; Rosendo Fraga, *San Martín y los británicos* (Buenos Aires, 2000), 17–21. Duff became M.P. for Banffshire in 1818, and was created Baron Fife in the British peerage and Kt. in 1827.

42. Earl of Fife to San Martín, Edinburgh, 3 June 1817, *SMC*, 309; San Martín to Earl of Fife, Santiago, 9 December 1817, in C.K. Webster, ed., *Britain and the Independence of Latin America 1812–1830: Select Documents from the Foreign Office Archives*, 2 vols (London, 1938), I, 556–8.

43. Esdaile, *The Peninsular War*, 488–96.

44. Bowles to Croker, *Aquilon*, off Buenos Ayres, 26 January 1813 [1814], in Graham and Humphreys, eds, *The Navy and South America*, 124.

45. Karen Racine, *Francisco de Miranda: A Transatlantic Life in the Age of Revolution* (Wilmington, DE, 2003), 194–5.

Chapter 2: The Revolution Calls

1. Baron de Montesquieu, *The Spirit of the Laws*, ed. Anne M. Cohlen and others (Cambridge, 1989), 396.

2. Príncipe de la Paz, *Memorias*, 2 vols (Biblioteca de Autores Españoles, 88–9, Madrid, 1956), I, 416.

3. Susan Migden Socolow, *The Merchants of Buenos Aires, 1778–1810: Family and Commerce* (Cambridge, 1978), 54–70, 124–35.

4. Samuel Amaral, *The Rise of Capitalism on the Pampas: The Estancias of Buenos Aires, 1785–1870* (Cambridge, 1998), 4–13, 59, 68.

5. Adrian J. Pearce, *British Trade with Spanish America, 1763–1808* (Liverpool, 2007), 249.

6. Antonio García-Baquero González, *Comercio colonial y guerras revolucionarias* (Seville, 1972), 182–3.

7. *Gaceta de Buenos Aires* [25 September 1810], in Noemí Goldman, *Historia y lenguaje: Los discursos de la Revolución de Mayo* (Buenos Aires, 1992), 33–4, 80.

8. Mark A. Burkholder and D.S. Chandler, *From Impotence to Authority: The Spanish Crown and the American Audiencias, 1687–1808* (Columbia, MO, 1977), 190–1.

9. Susan Migden Socolow, *The Bureaucrats of Buenos Aires, 1769–1810: Amor al Real Servicio* (Durham, NC, 1987), 132.

10. Juan Marchena Fernández, *Oficiales y soldados en el ejército de América* (Seville, 1983), 300.

11. Tulio Halperín Donghi, *Politics, Economics and Society in Argentina in the Revolutionary Period* (Cambridge, 1975), 128–32, and *Guerra y finanzas en los orígenes del estado argentino, 1791–1850* (Buenos Aires, 1982), 30, 84–5; Lyman L. Johnson, 'The Military as Catalyst of Change in Late Colonial Buenos Aires', in Mark D. Szuchman and Jonathan C. Brown, *Revolution and Restoration: The Rearrangement of Power in Argentina, 1776–1860* (Lincoln, NB, 1994), 27–53.

12. Manuel Belgrano, *Autobiografía*, in *Biblioteca de Mayo*, 19 vols (Senado de la Nación, Buenos Aires, 1960), II, 953–68.

13. Jorge Armando Pini, 'Perfiles culturales de la personalidad sanmartiniana', *PCIS*, VI, 43–72.

14. Goldman, *Historia y lenguaje*, 30–2.

15. Halperín Donghi, *Politics, Economics and Society in Argentina*, 186–7.

16. Merle E. Simmons, *Los escritos de Juan Pablo Viscardo y Guzmán, precursor de la independencia hispanoamericana* (Caracas, 1983), 363, 366–7, 369, 376.

17. Ricardo Levene, *Ensayo histórico sobre la Revolución de Mayo y Mariano Moreno*, 3 vols (4th edn, Buenos Aires, 1960), II, 36–72; Roberto H. Marfany, *El cabildo de Mayo* (Buenos Aires, 1961), 12, 38–42.

18. Fabian to Croker, *Mutine*, off Buenos Ayres, 3 June 1810, in Graham and Humphreys, eds, *The Navy and South America*, 49.
19. Carlos S.A. Segreti, 'Mariano Moreno y la independencia, los justos títulos de la Revolución de Mayo', *Boletín del Instituto de Historia Argentina Doctor Emilio Ravignani*, 5 (1960), 3–30.
20. John Lynch, *The Spanish American Revolutions 1808–1826* (2nd edn, London, 1986), 52–8.
21. Ricardo Piccirilli, *Rivadavia y su tiempo*, 3 vols (2nd edn, Buenos Aires, 1960), I, 117.
22. David Bushnell, *Reform and Reaction in the Platine Provinces 1810–1852* (Gainseville, FL, 1983), 8–19.
23. Halperín Donghi, *Politics, Economics and Society in Argentina*, 191, 200.
24. See José Luis Roca, *Ni con Lima ni con Buenos Aires: La formación de un estado nacional en Charcas* (Lima, 2007), 199–206, 301–34, for a modern analysis of developments in Upper Peru.
25. Pilar González Bernaldo de Quirós, *Civilité et Politique aux origines de la nation argentine* (Paris, 1999), 72–3; Noemí Goldman, 'Casos de continuidad y ruptura: Virreinato del Río de la Plata y Capitanía General de Chile, 1810–1830', in Germán Carrera Damas, *Historia general de América Latina*, vol. 5 (UNESCO, Paris, 2003), 186–94.
26. Quoted in Piccirilli, *Rivadavia y su tiempo*, I, 146.
27. *Gaceta de Buenos Aires 1810–1821*, 6 vols (Academia Nacional de la Historia, Buenos Aires, 1910–15), III, 13 March 1812.
28. Rivadavia to Pueyrredón, 9 March 1812, Museo Mitre, *Documentos del archivo de Pueyrredón*, 4 vols (Buenos Aires, 1912), I, 177–8.
29. Nina L. Kay Shuttleworth, *A Life of Sir Woodbine Parish* (London, 1910), 325.
30. Samuel Haigh, *Sketches of Buenos Ayres and Chile* (London, 1829), 11–17.
31. W.H. Hudson, *Far Away and Long Ago* (Everyman's Library, London, 1967), 54–5.
32. San Martín to Ramón Castilla, Boulogne, 11 September 1848, *SMC*, 296.
33. Staples to Castlereagh, London, 20 July 1812, National Archives, PRO, FO 72/157. An informant insinuated to Staples that the passengers from the *George Canning* 'were sent and supplied with money by the French Government'. Among them was 'a colonel St. Martin . . . who I have not the least doubt (from his past conduct) is in the pay of France.' M. Castilla to Staples, 13 August 1812, Ibid. FO 72/157.
34. Ricardo Piccirilli, *San Martín y la política de los pueblos* (Buenos Aires, 1957), 117–18.
35. Mitre, *Historia de San Martín*, I, 101.
36. Viana, chief of general staff, to government, 16 March 1812, *DHL*, I, 395, 398.
37. Government of Buenos Aires to San Martín, 16 March 1812, *DHL*, II, 1.
38. *DHL*, I, 406.
39. Ricardo Rodríguez Molas, 'La verdadera genealogía de San Martín', *Desmemoria, Revista de Historia*, no. 26 (2000), 37–40.
40. Héctor Juan Piccinali, *Vida de San Martín en Buenos Aires* (Buenos Aires, 1984), 53.
41. *DHL*, II, 37–40, 65–7.
42. *Gaceta de Buenos Aires*, III, 21 February 1812, no. 25, p. 98; J.P. and W.P. Robertson, *Letters on South America: comprising travels on the banks of the Paraná and Río de la Plata*, 3 vols (London, 1843), II, 172.
43. San Martín to Castilla, Boulogne, 11 September 1848, *SMC*, 296.
44. Juan Bautista Alberdi, *Escritos póstumos*, 16 vols (Buenos Aires, 1895–1901), IV, 330.
45. Klaus Gallo, *De la invasión al reconocimiento: Gran Bretaña y el Río de la Plata 1806–1826* (Buenos Aires, 1994), 151–62.
46. Heywood to Dixon, *Nereus*, off Buenos Ayres, 13 October 1812, in Graham and Humphreys, eds, *The Navy and South America*, 80.
47. Mark D. Szuchman, *Order, Family, and Community in Buenos Aires 1810–1860* (Stanford, CA, 1988), 214.

48. Edward Tagart, *A Memoir of the late Captain Peter Heywood R.N. with extracts from his Diaries and Correspondence* (London, 1832), 265.

49. San Martín to Pueyrredón, Pueyrredón to San Martín, 26 November 1812, in Piccirilli, *San Martín y la política de los pueblos*, 161–2.

50. See Piccirilli, *San Martín y la política de los pueblos*, 124–82, for the best traditional account, and Halperín Donghi, *Politics, Economics and Society in Argentina*, 216–21, for a modern analysis.

51. San Martín to General Miller, Brussels, 19 April 1827, in Piccirilli, *San Martín y la política de los pueblos*, 135–6.

52. John Street, *Artigas and the Emancipation of Uruguay* (Cambridge, 1959), 168–78.

53. Héctor Juan Piccinali, 'Tríptico de la campaña de San Lorenzo', *Investigaciones y Ensayos*, no. 34 (1983), 435–43.

54. San Martín to General Miller, 30 June 1827, *SMC*, 115–16.

55. J.P. and W.P. Robertson, *Letters on Paraguay: comprising an account of a four years' residence in that Republic, under the Government of the Dictator Francia*, 3 vols (2nd edn, London, 1839), II, 8–15.

56. Robertson, *Letters on Paraguay*, II, 14–15; see also Tagart, *A Memoir of the late Captain Peter Heywood*, 268.

57. Parte del coronel de granaderos a caballo D. José de San Martín al Gobierno Superior, 3 February 1813, *Gaceta de Buenos Aires*, 5 February 1813, vol. III, no. 44, 202; *DHL*, II, 9–10; San Martín to General Miller, 30 June 1827, *SMC*, 115–16.

58. Bowles to Croker, *Aquilon*, off Buenos Ayres, 26 January 1814, in Graham and Humphreys, eds, *The Navy and South America*, 123.

59. Bowles to Croker, 26 January 1814, ibid., 124.

60. Bowles to Croker, 22 September 1813, ibid., 107.

61. Belgrano to San Martín, 17 December 1813, *DHL*, II, 50.

Chapter 3: A Continental Strategy

1. Bowles to Croker, 22 June 1817, in Graham and Humphreys, eds, *The Navy and South America*, 202–3.

2. San Martín to Bowles, 7 September 1816, Ibid., 169.

3. Belgrano to San Martín, 25 September, 8 December 1813, *DHL*, II, 24, 44–6.

4. Belgrano to San Martín, Jujuy, 25 December 1813, *Epistolario belgraviano* (Buenos Aires, 2001), 247–50; Belgrano to San Martín, Jujuy, 2 January 1814, *DHL*, II, 73.

5. 'Voy a pasar el Río del Juramento, y respecto a hallarse V.S. con la tropa tan inmediato, sirvase esperarme con ella.' Belgrano to San Martín, Río de Juramento, 17 January 1814, *DHL*, II, 83. The meeting was not in Yatasto, as was long believed; see Julio Arturo Benencia, *Cómo San Martín y Belgrano no se conocieron en Yatasto* (Buenos Aires, 1973), 89.

6. San Martín to Supreme Director, 30 January, 11 February, 5 March 1814, in A.J. Pérez Amuchástegui, *San Martín y el Alto Perú, 1814* (Tucumán, 1976), 371–3, 340–1.

7. Pasquali, *San Martín*, 179.

8. José María Paz, *Memorias póstumas*, 3 vols (Buenos Aires, 1917), I, 146–7.

9. San Martín to Supreme Executive Power, Tucumán, 11 February 1814, in Pérez Amuchástegui, *San Martín y el Alto Perú*, 271–2.

10. San Martín to Supreme Director, Tucumán, 23 February 1814, in Gerónimo Espejo, *El paso de los Andes, Biblioteca de Mayo*, XVI, pt. 1 (Buenos Aires, 1960–9), 13, 854–5. *Obedezco pero no cumplo* ('I obey but I don't comply') was the classic formula by which Spanish colonial officials received orders that they did not intend to apply.

11. Posadas to San Martín, 10 March 1814, *DASM*, II, 54.

12. Belgrano to San Martín, Santiago del Estero, 6 April 1814, *DHL*, II, 123–4; *Epistolario belgraviano*, 273–5; Piccirilli, *San Martín y la política de los pueblos*, 154–5.
13. Posadas to San Martín, 2 March 1814, *DHL*, II, 120.
14. Mitre, *Historia de San Martín*, I, 166.
15. Paz, *Memorias póstumas*, I, 150; Mitre, *Historia de San Martín*, I, 203.
16. Raúl A. Bridondo, 'San Martín y la Guerra de Recursos en el Ejército del Norte, 1814', *PCIS*, II, 293–318; Alberto Crespo R., 'El ejército de San Martín y las guerrillas del Alto Perú', *PCIS*, II, 379–403.
17. San Martín to Supreme Director, Tucumán, 23 March 1814, in Pérez Amuchástegui, *San Martín y el Alto Perú*, 354–5.
18. Tulio Halperín Donghi, Politics, Economics and Society in Argentina in the Revolutionary Period (Cambridge, 1975), 64–9.
19. Roger M. Haigh, *Martin Güemes: Tyrant or Tool? A Study of the Sources of Power of an Argentine Caudillo* (Fort Worth, TX, 1968), 51–2.
20. Instructions to General Arenales, 28 February 1814, in José Everisto Uriburu, *Historia del General Arenales 1770–1831* (London, 1924), 169–71; Bridondo, *PCIS*, II, 303–4.
21. Pérez Amuchástegui, *San Martín y el Alto Perú*, 346–7.
22. Belgrano to San Martín, 21 April 1814, *DHL*, II, 131–2.
23. Antonio Alberto Guerrino, *La salud de San Martín: Ensayo de patografía histórica* (Buenos Aires, 1999), 65–8.
24. Posadas to San Martín, 24 June 1814, *DHL*, II, 154.
25. Paz, *Memorias póstumas*, 149–50.
26. Alvear to San Martín, Montevideo, 11 July 1814, *DHL*, II, 157.
27. Espejo, *El paso de los Andes, Biblioteca de Mayo*, XVI, pt. 1, 13, 856–7.
28. Mitre, *Historia de San Martín*, I, 198.
29. Argentine history has its share of controversial moments, replete with dodgy documents and passionate polemics. The letter from San Martín to Nicolás Rodríguez Peña, dated 22 April 1814 and published by Vicente Fidel López to claim an early date for San Martín's authorship of the *Plan Continental*, is not valid either for the text or the date, being a mere reconstruction from memory. It has been accepted by many historians, but not by Pérez Amuchástegui, *San Martín y el Alto Perú*, 200–01; see also Pasquali, *San Martín*, 197–8.
30. Plan del Teniente Coronel Don Enrique Paillardelle, 29 November 1813, Archivo General de la Nación, *Documentos referentes a la guerra de la independencia y emancipación política de la República Argentina (DGIRA)*, 3 vols (Buenos Aires, 1914–26), II, 223–4.
31. Tomás Guido, *Memoria*, 20 May 1816, *DHL*, III, 425–44.
32. Sir Thomas Maitland, Plan to capture Buenos Aires and Chile and then emancipate Peru and Quito, published by Rodolfo H. Terragno, *Maitland & San Martín* (Quilmes, 1998), 81–99.
33. Ibid., 18, 31, 126–7, 164–5, 224.
34. John Lynch, 'British Policy and Spanish America, 1783–1808', *Journal of Latin American Studies*, 1, 1 (1969), 1–30.
35. San Martín to Supreme Director, 29 February 1816, *DGIRA*, II, 256–7; Terragno, *Maitland & San Martín*, 219–20.
36. San Martín to Tomás Godoy Cruz, 12 May 1816, *DHL*, III, 392–6.
37. Guido, *Memoria*, 20 May 1816, *DHL*, III, 425–44; see also the version published in *DGIRA*, II, 263–8, dated 10 May 1816. Pasquali, *San Martín*, 237–42.
38. San Martín to Godoy Cruz, Mendoza, 12 May, 19 May 1816, *DHL*, III, 392–6, 419–20.
39. Alfredo Jocelyn-Holt Letelier, *La independencia de Chile: Tradición, modernización y mito* (Madrid, 1992), 163–4.
40. 'Memoriales útiles para la historia de la revolución sudamericana', Academia Chilena de la Historia, *Archivo de don Bernardo O'Higgins*, 28 vols (Santiago, 1946–68), I, 27.
41. San Martín to Carrera, Mendoza, 17 October 1814, *DHL*, II, 271–4.

42. J.M. Carrera to San Martín, Mendoza, 20 October 1814, San Martín to government, 21 October 1814, *DHL*, II, 285–90.
43. San Martín to J.J. Carrera, Mendoza, 2 January 1815, *DHL*, II, 389.
44. Bowles to Croker, 3 April 1819, in Graham and Humphreys, eds, *The Navy and South America*, 267–8.
45. Pasquali, *San Martín*, 216–18.
46. Street, *Artigas and the Emancipation of Uruguay*, 256–7.
47. Roca, *Ni con Lima ni con Buenos Aires*, 347–56.

Chapter 4: Power Base of Revolution

1. Bowles to Croker, *Amphion* at sea, 14 February 1818, in Graham and Humphreys, eds, *The Navy and South America*, 227–8. On the later career of Sir William Bowles, K.C.B., Admiral of the Fleet and writer on naval subjects, see ibid., 158.
2. Chamberlain to Castlereagh, 5 April 1817, in C.K. Webster, ed., *Britain and the Independence of Latin America 1812–1830: Select Documents from the Foreign Office Archives*, 2 vols (London, 1938), I, 103–4.
3. Bowles to Croker, Frigate *Amphion* at sea, Buenos Ayres, 21 August 1816, in Graham and Humphreys, eds, *The Navy and South America*, 163.
4. Posadas to San Martín, 16 September 1814, *DHL*, II, 195.
5. Posadas to San Martín, 1 October 1814, *DHL*, II, 238.
6. *Cabildo* of Mendoza to San Martín, 21 November 1815, *DHL*, III, 78–9.
7. San Martín to Guido, 31 August 1816, in Patricia Pasquali, ed., *San Martín confidencial* (Buenos Aires, 2000), 65–6.
8. Espejo, *El paso de los Andes, Biblioteca de Mayo*, XVI, pt. 1, 13,825–6.
9. Alfredo Estévez and Oscar Horacio Elía, *Aspectos económico-financieros de la campaña sanmartiniana* (Buenos Aires, 1961), 97–128.
10. Jorge Comadrán Ruiz, 'Cuyo y la formación del Ejército de los Andes', *PCIS*, VII, 575–610.
11. Pasquali, *San Martín*, 223–4, 240.
12. San Martín to *cabildo*, Mendoza, 12 August 1815, *DHL*, III, 9.
13. San Martín to *cabildo*, Mendoza, 22 November 1815, *DHL*, III, 83.
14. San Martín to *cabildo*, Mendoza, 26 January 1815, *DHL*, II, 414.
15. R.A. Humphreys, *Liberation in South America 1806–1827: The Career of James Paroissien* (London, 1952), 63–4.
16. José Pacífico Otero, *Historia del Libertador don José de San Martín*, 4 vols (Buenos Aires, 1932), IV, 490.
17. San Martín to Supreme Director, Mendoza, 21 October 1816, *DGIRA*, II, 449.
18. Chilean secret agents to San Martín, Concepción, Valparaíso, 17 December 1815, *DHL*, III, 93–5.
19. San Martín to Guido, Mendoza, 6 April 1816, in Pasquali, ed, *San Martín confidencial*, 236.
20. Roca, *Ni con Lima ni con Buenos Aires*, 355–7.
21. Mitre, *Historia de San Martín*, 349.
22. San Martín to Godoy Cruz, Mendoza, 19 January 1816, *DHL*, III, 178; Guerrino, *La salud de San Martín*, 70.
23. San Martín to Godoy Cruz, Mendoza, 24 August 1816, *DHL*, IV, 84.
24. Guido to San Martín, Buenos Aires, 1 January 1816, *DHL*, III, 131–2.
25. San Martín to Godoy Cruz, Mendoza, 19 January 1816, *DHL*, III, 183.
26. San Martín to Godoy Cruz, Mendoza, 24 February 1816, *DHL*, III, 239–40.
27. San Martín to Guido, Mendoza, 14 February 1816, in Pasquali, ed, *San Martín confidencial*, 45.
28. San Martín to Supreme Director, Mendoza, 29 February 1816, in Espejo, *El paso de los Andes, Biblioteca de Mayo*, XVI, pt. 1, 13, 998–9.

29. San Martín to Supreme Director, Mendoza, 20 March 1816, ibid., 14,000.
30. Alberto D.H. Scunio, 'San Martín, oficial de inteligencia', *Investigaciones y Ensayos*, 32 (1982), 225–42.
31. Reports of secret agent Manuel Rodríguez, alias El Español, to San Martín, Chile, 13 March 1816, *DHL*, III, 263–70, especially 268.
32. *Cabildo* to San Martín, Mendoza, 8 April 1816, *DHL*, III, 305–8.
33. *Cabildo* to National Congress, Mendoza, 24 April 1816, *DHL*, III, 350–3.
34. San Martín to Bowles, Mendoza, 7 September 1816, in Graham and Humphreys, eds, *The Navy and South America*, 169.
35. San Martín to Godoy Cruz, Mendoza, 12 April 1816, *DHL*, III, 318–19.
36. San Martín to Godoy Cruz, Mendoza, 12 March 1816, *DHL*, III, 258.
37. San Martín to Godoy Cruz, Mendoza, 12 May 1816, *DHL*, III, 392–6.
38. Guido, *Memoria*, Buenos Aires, 20 May 1816, *DHL*, III, 425–44.
39. Pueyrredón to San Martín, 6 June 1816, *DHL*, III, 472.
40. Pueyrredón to Marcos Balcarce, 24 June 1816, in Espejo, *El paso de los Andes, Biblioteca de Mayo*, XVI, pt. 1, 14,005–06.
41. San Martín to Supreme Director, Mendoza, 15 June 1816, ibid., 14,024.
42. San Martín to Godoy Cruz, Córdoba, 22 July 1816, *DHL*, IV, 13.
43. San Martín to Guido, in Pasquali, *San Martín*, 243.
44. *El Censeo*, 12 December 1816, in Espejo, *El paso de los Andes, Biblioteca de Mayo*, XVI, pt. 1, 14,037.
45. Declaration of Captain Francisco Bermúdez, Mendoza, 1 October 1816, *DHL*, IV, 201.
46. Army of the Andes, 5 September 1816, 30 September 1817, *DGIRA*, II, 437, 485.
47. I am indebted for the following to the recent work of Peter Blanchard, *Under the Flags of Freedom* (Pittsburgh, PA, 2008), 59–63.
48. San Martín to Godoy Cruz, Mendoza, 12 June 1816, *DHL*, III, 485.
49. Pueyrredón to San Martín, Buenos Aires, 9 October 1816, *DHL*, IV, 246.
50. Blanchard, *Under the Flags of Freedom*, 62, 147.
51. Belgrano to San Martín, Jujuy, 25 December 1813, in Pérez Amuchástegui, *San Martín y el Alto Perú*, 142–3; San Martín to Godoy Cruz, 12 May 1816, *DHL*, II, 52–3, III, 394.
52. John Miller, *Memoirs of General Miller in the Service of the Republic of Peru*, 2 vols (2nd edn, London, 1829), I, 271–2.
53. San Martín to secretary of war, Mendoza, 19 February 1816, *DGIRA*, II, 391–2.
54. José Luis Busaniche, *San Martín visto por sus contemporáneos* (Buenos Aires, 1942), 40–2; Miller, *Memoirs*, I, 92–103.
55. San Martín to Guido, Mendoza, 24 September 1816, in Pasquali, *San Martín confidencial*, 67.
56. 'Apuntes históricos del coronel Melián', *Biblioteca de Mayo*, II, 1, 657.
57. Miller, *Memoirs*, I, 90.
58. San Martín, Mendoza, September 1816, *DGIRA*, II, 442–3.
59. San Martín to secretary of war, Mendoza, 14 October 1816, *DGIRA*, II, 448.
60. Pueyrredón to San Martín, Buenos Aires, 2 November 1816, *DHL*, IV, 346.
61. Espejo, *El paso de los Andes, Biblioteca de Mayo*, XVI, pt. 1, 14,044–51; Piccirilli, *San Martín y la política de los pueblos*, 162–3.
62. San Martín to Guido, Mendoza, 15 December 1816, in Pasquali, *San Martín confidencial*, 77.

Chapter 5: Across the Andes

1. Bowles to Croker, frigate *Amphion*, off Buenos Ayres, 10 January 1817, in Graham and Humphreys, eds, *The Navy and South America*, 180.

2. Manuel Alejandro Pueyrredón, *Memorias inéditas: Historia de mi vida. Campañas del ejército de los Andes* (Buenos Aires, 1947), 150; Miller, *Memoirs*, I, 106.

3. Pueyrredón, *Memorias*, 152.

4. Mitre, *Historia de San Martín*, I, 421–2.

5. Miller, *Memoirs*, I, 107.

6. San Martín, Parte de la batalla de Chacabuco, 22 February 1817, *Biblioteca de Mayo*, XVI, pt. 1, 14,406.

7. Olazábal, 'Recuerdos de Chacabuco', quoted by Pasquali, *San Martín*, 274.

8. Pueyrredón, *Memorias*, 167.

9. San Martín, Contestación a las preguntas del General Miller, *Biblioteca de Mayo*, II, 1916.

10. San Martín, Parte de la batalla de Chacabuco, *Biblioteca de Mayo*, XVI, pt. 2, 14, 407.

11. San Martín, Contestación a las preguntas del General Miller, *Biblioteca de Mayo*, II, 1907; Pueyrredón, *Memorias*, 169; Miller, *Memoirs*, 131–2.

12. San Martín to Bowles, Santiago, 22 February 1817, in Graham and Humphreys, eds, *The Navy and South America*, 190–1.

13. Miller, *Memoirs*, II, 314.

14. Samuel Haigh, *Sketches of Buenos Ayres and Chile* (London, 1831), 133–5.

15. Pueyrredón, *Memorias*, 178–9. See above, p. 90.

16. San Martín to Bowles, Santiago, 22 February 1817, Webster, ed., *Britain and the Independence of Latin America*, I, 103.

17. Staples to Hamilton, Buenos Aires, 25 May 1817, National Archives, PRO, FO 72/202, and Webster, *Britain and the Independence of Latin America*, I, 553–4. Nine months later, 'General San Martín continues to press earnestly the solicitations communicated in my dispatch of 25 May last.' Staples to Hamilton, 16 February 1818, FO 72/215.

18. Bowles to Croker, *Amphion*, Buenos Ayres, 24 May 1817, San Martín to Bowles, Buenos Aires, 17 April 1817, in Graham and Humphreys, eds, *The Navy and South America*, 196–8. Staples to Hamilton, 3 July, 27 July, 16 August 1817, National Archives, PRO, FO 72/202, reported that Alvarez Condarco had 'extensive credit on the house of John McNeele & Co'.

19. Carlos Guido y Spano, *Vindicación histórica: Papeles del brigadier general Guido, 1817–1820* (Buenos Aires, 1882), 16–19.

20. Juan Isidro Zapata to Guido, Santiago, 16 July 1817, Guido to Director of United Provinces, Santiago, 18 July 1817, ibid., 24–5.

21. San Martín to Laprida, 31 August 1817, *DHL*, VI, 154.

22. San Martín to Godoy Cruz, Santiago, 22 July 1817, *DHL*, VI, 48.

23. Guerrino, *La salud de San Martín*, 84–96.

24. San Martín to Godoy Cruz, Santiago, 20 August 1817, *DHL*, VI, 132.

25. Damian Hudson, *Recuerdos históricos sobre la provincia de Cuyo*, 2 vols (Buenos Aires, 1898), 261.

26. San Martín to O'Higgins, Mendoza, 13 October 1818, *Archivo O'Higgins*, VIII, 180–1.

27. Pasquali, *San Martín*, 374–5, n. 46.

28. Staples to Hamilton, 16 August 1817, in Piccirilli, *San Martín y la política de los pueblos*, 434–5.

29. San Martín to Belgrano, Santiago, 20 August 1817, *DHL*, VI, 126.

30. Belgrano to San Martín, Tucumán, 26 September 1817, *DHL*, VI, 230.

31. Bowles to Croker, frigate *Amphion*, 4 January 1818, in Graham and Humphreys, eds, *The Navy and South America*, 218.

32. *DHL*, IV, 561–75, especially 572.

33. Belgrano to Guido, Tucumán, 10 April 1818, in Guido y Spano, *Vindicación histórica*, 105–6.

34. Mitre, *Historia de San Martín*, II, 75, 82–3. As he prepared to attack, the French general Brayer, a veteran of the Napoleonic wars but to San Martín a useless troublemaker and

alarmist, chose this time to request permission to leave the field and retire to the baths of Colonia for his health. 'You general are an old crock (*un carraco*),' replied San Martín. 'The least of my drummers has more honour than you,' and after the battle he took steps to have his military and political conduct judged and the man expelled. See Quintana, Declaration, 9 April 1818, *DHL*, VIII, 218; Haigh, *Sketches of Buenos Ayres and Chile*, 215.

35. San Martín, Contestación a las preguntas del General Miller, *Biblioteca de Mayo*, II, 1917.
36. Haigh, *Sketches of Buenos Ayres and Chile*, 235.
37. Oficio de San Martín, Santiago, 9 April 1818, *Biblioteca de Mayo*, XVI, pt. 2, 14, 632–5.
38. Humphreys, *Liberation in South America*, 73.
39. Juan Manuel Beruti, *Memorias curiosas, Biblioteca de Mayo*, IV, 3, 903–4.
40. San Martín to earl of Fife, 9 December 1817, in Webster, *Britain and the Independence of Latin America*, I, 557.
41. San Martín to Pezuela, Oficios, Santiago, 11 April 1818, *DHL*, VII, 181–4.
42. O'Higgins to Prince Regent, 20 November 1817, in Webster, *Britain and the Independence of Latin America*, I, 554–6.
43. Bowles to Croker, *Amphion*, at sea, 14 February 1818, in Graham and Humphreys, eds, *The Navy and South America*, 224–8.
44. Chamberlain to Castlereagh, Rio de Janeiro, 5 April 1817, 14 July 1818, in Webster, *Britain and the Independence of Latin America*, I, 103–4.
45. San Martín to Castlereagh, Santiago, 11 April 1818, Chamberlain to Castlereagh, Rio de Janeiro, 14 August 1818, ibid., I, 104, 558–9.
46. Joaquín Pérez, 'San Martín y el repaso de los Andes', *PCIS*, VIII, 339–430.
47. San Martín to Guido, Santiago, 12 January 1819, in Guido y Spano, *Vindicación histórica*, 174–5.
48. Haigh, *Sketches of Buenos Ayres and Chile*, 280.
49. San Martín to Supreme Director of United Provinces, 21 June 1819, *DASM*, IV, 465.
50. Pasquali, *San Martín*, 342–3.
51. San Martín to O'Higgins, 9 November 1819, *Archivo O'Higgins*, VIII, 193.
52. Bowles to Croker, Buenos Ayres, 31 August 1819, in Graham and Humphreys, eds, *The Navy and South America*, 275.
53. Acta de Reunión, 2 April 1820, *DASM*, VI, 191–9, *DHL*, XVI, 41–5; Miller, *Memoirs*, I, 270–1; Otero, *Historia del Libertador*, II, 667–71, who rejects the idea of disobedience and argues that it was simply a question of deciding whether San Martín's authority fell with that of the government, 'un punto de pura doctrina'; see also A.J. Pérez Amuchástegui, 'El Pacto de Rancagua', *PCIS*, VII, 191–206.
54. Mitre, *Historia de San Martín*, II, 256.
55. Proclama del General San Martín a los habitantes de las Provincias del Río de la Plata, Valparaíso, 22 July 1820, *DASM*, VII, 214.
56. Donald E. Worcester, *Sea Power and Chilean Independence* (Gainesville, FL., 1962), 18.
57. Staples to Hamilton, Buenos Aires, 12 June 1818, National Archives, PRO, FO 72/215.
58. Miller, *Memoirs*, I, 198.
59. Worcester, *Sea Power and Chilean Independence*, 17–35.
60. Brian Vale, *The Audacious Admiral Cochrane: The True Life of a Naval Legend* (London, 2004), 90–3.
61. Miller, *Memoirs*, I, 208; Thomas Cochrane, Earl of Dundonald, *Narrative of Services in the Liberation of Chile, Peru and Brazil from Spanish and Portuguese Domination*, 2 vols (London, 1859), I, 3.
62. San Martín to Lady Cochrane, 17 January 1819, in Alamiro de Avila Martel, 'La amistad de San Martín y Cochrane', *PCIS*, V, 16.
63. David Cordingly, *Cochrane the Dauntless: The Life and Adventures of Admiral Thomas Cochrane, 1775–1860* (London, 2007), 58–9.

64. Cordingly, *Cochrane the Dauntless*, 359–60, concludes that he was 'innocent of any involvement in the planning and execution' of the stock exchange fraud. For another view see Richard Dale, *Napoleon is Dead: Lord Cochrane and the Great Stock Exchange Scandal* (London, 2007).
65. Bowles to Croker, *Creole*, Buenos Ayres, 27 February 1819, in Graham and Humphreys, eds, *The Navy and South America*, 262–3.
66. Thomas Cochrane, *Narrative of Services*, I, 69–70.
67. Vale, *The Audacious Admiral Cochrane*, 103–5; Cordingly, *Cochrane the Dauntless*, 278–85; on Miller's role see Moises Enrique Rodriguez, *Freedom's Mercenaries: British Volunteers in the Wars of Independence of Latin America. Volume II: Southern South America* (Lanham, MD, 2006), 442–4.
68. Bowles to Croker, *Creole*, Buenos Ayres, 3 April 1819, in Graham and Humphreys, eds, *The Navy and South America*, 265–6; San Martín to Cochrane, repeated a year later on 13 August 1821, in Mitre, *Historia de San Martín*, II, 263.
69. Estévez and Elía, *Aspectos económico-financieros de la campaña sanmartiniana*, 155; Fritz C. Hoffman, 'The Financing of San Martín's Expeditions', *Hispanic American Historical Review*, 32 (1952), 634–8, who suggests that taking the two expeditions together Argentina and Chile contributed from 1.5 to 2 million pesos each; Joaquín Pérez, 'Las dificultades económicas de la alianza argentino-chileno y sus consecuencias', *Trabajos y comunicaciones*, 17 (1967), 153–83.
70. Estévez and Elía, ibid., 168–79.
71. Mitre, *Historia de San Martín*, II, 303–4.

Chapter 6: Peru, the Carthage of San Martín

1. Mitre, *Historia de San Martín*, II, 268–9.
2. Instrucciones reservadísimas a los Comisionados, José Fernández Paredes y José García, Santiago, 1 January 1819, *DHL*, X, 72–80, shows the kind of intelligence San Martín wanted from his agents, especially from sources close to the viceroy, 'not always reliable but at least containing material that can be tested'.
3. John R. Fisher, *Bourbon Peru 1750–1824* (Liverpool, 2003), 55–6. In 1827 the Indians formed 61.6 per cent of the population; see Cristóbal Aljovín de Losada, *Caudillos y constituciones: Perú, 1821–1845* (Lima, 2000), 61.
4. Alonso Carrió de la Vandera (Concolorcorvo, pseud.), *El Lazarillo de ciegos caminantes desde Buenos Aires hasta Lima* (1773) (Biblioteca de autores españoles, 122, Madrid, 1959), 379. The author was an inspector of posts.
5. Heraclio Bonilla and others, *La independencia en el Perú* (2nd edn, Lima, 1981), 88–92.
6. Alberto Flores Galindo, 'Independencia y clases sociales', *Independencia y revolución (1780–1840)*, 2 vols (Lima, 1987), I, 125–44.
7. López Aldana to Castelli, 10 March 1811, in Pablo Macera, *Tres etapas en el desarrollo de la conciencia nacional* (Lima, 1955), 88–9.
8. Timothy E. Anna, *The Fall of the Royal Government in Peru* (Lincoln, NB, 1979), 29–34; Mark A. Burkholder, *The Politics of a Colonial Career: José Baquijano and the Audiencia of Lima* (Albuquerque, NM, 1980), 79–80, 84–5.
9. *El argos constitucional*, in Macera, *Tres etapas*, 118; see also Ascensión Martínez Riaza, *La prensa doctrinal en la independencia del Perú 1811–1824* (Madrid, 1985), 117–26.
10. John Preston Moore, *The Cabildo in Peru under the Bourbons* (Durham, NC, 1966), 200–4.
11. John Fisher, *Minas y mineros en el Perú colonial 1776–1824* (Lima, 1977), 213–33.
12. Fisher, *Bourbon Peru*, 62–72.
13. Quoted by J.R. Fisher, *Government and Society in Colonial Peru: The Intendant System 1784–1814* (London, 1970), 154.

14. Hardy to Croker, *Creole*, Valparaíso, 17 May 1821, in Graham and Humphreys, eds, *The Navy and South America*, 331.

15. Armando Nieto Vélez, 'Contribución a la historia del fidelismo en el Perú (1808–1810)', *Boletín del Instituto Riva-Agüero*, 4 (1958–60), 9–146; José Fernando de Abascal y Sousa, *Memoria de gobierno*, eds Vicente Rodríguez Casado and José Antonio Calderón Quijano, 2 vols (Seville, 1944), I, 198.

16. María Teresa Berruezo, *La participación americana en las cortes de Cádiz 1810–1814* (Madrid, 1986), 28–9, 149–55, 310–11.

17. Fisher, *Bourbon Peru*, 118–21, who questions the existence of deep-seated ideological differences among the royalists.

18. Joaquín de la Pezuela, *Memoria de gobierno*, eds Vicente Rodríguez Casado and Guillermo Lohmann Villena (Seville, 1947), 279–80; report of Pezuela, 13 November 1818, in J.A. de la Puente Candamo, *San Martín y el Perú* (Lima, 1948), 9.

19. Miller, *Memoirs*, I, 277, who was one of the survivors. See also R.A. Humphreys, ed., 'James Paroissien's Notes on the Liberating Expedition to Peru', *HAHR*, 31 (1951), 254–68. Mitre, *Historia de San Martín*, II, 306–7.

20. O'Higgins to Cochrane, 19 August 1820, in Gonzalo Bulnes, *Historia de la expedición libertadora del Perú, 1817–1822*, 2 vols (Santiago, 1887), I, 345.

21. Cochrane, *Narrative of Services*, I, 79.

22. San Martín, Proclamation, September 1820, in Mitre, *Historia de San Martín*, II, 314. In March 2003, on leading his troops into Iraq, Colonel Tim Collins declared 'We go to liberate, not to conquer.' Reported in *The Times*, 13 March 2008.

23. San Martín, August 1821, in Puente Candamo, *San Martín y el Perú*, 3.

24. Bowles to Croker, 10 June 1818, in Graham and Humphreys, eds, *The Navy and South America*, 239.

25. San Martín to Torre Tagle, 19 January 1821, in Javier Ortiz de Zevallos, *Correspondencia de San Martín y Torre Tagle* (Lima, 1963), 34.

26. San Martín to Torre Tagle, 20 November 1820, ibid., 3–4.

27. Flores Galindo, *Independencia y revolución*, I, 139.

28. Fisher, *Bourbon Peru*, 117.

29. Puente Candamo, *San Martín y el Perú*, 12–14; Rubén Vargas Ugarte, *Historia del Perú: Emancipación. 1809–1825* (Buenos Aires, 1958), 186–92.

30. Alamiro de Avila, 'La amistad de San Martín y Cochrane', *PCIS*, V, 18–19.

31. Basil Hall, *Extracts from a Journal written on the coasts of Chile, Peru, and Mexico in the years 1820, 1821, 1822*, 2 vols (3rd edn, London, 1826), I, 66, 69. For an account of the action and subsequent recriminations see Vale, *The Audacious Admiral Cochrane*, 115–18, and Cordingly, *Cochrane the Dauntless*, 289–91, 293.

32. Searle to Hardy, *Hyperion*, Callao, 8 November 1820, in Graham and Humphreys, eds, *The Navy and South America*, 321.

33. Miller, *Memoirs*, I, 298.

34. Hardy to Croker, *Creole*, Valparaíso, 22 March 1821, in Graham and Humphreys, eds, *The Navy and South America*, 326.

35. Interview with San Martín, 25 June 1821, in Hall, *Journal*, I, 180–1.

36. José de la Riva Agüero to San Martín, 1820, quoted by Gustavo Montoya Rivas, *La independencia del Perú y el fantasma de la revolución* (Lima, 2002), 61.

37. Ibid., I, 79, 186–7.

38. Susy Sánchez, 'Clima, hambre y enfermedad en Lima durante la guerra independentista (1817–1826)', in Scarlett O'Phelan Godoy, ed., *La independencia en el Perú: De los Borbones a Bolívar* (Lima, 2001), 243–4.

39. Cochrane, *Narrative of Services*, 106.

40. Miller, *Memoirs*, I, 295–7.

41. San Martín to Abreu, Huaura, 6 March 1821, in Piccirilli, *San Martín y la política de los pueblos*, 262.

42. Hall, *Journal*, 265.
43. Puente Candamo, *San Martín y el Perú*, 19–23; Vargas Ugarte, *Historia del Perú: Emancipación*, 273–82.
44. Miller, *Memoirs*, I, 302–3.
45. Germán Leguía y Martínez, *Historia de la emancipación del Perú: El Protectorado*, 7 vols (Lima, 1972), IV, 41, 310–19, on the epidemics.
46. Hall, *Journal*, I, 243–4.
47. Ibid., I, 246–7.
48. Juan Isidro Quesada, *Memorias*, in Félix Luna, 'La personalidad de San Martín a través de las Memorias, parcialmente inéditas, de uno de sus oficiales', *PCIS*, V, 343.
49. Hall, *Journal*, I, 245.
50. Mitre, *Historia de San Martín*, II, 450.
51. Otero, *Historia del Libertador*, III, 350–1.
52. Quesada, *Memorias*, quoted in Luna, *PCIS*, V, 344.
53. Hall, *Journal*, I, 189–90.
54. Arenales to San Martín, Cachi-cachi, 20 July 1821, *DHL*, XVII, 182.
55. Arenales to San Martín, San Juan de Matucana, 27 July 1821, *DHL*, XVII, 203.
56. Arenales to San Martín, San Juan de Matucana, 30 July 1821, *DHL*, XVII, 211–13.
57. Hardy to Croker, *Creole*, off Ancón Bay, 14 September 1821, in Graham and Humphreys, eds, *The Navy and South America*, 347–8.
58. Hall, *Journal*, II, 53–4; Miller, *Memoirs*, I, 372.
59. Montoya Rivas, *La independencia del Perú*, 116–17.
60. Miller, *Memoirs*, I, 410–11.
61. Mitre, *Historia de San Martín*, II, 483.
62. Cochrane, *Narrative of Services*, 124–6.
63. Cochrane to San Martín, Callao Roads, 7 August 1821, in *Narrative of Services*, I, 129–32.
64. Basil Hall to Commodore Hardy, *Conway*, Mollendo, 14 June 1821, in Graham and Humphreys, eds, *The Navy and South America*, 334.
65. San Martín and Cochrane, in Cochrane, *Narrative of Services*, I, 77.
66. William Bennet Stevenson, *A Historical and Descriptive Narrative of Twenty Years Residence in South America*, 3 vols (London, 1825), III, 252–4. Stevenson was Cochrane's secretary and interpreter and not an impartial witness.
67. Cochrane, *Narrative of Services*, I, 127–8, and Stevenson, *A Historical and Descriptive Narrative*, are both hostile to San Martín and should be read accordingly.
68. San Martín to Cochrane, 9 August 1821, in Cochrane, *Narrative of Services*, 132–3.
69. 'Caudales que se apoderó Lord Cochrane', *Colección documental de la independencia del Perú*, *CDIP*, VII, 2, 203–7; Stevenson, *A Historical and Descriptive Narrative*, III, 386.
70. Worcester, *Sea Power and Chilean Independence*, 72.
71. San Martín to O'Higgins, Lima, 29 September 1821, *Archivo O'Higgins*, VIII, 198–9.
72. 11 March 1822, *CDIP*, VII, 3, 297–311.

Chapter 7: Monarchist in a World of Republics

1. For a narrative of the Protectorate see Leguía y Martínez, *Historia de la emancipación del Perú: El Protectorado*, vols IV–VII, and Otero, *Historia del Libertador*, III, 341–80, 512–49.
2. Decree of Protector of Peru, Lima, 3 August 1821, Mitre, *Historia de San Martín*, II, 457–8.
3. Joseph Dager Abra, 'Hipólito Unanue y la independencia del Perú', in Margarita Guerra Martinière, Oswaldo Holguín Callo and César Gutiérrez Muñoz, *Sobre el Perú: Homenaje a José Agustín de la Puente Candamo*, 2 vols (Lima, 2002), 455–73.
4. See below, Chapter 8.

5. Hardy to Croker, *Creole*, off Ancón Bay, 14 September 1821, in Graham and Humphreys, eds, *The Navy and South America*, 347.
6. Montoya Rivas, *La independencia del Perú*, 118–37, 145–6.
7. Bernardo Monteagudo, *Memoria política*, Quito, 1823, *Escritos* (Buenos Aires, Senado de la Nación, 1989), 46.
8. *Gaceta del Gobierno*, 2, 12, 26, 30 January 1822.
9. Monteagudo, 29 April 1822, *CDIP*, VI, 2, 370.
10. Gilbert F. Mathison, *Narrative of a Visit to Brazil, Chile, Peru and the Sandwich Islands during the Years 1821 and 1822* (London, 1825), 287–9.
11. Timothy Anna, *The Fall of the Royal Government in Peru* (Lincoln, NB, 1979), 183–5.
12. Hall, *Journal*, II, 87–8; on the political thought of Monteagudo and his influence in Peru see Montoya Rivas, *La independencia del Perú*, 152–88.
13. Mathison, *Narrative*, 260, 333–4.
14. Hall, *Journal*, I, 282–3.
15. Mathison, *Narrative*, 258–9, 290, 352–3.
16. Report of Guido, Lima, 19 May 1822, *CDIP*, VI, 2, 371.
17. Miller, *Memoirs*, I, 416–17.
18. Charles F. Walker, *Smoldering Ashes: Cuzco and the Creation of Republican Peru, 1780–1840* (Durham, NC, 1999), 109–16; Fisher, *Bourbon Peru*, 123–7.
19. Miller, *Memoirs*, I, 360–1, 366.
20. John Lynch, *Caudillos in Spanish America 1800–1850* (Oxford, 1992), 51.
21. Raúl Rivera Serna, *Los guerrilleros del Centro en la emancipación peruana* (Lima, 1958), 20–1, 80–92, 108–13; Alberto Flores Galindo, *Buscando un Inca: Identidad y utopia en los Andes* (Lima, 1987), 220–1; Peter Guardino, 'Las guerrillas y la independencia peruana: Un ensayo de interpretación', *Pasado y Presente*, 2–3 (1989), 101–17.
22. Miller, *Memoirs*, I, 377–8, II, 138–40.
23. Ibid., I, 365.
24. Ella Dunbar Temple, prologue, *Guerrillas y montoneros*, *CDIP*, tomo V, vol. 1, xix.
25. Ignacio Ninavilca, 30 December 1822, Ibid., *CDIP*, V, 1, xix.
26. Lynch, *Caudillos in Spanish America*, 52–3.
27. R.A. Humphreys, *British Consular Reports on the Trade and Politics of Latin America 1824–1826* (London, 1940), 128–9.
28. Estévez and Elía, *Aspectos económico-financieros de la campaña sanmartiniana*, 207–10.
29. Carlos Camprubí Alcázar, *El banco de la emancipación* (Lima, 1960), 27–31.
30. *Gaceta del Gobierno*, 2 October 1822.
31. Estatuto Provisional, 8 October 1821, *DASM*, XI, 489–99.
32. Hardy to Croker, *Creole*, Callao Bay, 23 December 1821, in Graham and Humphreys, eds, *The Navy and South America*, 353.
33. Leguía y Martínez, *Historia de la emancipación del Perú*, V, 66–70.
34. Miller, *Memoirs*, I, 370–1. Colonel Miller received twenty thousand dollars.
35. *Gaceta del Gobierno*, 12 January 1822.
36. Monteagudo, *Gaceta de Buenos Aires*, 27 December 1811, in *Escritos*, 105.
37. Goldman, *Historia y lenguaje: Los discursos de la Revolución de Mayo*, 54.
38. Monteagudo, *Memoria política*, in *Escritos*, 42–4, 47. See also Puente Candamo, *San Martín y el Perú*, 19–23, 34–42.
39. Aljovín de Losada, *Caudillos y constituciones*, 100–2.
40. Martínez Riaza, *La prensa doctrinal en la independencia del Perú*, 56–7, 93–4.
41. Aljovín de Losada, *Caudillos y constituciones*, 96–9.
42. Hall, *Journal*, I, 246–7.
43. Leguía y Martínez, *Historia de la emancipación del Perú*, II, 327, V, 531.
44. Miller, *Memoirs*, I, 426.
45. Ibid., I, 425.
46. Hall, *Journal*, I, 179–80.

47. Juan Isidro Quesada, *Memorias*, in Luna, *PCIS*, V, 346–7.
48. Maria Graham, *Journal of a Residence in Chile, during the year 1822, and a Voyage from Chile to Brazil in 1823* (London, 1824), 281.
49. San Martín to Guido, 6 January 1827, *DASM*, VI, 513–14.
50. San Martín to Godoy Cruz, 24 May 1816, *DHL*, III, 451–9.
51. San Martín to Godoy Cruz, Córdoba, 22 July 1816, *DHL*, IV, 13.
52. San Martín to Godoy Cruz, Mendoza, 24 May 1816, *DHL*, III, 452.
53. San Martín to earl of Fife, 9 December 1817, in Webster, *Britain and the Independence of Latin America*, I, 557.
54. Quoted by Humphreys, *Liberation in South America*, 87.
55. Piccirilli, *San Martín y la política de los pueblos*, 271; Puente Candamo, *San Martín y el Perú*, 316–17; Pasquali, *San Martín confidencial*, 178.
56. Humphreys, *Liberation in South America*, 95.
57. María Teresa Berruezo León, *La lucha de Hispanoamérica por su independencia en Inglaterra, 1800–1830* (Madrid, 1989), 351–60. Humphreys, *Liberation in South America*, 99, 101, 115.
58. Leguía y Martínez, *Historia de la emancipación del Perú*, V, 2.
59. San Martín to Guido, Brussels, 6 January 1827, in Pasquali, *San Martín confidencial*, 213–14.
60. San Martín to Godoy Cruz, Mendoza, 24 February 1816, *DHL*, III, 239.
61. San Martín to Bowles, 7 September 1816, in Graham and Humphreys, eds, *The Navy and South America*, 169.
62. Bowles to Croker, *Amphion*, at sea, 14 February 1818, ibid., 226–7.
63. San Martín to Torre Tagle, 13 January 1821, in Ortiz de Zevallos, *Correspondencia de San Martín y Torre Tagle*, 32.
64. Address to Peruvians, in Hall, *Journal*, I, 212–14; for a shorter version see Mitre, *Historia de San Martín*, II, 448–9, who attributes it to Monteagudo.
65. Leguía y Martínez, *Historia de la emancipación del Perú*, V, 268.
66. Mitre, *Historia de San Martín*, II, 498.
67. O'Higgins to San Martín, 6 August 1821, *Archivo O'Higgins*, VIII, 137.
68. San Martín to O'Higgins, Magdalena, 30 November 1821, *Archivo O'Higgins*, VIII, 204.
69. Piccirilli, *San Martín y la política de los pueblos*, 281–2.
70. García del Río to San Martín, Santiago, 21 March 1822, *DASM*, VII, 456.
71. Puente Candamo, *San Martín y el Perú*, 244.
72. Lord Ponsonby to George Canning, 20 July 1827, National Archives, PRO, FO 6/18.
73. Miller, *Memoirs*, II, 419.
74. Otero, *Historia del Libertador*, III, 647.
75. Woodbine Parish to Canning, Buenos Ayres, 25 April 1824, in Webster, *Britain and the Independence of Latin America*, I, 112; Humphreys, *Liberation in South America*, 107.
76. Humphreys, ibid., 111; J.A. Pérez Amuchástegui, *Ideología y acción de San Martín* (Buenos Aires, 1979), 59–60.
77. Frank Griffith Dawson, *The First Latin American Debt Crisis: The City of London and the 1822–25 Loan Bubble* (London, 1990), 34–7.
78. Letter in a London newspaper, dated Lima, 20 May 1823, National Archives, PRO, FO 61/2.
79. Captain Prescott to Commodore Hardy, 23 August 1822, National Archives, PRO, FO 61/1; Miller, *Memoirs*, I, 410–11.

Chapter 8: Liberal in a Conservative Society

1. San Martín to Castlereagh, 11 April 1818, in Webster, *Britain and the Independence of Latin America*, I, 558.

2. Otero, *Historia del Libertador*, III, 513–49.
3. Juan Pablo Viscardo y Guzmán, *Lettre aux Espagnols Américains*, in Merle E. Simmons, *Los escritos de Juan Pablo Viscardo y Guzmán* (Caracas, 1983), 372.
4. Martínez Riaza, *La prensa doctrinal en la independencia del Perú*, 119, 158, 198.
5. Estatuto Provisional, 8 October 1821, *DASM*, XI, 489–99.
6. San Martín to General Pinto, 26 September 1846, *SMC*, 191–2. Compare this conclusion with that of Bolívar, Jamaica Letter, 1815, *Escritos* (Caracas, 1972), VIII, 241: 'Let us not adopt the best system of government, but the one that is most likely to work.'
7. Otero, *Historia del Libertador*, III, 43–4.
8. *Gaceta del Gobierno*, 17 January 1821, quoted by Montoya, *La independencia del Perú*, 78.
9. Leguía y Martínez, *Historia de la emancipación del Perú*, IV, 303.
10. San Martín to European Spaniards, 4 August 1821, *DASM*, XI, 424–5.
11. Reglamento Provisional, Huaura, 12 February 1821, *DASM*, XI, 331–5.
12. José A. de la Puente Candamo, 'Contenido social de la obra de San Martín en el Perú', *PCIS*, VI, 457–81.
13. Otero, *Historia del Libertador*, III, 536.
14. Estatuto Provisional, 8 October 1821, Texto legal, 13 October 1821, *CDIP*, XIII, 1, 335–6; *DASM*, XI, 489–99.
15. Charles Milner Ricketts to Canning, Lima, 27 December 1826, in Humphreys, *British Consular Reports on the Trade and Politics of Latin America 1824–1826*, 107–95, 195–206.
16. Hall, *Journal*, I, 268.
17. Frank Griffith Dawson, *The First Latin American Debt Crisis: The City of London and the 1822–25 Loan Bubble*, 35–8; Humphreys, *Liberation in South America*, 122–32.
18. On Indian demography see Fisher, *Bourbon Peru*, 55–9.
19. Miller, *Memoirs*, II, 93.
20. Ibid., II, 285.
21. Ibid., I, 328–9.
22. *DASM*, XI, 440–1; Otero, *Historia del Libertador*, III, 364.
23. Anna, *The Fall of the Royal Government in Peru*, 62–3.
24. Miller, *Memoirs*, II, 191–2, 200.
25. José Santos Vargas, *Diario de un comandante de la independencia americana 1814–1825*, ed. Gunnar Mendoza L. (Mexico, 1982), June 1816, 88 and 30 December 1816, 118.
26. *DASM*, VIII, 239–40.
27. Instrucciones reservadísimas a los comisionados, José Fernández Paredes y José García. Santiago, 1 January 1819, *DHL*, X, 76–7.
28. Miller, *Memoirs*, I, 280, 305, 352–3. San Martín, Pisco, 20 September 1820, *CDIP*, VI, 2, 145. I am grateful for guidance on slavery and abolition to Peter Blanchard, whose book is cited below.
29. San Martín to Torre Tagle, 13 February 1821, *Correspondencia de San Martín y Torre Tagle*, 46.
30. Christine Hünefeldt, *Paying the Price of Freedom: Family and Labor among Lima's Slaves, 1800–1854* (Berkeley, CA, 1994), 87–8, 90.
31. Miller to San Martín, 9 April 1827, *SMC*, 70.
32. Decree of 12 August 1821, *DASM*, XI, 430–1; Otero, *Historia del Libertador*, III, 363–4.
33. *CDIP*, V, 1, pp. 24, 65, 74–5, 80, 106–7.
34. Peter Blanchard, *Slavery and Abolition in Early Republican Peru* (Wilmington, DE, 1992), 6–9, 15.
35. Hünefeldt, *Paying the Price of Freedom*, 149–66, 211–15.
36. *El Depositario*, 20 October 1820, quoted in Montoya, *La independencia del Perú*, 83.
37. *DASM*, I, 35.

38. Guido to San Martín, Buenos Aires, 27 March 1833, *DASM*, VI, 576.
39. Martínez Riaza, *La prensa doctrinal en la independencia del Perú*, 212–13.
40. Provisional Statute, *DASM*, XI, 490–1.
41. See Jeffrey Klaiber, 'La Iglesia ante la emancipación en el Perú', *Historia general de la Iglesia en América Latina*, VIII, *Perú, Bolivia y Ecuador* (Salamanca, 1987), 159–82.
42. Toribio Dabalos, commander of guerrilla bands, to San Martín, Yantac, 2 October 1821, *CDIP*, V, 1, 382.
43. Pedro de Leturia, *Relaciones entre la Santa Sede e Hispanoamérica*, 3 vols (Rome, Caracas, 1959–60), II, 110–13, 215, III, 432.
44. Otero, *Historia del Libertador*, III, 166.
45. Cayetano Bruno, 'El Protector del Perú, General José de San Martín, y la relación del arzobispo de Lima, Bartolomé María de Las Heras', *PCIS*, VI, 405–39; Rubén Vargas Ugarte, *Historia del Perú: Emancipación, 1809–1825* (Buenos Aires, 1958), 300–7.
46. *CDIP*, XX, 1–2; Aljovín de Losada, *Caudillos y constituciones*, 113.
47. Klaiber, 'La Iglesia ante la emancipación en el Perú', *Historia general de la Iglesia en América Latina*, VIII, 180, and in O'Phelan Godoy, ed., *La independencia del Perú*, 134–5.
48. Martínez Riaza, *La prensa doctrinal en la independencia del Perú*, 213–14.
49. Graham, *Journal of a Residence in Chile*, 83, 281–3.
50. San Martín to Guido, Brussels, 6 April 1830, in Piccirilli, *San Martín y la política de los pueblos*, 158–9.
51. Otero, *Historia del Libertador*, IV, 469–71.
52. *CDIP*, XIII, 1, 291–300.
53. *Gaceta del Gobierno*, 29 August 1821, 16 September 1822.
54. Jorge Armando Pini, 'Perfiles culturales de la personalidad sanmartiniana', *PCIS*, VI, 43–72.
55. *CDIP*, XIII, 1, 45–6, 483–500; Otero, *Historia del Libertador*, 534–9.
56. *Gaceta del Gobierno*, 10 October 1821.
57. Otero, *Historia del Libertador*, III, 535.

Chapter 9: Last Chance in Guayaquil

1. Bowles to Croker, *Creole*, Buenos Aires, 27 February 1819, in Graham and Humphreys, eds, *The Navy and South America*, 261.
2. San Martín's replies to various questions of General Miller, 9 April 1827, *SMC*, 103.
3. Royalist numbers from *CDIP*, VI, 1, 53, 212–13, 215; a British estimate from Commodore Hardy to Croker, *Creole*, Valparaiso, 22 March 1821, 17 May 1821, in Graham and Humphreys, eds, *The Navy and South America*, 326, 330. On patriot strength see above, Chapter 6, pp. 120–1.
4. Bowles to Croker, *Amphion*, Buenos Ayres, 10 June 1818, in Graham and Humphreys, eds, *The Navy and South America*, 239.
5. San Martín to Miller, Brussels, 8 September 1826, *SMC*, 65.
6. Bolívar to Santander, Tocuyo, 16 August 1821, *Cartas Santander-Bolívar*, Biblioteca de la Presidencia de la República, 6 vols (Bogotá, 1988–90), III, 132.
7. Sucre to San Martín, Guayaquil, 29 October 1821, in Daniel Florencio O'Leary, *Memorias del General O'Leary*, 34 vols (Caracas, 1981), XIX, 77–9.
8. Bolívar to San Martín, Quito, 17 June 1822, in O'Leary, *Memorias*, XIX, 307.
9. Bolívar to Santander, Quito, 21 June 1822, *Cartas Santander-Bolívar*, III, 235.
10. The *'Detached Recollections' of General D.F. O'Leary*, ed. R.A. Humphreys (London, 1969), 31.
11. San Martín to Bolívar, Lima, 13 July 1822, in O'Leary, *Memorias*, XIX, 335–6.

12. Bolívar to San Martín, Guayaquil, 25 July 1822, in O'Leary *Memorias*, XIX, 338, XXIX, 251.
13. On the Guayaquil interview, see Vicente Lecuna, *La entrevista de Guayaquil*, 2 vols (4th edn, Caracas, 1962–3); A.J. Pérez Amuchástegui, *La 'Carta de Lafond' y la preceptiva historiográfica* (Córdoba, 1962); Gerhard Masur, 'The Conference of Guayaquil', *HAHR*, 31 (1951), 189–229.
14. J.G. Pérez to Pedro Gual, Guayaquil, 29 July 1822, in Simón Bolívar, *Obras completas*, eds Vicente Lecuna and Esther Barret de Nazaris, 3 vols (2nd edn, Havana, 1950), I, 655–9.
15. Pérez Amuchástegui, *La 'Carta de Lafond'*, 4–10.
16. J.G. Pérez to Sucre, 29 July 1822, in Vicente Lecuna, *Selected Writings of Bolívar*, ed. Harold A. Bierck, trans. Lewis Bertrand, 2 vols (New York, 1951), I, 340–3.
17. San Martín to Miller, Brussels, 19 April 1827, *SMC*, 72–3.
18. San Martín to Miller, Brussels, 19 April 1827, *SMC*, 73; Lecuna, *La entrevista de Guayaquil*, II, 467.
19. Bolívar to Santander, Guayaquil, 29 July 1822, *Cartas Santander-Bolívar*, III, 243.
20. San Martín to Bolívar, 29 August 1822, in Pérez Amuchástegui, *La 'Carta de Lafond'*, 141–50.
21. San Martín to Guido, 18 December 1826, 21 June 1827, *DASM*, VI, 504, 529.
22. San Martín to O'Higgins, Lima, 25 August 1822, in Otero, *Historia del Libertador*, III, 786; Martínez Riaza, *La prensa doctrinal en la independencia del Perú*, 294–5.
23. Captain Prescott to Commodore Hardy, *Aurora*, Callao Bay, 23 August 1822, National Archives, PRO FO 61/1.
24. José Luis Roca, *Ni con Lima ni con Buenos Aires: La formación de un estado nacional en Charcas* (La Paz, 2007), 456–9, 468.
25. Monteagudo, *Memoria política*, in *Escritos*, 42–4.
26. Hall, *Journal*, I, 233.
27. San Martín to O'Higgins, 6 July 1821, in Mitre, *Historia de San Martín*, III, 177.
28. San Martín to O'Higgins, 20 August, 25 August 1822, in Leguía y Martínez, *Historia de la emancipación del Perú*, VII, 501.
29. Guerrino, *La salud de San Martín*, 113–14, 166.
30. Jorge Basadre, *Historia de la República del Perú*, 10 vols (5th edn, Lima, 1961–4), I, 5.
31. García del Río to San Martín, Santiago, 21 March 1822, *SMC*, 320–4.
32. Bolívar to Sucre, 21 February 1825, in O'Leary, *Memorias*, XXX, 41–5.
33. Bolívar to president of Congress of Peru, first days of February 1824, in *Papeles de Bolívar*, publicados por Vicente Lecuna, 2 vols (Madrid, 1920), I, 73–5.
34. Una mirada sobre la América Española, April–June 1829, in Simón Bolívar, *Doctrina del Libertador*, ed. Manuel Pérez Vila (Caracas, 1979), 286–7.
35. Arenales to San Martín, Santiago, 9 April 1823, *DASM*, VIII, 142–4.
36. Maria Graham, *Journal of a Residence in Chile*, 281.
37. Hardy to Croker, 7 March 1823, National Archives, PRO 61/l.
38. José de San Martín, Proclama, 20 September 1822, *DASM*, X, 356.
39. Tomás Guido, 'El General San Martín; su retirada del Perú', *Revista de Buenos Aires*, no. 13 (May 1864). San Martín talking to Guido on the night of his departure, 20 September 1822, reproduced in Leguía y Martínez, *Historia de la emancipación del Perú*, VII, 510–12; see also Pasquali, *San Martín*, 389.
40. San Martín to Guido, on board *Belgrano*, 2 a.m, 21 September 1822, in Pasquali, *San Martín confidencial*, 189.
41. Otero, *Historia del Libertador*, IV, 6–7.
42. Guido to San Martín, Lima, 11 June 1823, *DASM*, VI, 450–4.
43. Roca, *Ni con Lima ni con Buenos Aires*, 467–8.
44. Graham, *Journal of a Residence in Chile*, 282–4. See the recent edition of the *Journal*, edited by Jennifer Hayward (Charlottsville, VA, 2003), 302–7, for an evaluation of Maria Graham's views and those of other observers (William Bennet Stevenson, John Mier and Basil Hall).

45. Gonzalo Pereyra de Olazábal, 'Manuel de Olazábal—su amistad al General San Martín', *Investigaciones y Ensayos*, 26 (1979), 453–68.
46. San Martín to O'Higgins, Mendoza, 9 February 1823, *SMC*, 1.
47. San Martín to O'Higgins, Mendoza, 1 April 1823, *SMC*, 3.
48. Roca, *Ni con Lima ni con Buenos Aires*, 513–17.
49. San Martín to Guido, Mendoza, 11 March 1823, in Pasquali, *San Martín confidencial*, 193.
50. San Martín to Riva Agüero, Mendoza, 23 October 1823, *SMC*, 338–9.
51. Robert Proctor, *Narrative of a Journey across the Cordillera of the Andes and of a residence in Lima and parts of Peru, in the years 1823 and 1824* (London, 1825), 51–2.
52. Corvalán to San Martín, Mendoza, 29 December 1823, *SMC*, 177.
53. L. Peru de Lacroix, *Diario de Bucaramanga* (Ediciones Centauro, Caracas, 1976), 62–6.
54. San Martín to Guido, Montevideo, 3 April 1829, *DASM*, VII, 538.
55. Piccirilli, *San Martín y la política de los pueblos*, 359–65; see also Ana Teresa Zigon and Marta Verdenelli de van Gelder, 'San Martín y Rivadavia', *PCIS*, IV, 563–75.
56. San Martín to Guido, Mendoza, 31 July 1823, in Piccirilli, *San Martín y la política de los pueblos*, 369.
57. San Martín to Chilavert, Brussels, 1 January 1825, *SMC*, 148.
58. San Martín to O'Higgins, Brussels, 20 October 1827, *DASM*, X, 17.
59. San Martín to Guido, 22 September 1823, quoted in Pasquali, *San Martín*, 396.
60. Piccirilli, *San Martín y la política de los pueblos*, 370–1.
61. Avelino Ignacio Gómez Ferreyra, ed., *Viajeros pontificios al Río de la Plata y Chile (1823–1825)* (Córdoba, 1970), 295, 502, 543–4, 573.
62. Woodbine Parish to Canning, Buenos Aires, 25 April 1824, in Webster, *Britain and the Independence of Latin America*, I, 110–13; the interview is also described by Piccirilli, *San Martín y la política de los pueblos*, 375–6, who takes Rivadavia's views at their face value.
63. Guido to San Martín, Lima, 22 January 1824, *DASM*, VI, 494.
64. San Martín to Miller, Brussels, 10 October 1828, *SMC*, 88.

Chapter 10: Exile

1. Peter Heywood was confined by the mutineers and convicted with them; subsequently pardoned and promoted lieutenant and captain. See Edward Tagart, *A Memoir of the late Captain Peter Heywood, R.N. with extracts from his Diaries and Correspondence* (London, 1832).
2. Frank Griffith Dawson, *The First Latin American Debt Crisis* (New Haven and London, 1990) 76.
3. Arranged by a nephew of Paroissien: San Martín to Paroissien, London, 12 June 1824, Paroissien Papers.
4. Luis Santiago Sanz, 'El general San Martín en Bruselas', *Investigaciones y Ensayos*, 14 (1973), 527–55.
5. Quoted by Piccirilli, *San Martín y la política de los pueblos*, 380.
6. Ibid., 383.
7. San Martín to Chilavert, Brussels, 1 January 1825, *SMC*, 148.
8. San Martín to O'Higgins, Brussels, 8 February 1825, *SMC*, 4; San Martín to Guido, n.d., *DASM*, VI, 516.
9. San Martín to Guido, Brussels, 6 January 1827, in Pasquali, *San Martín confidencial*, 216.
10. Mendoza, 1826, *DASM*, IX, 326.
11. San Martín, 1825, *DASM*, I, 35.
12. Quoted in Humphreys, *Liberation in South America*, 141, n.1.
13. Miller to San Martín, 22 August 1826, *SMC*, 64.

14. San Martín to Miller, 8 September 1826, *SMC*, 65.
15. Carlos Alberto Guzmán, *San Martín 1824–1850* (Buenos Aires, 1953), 38.
16. Guido to San Martín, Buenos Aires, 30 August 1826, *DASM*, VI, 500–2.
17. San Martín to Guido, Brussels, 18 December 1826, *DASM*, VI, 503–6.
18. San Martín to Guido, Brussels, 21 June 1827, *DASM*, VI, 527–8.
19. San Martín to O'Higgins, 20 October 1827, *SMC*, 11.
20. Piccirilli, *San Martín y la política de los pueblos*, 390–1.
21. On the financial state of San Martín see Otero, *Historia del Libertador*, IV, 340–52, and Raúl de Labougle, 'San Martín en el ostracismo: Sus recursos', *Investigaciones y Ensayos*, 12 (1972), 167–92.
22. San Martín to Pedro Moyano, Brussels, 3 August 1826, *SMC*, 181–3.
23. San Martín to O'Higgins, Brussels, 20 October 1827, *DASM*, X, 16–18.
24. San Martín to Miller, 16 October 1827, *SMC*, 80.
25. See letters from San Martín to Miller, May–October 1828, *SMC*, 82–9.
26. Halperín Donghi, *Politics, Economics and Society in Argentina*, 211–15, 382–91.
27. John Lynch, *Argentine Dictator: Juan Manuel de Rosas 1829–1852* (Oxford, 1981), 43–7.
28. Domingo Faustino Sarmiento, *Facundo* (La Plata, 1938), 32.
29. San Martín to Díaz Vélez, rada de Buenos Aires, 6 February 1829, *DASM*, X, 69.
30. On the reaction in Buenos Aires see Pasquali, *San Martín*, 410–11.
31. San Martín to Guido, Montevideo, 19 March 1829, in Flavio A. García, 'Presencia rioplatense de San Martín en 1829', *Investigaciones y Ensayos*, 8 (1970), 194–5.
32. Ibid., 192.
33. Guido to San Martín, Buenos Aires, 12 March 1829, ibid., 197.
34. San Martín to Guido, Montevideo, 3 April 1829, *DASM*, VI, 553–6; Pasquali, *San Martín confidencial*, 241–5.
35. San Martín to López Planes, Brussels, 8 May 1830, *DASM*, IX, 353–5.
36. Pasquali, *San Martín*, 418–19.
37. San Martín to Guido, Brussels, 6 April 1830, Pasquali, *San Martín confidencial*, 259–61.
38. San Martín to Guido, Montevideo, 27 April 1829, Pasquali, *San Martín*, 419.
39. San Martín to O'Higgins, Brussels, 12 February 1830, *SMC*, 20.
40. San Martín to O'Higgins, Paris, 22 December 1832, *SMC*, 34–5.
41. San Martín to Guido, 1 February 1834, Pasquali, *San Martín confidencial*, 274–6.
42. 'Declaro no deber ni haber jamás debido nada a nadie.' The Will of San Martín, Paris, 23 January 1844, in Guzmán, *San Martín 1824–1850*, 139–43.
43. San Martín to Moreno, Grand Bourg, 30 July 1834, *DASM*, X, 84; Pasquali, *San Martín confidencial*, 285–9.
44. San Martín to Guido, Grand Bourg, 3 October 1834, *DASM*, X, 104.
45. San Martín to Guido, Grand Bourg, 17 December 1835, Pasquali, *San Martín confidencial*, 310–11.
46. San Martín to Guido, 26 October 1836, Pasquali, *San Martín confidencial*, 312–14.
47. Juan Manuel Beruti, *Memorias curiosas, Biblioteca de Mayo*, IV, 4,059, 4,066, 4,114.
48. Lynch, *Argentine Dictator*, 288–9.
49. San Martín to Rosas, 5 August 1838, Rosas to San Martín, 24 January 1839, *SMC*, 125–6.
50. Rosas to San Martín, Buenos Aires, 24 February 1840, *Cartas de Juan Manuel de Rosas*, 3 vols (Buenos Aires, 2004), III, 26.
51. San Martín to Gregorio Gómez, Grand Bourg, 21 September 1839, *DASM*, IX, 500–1. Manuel Vicente de Maza was president of the House of Representatives and of the Supreme Court, and a traditional collaborator of the regime; but that did not protect him from suspicion of conspiracy and assassination by the *mazorca*. San Martín's remark appears to suggest that he accepted the charge of conspiracy by Maza and others with the French intervention.

52. San Martín to Rosas, Naples, 11 January 1846, *SMC*, 134–5.
53. San Martín to E.F Dickson, Naples, 28 December 1845, *DASM*, X, 125–7. The dictator appreciated San Martín's support: Rosas to San Martín, Palermo de San Benito, 20 May 1846, *Cartas de Juan Manuel de Rosas*, III, 264.
54. Lynch, *Argentine Dictator*, 285–8.
55. San Martín to Rosas, Boulogne, 2 November 1848, *SMC*, 136, Rosas to San Martín, Buenos Aires, 19 March 1849, *SMC*, 138–9.
56. San Martín to Rosas, Boulogne, 6 May 1850, *SMC*, 143.
57. Otero, *Historia del Libertador*, IV, 340.
58. Alberdi, 'El general San Martín en 1843', *Obras completas*, II, 335–6.
59. Domingo Faustino Sarmiento, *Escritos sobre San Martín* (Buenos Aires, 1966), 96, 99; *Obras de D.F. Sarmiento*, 53 vols (Santiago and Buenos Aires, 1887–1903), V, 129, 138, XLIX, 17–23; Otero, *Historia del Libertador*, IV, 455.
60. San Martín to Rosas, Boulogne, 2 November 1848, *SMC*, 136.
61. Patriotic Society, Lima, 1848, *SMC*, 347.
62. San Martín, Boulogne, 15 March 1849, *SMC*, 348.
63. Pierre-André Wimet, 'Estada y muerte de San Martín en Boulogne-sur-Mer (1848–1850)', *PCIS*, V, 61–76.
64. Guerrino, *La salud de San Martín*, 174–5, 182–3.
65. Félix Frías, *El General José de San Martín: Sus últimos años y la noticia de su muerte 17 de agosto de 1850* (Buenos Aires, 1944).
66. See his letter to Guido, Brussels, 18 December 1826, Pasquali, *San Martín confidencial*, 207–11.
67. San Martín to Ramón Castilla, Boulogne, 11 September 1848, *SMC*, 296–8.
68. San Martín to Guido, Brussels, 18 December 1826, Pasquali, *San Martín confidencial*, 208.
69. See for example Bolívar to Santander, Pativilca, 23 January 1824, O'Leary, *Memorias*, XXIX, 400–1.
70. San Martín to Guido, Brussels, 18 December 1826, *DASM*, VI, 503; Pasquali, *San Martín confidencial*, 207–11.
71. Daniel Florencio O'Leary, *Memorias del General Daniel Florencio O'Leary: Narración*, 3 vols (Caracas, 1952), II, 240.
72. O'Leary, *Narración*, II, 155.
73. Miller, *Memoirs*, I, 424.
74. San Martín to Miller, Brussels, 30 June 1827, *SMC*, 77.
75. San Martín to Rosas, 5 August 1838, Rosas to San Martín, 24 January 1839, *SMC*, 125–6.
76. 'el hombre Americano, el hombre necesario.' Mitre, *Historia de San Martín*, II, 40, 258.
77. San Martín to Guido, 14 February 1816, Pasquali, *San Martín confidencial*, 45.
78. San Martín to Guido, 6 January 1827, *DASM*, VI, 513.
79. Thomas Carlyle, *On Heroes, Hero-Worship and the Heroic in History* (1841) (Lincoln, NE, 1966), 224–5.

Bibliography

Sources

San Martín did not write his memoirs or leave any significant autobiographical writings. During his brief return to the Río de la Plata in 1829 he went out of his way to collect his papers, which he took back with him to Europe and left in an ordered state for preservation in Argentina. These served Bartolomé Mitre for much of his *Historia de San Martín*. The Archive of San Martín was preserved in the Museo Mitre, and has been published in successive volumes of *Documentos del Archivo de San Martín*, 12 vols (Buenos Aires, 1910–11). Further collections, including documents from other archives and documents which subsequently came to light are published in the ongoing *Documentos para la historia del Libertador General San Martín*, 18 vols (Buenos Aires, 1953–2001). His correspondence with individual friends, colleagues and others can be found in the volume from the Museo Histórico Nacional, *San Martín: Su correspondencia, 1823–1850* (3rd edn, Madrid, 1911). In the Archivo General de la Nación *Documentos referentes a la guerra de la independencia y emancipación política de la República Argentina*, 3 vols (Buenos Aires, 1914–26), contain basic documentation from the Argentine national archives on the origins, development and participants of the wars of independence; volume 2 includes San Martín's continental project in its chronological sequence. The Chilean dimension of the story and San Martín's correspondence with O'Higgins is contained in Academia Chilena de la Historia, *Archivo de don Bernardo O'Higgins*, 35 vols (Santiago, 1942–68), particularly volumes 5, 6, 7 and 8. The Peruvian documentation of San Martín is collected in various volumes published by the Comisión Nacional del Sesquincentenario de la Independencia del Perú, *Colección documental de la independencia del Perú*, 17 vols (Lima, 1971–), and especially in volume 13, *Obra gubernativa y epistolario de San Martín*. Patricia Pasquali has edited the personal correspondence of San Martín with his friend Tomás Guido in *San Martín confidencial: Correspondencia personal del Libertador con su amigo Tomás Guido (1816–1849)* (Buenos Aires, 2000).

In the National Archives, Public Record Office, London, the following files have been consulted for relevant material: FO 72/157, 202, 215 (Spain), FO 6/18 (Argentina), FO 62/1. 2 (Peru).

Published Documents and Contemporary Works

Academia Chilena de la Historia, *Archivo de don Bernardo O'Higgins*, 35 vols (Santiago, 1942–68).

Academia Nacional de la Historia, *Gaceta de Buenos Aires, 1810–1821*, 6 vols (Buenos Aires, 1910–15).

Alberdi, Juan Bautista, 'El general San Martín en 1843', *Obras completas*, 8 vols (Buenos Aires, 1886–7), II, 335–6.

— Escritos póstumos, 16 vols (Buenos Aires, 1895–1901).

Archivo General de la Nación, *Documentos referentes a la guerra de la independencia y emancipación política de la República Argentina*, 3 vols (Buenos Aires, 1914–26).

Argentina: Congreso de la Nacíon. Senado de la Nación, *Biblioteca de Mayo*, 19 vols (Buenos Aires, 1960–8).

Belgrano, Manuel, *Epistolario Belgraviano* (Buenos Aires, 2001).

Beruti, Juan Manuel, *Memorias curiosas, Biblioteca de Mayo*, IV, 3,647–4,150.

Bolívar, Simón, *Papeles de Bolívar. Publicados por Vicente Lecuna*, 2 vols (Madrid, 1920).

Busaniche, José Luis, *San Martín visto por sus contemporáneos* (Buenos Aires, 1942).

Caillet-Bois, Ricardo and Julio César González, eds, *El 'Diario' y documentos de la misión sanmartiniana de Gutiérrez de la Fuente (1822)*, 2 vols (ANH, Buenos Aires, 1978).

Cochrane, Thomas, 10th Earl of Dundonald, *The Autobiography of a Seaman*, 2 vols, 1860 (London, 2000).

— *Manifiesto de las acusaciones que a nombre del General San Martín hicieron sus legados ante el gobierno de Chile contra el Vice-Almirante Lord Cochrane, y vindicación de este dirigido al mismo San Martín* (Lima, 1823).

— *Narrative of Services in the Liberation of Chili, Peru and Brazil from Spanish and Portuguese Domination*, 2 vols (London, 1859).

Comisión Nacional del Centenario, Museo Mitre, *Documentos del Archivo de San Martín*, 12 vols (Buenos Aires, 1910–11).

Comisión Nacional del Sesquincentenario de la Independencia del Perú, *Colección documental de la independencia del Perú*, 17 vols (Lima, 1971–).

Espejo, Gerónimo, *Apuntes históricos sobre la expedición libertadora del Perú, 1820, Biblioteca de Mayo*, XVII, 1ª parte.

— *El paso de los Andes: Crónica histórica de las operaciones del ejército de los Andes para la restauración de Chile en 1817, Biblioteca de Mayo*, XVI, 1ª parte.

— *Recuerdos: San Martín y Bolívar. Entrevista de Guayaquil, 1822, Biblioteca de Mayo*, XVII, 2ª parte.

Font Ezcurra, Ricardo, *San Martín y Rosas: Su correspondencia* (Buenos Aires, 1940).

Frías, Félix, *El General José de San Martín: Sus últimos años y la noticia de su muerte 17 de agosto de 1850* (Buenos Aires, 1944).

Gaceta del Gobierno de Lima Independiente, 3 vols (Buenos Aires, 1950).

Graham, Gerald S. and R.A. Humphreys, eds, *The Navy and South America 1807–1823: Correspondence of the Commanders-in-Chief on the South American Station* (London, 1962).

Graham, Maria, *Journal of a Residence in Chile, during the year 1822, and a Voyage from Chile to Brazil in 1823* (London, 1824).

— Edited by Jennifer Hayward (University of Virginia Press, Charlottesville, 2003).

Guido, Tomás, *San Martín y la gran epopeya* (Buenos Aires, 1928).

Guido y Spano, Carlos, ed., *Vindicación histórica: Papeles del brigadier general Guido, 1817–1820* (Buenos Aires, 1881).

Haigh, Samuel, *Sketches of Buenos Ayres and Chile* (London, 1831).

Hall, Basil, *Extracts from a Journal written on the coasts of Chile, Peru and Mexico in the years 1820, 1821, 1822*, 2 vols (Edinburgh, 1824).

Instituto de Historia Argentina 'Doctor Emilio Ravignani', *Mayo Documental*, 8 vols (Buenos Aires, 1962–4).

Instituto Nacional Sanmartiniano, *La conducción política del General San Martín durante el Protectorado del Perú*, 3 vols (Buenos Aires, 1982).

Lecuna, Vicente, ed., *Relaciones diplomáticas de Bolívar con Chile y Buenos Aires*, 2 vols (Caracas, 1954).

Mathison, Gilbert Farquar, *Narrative of a Visit to Brazil, Chile, Peru and the Sandwich Islands during the Years 1821 and 1822* (London, 1825).

Miller, John, *Memoirs of General Miller in the Service of the Republic of Peru*, 2 vols (2nd edn, London, 1829).

Ministerio de Educación de la Nación, Instituto Nacional Sanmartiniano, Museo Histórico Nacional, *Documentos para la historia del Libertador General San Martín*, 18 vols (Buenos Aires, 1953–2001).

Monteagudo, Bernardo, *Escritos* (Senado de la Nación, Buenos Aires, 1989).

Museo Mitre, *Documentos del Archivo de Belgrano*, 7 vols (Buenos Aires, 1913–17).

— *Documentos del Archivo de Pueyrredón*, 4 vols (Buenos Aires, 1912).

O'Leary, Daniel Florencio, *The 'Detached Recollections' of General D.F. O'Leary*, ed. R.A. Humphreys (London, 1969).

— *Memorias del General O'Leary*, 34 vols (Caracas, 1981).

— *Memorias del General Daniel Florencio O'Leary: Narración*, 3 vols (Caracas, 1952).

Pasquali, Patricia, ed., *San Martín confidencial: Correspondencia personal del Libertador con su amigo Tomás Guido (1816–1846)* (Buenos Aires, 2000).

Paz, José María, *Memorias póstumas*, 3 vols (Buenos Aires, 2000).

Proctor, Robert, *Narrative of a Journey across the Cordillera of the Andes and of a residence in Lima and other parts of Peru, in the years 1823 and 1824* (London, 1825).

Pueyrredón, Manuel Alejandro, *Memorias inéditas: Historia de mi vida. Campañas del ejército de los Andes* (Buenos Aires, 1947).

Robertson, J.P. and W.P., *Letters on South America, comprising travels on the banks of the Paraná and Río de la Plata*, 3 vols (London, 1843).

San Martín, José de, *Correspondencia de San Martín y Rosas*, ed. Fermín Chávez (Buenos Aires, 1975).

— *Correspondencia entre San Martín y Rosas (1838–1850)*, ed. Jordán B. Genta (Buenos Aires, 1950).

— *Correspondencia de San Martín y Torre Tagle*, ed. Javier Ortiz de Cevallos (Lima, 1963).

— *Manifiesto de las acusaciones que a nombre del General San Martín hicieron sus legados ante el gobierno* (Lima, 1823).

— *Proclama a los Americanos, inserta en la Gaceta de Lima* (Lima, 1822).

Sarmiento, Domingo Faustino, *Escritos sobre San Martín* (Buenos Aires, 1966).

Stevenson, William Bennet, *A Historical and Descriptive Narrative of Twenty Years Residence in South America*, 3 vols (London, 1825).

Tagart, Edward, *A Memoir of the late Captain Peter Heywood R.N. with extracts from his Diaries and Correspondence* (London, 1832).

Torre Revello, José M.A., *Don Juan de San Martín: Noticia biográfica con apéndice documental* (Buenos Aires, 1927).

Townsend, Joseph, *A Journey through Spain, in the Years 1786 and 1787*, 2 vols (3rd edn, London, 1814).

Universidad de Buenos Aires, Facultad de Filosofía y Letras, *Mayo Documental*, 12 vols (Buenos Aires, 1961–5).

Vargas, José Santos, *Diario de un comandante de la independencia americana 1814–1825*, ed. Gunnar Mendoza L. (Mexico, 1982).

Webster, C.K., ed., *Britain and the Independence of Latin America 1812–1830*, 2 vols (London, 1938).

Secondary Works

Academia Nacional de la Historia, *San Martín: Homenaje de la Academia Nacional de la Historia en el centenario de su muerte (1850–1950)*, 2 vols (Buenos Aires, 1951).

Aljovín de Losada, Cristóbal, *Caudillos y constituciones: Perú, 1821–1845* (Lima, 2000).

Amaral, Samuel, *The Rise of Capitalism on the Pampas: The Estancieros of Buenos Aires, 1785–1870* (Cambridge University Press, 1998).

Anna, Timothy E., 'Economic Causes of San Martín's Failure in Lima', *HAHR*, 54, 4 (1974), 657–81.

— *The Fall of the Royal Government in Peru* (Lincoln, NE, 1974).

Avila Martel, Alamiro de, 'La amistad de San Martín y Cochrane', *PCIS*, V (1978), 13–20.

— *San Martín y O'Higgins* (Santiago, 1978).

Barcia Trelles, Augusto, *San Martín en España, en América*, 5 vols (Buenos Aires, 1941–8).

Benencia, Julio Arturo, *Cómo San Martín y Belgrano no se conocieron en Yatásto* (Buenos Aires, 1973).

Berruezo León, María Teresa, *La lucha en Hispanoamérica por su independencia en Inglaterra, 1800–1830* (Madrid, 1989).

Bidondo, Raúl A., 'San Martín y la Guerra de Recursos en el Ejército del Norte, 1814', *PCIS*, II, 293–318.

Blanchard, Peter, *Slavery and Abolition in Early Republican Peru* (Wilmington, DE, 1992).

— *Under the Flags of Freedom: Slave Soldiers and the Wars of Independence in Spanish South America* (Pittsburgh, PA, 2008).

Carrera Damas, Germán, ed., *Historia general de América Latina: Volumen V, La crisis estructural de las sociedades implantadas* (UNESCO, Paris, 2003).

Chumbita, Hugo, 'El origen de San Martín y su proyecto americano', *Desmemoria: Revista de Historia*, año 7, no. 26 (2000), 8–27.

Cordingly, David, *Cochrane the Dauntless: The Life and Adventures of Admiral Thomas Cochrane, 1775–1860* (London, 2007).

Cuccorese, Horacio Juan, *San Martín, catolicismo y masonería* (Buenos Aires, 1993).

Dale, Richard *'Napoleon is Dead': Lord Cochrane and the Great Stock Exchange Scandal* (Stroud, 2006).

Dawson, Frank Griffith, *The First Latin American Debt Crisis: The City of London and the 1822–25 Loan Bubble* (New Haven and London, 1990).

Esdaile, Charles, *The Peninsular War: A New History* (London, 2002).

Estévez, Alfredo and Oscar H. Elía, *Aspectos económico-financieros de la campaña sanmartiniana* (Buenos Aires, 1961).

Fisher, John R., *Bourbon Peru 1750–1824* (Liverpool, 2003).

— *The Economic Aspects of Spanish Imperialism in America, 1492–1810* (Liverpool, 1997).

— *Government and Society in Colonial Peru: The Intendant System 1784–1814* (London, 1970).

— *Silver Mines and Silver Miners in Colonial Peru, 1776–1824* (Liverpool, 1977).

Fontaneda Pérez, Eugenio, *Raíces castellanas de José de San Martín* (Madrid, 1980).

Fraga, Rosendo, *San Martín y los británicos* (Buenos Aires, 2000).

Gallo, Klaus, *De la invasión al reconocimiento: Gran Bretaña y el Río de la Plata 1806–1826* (Buenos Aires, 1994).

— '¿Reformismo radical o liberal? La política rivadaviana en una era de conservadurismo europeo, 1815–1830', *Investigaciones y Ensayos*, 49 (1999), 287–313.

García, Flavio A., 'Presencia rioplatense de San Martín en 1829', *Investigaciones y Ensayos*, 8 (1970), 173–207.

García Godoy, Cristián, 'Jefes españoles en la formación militar de San Martín', *Investigaciones y Ensayos*, 44 (1994), 113–47.

Guerra Martinière, Margarita, Osvaldo Holguín Callo, César Gutiérrez Muñoz, *Sobre el Perú: Homenaje a José Agustín de la Puente Candamo*, 2 vols (Lima, 2002).

Guerrino, Antonio Alberto, *La salud de San Martín: Ensayo de patografía histórica* (Buenos Aires, 1999).

Guillén, Julio and Jorge Juan Guillén, *Las campañas de San Martín en la fragata 'Santa Dorotea' cuando era subteniente del Regimiento de Murcia* (Madrid, 1966).

Guzmán, Carlos Alberto, *San Martín 1824–1850* (Buenos Aires, 1993).

Halperín Donghi, Tulio, *Guerra y finanzas en los orígines del estado argentino, 1791–1850* (Buenos Aires, 1982).

— 'Militarización revolucionaria en Buenos Aires, 1805–1815', *El ocaso del orden colonial en Hispanoamérica* (Buenos Aires, 1978).

— *Politics, Economics and Society in Argentina in the Revolutionary Period* (Cambridge, 1975).

— *Reforma y disolución de los imperios ibéricos* (Madrid, 1985).

Harvey, Robert, *Liberators: Latin America's Struggle for Independence 1810–1830* (London, 2000).

Humphreys, R.A., *Liberation in South America 1806–1827: The Career of James Paroissien* (London, 1952).

Hünefeldt, Christine, *Paying the Price of Freedom: Family and Labour among Lima's Slaves, 1800–1854* (Berkeley, CA, 1994).

Labougle, Raúl de, 'San Martín en el ostracismo: Sus recursos', *Investigaciones y Ensayos*, 12 (1972), 167–92.

Langley, Lester D., *The Americas in the Age of Revolution, 1750–1850* (New Haven, CT, 1996).

Lecuna, Vicente, *La entrevista de Guayaquil: Restablecimiento de la verdad histórica*, 2 vols (4th edn, Caracas, 1962–3).

Leguía y Martínez, Germán, *Historia de la emancipación del Perú: El Protectorado*, 7 vols (Lima, 1972).

Leturia, Pedro de, *Relaciones entre la Santa Sede e Hispanoamérica, 1493–1835*, 3 vols (Rome, Caracas, 1959–60).

Levene, Ricardo, *El genio político de San Martín* (2nd edn, Buenos Aires, 1970).

— *Ensayo histórico sobre la Revolución de Mayo y Mariano Moreno*, 2 vols (4th edn, Buenos Aires, 1960).

Lynch, John, 'British Policy and Spanish America, 1783–1808', *JLAS*, 1, 1 (1969), 1–30.

— *Caudillos in Spanish America 1800–1850* (Oxford, 1992).

— 'Los factores estructurales de la crisis: La crisis del orden colonial', ed. Germán Carrera Damas, *Historia general de América Latina: Volumen V, la crisis estructural de las sociedades implantadas* (UNESCO, Paris, 2003), 31–54.

— *San Martín: Argentine Patriot, American Liberator* (Institute of Latin American Studies, London, 2001).

— *The Spanish American Revolutions 1808–1826* (2nd edn, New York, 1986).

McFarlane, Anthony, 'Identity, Enlightenment and Political Dissent in Late Colonial Spanish America', *Transactions of the Royal Historical Society*, Sixth series, 8 (1998), 309–35.

McFarlane, Anthony and Eduardo Posada-Carbó, eds, *Independence and Revolution in Spanish America: Perspectives and Problems* (London, 1999).

Masur, Gerhard, 'The Conference of Guayaquil', *HAHR*, 31, 2 (1951), 189–229.

Mayochi, Enrique Mario, *San Martín en la Argentina* (Buenos Aires, 1978).

Metford, J.C.J., *San Martín the Liberator* (Oxford, 1950).

Mitre, Bartolomé, *The Emancipation of South America: Being a condensed translation by W. Pilling of the 'History of San Martín'* (London, 1893).

— *Historia de Belgrano*, 4 vols (6th edn, Buenos Aires, 1927).

— *Historia de San Martín y de la emancipación Sud-Americana* [1887], 3 vols (Buenos Aires, 1950).

Montoya Rivas, Gustavo, *La independencia del Perú y el fantasma de la revolución* (Lima, 2002).

O'Phelan Godoy, Scarlett, ed., *La independencia en el Perú: De los Borbones a Bolívar* (Lima, 2001).

Otero, José Pacífico, *Historia del Libertador don José de San Martín*, 4 vols (Buenos Aires, 1932).

Oxford, *Dictionary of National Biography*, 61 vols (Oxford, 2004).

Pasquali, Patricia, *San Martín: La fuerza de la misión y la soledad de la gloria. Biografía* (3rd edn, Buenos Aires, 1999).

Paz Soldán, Mariano F., *Historia del Perú independiente*, 3 vols (Lima, 1869–74).

Pereyra de Olazábal, Gonzalo, 'Manuel de Olazábal—su amistad al General San Martín', *Investigaciones y Ensayos*, 26 (1979), 453–68.

Pérez, Joaquín, 'San Martín y el repaso de los Andes', *PCIS*, VIII, 339–430.

Pérez Amuchástegui, A.J., *La 'Carta de Lafond' y la preceptiva historiográfica* (Córdoba, 1962).

— *Ideología y acción de San Martín* (Buenos Aires, 1966).

— 'El Pacto de Rancagua', *PCIS*, VII, 191–206.

— *San Martín y el Alto Perú, 1814* (Tucumán, 1976).

Piccinali, Héctor Juan, 'Tríptico de la campaña de San Lorenzo', *Investigaciones y Ensayos*, 34 (1983), 435–43.

— *Vida de San Martín en España* (Buenos Aires, 1977).

— *Vida de San Martín en Buenos Aires* (Buenos Aires, 1984).

Piccirilli, Ricardo, *Rivadavia y su tiempo*, 3 vols (2nd edn, Buenos Aires, 1960).

— *San Martín y la política de los pueblos* (Buenos Aires, 1957).

Primer Congreso Internacional Sanmartiniano, 8 vols (Buenos Aires, 1979).

Puente Candamo, José Agustín de la, *San Martín y el Perú: Planteamiento doctrinario* (Lima, 1948).

Ramos, Demetrio, *España en la independencia de América* (Madrid, 1996).

Rivera Serna, Raúl, *Los guerrilleros del centro en la emancipación peruana* (Lima, 1958).

Robertson, William Spence, *Rise of the Spanish-American Republics as told in the Lives of their Liberators* (New York and London, 1918).

Roca, José Luis, *Ni con Lima ni con Buenos Aires: La formación de un estado nacional en Charcas* (Lima, 2007).

Rodriguez, Moises Enrique, *Freedom's Mercenaries: British Volunteers in the Wars of Independence of Latin America. Volume II: Southern South America* (Lanham, MD, 2006).

Rojas, Ricardo, *El santo de la espada: Vida de San Martín* (Buenos Aires, 1933).

Sanz, Luis Santiago, 'El general San Martín en Bruselas', *Investigaciones y Ensayos*, 14 (1973), 527–55.

Scunio, Alberdo D.H., 'San Martín, oficial de inteligencia', *Investigaciones y Ensayos*, 32 (1982), 225–42.

Segreti, Carlos S.A., *La acción política de Güemes* (Córdoba, 1991).

— *La máscara de la monarquía, 1808–1819* (Córdoba, 1994).

Terragno, Rodolfo H., *Maitland & San Martín* (Universidad Nacional de Quilmes,1998).

Uriburu, José Evaristo, *Historia del General Arenales 1770–1831* (London, 1924).

Vale, Brian, *The Audacious Admiral Cochrane: The True Life of a Naval Legend* (London, 2004).

Vargas Ugarte, Rubén, *Historia del Perú: Emancipación, 1809–1825* (Buenos Aires, 1958).

— *Historia general del Perú*, 6 vols (Barcelona, 1966–71).

Vicuña MacKenna, Benjamín, *El General Don José de San Martín* (3rd edn, Santiago, 1971).

— *La revolución de la independencia del Perú desde 1809 a 1819* (Lima, 1860).

Villegas, Alfredo G., *Juan de San Martín: El padre de un libertador* (Buenos Aires, 1948).

— *San Martín y su época* (Buenos Aires, 1976).

Worcester, Donald E., *Sea Power and Chilean Independence* (Gainesville, FA, 1962).

Glossary

altiplano	high plateau
amable loca	lovable crazy girl
audiencia	high court of justice with administrative functions
Banda Oriental	'the east shore', i.e. of the River Uruguay and the Río de la Plata, equivalent to modern Uruguay
cabildo	town council (*cabildo abierto*: a *cabildo* augmented with selected citizens for an extraordinary meeting)
cacique	Indian chieftain
campesino	peasant
caudillo	leader, whose rule is based on personal power rather than constitutional form
cholo	mestizo, near-Indian
corregidor	district officer
correntino	of Corrientes
cortes	parliament, assembly
cotorrana	older lady
creole	Spaniard born in America
doctrina	Indian parish
encomienda	grant of Indians, especially as tribute payers
estancia	large cattle ranch (*estanciero*: owner of an *estancia*)
fueros	right, privilege, immunity
gaucho	mounted nomad, free cowboy, inhabitant of the pampas of Argentina
golpe; golpista	blow, coup; participant in a coup
guayaquileños	people of Guayaquil
hacienda	large landed estate, plantation (*hacendado*: owner of a hacienda)

indio	Indian
jornalero	rural day labourer
junta	committee, board
kuraka	Andean Indian chief
limeño	inhabitant of Lima
llanos	plains
logista	member of Lodge
maricón de cazoleta	perfumed pansy
mate	maté, Paraguayan tea
mayorazgo	entail, entailed estate
mazorca	semi-official terrorist squad
mendocino	inhabitant of Mendoza
mestizo	of mixed white and Indian descent
mita	Quechua word meaning 'turn'; forced recruitment of Indians in rotation for public or private work, especially in the silver mines of Potosí (*mitayo*: an Indian so conscripted)
montonero	guerrilla fighter
mulato	of mixed white and black descent ('mulatto' in English)
novia	fiancée
obraja	workshop
pampa	plains, prairie; in Andes a grassy plateau
pardo	of mixed white and black descent, free coloureds
pasión de mando	a passion for command
patria	native land, mother country, fatherland
peninsular	Spaniard born in Spain
peon	rural labourer, employee of hacienda or estancia
perulero	Peruvian
populacho	populace, mob
porteño	of Buenos Aires, inhabitant of Buenos Aires
pueblo	people, village
pulpería	general store and bar
rosismo	policy or movement of Rosas (*rosista*: follower of Rosas)
soledad	solitude
soroche	altitude sickness
tertulia	social gathering, literary *salon*
unitarios	unitarians (political), as opposed to federalists, especially in Argentina.
yanacona	tenant in Andean America, holding land in return for labour service *yanaconazgo*: such tenancy

Index